T0202901

Lecture Notes in Computer Science 13910

Founding Editors

Gerhard Goos
Juris Hartmanis

The series Lecture Notes in Computer Science (LNCS), including its subseries Lecture Notes in Artificial Intelligence (LNAI) and Lecture Notes in Bioinformatics (LNBI), has established itself as a medium for the publication of new developments in computer science and information technology research, teaching, and education.

LNCS enjoys close cooperation with the computer science R & D community, the series counts many renowned academics among its volume editors and paper authors, and collaborates with prestigious societies. Its mission is to serve this international community by providing an invaluable service, mainly focused on the publication of conference and workshop proceedings and postproceedings. LNCS commenced publication in 1973.

Marieke Huisman · António Ravara
Editors

Formal Techniques for Distributed Objects, Components, and Systems

43rd IFIP WG 6.1 International Conference, FORTE 2023
Held as Part of the 18th International Federated Conference
on Distributed Computing Techniques, DisCoTec 2023
Lisbon, Portugal, June 19–23, 2023
Proceedings

 Springer

Editors
Marieke Huisman 🆔
University of Twente
Enschede, The Netherlands

António Ravara 🆔
NOVA School of Science and Technology
and NOVA LINCS
Caparica, Portugal

ISSN 0302-9743   ISSN 1611-3349 (electronic)
Lecture Notes in Computer Science
ISBN 978-3-031-35354-3   ISBN 978-3-031-35355-0 (eBook)
https://doi.org/10.1007/978-3-031-35355-0

This Springer imprint is published by the registered company Springer Nature Switzerland AG
The registered company address is: Gewerbestrasse 11, 6330 Cham, Switzerland

Foreword

The 18th International Federated Conference on Distributed Computing Techniques (DisCoTec) took place in Lisbon, Portugal, from June 19 to June 23, 2023. It was organized by the Department of Computer Science of NOVA School of Science and Technology, NOVA University Lisbon. The DisCoTec series is one of the major events sponsored by the International Federation for Information Processing (IFIP). It comprises three conferences:

– COORDINATION, the IFIP WG 6.1 25th International Conference on Coordination Models and Languages
– DAIS, the IFIP WG 6.1 23rd International Conference on Distributed Applications and Interoperable Systems
– FORTE, the IFIP WG 6.1 43rd International Conference on Formal Techniques for Distributed Objects, Components and Systems

Together, these conferences cover a broad spectrum of distributed computing subjects, ranging from theoretical foundations and formal description techniques to systems research issues. In addition to the individual sessions of each conference, the event also included plenary sessions that gathered attendees from the three conferences. These included joint invited speaker sessions and a joint session for the best papers and artefacts from the three conferences. The keynote speakers of DisCoTec 2023 are listed below:

– Azalea Raad, Imperial College London, UK
– Frank Pfenning, Carnegie Mellon University, USA
– Peter Pietzuch, Imperial College London, UK

Associated with the federated event were also the following satellite events:

– ICE, the 16th Interaction and Concurrency Experience
– BehAPI Tutorial Day, a series of three tutorials covering results from the BehAPI project

in addition to other short tutorials on relevant topics to DisCoTec.

I would like to thank the Program Committee chairs of the different events for their help and cooperation during the preparation of the conference, and the Steering Committee and Advisory Boards of DisCoTec for their guidance, patience, and support. The organization of DisCoTec 2023 was only possible thanks to the work of the Organizing Committee, including João Costa Seco, João Leitão, Mário Pereira, Carlos Baquero (publicity chair), Simão Melo de Sousa (workshops and tutorials chair), Joana Dâmaso (logistics and finances), as well as all the students who volunteered their time to help. Finally, I would like to thank IFIP WG 6.1 and NOVA LINCS for sponsoring this event,

Springer's Lecture Notes in Computer Science team for their support and sponsorship, and EasyChair for providing the reviewing infrastructure.

June 2023   Carla Ferreira

Preface

This volume contains the papers presented at the 43rd IFIP WG 6.1 International Conference on Formal Techniques for Distributed Objects, Components, and Systems (FORTE 2022), held as one of three main conferences of the 18th International Federated Conference on Distributed Computing Techniques (DisCoTec 2023) during June 19–23, 2023. The conference was organized by the NOVA University Lisbon.

FORTE is a well-established forum for fundamental research on theory, models, tools, and applications for distributed systems. It solicits submissions focused on foundational aspects of distributed software systems, presenting approaches or tools to formally model, soundly implement, and rigorously validate these demanding but ever more necessary systems and applications. As our dependency on such software systems grows, also our responsibility as researchers grows to provide both trustworthy and usable solutions.

The main topics of interest include:

- Language concepts for concurrency and distribution, supported by rigorous semantics, well-supported pragmatics, and/or expressive illustrative use-cases.
- Analysis techniques, methodologies, and/or algorithms, using testing and/or verification, to validate (aspects of) the soundness of various types of concurrent and distributed systems, including communication and network protocols, service-oriented systems, adaptive distributed systems, cyber-physical systems, and sensor networks.
- Principles for qualitative and quantitative security analysis of distributed systems.
- Applications of formal methods and techniques for studying the quality, reliability, availability, and safety of concrete distributed systems. We are especially interested in "real-life" case studies and industrial applications involving real distributed systems.
- Emerging challenges and hot topics in distributed systems (broadly construed), such as software-defined networks, distributed ledgers, smart contracts, and blockchain technologies, etc.

Papers in three different categories were solicited: regular research papers, long tool papers, and short papers describing innovative and promising ideas. For tool papers, artefact submission was required, and artefact acceptance was mandatory. For regular papers, artefact submission was also enabled.

The Program Committee received a total of 26 submissions, written by authors from 15 different countries. Of these, 13 papers were selected for inclusion in the scientific program (an acceptance rate of 50 %). Each submission was single-blind reviewed by at least three Program Committee members with the help of 15 external reviewers. In addition, 4 description paper were submitted, and 3 of them were accepted. These papers are marked with a badge in the proceedings. For the first time, FORTE introduced a partial rebuttal phase, for papers that raised questions that the reviewers would like to clarify before deciding about acceptance. The option to rebut was provided to the authors of 9 papers. The selection of accepted submissions was based on electronic discussions via the EasyChair conference management system.

As program chairs of FORTE 2022, we actively contributed to the selection of the keynote speakers for DisCoTec 2023:

– Azalea Raad, Imperial College London, UK
– Frank Pfenning, Carnegie Mellon University, USA
– Peter Pietzuch, Imperial College London, UK

We are most grateful to Azalea Raad for accepting our invitation to be the FORTE-related keynote speaker. This volume contains the abstract of her talk entitled "Principles of Persistent Programming".

We wish to thank all the authors of submitted papers, all the members of the Program Committee for their thorough evaluations of the submissions, and the external reviewers who assisted the evaluation process. We would also like to express our appreciation to the Steering Committee of FORTE for their advice and suggestions. Last but not least, we thank the DisCoTec General Chair, Carla Ferreira, and her organization team for their hard, effective work in providing an excellent environment for FORTE 2023 and all other conferences and workshops.

June 2023   Marieke Huisman
                                                                   António Ravara

Organization

Program Committee

Elvira Albert	Universidad Complutense de Madrid, Spain
Jiri Barnat	Masaryk University, Czech Republic
Georgiana Caltais	University of Twente, The Netherlands
Silvia Crafa	University of Padova, Italy
Mariangiola Dezani-Ciancaglini	Università di Torino, Italy
Adrian Francalanza	University of Malta, Malta
Hongfei Fu	Shanghai Jiao Tong University, China
Fatemeh Ghassemi	University of Tehran, Iran
Rob van Glabbeek	University of Edinburgh, UK
Helle Hvid Hansen	University of Groningen, The Netherlands
Marieke Huisman (Co-chair)	University of Twente, The Netherlands
Sung-Shik Jongmans	Open University of the Netherlands; Centrum Wiskunde & Informatica (CWI), The Netherlands
Jan Kofron	Charles University, Czech Republic
Alfons Laarman	Leiden University, The Netherlands
Claudio Antares	Mezzina Università di Urbino, Italy
Mohammadreza Mousavi	King's College London, UK
Daniele Nantes-Sobrinho	Imperial College London, UK
Luca Padovani	Università di Camerino, Italy
Kirstin Peters	Universität Augsburg, Germany
Anna Philippou	University of Cyprus, Cyprus
António Ravara (Co-chair)	NOVA University Lisbon, Portugal
Anne Remke	WWU Münster, Germany
Vasco T. Vasconcelos	LaSiGE and University of Lisbon, Portugal
Yuting Wang	Shanghai Jiao Tong University, China

Artefact Evaluation Committee

Tom van Dijk (Co-chair)	University of Twente, The Netherlands
Andrea Esposito	Università di Urbino, Italy
Ludovico Fusco	University of Urbino "Carlo Bo", Italy
Luís Horta	NOVA LINCS, University of Beira Interior, Portugal

Milan Lopuhaä-Zwakenberg   University of Twente, The Netherlands
Mário Pereira (Co-chair)   NOVA University Lisbon, Portugal
Peixin Wang   University of Oxford, UK

Additional Reviewers

Attard, Duncan Paul
Barkaoui, Kamel
Bartolo Burlò, Christian
Ciardo, Gianfranco
Edixhoven, Luc
Gheri, Lorenzo
Le Brun, Matthew Alan
Lopuhaä-Zwakenberg, Milan
Lööw, Andreas
Nazirkhanova, Kamilla
Psara, Kyriaki
Quadrini, Michela
Rot, Jurriaan
Villoria Gonzalez, Alejandro
Wißmann, Thorsten

Principles of Persistent Programming (Keynote Talk)

Azalea Raad

Imperial College London, UK

Persistent programming is the art of developing programs that operate on persistent (non-volatile) states that survive program termination, be it planned or abrupt (e.g. due to a power failure). Persistent programming poses several important challenges: 1) persistent systems have complex—and often unspecified—semantics in that operations do not generally persist in their execution order; 2) software bugs in persistent settings can lead to permanent data corruption; and 3) traditional testing techniques are inapplicable in persistent settings. Can formal methods come to the rescue?

Contents

Model-Based Testing and Petri Nets

Concurrent Programming

An Experimental Evaluation of Tools for Grading Concurrent Programming Exercises

Manuel Barros$^{(\boxtimes)}$ ⓘ, Maria Ramos ⓘ, Alexandre Gomes ⓘ, Alcino Cunha ⓘ,
José Pereira ⓘ, and Paulo Sérgio Almeida ⓘ

INESC TEC & U. Minho, Braga, Portugal
{manuel.q.barros,maria.j.ramos}@inesctec.pt, pg46950@alunos.uminho.pt,
{alcino,jop,psa}@di.uminho.pt

Abstract. Automatic grading based on unit tests is a key feature of massive open online courses (MOOC) on programming, as it allows instant feedback to students and enables courses to scale up. This technique works well for sequential programs, by checking outputs against a sample of inputs, but unfortunately it is not adequate for detecting races and deadlocks, which precludes its use for concurrent programming, a key subject in parallel and distributed computing courses. In this paper we provide a hands-on evaluation of verification and testing tools for concurrent programs, collecting a precise set of requirements, and describing to what extent they can or can not be used for this purpose. Our conclusion is that automatic grading of concurrent programming exercises remains an open challenge.

Keywords: Concurrent programming · Testing · Verification · e-Learning

1 Introduction

Learning concurrent programming is hard. For students coming from a sequential programming background, writing programs with multiple threads that share data is confusing and difficult to get right. Concurrent programming gives rise to new classes of bugs, such as deadlocks [24] and race conditions [34].

When learning to program, students are often presented with a system such as *Codeboard* [1], with a variety of coding exercises, accompanied by unit tests. Students can submit solutions and find out how they perform based on the number of tests passed. Unit testing proves to be a valuable technique for autograding simple sequential programs. It lets students experiment and get instant feedback, exposing problems and guiding them to correct solutions.

This work is financed by National Funds through the Portuguese funding agency, FCT
- Fundação para a Ciência e a Tecnologia, within project LA/P/0063/2020.

M. Huisman and A. Ravara (Eds.): FORTE 2023, LNCS 13910, pp. 3–20, 2023.
https://doi.org/10.1007/978-3-031-35355-0_1

Unlike for sequential code, identifying incorrect concurrent code is not trivial. Even for sequential programs testing is non-exhaustive, but it is relatively easy to define a set of unit tests that almost always detects incorrect solutions. However, unit tests are much less reliable when checking concurrent programs, where errors are often subtle and may manifest into visible bugs only after many program executions. This non-determinism may lead students to falsely assume that their programs are correct when tests show no anomalies.

Given the benefits of autograders for learning sequential programming, we would like to deploy similar learning strategies for concurrent programming. For that purpose, we would need tools that automatically detect common concurrency anomalies, like race conditions and deadlocks, and provide accurate and helpful feedback. As unit testing is generally inappropriate for concurrent code, we turn to more sophisticated techniques, such as automatic race detectors.

The main goal of this work is to evaluate existing tools that perform automatic analysis of multi-threaded Java code. Focusing on Java, instead of a more verification friendly pseudo-code specification language such as Promela [25] or PlusCal [29], enables a systems approach that considers the interaction of concurrency with all the complications of the language and platform. For instance, reference aliasing and exceptions in the Java language can contribute to races (by exposing supposedly encapsulated state) and deadlocks (by preventing locks from being released), respectively.

In particular, we want to evaluate the possibility of using these tools in an educational context, to automatically grade and give prompt feedback on student submissions to concurrent programming exercises regarding races and deadlocks. Although, being race and deadlock free is not the same as being optimal, as solutions might, for instance, overly restrict concurrency to meet tests. The possibility that an inadequate solution is accepted by automatic testing also exists in sequential programming exercises but can be mitigated by judicious problem statements. The same care should be taken when devising concurrency problems.

The rest of this paper is structured as follows. Section 2 establishes the scope of this experiment by describing the requirements for automatic grading. Section 3 introduces a set of typical concurrent programming problems and corresponding solutions containing various errors. Then, Sect. 4 introduces currently available tools that can be repurposed for automatically grading these solutions. Section 5 presents the results of the experiments and Sect. 6 uses them to compare the tools. Finally, Sect. 7 concludes the paper by summarizing the main lessons learned and proposing future work.

2   Scope

Since we are interested in tools for an educational setting, our requirements are different than those regarding tools suitable for production settings. Our main use case is finding concurrency bugs in submissions to proposed exercises. Normally, students are given a specification in the form of some interface methods and are asked to write thread-safe Java classes that implement them. Our analysis targets will be small, self-contained programs, with just a few Java classes.

We are not interested in tools that require thoughtfully annotating or modifying parts of the code. The analysis of hundreds of submissions needs to be automatic and require at most a one-time set-up, such as writing a script or defining some sort of specification. Tools that require the tester to manually analyze each submission fall outside of our scope, but tools that require simple annotations can be considered, as long as annotating code can be automated.

We will take into consideration the rates of false-positives/negatives. A false-negative is a result where a tool does not report a bug when it exists and a false-positive is when a tool reports a bug that does not exist. When automatic analyzers are being used to give students feedback on potential concurrency problems, it is important to have a small rate of false-negatives, so students are not mislead into thinking that there is nothing wrong with their code, which could cause them to develop bad programming habits. But when grading students assignments, we are mostly concerned with the false-positive rate, as we cannot afford to falsely classify a program as incorrect when a student grade depends on it.

For the purpose of this evaluation, we are interested in two types of bugs: data races and deadlocks. A data race occurs when two threads access the same data item without using some synchronization mechanism, one access being a write. A deadlock corresponds to a situation where every member of a set of threads is waiting for some action to be taken by another thread of the same set. In most deadlock scenarios, a thread is waiting for a signal to be sent or a lock to be released. In this situation, every thread is prevented from making progress. It is important to note that data races and deadlocks are a subset of the possible concurrency anomalies. There are even subtler concurrency bugs that silently (with no crash or stall) violate the intended semantics of a program, but we choose to focus on these since they often occur when first learning concurrent programming.

3 Dataset

Our dataset for evaluating analysis tools mainly consists of two collections of concurrent programs. The first one contains different implementations of a thread-safe `Bank` class, mostly written by students, with operations such as fetching the balance of an account or transferring money between accounts. The other one is made up of different implementations of a `BoundedBuffer`. Each program was manually revised and labeled based on which bugs (deadlocks and/or data races) were present. For each of the two datasets we created tests that exercised the different methods of the supposedly thread-safe classes under workloads of multiple threads. This was necessary for the evaluation of the dynamic checking tools. Both collections of programs are available in an online repository.[1]

---

[1] https://github.com/mj-ramos/FORTE2023.

```
class Bank {
    private static class Account {
        private int balance;
        private ReentrantLock account_lock;

        int balance();
        boolean deposit(int value);
        boolean withdraw(int value);
    }

    private Map<Integer, Account> accounts;
    private int nextId;
    private ReentrantLock bank_lock;

    int createAccount(int balance);
    int closeAccount(int id);
    int balance(int id);
    boolean deposit(int id, int value);
    boolean withdraw(int id, int value);
    boolean transfer(int from, int to, int value);
    int totalBalance(int[] ids);
}
```

Fig. 1. Bank class variables and methods.

Additionally, we use the JBench [23] benchmark to evaluate data race detection tools. It consists of a collection of programs containing data races, specifically curated for evaluating data race detection tools. Although JBench will be part of our dataset, we will mostly use the Bank and BoundedBuffer for qualitatively evaluating the tools we explore, since these examples have been carefully revised and better resemble the kind of concurrent programming exercises presented to students. Also, it is easier to manually evaluate each tool by running it on a collection of small programs sharing the same interface and whose semantics we understand clearly. JBench will mostly serve as an extra benchmark to assess how each tool performs when ran with no special configuration against an existing set of programs known to contain data races.

3.1 The Bank dataset

Part of our dataset is composed of submissions to an exercise that asked students to implement a Bank class that manages a set of client accounts, as shown in Fig. 1. This problem statement is aimed at applying multiple locks and the two-phase locking protocol when traversing and modifying collections, a key learning outcome for concurrent programming. It is useful also to demonstrate the usefulness and applicability of different locking primitives.

A correct implementation should be thread-safe: it should work correctly when used by multiple threads concurrently. A correct implementation should allow concurrency, but the result of running multiple concurrent operations must correspond to the outcome of some sequential execution. This implies, for example, that a thread cannot observe the state of the bank in the middle of a transfer.

Besides the simplistic solution that uses a single lock and overly restricts concurrency, the assignment then suggests two different implementations. The first one uses `ReentrantLock` instances for protecting accesses to each account and accesses to the collection of accounts. Alternatively, `ReentrantReadWriteLock` can be used to synchronize accesses to the collection of accounts (the main point of contention), allowing more concurrency. Writing such a thread-safe class, that maximizes concurrency by applying two-phase locking and using `ReentrantReadWriteLock`, is not trivial. There is a lot of room for introducing concurrency bugs.

In addition to bugs caused by unprotected accesses to the collection of accounts, or to the accounts themselves, there is a particularly subtle class of problems that can lead to deadlocks. It corresponds to the scenario where two threads attempt to acquire the same two locks but in reverse orders. This may cause the two threads to block indefinitely waiting for each other's lock to be released. This type of bug can arise in implementations that use `ReentrantReadWriteLock` to protect accesses to the collection, particularly in methods involving multiple accounts (`transfer` or `totalBalance`).

In total, the `Bank` dataset is composed of seventeen different implementations. Eight of them contain data races and five contain deadlocks. Ten of them are actual student submissions. The remaining seven variants were inspired by typical student errors collected over many years of teaching concurrent programming.

3.2   The `BoundedBuffer` dataset

The *bounded buffer* is a classical problem in concurrent programming and a construct that can be used as a building block for inter-thread synchronization and communication. It is thus widely available in various forms, such as operating system *pipes* and in concurrent programming libraries. It is also a good example of how synchronization primitives such as semaphores or monitors can be used.

The `BoundedBuffer` dataset was developed specifically for the purpose of this study based on well-known pitfalls and the experience of authors teaching concurrent programming. The first step was writing a correct implementation, as shown in Fig. 2, using a single `ReentrantLock` and two `Conditions` for concurrency control.

The two main methods are `pop` and `push`. The first one is responsible for removing an element from the array. The lock is acquired and an element is removed if the array is not empty, signaling a producer that is waiting for space to be freed and freeing the lock. If the array is empty, then the consumer will free the lock and wait for a producer to add an element to the array. As soon as the consumer is signaled by a producer, it acquires the lock, checking again if the array is empty and repeating the process. The `push` method works in the same way, but for the addition of an item instead.

The second step was identifying possible ways in which bugs could arise. For example, data races can occur when the array is accessed outside the scope of

```java
class BoundedBuffer<T> {
    private final int max;
    private List<T> queue = new ArrayList<>();
    private Lock lock = new ReentrantLock();
    private Condition notFull = lock.newCondition();
    private Condition notEmpty = lock.newCondition();

    public BoundedBuffer(int size) { this.max = size; }

    public T pop() throws InterruptedException {
        try {
            lock.lock();
            while (queue.isEmpty()) notEmpty.await();
            notFull.signal();
            return queue.remove(0);
        } finally {
            lock.unlock();
        }
    }

    public void push(T value) throws InterruptedException {
        try {
            lock.lock();
            while (queue.size()>=max) notFull.await();
            notEmpty.signal();
            queue.add(value);
        } finally {
            lock.unlock();
        }
    }
}
```

Fig. 2. Correct implementation of the Bounded Buffer class.

a lock. There are also ways in which deadlocks can arise, such as when using a single Condition and signal, or signaling only if the buffer is empty or full. Not retesting predicates (i.e., using if instead of while) can lead to exceptions, either due to spurious wake-ups (which may or may not happen), or the usage of signalAll. Table 1 shows different ways in which a bounded buffer implementation can be wrong.

The third step was to create multiple permutations of the identified possible mistakes, with eleven classes being created using this method. Two other correct classes were created by changing the way in which the condition in the push and pop methods is checked and the way the threads are signaled. Together with the original class, we ended up with a total of fourteen classes in our dataset.

Table 1. Concurrency bugs in a Bounded Buffer implementation.

Method	Buggy code	Outcome
pop	remove after lock release	data race, deadlock
pop	remove before lock acquisition	data race
push	insert after lock release	data race, deadlock
push	insert before lock acquisition	data race
pop, push	only one Condition and signal	deadlock
pop, push	signal only if empty/full	deadlock
pop, push	test with if (instead of while)	exception
pop, push	test with if and signalAll	exception

3.3　JBench

JBench is a collection of multi-threaded programs specifically targeted at benchmarking data race detectors. It is composed of several small programs and some real-world applications, each with a number of known data races. Every program in this repository has been manually verified by its creators, and every data race has been properly documented.

The types of programs contained in JBench vary in size and nature. It contains 6 real-world examples, consisting of actual applications, and 42 small, academic programs. Since our targets are small programs with few classes, we excluded the real-world programs from our dataset. Among the remaining programs, there are some whose format better resembles the kind of programs students are asked to develop (thread-safe implementations of some interface) and others that mainly consist of a main method that launches several threads that exercise some sequence of statements that possibly leads to data races.

4　Tools

Our method for finding tools for automatic analysis of concurrent programs mainly consisted in scanning through scientific papers related to this topic. As a starting point, we analyzed a survey of tools [32], to find potential candidates for testing. Additionally, most papers we analysed were found either by searching through Google Scholar, using terms like "deadlock detection" and "data race detection", or by following references in relevant works.

Our experience shows that, despite the large amount of published work on automatic analysis of concurrent programs, there are not many publicly available tools with active support that can easily be downloaded and ran on current Java code. Many articles describe tools or algorithms for detecting concurrency anomalies but do not present a publicly available artifact [15,17,18,20,22,30,31, 37–39,42]. In other cases, where a link for the tool was provided, the tool was no longer available [3,11,12,19,27,35,40]. Some tools were developed for now

```
src/RacyDict.java:20: warning: Thread Safety Violation
   Read/Write race. Non-private method 'RacyDict.get(...)'
      reads without synchronization from container 'this.dict
      ' via call to 'Map.get(...)'. Potentially races with
      write in method 'RacyDict.put(...)'.
 Reporting because another access to the same memory occurs
    on a background thread, although this access may not.
   18.
   19.         public String get(String key) {
   20. >          return dict.get(key);
   21.       }
   22.   }


Found 1 issue
                   Issue Type(ISSUED_TYPE_ID): #
  Thread Safety Violation(THREAD_SAFETY_VIOLATION): 1
```

Fig. 3. RacerD output report example.

deprecated Java versions [21, 28, 33] and others do not work with the package java.util.concurrent [5, 8].

Excluding all the tools that we were unable to run for the reasons mentioned above resulted in a set of four tools: Infer, Java Pathfinder, RV-Predict, and MultithreadedTC. We believe these four tools are representative of the current panorama of mature tools for data race and deadlock detection for Java programs.

4.1 Infer

Facebook's Infer [16] is a static analysis tool for Java, C, and Objective-C, able to find several types of bugs in a program. For this evaluation, we explored its ability to detect data races and deadlocks.

Infer checks Java programs for the existence of data races using a static race detector called RacerD [14]. RacerD looks for potential data races between non-private methods of a Java class when run in parallel with one another. RacerD starts from non-private methods but will recursively analyze each method call it encounters. Given a program, RacerD will run this analysis for classes annotated with @ThreadSafe and classes that it can infer are intended to run in a concurrent context (classes that use locks, for example).

The generated reports provide a detailed description of the data races found, intended to give a clear understanding of their location, as well as the original method calls that gave rise to each bug. For example, when ran against a supposedly thread-safe class called RacyDict, containing a get method that reads from a Map without synchronization, RacerD outputs the report on Fig. 3.

RacerD was designed to be used at Facebook. It is suited for large code bases that evolve rapidly over time. Its design favours speed, scalability, low friction (meaning it demands little effort from the tester) and effective signaling (meaning it only reports high-confidence bugs, aiming at reducing false-positives and always providing meaningful reports). The detection of some data races is purposely compromised in order to achieve these goals. As such, false-negatives are possible.

Infer is also able to analyze a program in search of starvation issues. One of the issues it tries to find is the possibility of deadlocks. To trigger this analysis, Infer must be run with the -starvation flag. It will report a deadlock if there is the possibility of two threads attempting to acquire two locks in reverse orders.

4.2   Java Pathfinder

Java Pathfinder (JPF) core [6] is a Java Virtual Machine that executes the system under test (SUT) checking for properties such as unhandled exceptions, deadlocks and user-defined assertions. JPF is a model checker, therefore it does not simply test the SUT. Instead, it explores all potential execution paths, identifying points in programs which represent execution choices, from which the program could proceed differently. Execution choices can be due to different scheduling sequences or random values, and JPF allows the user to control which choices are explored if some of them are known to be uninteresting.

One of the main problems of model checking is the state space explosion. In order to mitigate this problem, JPF uses Partial Order Reduction (POR) to minimize context switches between threads that do not result in interesting new program states. This is done without prior analysis or annotation of the program, only by examining which instructions can have inter-thread effects.

To extract information from JPF while exploring all execution paths, JPF uses event-driven programming, through listeners for handling events. In particular, to allow data race detection, we need to extend JPF with a listener called PreciseRaceDetector.

One important aspect of this tool is the fact that it is highly extensible. Besides allowing users to create their own listeners or choice generators, is possible to define publishers, to produce different output formats, or bytecode factories, to provide alternative execution semantics of bytecode instructions. In our evaluation, we only extended it with simple listeners.

4.3   RV-Predict

RV-Predict [10] is a dynamic data race detector that is both sound and maximal. Dynamic means that it executes the program in order to extract an execution trace to analyze. Sound means that it only reports races that are real (no false-positives). And maximal means that it finds all the races that can be found by any other sound race detector analyzing the same execution trace.

RV-Predict works by analyzing a sequentially consistent execution trace and changing the order of events to create a new set of traces, which are then analyzed in order to find traces that are consistent and manifest a data race [26,41].

4.4 MultithreadedTC

MultithreadedTC [36] is a framework that allows exercising specific interleavings of threads in Java applications. Threads are scheduled unpredictably by operating systems, making failures in concurrent applications non-deterministic, since they might not occur every time the application is run. The idea behind this framework is to make it possible to have deterministic and reproducible tests for concurrent code, despite some critical interleavings being hard to exercise because of the presence of blocking and timing.

To coordinate threads, MultithreadedTC uses a clock that runs in a separate thread. The clock advances when all threads are blocked and at least one is waiting for a tick. This simple mechanism makes it possible to delay operations within a thread without using functions like `Thread.sleep()`, which make the test timing dependent. These delays are crucial to define specific interleavings and allow the detection of deadlocks. When threads are blocked and none of them are waiting for a tick or a timeout, the test is declared to be in deadlock.

One of the main features of MultithreadedTC is its integration with JUnit [9]. JUnit assertions can be used to verify, for example, the current clock tick.

To fully utilize the potential of MultithreadedTC to verify a concurrent program, the source code needs to be changed. The task of specifying concrete thread interleavings requires threads to be programmed as individual methods, like `void thread1() {...}` and extra code to be written that defines the desired interleaving. This is not suitable for our case study, since we want the testing to be automated. Automation may be possible to achieve, but given the variety of ways in which students can program, adding lines of code to define interleavings might not be that simple.

It is possible to use MultithreadedTC without defining interleavings, by simply running multiple tests systematically and, through JUnit, define assertions for the desired results. However, this type of testing gives no guarantees about the results – they are non-deterministic. There is also the possibility of those assertions failing for reasons other than concurrency anomalies. Since every test will give different results, we decided to exclude MultithreadedTC from the quantitative results presented in the next section.

5   Results

Tables 2 and 3 present the quantitative results obtained by running each tool against our dataset, excluding MultithreadedTC, as mentioned above. It is important to note that no tool ever reported a false-positive. Since every program without concurrency bugs was always correctly labeled as bug-free, results only highlight the ratio of files reported to have bugs over the actual number of programs with bugs. Table 4 shows the average run time of each tool for each dataset.

We used Infer v1.1.0, RV-Predict v2.1.3, MultithreadedTC v1.01 with JUnit v4.13.2, and the latest version of JPF from GitHub [7]. MultithreadedTC was tested with jdk-11 and the rest of them with jdk-8.

Table 2. Ratio of programs with data races reported over programs with data races. Elements marked with * mean that some data races might not have been caught because of other problems in the programs.

Dataset	Tool		
	Infer	Pathfinder	RV-Predict
Bank	5/8	5*/8	8/8
Bounded buffer	9/9	0/9	9/9
JBench	15/30	30*/42	26*/42

Table 3. Ratio of programs with deadlocks reported over programs with deadlocks. Elements marked with * mean that some deadlocks might not have been caught because of other problems in the programs.

Dataset	Tool		
	Infer	Pathfinder	RV-Predict
Bank	0/5	4*/5	N/A
Bounded buffer	0/10	9/10	N/A

5.1   Infer

In the `Bank` dataset, Infer's RacerD misses three of the faulty programs, revealing two limitations of RacerD. The first limitation, already known [14], caused RacerD to miss races in two programs, caused by wrong usage of `Reentrant-ReadWriteLock`: `closeAccount` acquires a read lock instead of a write lock, even though it updates the map. The other missed race reveals another limitation of RacerD: it fails to detect races caused by unsynchronized accesses to the `balance` field of an `Account`. Further testing revealed that RacerD is unable to detect data races on fields of objects stored in a container in the class being tested.

Since Infer depends on a working compilation command to work, for testing RacerD we reduced the JBench dataset to only those examples with a valid compilation command. This excludes 12 from the 42 small programs in JBench. From the remaining 30 examples, RacerD detects data races in 15 of them.

It is worth mentioning that RacerD is fast. It takes around 600 ms per `Bank` example (each of these examples has around 200 lines of code), and around 160 ms per `BoundedBuffer` example (each example has around 40 lines of code).

Infer's documentation mentions that it can detect deadlocks when run with the `starvation` flag activated. However, it did not detect any of the deadlocks present in our dataset. For the `Bank` in particular, it failed to detect any problems in examples containing the following issues:

Table 4. Average run time in seconds for each tool and each dataset. For JPF we also show the number of examples for which the analysis was interrupted after the chosen 4m time limit.

Dataset	Tool		
	Infer	Pathfinder	RV-Predict
Bank	0.6	95.9 (2)	4.6
Bounded buffer	0.2	240.0 (14)	9.8
JBench	1.3	87.2 (14)	9.3

```
public int totalBalance(int[] ids) {
    int total = 0;
    Account1[] acs =new Account1[ids.length];
    rlock.lock();
    try {
        for (int i : ids) {
            Account1 c = map.get(i);
            if (c == null)
                return 0;
            acs[i]=c;
        }
        ...
}
```

Fig. 4. Common error in the Bank example

1. Methods that can cause two concurrent threads to try to acquire the same two locks in reverse order.
2. Methods that do not call unlock() on a previously acquired Lock object.

5.2 Java Pathfinder

In many tests, JPF was not able to detect data races or deadlocks because the programs had other bugs, causing exceptions to be thrown. This happened frequently in the JBench examples, especially in the more complex ones.

There is a very common error in the bank examples, in the totalBalance method, where many students confuse array indexes with account identifiers, as shown in the code fragment in Fig. 4. If the array ids is [2,3,4], an index out of bounds exception is thrown at line 10. JPF reports this exception and stops the execution, as expected. After correcting this error, JPF successfully found the deadlock related to the out-of-order acquisition of the locks. This is why the tables above may mislead the reader into thinking that JPF is not capable of detecting some concurrency anomalies. For the deadlock cases in the bank samples, we corrected the code that was interfering with the deadlock detection, and all deadlocks were found.

Regarding data race detection, even with examples that were correctly implemented, apart from the concurrency problems, JPF could not find all the anomalies. One interesting outcome is that JPF never explicitly reported a data race in the bounded buffer examples, although in many examples it is possible to see the exception of index out of bounds being thrown, that, in the case of the bounded buffer, is potentially caused by data races.

JPF found all deadlocks but one: the deadlock that was already explained in Sect. 3.2 and is related to the use of `signal()` instead of `signalAll()`.

It is important to mention that, in many cases, JPF takes a long time to analyze the code, and we decided to impose a time limit of 4 min. In nine of the JBench samples the analysis timed out. The test class used for the `Bounded Buffer` with the RV-predict tool could not be used with JPF, because it cannot handle many threads, even with the partial order reduction enabled. For this reason, in almost all of the tests in this example, JPF timed out, even in those using only four threads.

5.3   RV-Predict

RV-Predict is exclusively a data race detector, and therefore not applicable to deadlock detection. In theory, RV-Predict does not report any false-positives, thus only the examples where data races could occur were tested.

RV-Predict was able to detect all of the races in `Bank` and `Bounded Buffer` datasets and being rather quick too. In the JBench dataset, RV-Predict did not detect races in some of the more complex programs: increasing the window of detection, that determines the largest distance between events where RV-Predict is going to try and find races, would make it possible to detect more races, but the prediction phase would take much longer to finish. In some examples RV-Predict could not find any trace that executed correctly – in these cases RV-Predict did not detect any races. When RV-Predict finishes the prediction phase, it will always run one trace of the execution. If a deadlock is encountered, or an exception is thrown, then the execution of the trace will not finish correctly, but if a log directory is specified, all of the races encountered will be logged.

6   Discussion

Infer is easy to use and requires a minimal set-up to make it work. Although its `starvation` analysis failed to detect any deadlock in our dataset, its race detection component, RacerD, showed several desirable qualities for our use case, namely:

- No need to manually inspect and modify the code under test. In some cases, some classes might need to be marked with the `ThreadSafe` annotation, but that can be automated for multiple files.
- Can easily be used to automatically check several programs and generate an aggregated report with the bugs found.

– Its reports provide detailed and understandable explanations regarding the source of the detected races (this is a really desirable feature for a tool meant to be used by students).
– Absence of false-positives, meaning that it could be safely used in automatic evaluation.
– The analysis is fast, which makes the tool viable to use on a large number of examples at once.

Another important feature is that Infer is already present in some e-Learning platforms, namely *Codeboard*, and can be used out of the box to provide automatic feedback on solutions to concurrent programming exercises.

RacerD shines when it comes to ease of use, but there were some data races it was unable to identify. RacerD highlights how our evaluation criteria might differ from those one would use to choose a tool to employ in an industrial setting. This tool sacrifices soundness for scalability. Since our use case involves small programs, we would rather have a less efficient tool, but that does not have false-negatives.

MultithreadedTC is an interesting tool for testing concurrent code, but it has some downsides. For instance, there is no specific mechanism to detect data races. What can be done to hopefully find data races is to define some assertions that express what are the expected results and run the code multiple times so that possibily many interleavings are exercised. One of the problems with this approach is the false-negatives because it is possible that the scenario which leads to wrong results does not come up. In fact, even for deadlock testing, when following this strategy, this can happen. Another downside is the lack of information given when a deadlock is found.

One important aspect of this framework is the fact that the testing methodology follows a *white box approach* [13]. This means that one needs to know the internal design of the application to be able to do more sophisticated tests. To define a specific interleaving, it is sometimes necessary to add lines of code inside a method. This can be seen as a downside since it is essential to have knowledge of how classes are coded, which is particularly undesirable in our use case of testing students' submissions. It is possible to use this tool without the methods that allow the definition of specific interleavings, as we did in some tests we performed, but this is not using the tool to its full potential and has the problem of non-determinism in the results, as described above.

Configuring JPF was not an easy task. Also, in early experiments, it never detected any deadlocks. Later, with the help of another user [2], we were able to find out that JPF was not really adapted to work with `ReentrantReadWrite-Locks`. Luckily, someone already had encountered this problem and we managed to fix it by modifying some of the source code of JPF [4].

One downside of JPF is the amount of output generated when the property that allows finding multiple errors (`search.multiple_errors`) is enabled, since all the paths of execution that exhibit a particular data race will be reported as an error. At the end of the execution, the output can have thousands of lines pointing the occurrence of the same data race. Another aspect related to the output is the poor information provided regarding detected deadlocks. In some cases, where the same example had two different deadlocks, it was difficult to understand if both deadlocks were being reported. For this reason, we had to perform tests separately to understand if a specific deadlock was detected.

Although JPF presented good results in detecting deadlocks, testing was extremely slow, even considering simple programs with a reduced number of threads. This makes it somewhat unsuitable for the purpose of our study, which is to find a tool that students can use to test their programs. It is not reasonable to expect that a student will wait more than 20 min for the result of a test of an implementation of a simple exercise.

RV-Predict shows great promise. It is very easy to install and use, and only requires writing a main test program. This main program does not even need to be complicated, in fact, the more simplistic the better since RV-Predict will take care of finding the traces where a data race could occur and still be fast. The only downside of RV-Predict is testing complex programs. A program where multiple methods need to be tested for data races means that the prediction phase will take much longer to complete since multiple combinations of states need to be tested. This could be circumvented by dividing the main test into smaller tests, which will accelerate the prediction process but, in turn, less data races might be detected.

7   Conclusions

The main goal of this work was to evaluate existing tools for automatic detection of concurrency bugs in Java programs, to determine their potential for being used in automatic grading of concurrency programming exercises. We focused on analysing tools for detecting data races and deadlocks.

One of our main takeaways is that, despite the amount of academic research on automatic analysis of concurrent code, there are not many mature and readily available tools for detecting concurrency problems in Java programs. In particular, we found no tool that excelled in detecting both data races and deadlocks.

Regarding data race detection, we were most impressed by Infer's RacerD and RV-Predict. Infer does static analysis, while presenting no false-positives and reporting errors in a comprehensible and educational fashion. However, it is unable to catch some problems that might arise in students' code. RV-Predict requires constructing a small testing program to exercise the code under evaluation (since it is does dynamic analysis) but performed very well with our dataset. We believe that RV-Predict is a good fit for a tool to be used in an educational setting for automatic detection of data races in students' code.

As for deadlock detection, we struggled to find a tool that completely satisfied our criteria. We had the most success with Java Pathfinder. It found most of the deadlocks in our dataset, however its run time makes it unfit to be used to evaluate hundreds of students' submissions. We can thus conclude that the subject of automatic deadlock detection for small Java programs is still a promising field of investigation.

One interesting future step would be to conduct a more precise analysis of the results obtained with each tool. For each type of bug (data race or deadlock) and for each program in our dataset, we only tested if a given tool labelled that program as erroneous or bug-free. This leaves room for undetected false-negatives (in case the analysis tool detects only a portion of the existing bugs) as well as false-positives (in case the tool reports more bugs than there really exist). Conducting such analysis is not trivial, since the way static tools and dynamic tools report errors is fundamentally different (for example, a single race reported by RacerD might be exercised more than once in some test method used by a dynamic race detector like RV-Predict, which would cause it to report more than one race).

References

1. Codeboard. https://codeboard.io/. Accessed 30 Apr 2023
2. Deadlock not being detected. https://groups.google.com/g/java-pathfinder/c/rzkaeuNDZCY. Accessed 04 Jan 2023
3. Dl-Check. https://github.com/devexperts/dlcheck. Accessed 02 Jan 2023
4. Google groups thread: java.lang.error: java.lang.nosuchfieldexception: tid. https://groups.google.com/g/java-pathfinder/c/t1n73xdyrFI. Accessed 29 April 2023
5. JaDA. http://jada.cs.unibo.it/demo.html. Accessed 30 Apr 2023
6. Java Pathfinder. https://github.com/javapathfinder/jpf-core
7. Java Pathfinder (master branch). https://github.com/javapathfinder/jpf-core/tree/45a4450cd0bd1193df5419f7c9d9b89807d00db6. Accessed 04 Jan 2023
8. JCarder. http://www.jcarder.org/download.html. Accessed 30 Apr 2023
9. JUnit. https://junit.org/junit5/. Accessed 30 Apr 2023
10. RV-Predict. https://runtimeverification.com/predict/. Accessed 30 Apr 2023
11. ThreadSafe. http://www.contemplateltd.com/. Accessed 27 Dec 2022
12. Visual Threads. http://www.unix.digital.com/visualthreads/index.html. Accessed 30 Apr 2023
13. White box testing techniques, tools and advantages – a quick guide (2022). https://www.xenonstack.com/insights/what-is-white-box-testing. Accessed 03 Jan 2023
14. Blackshear, S., Gorogiannis, N., O'Hearn, P., Sergey, I.: RacerD: compositional static race detection. In: Proceedings of the ACM Conference on Programming Languages 2(OOPSLA), pp. 1–28 (2018). https://doi.org/10.1145/3276514
15. Cai, Y., Wu, S., Chan, W.: ConLock: a constraint-based approach to dynamic checking on deadlocks in multithreaded programs. In: Proceedings of the 36th International Conference on Software Engineering, pp. 491–502. ACM (2014). https://doi.org/10.1145/2568225.2568312
16. Calcagno, C., et al.: Moving fast with software verification. In: Havelund, K., Holzmann, G., Joshi, R. (eds.) NFM 2015. LNCS, vol. 9058, pp. 3–11. Springer, Cham (2015). https://doi.org/10.1007/978-3-319-17524-9_1
17. Elmas, T., Qadeer, S., Tasiran, S.: Goldilocks: a race-aware Java runtime. Commun. ACM **53**, 85–92 (2010). https://doi.org/10.1145/1839676.1839698
18. Engler, D., Ashcraft, K.: RacerX: effective, static detection of race conditions and deadlocks. In: Proceedings of the19th ACM Symposium on Operating Systems Principles, pp. 237–252. ACM (2003). https://doi.org/10.1145/945445.945468
19. Erickson, J., Musuvathi, M., Burckhardt, S., Olynyk, K.: Effective data-race detection for the kernel, pp. 151–162 (2010)

20. Eslamimehr, M., Palsberg, J.: Sherlock: scalable deadlock detection for concurrent programs. In: Proceedings of the 22nd ACM SIGSOFT International Symposium on Foundations of Software Engineering, pp. 353–365. FSE 2014, Computing Machinery (2014). https://doi.org/10.1145/2635868.2635918
21. Flanagan, C., Leino, K., Lillibridge, M., Nelson, G., Saxe, J., Stata, R.: Extended static checking for Java. In: Proceedings of the ACM SIGPLAN 2002 Conference on Programming Language Design and Implementation, pp. 234–245. ACM (2002). https://doi.org/10.1145/512529.512558
22. Flanagan, C., Freund, S.N.: FastTrack: efficient and precise dynamic race detection. SIGPLAN Not. 44(6), 121–133 (2009). https://doi.org/10.1145/1543135.1542490
23. Gao, J., Yang, X., Jiang, Y., Liu, H., Ying, W., Zhang, X.: Jbench: a dataset of data races for concurrency testing. In: Proceedinsg of the 15th IEEE/ACM 15th International Conference on Mining Software Repositories, pp. 6–9. ACM (2018). https://doi.org/10.1145/3196398.3196451
24. Holt, R.: Some deadlock properties of computer systems. ACM Comput. Surv. 4(3), 179–196 (1972). https://doi.org/10.1145/356603.356607
25. Holzmann, G.: The SPIN Model Checker: Primer and Reference Manual. Addison-Wesley Professional, Boston (2011)
26. Huang, J., Meredith, P., Roşu, G.: Maximal sound predictive race detection with control flow abstraction. In: Proceedings of the 35th ACM SIGPLAN Conference on Programming Language Design and Implementation, pp. 337–348. ACM (2014). https://doi.org/10.1145/2666356.2594315
27. Huang, J., Zhang, C.: Persuasive prediction of concurrency access anomalies. In: Proceedings of the 2011 International Symposium on Software Testing and Analysis, pp. 144–154. ISSTA 2011. Association for Computing Machinery (2011). https://doi.org/10.1145/2001420.2001438
28. Joshi, P., Naik, M., Park, C.-S., Sen, K.: CalFuzzer: an extensible active testing framework for concurrent programs. In: Bouajjani, A., Maler, O. (eds.) CAV 2009. LNCS, vol. 5643, pp. 675–681. Springer, Heidelberg (2009). https://doi.org/10.1007/978-3-642-02658-4_54
29. Lamport, L.: The PlusCal algorithm language. In: Leucker, M., Morgan, C. (eds.) ICTAC 2009. LNCS, vol. 5684, pp. 36–60. Springer, Heidelberg (2009). https://doi.org/10.1007/978-3-642-03466-4_2
30. Luo, Q., Zhang, S., Zhao, J., Hu, M.: A lightweight and portable approach to making concurrent failures reproducible. In: Rosenblum, D.S., Taentzer, G. (eds.) FASE 2010. LNCS, vol. 6013, pp. 323–337. Springer, Heidelberg (2010). https://doi.org/10.1007/978-3-642-12029-9_23
31. Marino, D., Musuvathi, M., Narayanasamy, S.: LiteRace: effective sampling for lightweight data-race detection. In: Proceedings of the 30th ACM SIGPLAN Conference on Programming Language Design and Implementation, pp. 134–143. PLDI 2009. Association for Computing Machinery (2009). https://doi.org/10.1145/1542476.1542491
32. Melo, S., Souza, S., Silva, R., Souza, P.: Concurrent software testing in practice: a catalog of tools. In: Proceedings of the 6th International Workshop on Automating Test Case Design, Selection and Evaluation, pp. 31–40. ACM (2015). https://doi.org/10.1145/2804322.2804328
33. Naik, M., Aiken, A., Whaley, J.: Effective static race detection for Java. In: Proceedings of the 27th ACM SIGPLAN Conference on Programming Language Design and Implementation, pp. 308–319. ACM (2006). https://doi.org/10.1145/1133981.1134018

34. Netzer, R., Miller, B.: What are race conditions? Some issues and formalizations. ACM Lett. Program. Lang. Syst. **1**(1), 74–88 (1992). https://doi.org/10.1145/130616.130623

35. Nir-Buchbinder, Y., Ur, S.: ConTest listeners: a concurrency-oriented infrastructure for Java test and heal tools. In: Pezzè, M. (ed.) Proceedings of the 4th International Workshop on Software Quality Assurance, SOQUA 2007, in conjunction with the 6th ESEC/FSE joint meeting, pp. 9–16. ACM (2007). https://doi.org/10.1145/1295074.1295077

36. Pugh, W., Ayewah, N.: Unit testing concurrent software. In: Proceedings of the 22nd IEEE/ACM International Conference on Automated Software Engineering, pp. 513–516. ASE 2007. Association for Computing Machinery (2007). https://doi.org/10.1145/1321631.1321722

37. Said, M., Wang, C., Yang, Z., Sakallah, K.: Generating data race witnesses by an SMT-based analysis, vol. 6617 (2011). https://doi.org/10.1007/978-3-642-20398-5_23

38. Samak, M., Ramanathan, M.K.: Trace driven dynamic deadlock detection and reproduction. SIGPLAN Not. **49**(8), 29–42 (2014). https://doi.org/10.1145/2692916.2555262

39. Savage, S., Burrows, M., Nelson, G., Sobalvarro, P., Anderson, T.: Eraser: a dynamic data race detector for multithreaded programs. ACM Trans. Comput. Syst. **15**(4), 391–411 (1997). https://doi.org/10.1145/265924.265927

40. Sen, K., Agha, G.: A race-detection and flipping algorithm for automated testing of multi-threaded programs. In: Bin, E., Ziv, A., Ur, S. (eds.) HVC 2006. LNCS, vol. 4383, pp. 166–182. Springer, Heidelberg (2007). https://doi.org/10.1007/978-3-540-70889-6_13

41. Şerbănuţă, T., Chen, F., Roşu, G.: Maximal causal models for sequentially consistent systems. In: Qadeer, S., Tasiran, S. (eds.) Proceedings of the 3rd International Conference on Runtime Verification. LNCS, vol. 7687, pp. 136–150. Springer, Heidelberg (2013). https://doi.org/10.1007/978-3-642-35632-2_16

42. Zhai, K., Xu, B., Chan, W., Tse, T.: CARISMA: a context-sensitive approach to race-condition sample-instance selection for multithreaded applications. In: Proceedings of the 2012 International Symposium on Software Testing and Analysis, pp. 221–231. ACM (2012). https://doi.org/10.1145/2338965.2336780

Towards an Automatic Proof
of the Bakery Algorithm

Aman Goel[1]([✉]), Stephan Merz[2], and Karem A. Sakallah[3]

[1] Amazon Web Services, Seattle, USA
amangoel@umich.edu
[2] University of Lorraine, CNRS, Inria, LORIA, Nancy, France
[3] University of Michigan, Ann Arbor, USA

Abstract. The Bakery algorithm is a landmark algorithm for ensuring mutual exclusion among N processes that communicate via shared variables. Starting from existing TLA$^+$ specifications, we use the recently-developed IC3PO parameterized model checker to automatically compute inductive invariants for two versions of the algorithm. We compare the machine-generated invariants with human-written invariants that were used in an interactive correctness proof checked by the TLA$^+$ Proof System. Our experience suggests that automated invariant inference is becoming a viable alternative to labor-intensive human-written proofs.

Keywords: parameterized verification · mutual exclusion · inductive invariant

1 Introduction

Concurrent and distributed programs are difficult to get correct because of the many possible ways that parallel processes can interfere with each other. It is therefore very important to design formal verification techniques that ensure the correctness of such programs in all possible executions. Whereas classical model checking techniques [4] can verify the correctness of finite-state systems, parameterized verification targets systems whose state space is unbounded. Although this problem is undecidable in general [1], a lot of progress has recently been made, either by considering particular classes of programs or by developing powerful heuristics. The recently-developed IC3PO model checker [8,10] targets the verification of parameterized systems that exhibit certain structural regularities. IC3PO extends the well-known IC3/PDR model checking technique [3,6] for verifying finite instances by generalizing clauses learned during the IC3 algorithm with quantifier inference performed by co-relating quantification with (a) *spatial* regularity over identical "replicas" that can be permuted arbitrarily, and (b) *temporal* regularity over ordered domains that capture unbounded, but regular, evolution of program behaviors "over time". The key insight underlying IC3PO is that protocol regularities and quantification are closely related concepts that

---

Work does not relate to Aman Goel's position at Amazon.

© IFIP International Federation for Information Processing 2023
M. Huisman and A. Ravara (Eds.): FORTE 2023, LNCS 13910, pp. 21–28, 2023.
https://doi.org/10.1007/978-3-031-35355-0_2

express protocol invariance under different rearrangements of its components or its evolution over time. Starting with an initial instance size, IC3PO systematically computes quantified inductive invariants over protocol instances of increasing sizes, until protocol behaviors *saturate*, concluding with an inductive proof that is correct for all instances of the protocol. The automatically-generated invariants help provide useful insights into why the algorithm is correct, and serve as independently-verifiable proof certificates.

IC3PO has been used successfully for verifying distributed fault-tolerant algorithms, including a version of Lamport's Paxos algorithm [9]. In this work, we target the Bakery algorithm [11]. Given that the algorithm is based on a substantially different computational paradigm (shared-variable concurrency instead of message passing) and solves a different problem (mutual exclusion instead of consensus), we believe that it constitutes an interesting target for invariant synthesis. The Bakery algorithm is parameterized by the number of processes, and even instances of the algorithm with a finite number of processes exhibit infinite state spaces because ticket numbers may grow beyond any bound. We also consider two versions of the algorithm that differ in the semantics of concurrent reads and writes.

We use existing specifications of the Bakery algorithm modeled in TLA$^+$ [14, 15] as the starting point of our work and translate them faithfully into Ivy [18], one of the input languages supported by IC3PO. This lets us compare the IC3PO machine-generated invariants with the human-written invariants used for an existing interactive proof contributed by Leslie Lamport. We show, using the TLA$^+$ Proof System TLAPS [5], that the machine-generated invariants are indeed inductive and imply mutual exclusion, and further analyze their similarities and differences with the human-written invariants.

2 Preliminaries

2.1 Incremental Induction

A major milestone in model checking was the introduction of incremental induction. The basic idea, first described as IC3 in [3] and re-implemented with several enhancements as PDR in [6], is to employ fast incremental SAT solving to learn quantifier-free clauses that systematically refine over-approximations of a sequence of reachability frontiers at increasing distances from the initial state(s). When applied to finite transition systems this algorithm converges *syntactically* and produces an inductive invariant or a counterexample. In contrast to the earlier SAT-based bounded model checking approach [2] that unrolled the transition relation to detect the presence of k-step counterexamples, the IC3/PDR verifiers operate on a single copy of the transition relation allowing for better scalability and the ability to generate a proof certificate.

2.2 IC3PO: IC3 for Proving Protocol Properties

Recognizing the spatial and temporal regularity in distributed protocols, IC3PO [7] automatically infers compact quantified inductive invariants by augmenting the incremental induction algorithm with the following enhancements:

- A *regularity-aware clause boosting* procedure that generalizes a single clause φ to a set of spatially- or temporally-equivalent clauses, referred as φ's *orbit*.
- A *quantifier inference* algorithm, based on a simple analysis of φ's *syntactic structure*, that encodes φ's orbit by a quantified predicate Φ involving a bounded prefix of universal and existential quantifiers.
- A systematic *finite convergence* procedure to determine a minimal protocol *cutoff* size sufficient for deriving a quantified inductive invariant that holds for all sizes.

Given a protocol specification, and starting from an initial base size, IC3PO iteratively invokes regularity-aware incremental induction on finite instances of increasing size, until it either a) converges on an inductive invariant that proves the property for the unbounded protocol, or b) produces a counterexample trace that serves as a finite witness to its violation in both the finite instance and the unbounded protocol. The reader is referred to [10] for complete details on IC3PO as well as a comparison of its performance against other state-of-the-art distributed protocol verifiers.

3   Modeling the Bakery Algorithm

The Bakery algorithm ensures mutual exclusion among a set of N processes by letting a process i draw a "ticket" num[i] whose number it believes to be larger than any ticket already in use. Access to the critical section is then ordered by ticket numbers. Since two processes may concurrently draw the same ticket number, the actual order is a lexicographic ordering on ticket numbers, followed by process identity. Formally, we define the set P of processes and the ordering LL(i,j) by

$$P \triangleq 1\,..\,N \qquad LL(i,\,j) \triangleq (num[i] < num[j]) \vee (num[i] = num[j] \wedge i \le j)$$

A pseudo-code representation of the Bakery algorithm appears in Fig. 1. Labels are used to indicate the grain of atomicity: for example, each iteration of the **for** loop at label p2 is assumed to be executed atomically. Importantly, every atomic block of instructions updates at most one shared variable. Label cs indicates the critical section.

We consider two versions of the Bakery algorithm. In the *atomic* version, reads and writes to the shared variables num[i] and flag[i] are assumed to happen atomically so they never overlap. In the *non-atomic* version, these variables are assumed to be safe registers [13]: reads that do not overlap a write return the actual value of the variable, while reads that overlap with a write may return an arbitrary (type-correct) value.

4   Proving Mutual Exclusion of the Bakery Algorithm

As our starting point for formally modeling and verifying the Bakery algorithm, we chose existing TLA$^+$ specifications of both versions of the algorithm.[1] Both

---

[1] https://github.com/tlaplus/tlapm/tree/main/examples.

variables num = [i ∈ P ↦ 0], flag = [i ∈ P ↦ **false**]
process self ∈ P:
  variables unread = {}, max = 0;
p1: **while true:**
   unread := P \ {self}; max := 0; flag[self] := **true**;
p2: **for** nxt ∈ unread:
   if num[nxt] > max: max := num[nxt];
   unread := unread \ {nxt};
p3: num[self] := max + 1;
p4: flag[self] := **false**; unread := P \ {self};
p5: **for** nxt ∈ unread:
   await ¬flag[nxt];
p6: **await** (num[nxt] = 0) ∨ LL(self, nxt);
   unread := unread \ {nxt}
cs: **skip**;
p7: num[self] := 0

Fig. 1. The Bakery algorithm as pseudo-code.

versions are also accompanied with a human-written inductive invariant that has been mechanically proved correct using TLAPS. We transcribe these TLA+ specifications in Ivy, with minimal changes, before we apply IC3PO in order to prove mutual exclusion. We then compare the invariants that IC3PO generates during this verification against the hand-written ones. Our findings are similar for both versions of the algorithm. Due to space limitations, we will only discuss the non-atomic version in the remainder of the paper.[2]

4.1 Human-Written Invariant

Figure 2a contains the invariant HInv used for the correctness proof of the Bakery algorithm checked by TLAPS.[3] It is the conjunction of a standard type-correctness predicate TypeOK, which we do not display here, and the main correctness invariant HIInv(i), asserted for every process i ∈ P. The first two conjuncts A1 and A2 delimit the control points where the ticket number num[i] is 0. Similarly, conjuncts B1 and B2 assert when process i may set its flag. The rest of the conjuncts involve the auxiliary formula After(j, i) that characterizes states from which it is certain that process j will enter the critical section later than process i. Conjunct C asserts that for any process i executing the final steps of its entry protocol (control points "p5" and "p6") and any process j different from i whose value num[j] process i has already read, j will enter the critical section later than i. Conjunct D concerns process i waiting at control point "p6" for process nxt[i] to satisfy the predicate (num[nxt[i]] = 0) ∨ LL(i, nxt[i]). It asserts that in case nxt[i] is about to draw a new ticket number then nxt[i] has

---

[2] All our models are available at https://github.com/aman-goel/BakeryProtocol.
[3] We use TLA+'s convention for displaying nested conjunctions and disjunctions as lists, with indentation reflecting precedence.

$\text{HInv} \triangleq \text{TypeOK} \land \forall i \in P : \text{HIInv}(i)$

$\text{HIInv}(i) \triangleq$

A1	$\land \; pc[i] \in \{\text{"p1"}, \text{"p2"}\} \Rightarrow num[i] = 0$
A2	$\land \; num[i] = 0 \Rightarrow pc[i] \in \{\text{"p1"}, \text{"p2"}, \text{"p3"}, \text{"p7"}\}$
B1	$\land \; pc[i] \in \{\text{"p2"}, \text{"p3"}\} \Rightarrow flag[i]$
B2	$\land \; flag[i] \Rightarrow pc[i] \in \{\text{"p1"}, \text{"p2"}, \text{"p3"}, \text{"p4"}\}$
C	$\land \; pc[i] \in \{\text{"p5"}, \text{"p6"}\}) \Rightarrow \forall j \in (P \setminus unread[i]) \setminus \{i\} : \text{After}(j, i)$

$$D \begin{cases} \land \; pc[i] = \text{"p6"} \land \; \lor \; pc[nxt[i]] = \text{"p2"} \land i \notin unread[nxt[i]] \\ \qquad\qquad\qquad\quad \lor \; pc[nxt[i]] = \text{"p3"} \\ \Rightarrow max[nxt[i]] \geq num[i] \end{cases}$$

E	$\land \; pc[i] = \text{"cs"} \Rightarrow \forall j \in P \setminus \{i\} : \text{After}(j, i)$

$\text{After}(j, i) \triangleq$
$$\begin{aligned} &\land \; num[i] > 0 \\ &\land \; \lor \; pc[j] = \text{"p1"} \\ &\qquad \lor \; pc[j] = \text{"p2"} \land (i \in unread[j] \lor max[j] \geq num[i]) \\ &\qquad \lor \; pc[j] = \text{"p3"} \land max[j] \geq num[i] \\ &\qquad \lor \; \land \; pc[j] \in \{\text{"p4"}, \text{"p5"}, \text{"p6"}\} \\ &\qquad\qquad \land \; LL(i, j) \\ &\qquad\qquad \land \; pc[j] \in \{\text{"p5"}, \text{"p6"}\} \Rightarrow i \in unread[j] \\ &\qquad \lor \; pc[j] = \text{"p7"} \end{aligned}$$

(a) Human-written invariant used for the interactive correctness proof with TLAPS.

$\text{MInv} \triangleq \forall i \in P : \text{MIInv}(i)$

$\text{MIInv}(i) \triangleq$

a	$\land \; pc[i] \in \{\text{"p4"}, \text{"p5"}, \text{"p6"}, \text{"cs"}\} \Rightarrow num[i] \neq 0$
b1	$\land \; pc[i] \in \{\text{"p2"}, \text{"p3"}\} \Rightarrow flag[i]$

$$b2 \begin{cases} \land \; pc[i] \in \{\text{"p5"}, \text{"p6"}\} \land flag[i] \Rightarrow \forall j \in P \setminus \{i\} : \\ \qquad \land \; pc[j] \in \{\text{"p5"}, \text{"p6"}\} \Rightarrow i \in unread[j] \\ \qquad \land \; pc[j] = \text{"p6"} \Rightarrow i \neq nxt[j] \\ \qquad \land \; pc[j] = \text{"cs"} \Rightarrow i = nxt[j] \lor j = nxt[j] \end{cases}$$

$$c \begin{cases} \land \; pc[i] \in \{\text{"p5"}, \text{"p6"}\} \Rightarrow \forall j \in P \setminus unread[i] : \\ \qquad \land \; pc[j] = \text{"p2"} \Rightarrow i \in unread[j] \lor max[j] \geq num[i] \\ \qquad \land \; pc[j] = \text{"p3"} \Rightarrow max[j] \geq num[i] \\ \qquad \land \; pc[j] \in \{\text{"p4"}, \text{"p5"}, \text{"p6"}\} \Rightarrow LL(i, j) \end{cases}$$

d1	$\land \; pc[i] = \text{"p6"} \land pc[nxt[i]] = \text{"p2"} \Rightarrow i \in unread[nxt[i]] \lor max[nxt[i]] \geq num[i]$
d2	$\land \; pc[i] = \text{"p6"} \land pc[nxt[i]] = \text{"p3"} \land flag[nxt[i]] \Rightarrow max[nxt[i]] \geq num[i]$

$$e \begin{cases} \land \; pc[i] = \text{"cs"} \Rightarrow \forall j \in P \setminus \{i\} : \\ \qquad \land \; pc[j] = \text{"p2"} \Rightarrow i \in unread[j] \lor max[j] \geq num[i] \\ \qquad \land \; pc[j] = \text{"p3"} \Rightarrow max[j] \geq num[i] \\ \qquad \land \; pc[j] = \text{"p4"} \Rightarrow LL(i, j) \\ \qquad \land \; pc[j] \in \{\text{"p5"}, \text{"p6"}\} \Rightarrow LL(i, j) \land i \in unread[j] \\ \qquad \land \; pc[j] \neq \text{"cs"} \end{cases}$$

(b) Machine-generated invariant produced by IC3PO (pretty-printed).

Fig. 2. The two invariants used for the proof of the Bakery algorithm.

not read process i or it will draw a ticket higher than process i's ticket number. The last conjunct E asserts that if process i resides at the critical section then all other processes must enter their critical section later than i.

4.2 Machine-Generated Invariant

The Ivy version of the protocol specification is expressed in a typed, relational language, which subsumes most of the type correctness invariant of TLA$^+$. The target safety property given to IC3PO asserts mutual exclusion and the fact that each process resides at exactly one control point throughout the execution. Starting with an initial finite instance consisting of 3 processes and 3 ticket numbers, IC3PO converged at 4 processes and 3 ticket numbers and produced an inductive invariant consisting of 42 additional clausal conjuncts. This invariant, transcribed back to TLA$^+$ and slightly simplified by grouping identical formulas that apply at different control points, appears in Fig. 2b. In total, IC3PO took 23 min to produce this invariant, making 87,707 SAT solver calls to eliminate 3,358 counterexamples-to-induction. We used TLAPS to verify that our transcription to TLA$^+$ of IC3PO's machine-generated invariant is inductive.

4.3 Comparison of the Two Invariants

One obvious difference between the human-written and machine-generated invariants is that IC3PO does not introduce auxiliary predicates such as After(j,i) that appears in Fig. 2a. IC3PO generates predicates in clausal form that are pretty-printed as implications. Still, the two invariants are built from the same constituent predicates, and by expanding the definition of After and distinguishing the possible control points of processes we can compare them in detail.

The first two conjuncts A1 and A2 of the human-written invariant indicate where num[i] may or must be 0. The machine-generated invariant contains only one such conjunct (labeled a) that is equivalent to the condition A2 of the human-written invariant.

Conjuncts labeled B* or b* delimit the control points where flag[i] can be set. The conjunct B1 of the human-written invariant and b1 of the machine-generated invariant are identical. The conjunct B2 of the human-written invariant implies that the flag cannot be set at control points "p5" and "p6". The condition b2 of the machine-generated invariant is weaker, asserting certain predicates that must be true whenever control is at "p5" or "p6" and the flag is set.

Conjuncts labeled C and c assert what must be true of a process i at control points "p5" or "p6" and a process j whose num value has already been read by process i. Analyzing the meaning of the After predicate, we find that the two conditions are very similar. Again, the human-written invariant (labeled C) is stronger than the machine-generated one (labeled c): it implies that process j cannot be in the critical section, and also that if both processes are at "p5" or "p6" then i ∈ unread[j] or j ∈ unread[i] must hold.

Conjunct D of the human-written invariant is equivalent to the conjunction of d1 and d2 in the machine-generated invariant. (The extra condition flag[nxt[i]] in conjunct d2 is actually redundant due to B1/b1.) Similarly, conjuncts E and e are equivalent when the definition of After is expanded.

Overall, it can be seen that the two invariants express similar conditions, but that the machine-generated invariant is a little weaker, while still implying mutual exclusion. The most notable difference concerns the control points where the flag may be set: inspecting the code of the Bakery algorithm, one immediately realizes that the flag cannot be set after the instruction at "p4", but IC3PO generates weaker, albeit somewhat more complicated conditions. This appears to be due to the internal workings of the IC3 algorithm, where, starting with the main safety property, the overapproximation of the reachable state space is iteratively refined/strengthened by eliminating parts of the unreachable space (called counterexamples-to-induction) until the overapproximation becomes inductive. It should be possible to add a post-processing step to IC3PO that iteratively shrinks the generated strengthening assertions by dropping redundant literals while ensuring induction relative to the property, similar to minimal unsatisfiable subset extraction algorithms [17].

5   Conclusions

The Bakery algorithm is an iconic algorithm for ensuring mutual exclusion between processes. Despite its apparent simplicity, its details are quite intricate, in particular when non-atomic access to memory is considered. The algorithm has long served as a testbed for formal verification techniques. We have shown that IC3PO, a state-of-the-art algorithm for parameterized verification is able to infer inductive invariants for the Bakery algorithm. Because they are constructed by iteratively refining the initially provided invariant, the invariants generated by IC3PO will generally be weaker than human-written invariants, but the ones that we obtained for the Bakery algorithm are remarkably similar to those used in the human-written correctness proof. Although we have only shown the invariants for the non-atomic version of the algorithm, the results for the atomic version are very similar, and they are available online. Inductive invariants explain why the algorithm is correct, and they can serve as independently verifiable certificates of correctness. Our experience is a testimony to the maturity of state-of-the-art methods for invariant generation.

For this experiment, we manually transcribed the existing TLA$^+$ specifications to Ivy. Given that the languages are quite different (in particular because Ivy mostly relies on relational specifications), the transcription is not entirely mechanical, and is the reason why we do not yet consider the approach to be fully automatic. In future work, we intend to develop a front-end that would enable us to run IC3PO on a substantial fragment of TLA$^+$.

Lamport recently published [16] a generalized version of the Bakery algorithm and showed that the distributed mutual-exclusion algorithm of [12] could be understood as a refinement of that version of the Bakery algorithm. These algorithms would make interesting targets for automatic invariant inference.

References

1. Apt, K.R., Kozen, D.: Limits for automatic verification of finite-state concurrent systems. Inf. Process. Lett. **22**(6), 307–309 (1986)
2. Biere, A., Cimatti, A., Clarke, E., Zhu, Y.: Symbolic model checking without BDDs. In: Cleaveland, W.R. (ed.) TACAS 1999. LNCS, vol. 1579, pp. 193–207. Springer, Heidelberg (1999). https://doi.org/10.1007/3-540-49059-0_14
3. Bradley, A.R.: SAT-based model checking without unrolling. In: Jhala, R., Schmidt, D. (eds.) VMCAI 2011. LNCS, vol. 6538, pp. 70–87. Springer, Heidelberg (2011). https://doi.org/10.1007/978-3-642-18275-4_7
4. Clarke, E.M., Emerson, E.A.: Design and synthesis of synchronization skeletons using branching time temporal logic. In: Kozen, D. (ed.) Logic of Programs 1981. LNCS, vol. 131, pp. 52–71. Springer, Heidelberg (1982). https://doi.org/10.1007/BFb0025774
5. Cousineau, D., Doligez, D., Lamport, L., Merz, S., Ricketts, D., Vanzetto, H.: TLA⁺ proofs. In: Giannakopoulou, D., Méry, D. (eds.) FM 2012. LNCS, vol. 7436, pp. 147–154. Springer, Heidelberg (2012). https://doi.org/10.1007/978-3-642-32759-9_14
6. Een, N., Mishchenko, A., Brayton, R.: Efficient implementation of property directed reachability. In: Formal Methods in Computer Aided Design (FMCAD 2011), pp. 125–134, October 2011
7. Goel, A., Sakallah, K.: On symmetry and quantification: a new approach to verify distributed protocols. In: Dutle, A., Moscato, M.M., Titolo, L., Muñoz, C.A., Perez, I. (eds.) NFM 2021. LNCS, vol. 12673, pp. 131–150. Springer, Cham (2021). https://doi.org/10.1007/978-3-030-76384-8_9
8. Goel, A., Sakallah, K.A.: IC3PO: IC3 for proving protocol properties. https://github.com/aman-goel/ic3po
9. Goel, A., Sakallah, K.A.: Towards an automatic proof of Lamport's Paxos. In: Formal Methods in Computer Aided Design (FMCAD 2021), pp. 112–122. IEEE, New Haven, CT, U.S.A. (2021)
10. Goel, A., Sakallah, K.A.: Regularity and quantification: a new approach to verify distributed protocols. Innov. Syst. Softw. Eng. 1–19 (2022). https://doi.org/10.1007/s11334-022-00460-8
11. Lamport, L.: A new solution of Dijkstra's concurrent programming problem. Commun. ACM **17**(8), 453–455 (1974)
12. Lamport, L.: Time, clocks, and the ordering of events in a distributed system. Commun. ACM **21**(7), 558–565 (1978)
13. Lamport, L.: On interprocess communication. Distrib. Comput. **1**, 77–101 (1986)
14. Lamport, L.: The temporal logic of actions. ACM Trans. Program. Lang. Syst. (TOPLAS) **16**(3), 872–923 (1994)
15. Lamport, L.: Specifying Systems: The TLA+ Language and Tools for Hardware and Software Engineers. Addison-Wesley Longman Publishing Co., Boston (2002)
16. Lamport, L.: Deconstructing the bakery to build a distributed state machine. Commun. ACM **65**(9), 58–66 (2022)
17. Liffiton, M.H., Sakallah, K.A.: Algorithms for computing minimal unsatisfiable subsets of constraints. J. Autom. Reason. **40**(1), 1–33 (2008)
18. Padon, O., McMillan, K.L., Panda, A., Sagiv, M., Shoham, S.: Ivy: safety verification by interactive generalization. In: Proceedings 37th ACM SIGPLAN Conference on Programming Language Design and Implementation, pp. 614–630 (2016)

Certified Compilation of Choreographies with hacc

Luís Cruz-Filipe⬡, Lovro Lugović$^{(\boxtimes)}$⬡, and Fabrizio Montesi⬡

Department of Mathematics and Computer Science, University of Southern Denmark,
Odense, Denmark
{lcf,lugovic,fmontesi}@imada.sdu.dk

Abstract. Programming communicating processes is challenging, because it requires writing separate programs that perform compatible send and receive actions at the right time during execution. Leaving this task to the programmer can easily lead to bugs. *Choreographic programming* addresses this challenge by equipping developers with high-level abstractions for codifying the desired communication structures from a global viewpoint. Given a choreography, implementations of the involved processes can be automatically generated by *endpoint projection (EPP)*.

While choreographic programming prevents manual mistakes in the implementation of communications, the correctness of a choreographic programming framework crucially hinges on the correctness of its complex compiler, which has motivated formalisation of theories of choreographic programming in theorem provers. In this paper, we build upon one of these formalisations to construct a toolchain that produces executable code from a choreography.

Keywords: Choreographic programming · Certified compilation · Jolie · Formal verification

1 Introduction

In traditional distributed programming, the programmer is tasked with writing the implementation of each *process* (endpoint) as a separate program, taking care of correctly matching send and receive actions in the different programs. This approach is known to be cumbersome and error-prone [7].

In *Choreographic programming* [8], developers specify the desired communications between processes from a global viewpoint. Given a choreographic program (called *choreography*), correct implementations for all involved processes can be automatically generated by a procedure known as *endpoint projection (EPP)* [9]. This avoids manual mistakes in the programming of communication actions, and provides important theoretical advantages, like deadlock-freedom by design—distributed code generated from a choreography is always deadlock-free, as choreographic languages do not have syntax for unmatched communications [1]. In addition to these correctness advantages, this also saves time and lets the programmer focus on the bigger picture of the protocol being developed.

M. Huisman and A. Ravara (Eds.): FORTE 2023, LNCS 13910, pp. 29–36, 2023.
https://doi.org/10.1007/978-3-031-35355-0_3

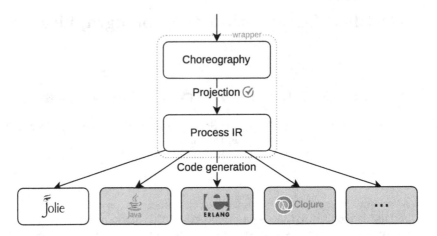

Fig. 1. The architecture of hacc's compilation pipeline. In this work we target the Jolie programming language, but the architecture is designed with extensibility in mind. The languages with a grey background are given as examples of potential future targets.

Defining and implementing EPP is technically involved [13], which motivated mechanising theories of choreographic programming using interactive theorem provers [3,4,6,12]. Among these, the formalisation of *Core Choreographies (CC)* and its EPP to the process calculus of *Stateful Processes (SP)* was designed with broad applicability in mind [5]. Specifically, its design allows for annotating communications with arbitrary metadata and is parametric on the languages used to express local computation, data, process identifiers, etc.

In this work, for the first time, we reap the benefits of [5] to develop hacc (Haskell Core Choreographies, pronounced "hack"): a tool for compiling choreographies in CC to executable code. As target language for this executable code, we use the service-oriented programming language Jolie [10]. Additionally, hacc is designed with extensibility in mind, so that new target languages can be added.

The architecture of hacc consists of two compilation phases (Fig. 1). The first phase (projection) uses EPP to translate a choreography in CC into an abstract representation of process programs given in SP, used as an intermediate representation (IR). This phase is certified: it uses a Haskell program extracted from the Coq formalisation [3]. The second phase (code generation) translates the abstract actions of SP into an executable programming language. This phase is not formally verified: since it is a homomorphic transformation that follows the term structure of SP in a straightforward fashion, its correctness is easy to establish directly by manual inspection.

Our development allows for writing and executing CC choreographies [2–4,9]. Also, it confirms the informal claim that the formalisation of CC was made with flexibility in mind for this kind of applications [5]. In particular, our application to Jolie did not require any modification of the formalisation, but just an appropriate instantiation of its parameters and a simple interfacing of its extracted data types with the other components of our compilation pipeline in Haskell.

Structure. Section 2 gives an overview of our compiler's architecture and describes its implementation. Section 3 explains how we map the process language to Jolie in order to generate executable Jolie code consisting of multiple independent services.

Related Work. There are two other formalisations of choreographic programming. Kalas [12] is a choreographic programming language formalised in the Hol4 proof assistant. It comes with an end-to-end certified compiler that targets CakeML [11], a formally-verified subset of the ML language. By contrast, we take a technology-agnostic approach that allows for reusing our compiler infrastructure for different target languages. Pirouette [6] is a functional choreographic programming language formalised in Coq, which similarly to [4] can be instantiated with different languages for local computation. However, it has not yet been used to implement a choreographic compiler that targets executable code.

2   Choreographies in hacc

We represent choreographies and processes (terms of CC and SP, respectively) by Haskell data types that have been automatically extracted from the Coq formalisation. However, a few considerations are necessary, given that Coq is a dependently-typed language, while all of the languages it can extract to are not. As mentioned before, the formalisation is parametric over the types used to represent process identifiers, (recursion) variables, terms of the local computation language, etc. Because this is done using the dependently-typed features of Coq, the extracted Haskell code has some peculiarities.

In particular, instead of using Haskell's type system and parametric polymorphism, the extracted code uses Haskell's Any type to achieve genericity. As a consequence, interfacing the extracted code requires using the unsafeCoerce function. To deal with the verbosity we provide a more ergonomic interface with a thin *wrapper* (Fig. 1) around the extracted code. The wrapper hides the necessary coercions and models the terms using Haskell's parametric polymorphism. This step is not formally verified, but the wrapper again follows the term structure of CC and SP, so checking it for correctness manually is not a problem.

Figure 2 shows our interface. We fix the types of process identifiers (Pid), variable names (Var, RecVar), selection labels (Label) and annotations (Ann) for simplicity. The Label type is a binary sum type with CLeft and CRight as its constructors, while others are wrappers around **String**s, used as identifiers.

Choreographies have type Choreography e b, parametric on the local computation and Boolean expression languages (e and b). Processes can perform point-to-point interactions (Interaction)—value communications (Com), where a process evaluates an expression and sends the result to another, or selections (Sel), where a process selects how another process should behave by communicating a label.

```
                                                                    Haskell
data Eta e = Com Pid e Pid Var | Sel Pid Pid Label

data Choreography e b
  = CEnd
  | Interaction (Eta e) Ann (Choreography e b)
  | CCond Pid b (Choreography e b) (Choreography e b)
  | CCall RecVar

newtype CDefSet e b = CDefSet [(RecVar, Choreography e b)]
newtype CProgram e b = CProgram (CDefSet e b, Choreography e b)
```

Fig. 2. Datatypes for choreographies in hacc.

Interactions include an annotation (Ann), discussed below. Conditionals (CCond) are based on Boolean expressions, and CCall invokes a named procedure.[1] CProgram is the type of choreographic programs, which includes definitions of named procedures (CDefSet) as well as the main choreography.[2]

Instead of working with our data types directly we define a convenient set of combinators for building choreographies. We provide a prog combinator that returns a CProgram given a pair of recursive procedure definitions and the main choreography. A choreography is given as a list of instructions (communications, selections of CLeft or CRight, conditionals and calls), all built using the corresponding combinators (com, left, right, cond and call, respectively), which are strung together to produce a CC term in our representation.

When compiling to Jolie, the programmer can configure the generated code by annotating interactions using the ann combinator. These annotations will be used to override the default names of the Jolie operations that implement them.

Example 1 (Distributed authentication). Fig. 3 shows the distributed authentication choreography from [3] encoded as a CProgram.

Here, Client wishes to authenticate with Ip (identity provider) in order to receive a token from Server. Client sends its credentials to Ip, which checks them and communicates the result to both Client and Server. If the authentication was successful, Server sends a token to Client, otherwise the protocol terminates.

The terms of the local computation and Boolean expression languages are simply strings, which are included as-is into the generated executable code.   ◁

---

[1] CC includes runtime terms, needed for the semantics. Programmers should not write them explicitly, so we do not include them in our datatype.

[2] In Coq, DefSet also includes the set of processes involved in each procedure. In theory, this set might not be computable, as there may be infinitely many procedures. This cannot happen in hand-written choreographies, so our wrapper computes this set.

```Haskell
auth :: CProgram String String
auth = prog ([],
  [ann "authenticate" $ com c "credentials" ip credentials,
  cond ip "check@Util( credentials )"
    ([ann "authOk" $ left ip s, ann "authOk" $ left ip c,
      ann "acceptToken" $ com s "makeToken@Util()" c token],
    [ann "authFail" $ right ip s, ann "authFail" $ right ip c])])
  where [ip, s, c] = pids ["Ip", "Server", "Client"]
        [credentials, token] = vars ["credentials", "token"]
```

Fig. 3. The distributed authentication choreography in CC.

3 Code Generation

The projected behaviour of a process has type Behaviour e b, again parametric on the local languages (Fig. 4) Send and Recv correspond to the respective communication actions, while BCond and BCall are as in CC. The remaining terms Choose and Offer are used to implement selections, where one process can *choose* which of the *offered* behaviours another process should execute. Note that a process does not have to offer behaviours for both labels.

```Haskell
data Behaviour e b
  = BEnd
  | Send Pid e Ann (Behaviour e b)
  | Recv Pid Var Ann (Behaviour e b)
  | Choose Pid Label Ann (Behaviour e b)
  | Offer Pid (Maybe (Ann, Behaviour e b)) (Maybe (Ann, Behaviour e b))
  | BCond b (Behaviour e b) (Behaviour e b)
  | BCall (RecVar, Pid)

newtype BDefSet e b = BDefSet [((RecVar, Pid), Behaviour e b)]
newtype Network e b = Network [(Pid, Behaviour e b)]
newtype BProgram e b = BProgram (BDefSet e b, Network e b)

epp :: CProgram e b -> Maybe (BProgram e b)
```

Fig. 4. Datatypes for processes in hacc.

Processes are named by identifiers and grouped into a Network, which is then paired with the projections of recursive procedures for each process (BDefSet) to form a BProgram. Finally, epp performs the projection of a CProgram to a BProgram using the extracted EPP as its foundation. We use the **Maybe** type to handle the case when a choreography is not projectable.

Example 2. Projecting the distributed authentication choreography from Example 1 gives us the SP program seen in Fig. 5. Note how the annotations from the choreography have been preserved and propagated to the projection.   ◁

```
                                                                    Haskell
BProgram (BDefSet [], Network [
  (Pid "Client",
   Send (Pid "Ip") "credentials" (Ann "authenticate")
    (Offer (Pid "Ip")
      (Just (Ann "authOk",
             Recv (Pid "Server") (Var "token") (Ann "acceptToken") BEnd))
      (Just (Ann "authFail", BEnd)))),
  (Pid "Ip",
   Recv (Pid "Client") (Var "credentials") (Ann "authenticate")
    (BCond "check@Util( credentials )"
      (Choose (Pid "Server") CLeft (Ann "authOk")
        (Choose (Pid "Client") CLeft (Ann "authOk") BEnd))
      (Choose (Pid "Server") CRight (Ann "authFail")
        (Choose (Pid "Client") CRight (Ann "authFail") BEnd)))),
  (Pid "Server",
   Offer (Pid "Ip")
    (Just (Ann "authOk",
           Send (Pid "Client") "makeToken@Util()" (Ann "acceptToken") BEnd))
    (Just (Ann "authFail", BEnd)))])
```

Fig. 5. The projection of the choreography in Example 1.

Example 3. The SP program from Example 2 can now be compiled down to executable code (Fig. 6). For each process, the backend generates a corresponding **service** block in Jolie. We omit the deployment configuration and show only the behaviour, whose structure follows that of the SP program.

Note how the strings used for the local computation and Boolean expressions (makeToken@Util() at Client and check@Util(credentials) at Ip) were incorporated into the generated code. Both make use of the Util module which we **embed** into all of the main services to provide a way for the user to supply local code that can be called out to if necessary – **embed** is Jolie for loading an internal service and is often used for encapsulating internal functions [10].

The annotations were used to specify the operation names exposed by the services (authOk and acceptToken for Client, authenticate for Ip, and authOk and authFail for Server). In general, they can specify arbitrary metadata that allows the programmer to control and guide the backend's code generation.   ◁

```
service Client {                         service Ip {                    Jolie
  embed Util as Util                       embed Util as Util

  ...                                      ...

  main {                                   main {
    authenticate@Ip( credentials )           authenticate( credentials )
    [ authOk() ] {                           if( check@Util( credentials ) ) {
      acceptToken( token )                     authOk@Server()
    }                                          authOk@Client()
    [ authFail() ] {                         } else {
      nullProcess                              authFail@Server()
    }                                          authFail@Client()
  }                                          }
}                                          }
                                         }


service Server {
  embed Util as Util
  main {
    [ authOk() ] {
      acceptToken@Client( makeToken@Util() )
    }
    [ authFail() ] {
      nullProcess
    }
  }
}
```

Fig. 6. The executable Jolie code generated for Client, Ip, and Server.

4   Conclusion

We implemented a toolchain for compiling choreographies to executable code in Jolie. The complex step, computing the endpoint projection, is handled by certified code extracted from the Coq formalisation in [3]. This certified code is then combined with uncertified wrappers whose correctness is easy to check by hand. We illustrated the toolchain with a protocol for distributed authentication.

Acknowledgements. This work was partially supported by Villum Fonden, grant no. 29518, and the Independent Research Fund Denmark, grant no. 0135-00219.

References

1. Carbone, M., Montesi, F.: Deadlock-freedom-by-design: multiparty asynchronous global programming. ACM SIGPLAN Notices **48**(1), 263–274 (2013). https://doi.org/10.1145/2429069.2429101

2. Cruz-Filipe, L., Montesi, F.: A core model for choreographic programming. Theor. Comput. Sci. **802**, 38–66 (2020). https://doi.org/10.1016/j.tcs.2019.07.005. https://doi.org/10.1016/j.tcs.2019.07.005

3. Cruz-Filipe, L., Montesi, F., Peressotti, M.: Certifying choreography compilation. In: Cerone, A., Ölveczky, P.C. (eds.) ICTAC 2021. LNCS, vol. 12819, pp. 115–133. Springer, Cham (2021). https://doi.org/10.1007/978-3-030-85315-0_8

4. Cruz-Filipe, L., Montesi, F., Peressotti, M.: Formalising a turing-complete choreographic language in coq. In: Cohen, L., Kaliszyk, C. (eds.) 12th International Conference on Interactive Theorem Proving, ITP 2021, 29 June to 1 July 2021, Rome, Italy (Virtual Conference). LIPIcs, vol. 193, pp. 15:1–15:18. Schloss Dagstuhl - Leibniz-Zentrum für Informatik (2021). https://doi.org/10.4230/LIPIcs.ITP.2021.15

5. Cruz-Filipe, L., Montesi, F., Peressotti, M.: A formal theory of choreographic programming. CoRR **abs/2209.01886** (2022). https://doi.org/10.48550/arXiv.2209.01886. https://doi.org/10.48550/arXiv.2209.01886

6. Hirsch, A.K., Garg, D.: Pirouette: higher-order typed functional choreographies. Proc. ACM Program. Lang. **6**(POPL), 1–27 (2022). https://doi.org/10.1145/3498684. https://doi.org/10.1145/3498684

7. Leesatapornwongsa, T., Lukman, J.F., Lu, S., Gunawi, H.S.: TaxDC: A taxonomy of non-deterministic concurrency bugs in datacenter distributed systems. In: Proceedings of ASPLOS, pp. 517–530 (2016)

8. Montesi, F.: Choreographic Programming. Ph.D. Thesis, IT University of Copenhagen (2013). http://www.fabriziomontesi.com/files/choreographic-programming.pdf

9. Montesi, F.: Introduction to Choreographies. Cambridge University Press, Cambridge (2023)

10. Montesi, F., Guidi, C., Zavattaro, G.: Service-oriented programming with Jolie. In: Bouguettaya, A., Sheng, Q.Z., Daniel, F. (eds.) Web Services Foundations, pp. 81–107. Springer, Cham (2014). https://doi.org/10.1007/978-1-4614-7518-7_4

11. Myreen, M.O., Owens, S.: Proof-producing synthesis of ML from higher-order logic. In: International Conference on Functional Programming (ICFP), pp. 115–126. ACM Press (2012). https://doi.org/10.1145/2364527.2364545. https://cakeml.org/icfp12/index.html

12. Pohjola, J.Å., Gómez-Londoño, A., Shaker, J., Norrish, M.: Kalas: A verified, end-to-end compiler for a choreographic language. In: Andronick, J., de Moura, L. (eds.) 13th International Conference on Interactive Theorem Proving, ITP 2022, 7-10 August 2022, Haifa, Israel. LIPIcs, vol. 237, pp. 27:1–27:18. Schloss Dagstuhl - Leibniz-Zentrum für Informatik (2022). https://doi.org/10.4230/LIPIcs.ITP.2022.27

13. Scalas, A., Yoshida, N.: Less is more: multiparty session types revisited. Proc. ACM Program. Lang. **3**(POPL), 30:1–30:29 (2019). https://doi.org/10.1145/3290343

Implementing a CTL Model Checker with $\mu\mathcal{G}$, a Language for Programming Graph Neural Networks

Matteo Belenchia[(⊠)][iD], Flavio Corradini[iD], Michela Quadrini[iD], and Michele Loreti[iD]

University of Camerino, Camerino, Italy
{matteo.belenchia,flavio.corradini,michela.quadrini,
michele.loreti}@unicam.it

Abstract. A graph neural network is a deep learning architecture operating on graph-structured data. While they have achieved impressive results in many application domains, their applicability is limited when one needs to perform symbolic and semantic reasoning, for example, in model checking. We propose an approach based on the idea that graph neural networks can be programmed. We introduce $\mu\mathcal{G}$, a simple language inspired by modal μ-calculus that can be *compiled*, via TensorFlow, in a graph neural network that can be efficiently run on parallel architectures. To demonstrate our method, we use our language to implement a Computation Tree Logic model checker. A benchmark from the Model Checking Contest is used to show that the performance of the resulting tool outperforms that of other model checkers.

Keywords: Graph Neural Networks · Model checking · Computation Tree Logic

1 Introduction

Artificial Intelligence (AI) systems are being deployed in an increasing number of different tasks. In the last decade, there has been a renewed interest in Deep Learning (DL) models, such as neural networks, due to the increased computational capabilities of modern computers and the vast abundance of data in the Digital Age. Neural Networks [18] had stunning success in various tasks spanning computer vision, natural language processing, autonomous driving, software engineering, and more. Out of the many classes of neural network architectures, Graph Neural Networks (GNNs) emerged to deal specifically with graph-based data in the fields mentioned above. On the other hand, symbolic AI systems, which dominated the early years of AI, proved to be too brittle and unable to adapt to many of the tasks that nowadays machine learning systems can perform exceptionally well, and therefore gathered little interest from the industry and research community.

© IFIP International Federation for Information Processing 2023
M. Huisman and A. Ravara (Eds.): FORTE 2023, LNCS 13910, pp. 37–54, 2023.
https://doi.org/10.1007/978-3-031-35355-0_4

Our work stems from a simple question: *Can GNNs be used to improve model checking procedures?* Unfortunately, DL algorithms still have several limitations, including adversarial perturbations, unexplainability, catastrophic forgetting, and the inability to distinguish causation from correlation, to mention a few [29]. These issues make DL unsuitable for domains such as model-checking, where semantic and rule-based reasoning plays an important role. This is witnessed by the fact that neuro-symbolic computing has been proposed as an approach to combine the strengths of deep learning with those of symbolic AI [28,30,36].

In this paper, we propose combining neural and symbolic AI by defining $\mu\mathcal{G}$, a formal language for the specification of graph neural networks. A $\mu\mathcal{G}$ graph neural network consists of a composition of layers assembled according to the formal rules of the language, which may also be optimized during training in a supervised manner. The rules of $\mu\mathcal{G}$ specify what transformations to perform on the input node-labeling of a graph and are loosely inspired from modal μ-calculus [26]. Using our language allows the specification of graph neural networks that partly mitigate the problems typically associated with deep learning models outlined above.

For example, the outputs of a GNN can be explained according to the $\mu\mathcal{G}$ terms that have been used to specify it. This approach does not make a $\mu\mathcal{G}$ GNN completely explainable since it might still include opaque trainable components. Still, it is an improvement over the usual black-box approach of standard deep learning models.

More generally, our programming language allows selecting a reasonable trade-off between symbolic and neural computation. Once an appropriate level of detail has been chosen for a task [9], one could choose to use trainable functions (e.g., neural networks) to perform the sub-tasks where deep-learning usually excels, then use $\mu\mathcal{G}$ to specify a GNN that performs the complete task using these functions as building blocks. The simpler the sub-tasks delegated to the trainable functions, the closer the final composite GNN resembles a purely symbolic algorithm. On the other hand, the more complex these sub-tasks, the more the final composite GNN resembles an ensemble of neural networks.

Furthermore, it is possible to avoid using trainable functions and completely specify a GNN without training it. A GNN of this kind can be used to implement any algorithm while also enjoying the computational benefits of deep learning models, namely the possibility of efficient computation on parallel architectures such as Graphic Processor Units (GPUs) and the portability of the code on any such architecture.

To show the advantages of the proposed approach, we apply $\mu\mathcal{G}$ to develop a model checker for Computation Tree Logic (CTL [17]).

Contributions. Our main contributions are:

- We define the $\mu\mathcal{G}$ language, its denotational semantics, and the typing of its expressions.
- We show how the $\mu\mathcal{G}$ language can be implemented in Python using Tensor-Flow/Keras as the backend.

- We demonstrate how to use $\mu\mathcal{G}$ to program graph neural networks for CTL model checking.
- We show that the obtained tool outperforms two other existing tools, pyModelChecking and μCRL2, on a benchmark of the Model Checking Contest.

Structure of the Paper. In Sect. 2, we introduce the notation and preliminary information about graphs and graph neural networks. Then the $\mu\mathcal{G}$ language is described in Sect. 3 by its denotational semantics, while its Python implementation in TensorFlow is shown in Sect. 4. We evaluate the $\mu\mathcal{G}$ language on the task of CTL model checking in Sect. 5. Finally, we conclude with related work in Sect. 6 and future directions in Sect. 7.

2   Preliminaries and Notation

Graphs and their Labelings. A directed graph is a pair $\mathsf{G} = (\mathsf{V}, \mathsf{E})$ where V is a collection of vertices (which we also refer to as "nodes") and E is a collection of ordered pairs of vertices, called edges. For any $u, v \in \mathsf{V}$, whenever $(u, v) \in \mathsf{E}$ we say that u is a *predecessor* of v and that v is a *successor* of u. We also say that (u, v) is an *incoming edge* for v and an *outgoing edge* for u. Moreover, let $\overleftarrow{N}_{\mathsf{G}}(v)$ denote the set of *predecessors* of v, formally $\overleftarrow{N}_{\mathsf{G}}(v) = \{u \mid (u, v) \in \mathsf{E}\}$, while $\overrightarrow{N}_{\mathsf{G}}(u)$ denotes the set of *successors* of u, namely $\overrightarrow{N}_{\mathsf{G}}(u) = \{v \mid (u, v) \in \mathsf{E}\}$. Similarly, let $I_{\mathsf{G}}(v)$ denote the set of *incoming edges* for v, formally $I_{\mathsf{G}}(v) = \{(u, v) \mid u, v \in \mathsf{V}\}$, and let $O_{\mathsf{G}}(u)$ denote the set of *outgoing edges* for u, formally $O_{\mathsf{G}}(u) = \{(u, v) \mid u, v \in \mathsf{V}\}$.

Sometimes it is useful to associate nodes and edges with values. Given a graph $\mathsf{G} = (\mathsf{V}, \mathsf{E})$, we can consider its *node-labeling* and *edge-labeling*. The former is a function $\eta : \mathsf{V} \to T_v$ associating each node $v \in \mathsf{V}$ with a value in the set T_v. Similarly, an *edge-labeling* is a function $\xi : \mathsf{E} \to T_e$ that maps an edge to its label in the set T_e. Let $V \subseteq \mathsf{V}$ (resp. $E \subseteq \mathsf{E}$), we let $\eta(V)$ (resp. $\xi(E)$) denote the *multi-set* of labels associated to the elements of V (resp. E) by η (resp. ξ). Likewise, we let $(\eta, \xi)(E)$ denote the *multi-set* of tuples $(\eta(u), \xi((u, v)), \eta(v))$ for each $(u, v) \in E$.

Encoding of Graphs and Labels. One way to represent graphs and their labeling functions on a computer is in the form of a matrix of node features $\mathbf{X}$, an adjacency matrix $\mathbf{A}$ and a matrix of edge features $\mathbf{E}$. The node features matrix $\mathbf{X}$ stores the features associated with each node in the graph. The i-th row of the matrix contains a value of type $\mathbf{x}_i \in T_v$ that represents the information associated with the i-th vertex of the graph in a given ordering. The adjacency matrix $\mathbf{A}$ encodes the architecture of the graph, with each non-zero element $a_{ij} \in \mathbb{R}$ denoting the presence of an edge from a node i to a node j with weight a_{ij}. The edge features matrix $\mathbf{E}$ stores the features associated with each edge, much like the node features matrix. The i-th row of $\mathbf{E}$ is a value of type T_e that represents the information associated with the i-th edge in the row-major (or any other) ordering of the edges in $\mathbf{A}$.

Graph Neural Networks. A Graph Neural Network (GNN) is a deep learning model that operates on graph-structured data. Introduced by [35], it emerged to overcome the limitations of graph kernel methods [31]. GNNs are one of the most general classes of deep learning architecture: many other deep learning models can be seen as a particular case of graph neural networks [14].

Graph neural networks can be used for many tasks, which can be roughly categorized according to the subject of prediction: nodes, edges, or entire graphs. As with other machine learning models, there are two main kinds of tasks, namely classification and regression, where the goal is to predict the class or some numerical quantity associated with the nodes in the graph, edges, or entire graphs. What is different from other machine learning models is that the success of graph neural networks stems not from the assumption of independent and identically distributed data, but rather from the information that can be obtained from the dependencies of the data. GNNs may exploit concepts such as homophily, heterophily, the structural equivalence of nodes, or the small-world phenomenon [24].

The most general form of graph neural network, which subsumes most of the GNN variants that have been developed over the years [14], is the message passing neural network (MPNN) variant [8,21]. A typical MPNN comprises a fixed number of convolutional layers stacked in sequence, each updating the node features matrix. A convolution operation updates the features of all nodes in the graph at the same time, according to the following equation:

$$\mathbf{x}'_i = u\left(\mathbf{x}_i, \oplus_{j \in N_G(i)} \varphi(\mathbf{x}_i, \mathbf{e}_{ij}, \mathbf{x}_j)\right) \tag{1}$$

where $N_G(i)$ is the set of neighbours of node i, $\oplus$ is a permutation-invariant function and u, φ are learnable functions. The function φ generates the message sent from node j to node i, which in the simplest case might be the value of $\mathbf{x}_j$. The function $\oplus$ aggregates the multiset of messages obtained by φ in a way that is independent of the order they are evaluated and is usually a non-learnable function such as the sum, product or mean, but, more generally, it can also be defined as a neural network. The function u updates the embedding of node i by considering both the current embedding $\mathbf{x}_i$ and the new embedding that was just computed.

Graph neural networks composed by layers described by Eq. 1 are permutation-equivariant functions that take as input a tuple $(\mathbf{X}, \mathbf{A}, \mathbf{E})$ and return a new node features matrix $\mathbf{X}'$. This characterization leaves out some types of graph neural networks, namely, the graph neural networks that use pooling layers (which therefore change the architecture of the graph by removing elements from V and E) and the graph neural networks that learn edge features rather than node features (which therefore produce a new edge features matrix $\mathbf{E}'$ instead). At any rate, the standard graph neural network model we have just described is general enough to encompass these two special cases as well. A graph neural network that uses pooling layers can be represented by allowing the node-labeling function to label each node with an additional Boolean value that specifies whether the node has been deleted or not and by ruling that an edge is valid if and only if both the source and destination nodes have not been deleted. A graph neural network that learns edge features can instead be modeled by reifying edges into nodes and by having the graph's node-labeling function label each node with an additional Boolean value that specifies whether the node represents an edge or a node of the original graph.

Types. We denote the set of all labeling functions with codomain T as $H[T]$, and we say that this set specifies its *type*. As examples, labeling functions of type $H[\mathbb{B}]$ map vertices to Boolean values, while functions of type $H[\mathbb{N}^k]$ with $k \in \mathbb{N}$ map vertices to k-tuples of natural numbers. Given a graph G together with its edge-labeling function ξ, we consider a graph neural network as a function $\phi_{\mathsf{G},\xi} : H[T_1] \rightarrow H[T_2]$ that maps a node-labeling function to another node-labeling function. We denote the set of graph neural networks as $\Phi_{\mathsf{G},\xi}[T_1, T_2]$ or, more succinctly, as $\Phi_{\mathsf{G},\xi}$. The subscript G, ξ indicates that each graph neural network is parametrized by a graph and the edge-labeling function.

3 A Calculus of Graph Neural Networks

This section introduces the syntax of $\mu\mathcal{G}$ as a programming language for graph neural networks. After defining the syntax (Definition 1), we show its denotational semantics (Definition 2).

Definition 1. *(Syntax) Given a set $\mathcal{X} = \{X, Y, Z, \ldots\}$ of variable symbols and a set $\mathcal{S}$ of function symbols, we define an algebra of Graph Neural Networks with the following abstract syntax:*

$$\mathcal{N} ::= \psi \mid \lhd_\sigma^\varphi \mid \rhd_\sigma^\varphi \mid \mathcal{N}_1; \mathcal{N}_2 \mid \mathcal{N}_1 \| \mathcal{N}_2 \mid X \mid f(\mathcal{N}_1, \mathcal{N}_2, \ldots, \mathcal{N}_k) \mid$$
$$\texttt{let } X = \mathcal{N}_1 \texttt{ in } \mathcal{N}_2 \mid \texttt{def } f(\tilde{X})\{\mathcal{N}_1\} \texttt{ in } \mathcal{N}_2 \mid$$
$$\texttt{if } \mathcal{N}_1 \texttt{ then } \mathcal{N}_2 \texttt{ else } \mathcal{N}_3 \mid \texttt{fix } X = \mathcal{N}_1 \texttt{ in } \mathcal{N}_2$$

with $\varphi, \sigma, \psi, f \in \mathcal{S}$ and $X \in \mathcal{X}$.

Given a graph G and an edge-labeling ξ, the meaning of a $\mu\mathcal{G}$ expression is a graph neural network, a function between node-labeling functions. One of the basic $\mu\mathcal{G}$ terms is the *function application* ψ. This represents the application of a given function (referenced by ψ) to the input node-labeling function. Moreover, the *pre-image* operator $\lhd_\sigma^\varphi$ and the *post-image* operator $\rhd_\sigma^\varphi$ are used to compute the labeling of a node in terms of the labels of its predecessors and successors, respectively. Basic terms are composed by *sequential composition* $\mathcal{N}_1; \mathcal{N}_2$ and *parallel composition* $\mathcal{N}_1 \| \mathcal{N}_2$. Local *variables* X and *functions* $f(\tilde{X})$ can be defined using let and def. The *choice* operator if $\mathcal{N}_1$ then $\mathcal{N}_2$ else $\mathcal{N}_3$ allows to run different GNNs according to the result of a guard GNN. Finally, the *fixed point* operator fix $X = \mathcal{N}_1$ in $\mathcal{N}_2$ is used to program *recursive behavior*.

We say that a $\mu\mathcal{G}$ term is *well-formed* whenever it can be typed with the rules of Table 1. These rules guarantee that any *well-formed* $\mu\mathcal{G}$ term can be interpreted as a GNN. From now on, we will consider only *well-formed* terms.

Definition 2. *(Denotational semantics) Given a graph* G *and an environment* ρ *that comprises a variable evaluation function* $\rho_v : \mathcal{X} \to \Phi_{\mathsf{G},\xi}$ *and a function evaluation function* $\rho_f : \mathcal{S} \to ((\Phi_{\mathsf{G},\xi} \times \ldots \times \Phi_{\mathsf{G},\xi}) \to \Phi_{\mathsf{G},\xi})$ *we define the semantic interpretation function* $\llbracket \cdot \rrbracket_\rho^{\mathsf{G},\xi} : \mathcal{N} \to \Phi_{\mathsf{G},\xi}$ *on* $\mu\mathcal{G}$ *formulas* $\mathcal{N}$ *by induction in the following way:*

$$\llbracket \psi \rrbracket_\rho^{\mathsf{G},\xi}(\eta) = \lambda v.f_\psi(\eta(\mathsf{V}), \eta(v))$$

$$\llbracket \triangleleft_\sigma^\varphi \rrbracket_\rho^{\mathsf{G},\xi}(\eta) = \lambda v.f_\sigma(f_\varphi((\eta,\xi)(I_\mathsf{G}(v))), \eta(v))$$

$$\llbracket \triangleright_\sigma^\varphi \rrbracket_\rho^{\mathsf{G},\xi}(\eta) = \lambda v.f_\sigma(f_\varphi((\eta,\xi)(O_\mathsf{G}(v))), \eta(v))$$

$$\llbracket \mathcal{N}_1 ; \mathcal{N}_2 \rrbracket_\rho^{\mathsf{G},\xi} = \llbracket \mathcal{N}_2 \rrbracket_\rho^{\mathsf{G},\xi} \circ \llbracket \mathcal{N}_1 \rrbracket_\rho^{\mathsf{G},\xi}$$

$$\llbracket \mathcal{N}_1 || \mathcal{N}_2 \rrbracket_\rho^{\mathsf{G},\xi}(\eta) = \lambda v.\langle(\llbracket \mathcal{N}_1 \rrbracket_\rho^{\mathsf{G},\xi}(\eta))(v), (\llbracket \mathcal{N}_2 \rrbracket_\rho^{\mathsf{G},\xi}(\eta))(v)\rangle$$

$$\llbracket X \rrbracket_\rho^{\mathsf{G},\xi} = \rho(X)$$

$$\llbracket f(\mathcal{N}_1, \mathcal{N}_2, \ldots, \mathcal{N}_k) \rrbracket_\rho^{\mathsf{G},\xi} = \rho(f)(\llbracket \mathcal{N}_1 \rrbracket_\rho^{\mathsf{G},\xi}, \llbracket \mathcal{N}_2 \rrbracket_\rho^{\mathsf{G},\xi}, \ldots, \llbracket \mathcal{N}_k \rrbracket_\rho^{\mathsf{G},\xi})$$

$$\llbracket \texttt{let } X = \mathcal{N}_1 \texttt{ in } \mathcal{N}_2 \rrbracket_\rho^{\mathsf{G},\xi} = \llbracket \mathcal{N}_2 \rrbracket_{\rho[X \leftarrow \llbracket \mathcal{N}_1 \rrbracket_\rho^{\mathsf{G},\xi}]}^{\mathsf{G},\xi}$$

$$\llbracket \texttt{def } f(\tilde{X})\{\mathcal{N}_1\} \texttt{ in } \mathcal{N}_2 \rrbracket_\rho^{\mathsf{G},\xi} = \llbracket \mathcal{N}_2 \rrbracket_{\rho[f \leftarrow \lambda\tilde{X}'.\llbracket \mathcal{N}_1 \rrbracket_{\rho[\tilde{X} \leftarrow \tilde{X}']}^{\mathsf{G},\xi}]}^{\mathsf{G},\xi}$$

$$\llbracket \texttt{if } \mathcal{N}_1 \texttt{ then } \mathcal{N}_2 \texttt{ else } \mathcal{N}_3 \rrbracket_\rho^{\mathsf{G},\xi}(\eta) = cond(\llbracket \mathcal{N}_1 \rrbracket_\rho^{\mathsf{G},\xi}, \llbracket \mathcal{N}_2 \rrbracket_\rho^{\mathsf{G},\xi}, \llbracket \mathcal{N}_3 \rrbracket_\rho^{\mathsf{G},\xi})(\eta)$$

$$\llbracket \texttt{fix } X = \mathcal{N}_1 \texttt{ in } \mathcal{N}_2 \rrbracket_\rho^{\mathsf{G},\xi}(\eta) = g(\llbracket \mathcal{N}_1 \rrbracket_\rho^{\mathsf{G},\xi})(\eta)$$

For any $\psi, \varphi, \sigma, f \in \mathcal{S}$ *and any* $X \in \mathcal{X}$. *The functions cond and g are defined as follows:*

$$cond(t, f_1, f_2)(\eta) = \begin{cases} f_1(\eta) & \text{if } t(\eta) = \lambda v.\texttt{True} \\ f_2(\eta) & \text{otherwise} \end{cases}$$

$$g(\phi)(\eta) = \begin{cases} \phi(\eta) & \text{if } \phi(\eta) = \llbracket \mathcal{N}_2 \rrbracket_{\rho[X \leftarrow \phi]}^{\mathsf{G},\xi}(\eta) \\ g(\llbracket \mathcal{N}_2 \rrbracket_{\rho[X \leftarrow \phi]}^{\mathsf{G},\xi})(\eta) & \text{otherwise} \end{cases}$$

In the following paragraphs, we clarify the denotational semantics of $\mu\mathcal{G}$ expressions.

Function Application. The function symbols $\psi_1, \psi_2, \ldots \in \mathcal{S}$ are evaluated as the graph neural networks $\llbracket \psi_1 \rrbracket_\rho^{\mathsf{G},\xi}, \llbracket \psi_2 \rrbracket_\rho^{\mathsf{G},\xi}, \ldots$ that map a node-labeling function η to a new node-labeling function by applying a function on both local and global node information. The local information consists of applying η to the input node, while the global information is the multiset of the labels of all the nodes in the graph. The graph neural network we obtain applies a possibly trainable function f_ψ to these two pieces of information. Two particular cases arise if f_ψ decides to ignore either of the two inputs. If f_ψ ignores the global information, the GNN returns a node-labeling function η_l, a purely local transformation of the node labels. On the other hand, if f_ψ ignores the local information, the GNN returns a

Table 1. Typing of $\mu\mathcal{G}$ expressions.

ψ	$$\frac{}{f_\psi : T_1^* \times T_1 \to T_2, \Gamma \vdash \psi : \Phi_{\mathsf{G},\xi}[T_1, T_2]}$$
$\triangleleft_\sigma^\varphi$	$$\frac{}{f_\varphi : T_1 \times T_e \times T_1 \to T_2, f_\sigma : T_2^* \times T_1 \to T_3, \Gamma \vdash \triangleleft_\sigma^\varphi : \Phi_{\mathsf{G},\xi}[T_1, T_3]}$$
$\triangleright_\sigma^\varphi$	$$\frac{}{f_\varphi : T_1 \times T_e \times T_1 \to T_2, f_\sigma : T_2^* \times T_1 \to T_3, \Gamma \vdash \triangleright_\sigma^\varphi : \Phi_{\mathsf{G},\xi}[T_1, T_3]}$$
$\mathcal{N}_1 ; \mathcal{N}_2$	$$\frac{\Gamma \vdash \mathcal{N}_1 : \Phi_{\mathsf{G},\xi}[T_1, T_2], \mathcal{N}_2 : \Phi_{\mathsf{G},\xi}[T_2, T_3]}{\Gamma \vdash \mathcal{N}_1 ; \mathcal{N}_2 : \Phi_{\mathsf{G},\xi}[T_1, T_3]}$$
$\mathcal{N}_1 \| \mathcal{N}_2$	$$\frac{\Gamma \vdash \mathcal{N}_1 : \Phi_{\mathsf{G},\xi}[T_1, T_2], \mathcal{N}_2 : \Phi_{\mathsf{G},\xi}[T_1, T_2]}{\Gamma \vdash \mathcal{N}_1 \| \mathcal{N}_2 : \Phi_{\mathsf{G},\xi}[T_1, T_2 \times T_2]}$$
X	$$\frac{}{\Gamma \vdash X : \Phi_{\mathsf{G},\xi}[T_1, T_2]}$$
$f(\mathcal{N}_1, \ldots, \mathcal{N}_k)$	$$\frac{\Gamma \vdash \mathcal{N}_1 : \Phi_{\mathsf{G},\xi}[T_1, T_1'], \ldots, \mathcal{N}_k : \Phi_{\mathsf{G},\xi}[T_k, T_k']}{\Gamma \vdash f(\mathcal{N}_1, \ldots, \mathcal{N}_k) : \Phi_{\mathsf{G},\xi}[T, T']}$$
let $X = \mathcal{N}_1$ in $\mathcal{N}_2$	$$\frac{\Gamma \vdash \mathcal{N}_1 : \Phi_{\mathsf{G},\xi}[T_1, T_2], \Gamma \cup \{X : \Phi_{\mathsf{G},\xi}[T_1, T_2]\} \vdash \mathcal{N}_2 : \Phi_{\mathsf{G},\xi}[T, T']}{\Gamma \vdash \text{let } X = \mathcal{N}_1 \text{ in } \mathcal{N}_2 : \Phi_{\mathsf{G},\xi}[T, T']}$$
def $f(\tilde{X})\{\mathcal{N}_1\}$ in $\mathcal{N}_2$	$$\frac{\begin{array}{c} \Gamma \cup \{X_i : \Phi_{\mathsf{G},\xi}[T_i, T_i'] \mid i \in 1, \ldots, k\} \vdash \mathcal{N}_1 : \Phi_{\mathsf{G},\xi}[T_0, T_0'], \\ \Gamma \cup \{f : \Phi_{\mathsf{G},\xi}[T_1, T_1'] \times \cdots \times \Phi_{\mathsf{G},\xi}[T_k, T_k'] \to \Phi_{\mathsf{G},\xi}[T_0, T_0']\} \vdash \mathcal{N}_2 : \Phi_{\mathsf{G},\xi}[T, T'] \end{array}}{\Gamma \vdash \text{def } f(\tilde{X})\{\mathcal{N}_1\} \text{ in } \mathcal{N}_2 : \Phi_{\mathsf{G},\xi}[T, T']}$$
if $\mathcal{N}_1$ then $\mathcal{N}_2$ else $\mathcal{N}_3$	$$\frac{\Gamma \vdash \mathcal{N}_1 : \Phi_{\mathsf{G},\xi}[T_1, \mathbb{B}], \mathcal{N}_2 : \Phi_{\mathsf{G},\xi}[T_1, T_2], \mathcal{N}_3 : \Phi_{\mathsf{G},\xi}[T_1, T_3]}{\Gamma \vdash \text{if } \mathcal{N}_1 \text{ then } \mathcal{N}_2 \text{ else } \mathcal{N}_3 : \Phi_{\mathsf{G},\xi}[T_1, T_2 \cup T_3]}$$
fix $X = \mathcal{N}_1$ in $\mathcal{N}_2$	$$\frac{\Gamma \vdash \mathcal{N}_1 : \Phi_{\mathsf{G},\xi}[T_1, T_2], \Gamma \cup \{X : \Phi_{\mathsf{G},\xi}[T_1, T_2]\} \vdash \mathcal{N}_2 : \Phi_{\mathsf{G},\xi}[T_1, T_2]}{\Gamma \vdash \text{fix } X = \mathcal{N}_1 \text{ in } \mathcal{N}_2 : \Phi_{\mathsf{G},\xi}[T_1, T_2]}$$

node-labeling function η_g that assigns to each node a label that summarizes the entire graph, emulating what in the GNN literature is known as a *global pooling operator* [23].

Pre-image and Post-Image. The pre-image symbol $\triangleleft$ and the post-image symbol $\triangleright$, together with function symbols $\varphi \in \mathcal{S}$ and $\sigma \in \mathcal{S}$ are evaluated as the graph neural networks $[\![\triangleleft_\sigma^\varphi]\!]_\rho^{\mathsf{G},\xi}$ and $[\![\triangleright_\sigma^\varphi]\!]_\rho^{\mathsf{G},\xi}$ for any $\sigma, \varphi \in \mathcal{S}$. In the case of the pre-image, for any symbol $\varphi \in \mathcal{S}$ the corresponding function f_φ generates a *message* from a tuple $(\eta(u), \xi((u,v)), \eta(v))$, and this is repeated for each $(u,v) \in I_{\mathsf{G}}(v)$. Then for any symbol $\sigma \in \mathcal{S}$ the corresponding function f_σ generates a new label for a node v from the multiset of messages obtained from f_φ and the current label $\eta(v)$. The functions f_φ and f_σ may be trainable. The case of the post-image is analogous, with the difference that f_φ is applied to tuples $(\eta(v), \xi((v,u)), \eta(u))$ for each $(v,u) \in O_{\mathsf{G}}(v)$ instead.

Sequential Composition. An expression of the form $\mathcal{N}_1 ; \mathcal{N}_2$ for $\mu\mathcal{G}$ formulas $\mathcal{N}_1, \mathcal{N}_2$ is evaluated as the graph neural network $[\![\mathcal{N}_2 ; \mathcal{N}_1]\!]_\rho^{\mathsf{G},\xi}$ that maps a node-labeling function η to a new node-labeling function obtained from the function composition of $[\![\mathcal{N}_2]\!]_\rho^{\mathsf{G},\xi}$ and $[\![\mathcal{N}_1]\!]_\rho^{\mathsf{G},\xi}$.

Parallel Composition. An expression of the form $\mathcal{N}_1 || \mathcal{N}_2$ for $\mu\mathcal{G}$ formulas $\mathcal{N}_1, \mathcal{N}_2$ is evaluated as the graph neural network $[\![\mathcal{N}_2 || \mathcal{N}_1]\!]_\rho^{G,\xi}$ that maps a node-labelling function η to a new node-labelling function that maps a node v to the tuple $\langle [\![\mathcal{N}_1]\!]_\rho^{G,\xi}(\eta)(v), [\![\mathcal{N}_2]\!]_\rho^{G,\xi}(\eta)(v) \rangle$. Moreover, combining this operator with the basic function symbols $\psi_1, \psi_2, \ldots \in \mathcal{S}$ allows the execution of k-ary operations on the node-labelling functions: a k-ary function application $f_{op_k}(\mathcal{N}_1, \ldots, \mathcal{N}_k)$ is expressible as the $\mu\mathcal{G}$ expression $((\ldots (\mathcal{N}_1 || \mathcal{N}_2) || \ldots) || \mathcal{N}_k); op_k$.

Choice. The choice operator if $\mathcal{N}_1$ then $\mathcal{N}_2$ else $\mathcal{N}_3$ for $\mu\mathcal{G}$ formulas $\mathcal{N}_1, \mathcal{N}_2,$ $\mathcal{N}_3$ is evaluated as the graph neural network $[\![\mathcal{N}_2]\!]_\rho^{G,\xi}$ if $\eta' = [\![\mathcal{N}_1]\!]_\rho^{G,\xi}(\eta)$ is a node-labelling function such that $\forall v \in G, \eta'(v) = \texttt{True}$. Otherwise it is evaluated as the graph neural network $[\![\mathcal{N}_3]\!]_\rho^{G,\xi}$.

Fixed Points. The fixed point operator is evaluated as the graph neural network that is obtained by applying $[\![\mathcal{N}_1]\!]_\rho^{G,\xi}$ to the least fixed point of the functional $\mathcal{F}$ [32] associated to g. Formally, it is $\bigsqcup \{\mathcal{F}^n \mid n \geq 0\}([\![\mathcal{N}_1]\!]_\rho^{G,\xi})$ where

$$\mathcal{F}^0 = \lambda\phi.\lambda\eta.\bot$$
$$\mathcal{F}^{n+1} = \mathcal{F}(\mathcal{F}^n)$$

4   From $\mu\mathcal{G}$ to TensorFlow

One of the main advantages of using GNNs is related to the widespread availability of Python libraries that allow their development. We chose to implement $\mu\mathcal{G}$ using Spektral [22], based on the well-known TensorFlow/Keras framework, because of its easy-to-use APIs to represent graphs, implement new GNN layers and batch graphs together. Another advantage of libraries such as TensorFlow is that once we have a graph neural network model, it can be executed on any architecture without changes. This means a $\mu\mathcal{G}$ program can be run without modification on a CPU, GPU, or TPU. Furthermore, in TensorFlow, it is straightforward to distribute input data across multiple devices. Therefore, it is possible to split the input data to be run on multiple GPUs in parallel.

In the following paragraphs, we describe how each of the $\mu\mathcal{G}$ expressions is translated into TensorFlow/Keras layers using Spektral APIs. These layers can then be composed together into a single graph neural network model. Intermediate outputs of the model can be re-used: if the same $\mu\mathcal{G}$ sub-formula occurs more than once as part of the same $\mu\mathcal{G}$ expression, its results are computed only once and re-used wherever they are needed.

Function Application. The function application operator is implemented by a layer that applies the function f_ψ to the input node features matrix $\mathbf{X}$. Therefore, even though we defined f_ψ in two arguments, we really only provide the first: a local operation on every node-labeling value can be performed efficiently and in parallel because TensorFlow broadcasts arithmetic operations. For example, if we are interested in adding 1 to every label, a function $f_1(\mathbf{X}) = \mathbf{X} + 1$ suffices because 1 is broadcast to every row of $\mathbf{X}$.

Pre-image and Post-image. For the pre-image and post-image operators, we developed the corresponding layers that compute a multiset of messages for each node using f_φ and then aggregate them using f_σ. The sparse adjacency matrix $\mathbf{A}$ is stored in memory as a $(|\mathbf{E}|, 2)$ matrix, with each row representing an edge that originates in the node of the first column and ends in the node of the second column. Therefore the inputs for the function f_φ are three sequences: the labels of the nodes in the first column of $\mathbf{A}$, the edge labels $\mathbf{E}$ and the labels of the nodes in the second column of $\mathbf{A}$. The function will be applied row by row on these three input sequences in parallel using broadcasting. The messages are then passed to f_σ together with the nodes to which each message should be "sent": for the pre-image operator, this is the first column of $\mathbf{A}$, while for the post-image operator, it is the second column instead. Additionally, we make f_σ accept the total number of nodes in the graph because TensorFlow offers very efficient functions to aggregate values which require the number of aggregations to be performed.

Sequential Composition. The sequential composition of graph neural networks is straightforward: the model is built by composing in sequence the left-hand side graph neural network model with the right-hand side one, with the output of the former becoming the input of the latter.

Parallel Composition. The parallel composition of graph neural networks is a model that is built by concatenating the left-hand side graph neural network model with the right-hand side one. This type of operation is common enough that it is already available in TensorFlow with the `Concatenate` layer. Therefore it simply suffices to send the outputs of the two models as inputs to the `Concatenate` layer.

Choice Operator. The choice operator is a model that is built using TensorFlow's `cond` function: the arguments of this function are the output of the graph neural network that computes the Boolean test and the two graph neural networks that are to be run according to the condition.

Fixed Point Computation. For the fixed point operator `fix` $X = \mathcal{N}_1$ in $\mathcal{N}_2$, we first evaluate the argument $\mathcal{N}_2$. If no variable X occurs in $\mathcal{N}_2$, then `fix` $X = \mathcal{N}_1$ in $\mathcal{N}_2$ simplifies to $\mathcal{N}_2$. In all other cases, $\mathcal{N}_2$ will contain zero or more sub-expressions independent of X and one or more sub-expressions that depend on X. We build the parse tree for $\mathcal{N}_2$ and construct models $M_1, M_2, \ldots, M_k$ for any sub-tree that is independent of X. The values produced by these models become inputs of the fixed point layer. The fixed point layer is characterized by a model M in exactly $k + 1$ inputs, the first k of them to be bound to the outputs of models $M_1, \ldots, M_k$ and the last argument to be bound, initially, to the value produced by $\mathcal{N}_1$. The layer performs a looping operation, each time running M with the same k arguments but with the previously obtained output as the value of the $k+1$-th argument. When the output of M is the same as the value of $k+1$-th input argument, it is returned as output. For floating point labels, it is possible to specify an absolute tolerance value such that two labels are considered equal if they differ by less than the tolerance value.

5 $\mu\mathcal{G}$ in Action: A CTL Model Checker

This section shows how $\mu\mathcal{G}$ can be used to program a model checker for CTL formulas. To the best of our knowledge, neither GPU-accelerated CTL model-checking algorithms nor machine learning models for this task have been proposed. Our approach enables using GNNs for CTL model checking that can be executed on parallel architectures such as GPUs. Notably, we need not use trainable functions for this task. In Sect. 5.1, we recall the basics of Computation Tree Logic model checking, then in Sect. 5.2, we show how to translate each CTL formula to a $\mu\mathcal{G}$ term that labels each node of a graph with a Boolean value indicating if the formula is satisfied or not in the state represented by that node. Finally, in Sect. 5.3, we evaluate the $\mu\mathcal{G}$-programmed CTL model checker against two other model checking tools on Petri net models from the Model Checking Contest.

5.1   Basics of Computation Tree Logic

Computation Tree Logic (CTL) is a branching-time logic interpreted over Kripke structures. A Kripke structure is a directed graph whose nodes correspond to the states of a system and whose edges correspond to state transitions. More formally, let AP be a set of atomic propositions, then a Kripke structure is a tuple $\mathcal{K} = (S, I, R, L)$ where S is a finite set of states, $I \subseteq S$ is a set of initial states, $R \subseteq S \times S$ is a transition relation between states, and $L : S \to 2^{AP}$ is a labeling function that associates each state to a set of atomic propositions.

Let $p \in AP$, a CTL formula can be generated using the following grammar:

$$\phi ::= p \mid \neg\phi \mid \phi_1 \wedge \phi_2 \mid EX\phi \mid EG\phi \mid E\phi_1 U\phi_2$$

We recall that a path $\pi = s_1 s_2 \ldots$ is an infinite sequence of states such that $\forall i, (s_i, s_{i+1}) \in R$. We let $Path(s)$ denote the set of paths originating from s, while for any path π, $\pi[i]$ denotes the i-th state in π.

Given a Kripke structure $\mathcal{K} = (S, I, R, L)$, a set of atomic propositions AP and a well-formed CTL formula ϕ, we define the semantics of a CTL formula as a set of states $[\![\phi]\!]_{\mathcal{K}}$ in the following way:

Table 2. Recursive definition of the translation function $\mathcal{M} : \phi \to \mathcal{N}$.

$$\mathcal{M}(p) = \psi_p \qquad \mathcal{M}(\neg\phi) = \mathcal{M}(\phi); \psi_\neg$$

$$\mathcal{M}(\phi_1 \wedge \phi_2) = (\mathcal{M}(\phi_1)||\mathcal{M}(\phi_2)); \psi_\wedge \qquad \mathcal{M}(EX\phi) = \mathcal{M}(\phi); \triangleright_{\sigma_\vee}^{\varphi_{pr_3}}$$

$$\mathcal{M}(EG\phi) = \texttt{fix } X = \psi_{true} \texttt{ in } ((\mathcal{M}(\phi)||(X; \triangleright_{\sigma_\vee}^{\varphi_{pr_3}})); \psi_\wedge)$$

$$\mathcal{M}(E\phi_1 U\phi_2) = \texttt{fix } X = \psi_{false} \texttt{ in } (\mathcal{M}(\phi_2)||((\mathcal{M}(\phi_1)||(X; \triangleright_{\sigma_\vee}^{\varphi_{pr_3}})); \psi_\wedge); \psi_\vee)$$

$\llbracket p \rrbracket_\mathcal{K} = \{s \mid p \in L(s)\}$
$\llbracket \neg\phi \rrbracket_\mathcal{K} = S \setminus \llbracket \phi \rrbracket_\mathcal{K}$
$\llbracket \phi_1 \wedge \phi_2 \rrbracket_\mathcal{K} = \llbracket \phi_1 \rrbracket_\mathcal{K} \cap \llbracket \phi_2 \rrbracket_\mathcal{K}$
$\llbracket EX\phi \rrbracket_\mathcal{K} = \{s \mid \exists s' \text{ s.t. } (s,s') \in R \wedge s' \in \llbracket \phi \rrbracket_\mathcal{K}\}$
$\llbracket EG\phi \rrbracket_\mathcal{K} = \{s \mid \exists \pi \text{ s.t. } \pi[0] = s \wedge \forall i,\ \pi[i] \in \llbracket \phi \rrbracket_\mathcal{K}\}$
$\llbracket E\phi_1 U\phi_2 \rrbracket_\mathcal{K} = \{s \mid \exists \pi \text{ s.t. } \pi[0] = s \wedge \exists k \forall i < k\ \pi[i] \in \llbracket \phi_1 \rrbracket_\mathcal{K} \wedge \pi[k] \in \llbracket \phi_2 \rrbracket_\mathcal{K}\}$

5.2 Computation Tree Logic in $\mu\mathcal{G}$

Let ϕ be a CTL formula. Then we can define a graph neural network $\text{SAT}_\varphi : H[2^{AP}] \to H[\mathbb{B}]$ where the input node-labeling function is the Kripke structure's labeling function, and the output node-labeling function assigns a `True` label to every node that satisfies φ and a `False` label to every node that doesn't. The translation function $\mathcal{M} : \phi \to \mathcal{N}$ that maps CTL expressions to $\mu\mathcal{G}$ terms is shown in Table 2. The function symbols used in the table are to be intended as follows: ψ_p denotes a function

$$f_p(\cdot, l) = \begin{cases} \texttt{True} & \text{if } p \in l \\ \texttt{False} & \text{otherwise} \end{cases}$$

that maps a node's label l to `True` if and only if $p \in L(s)$, and we have one such function for any $p \in AP \cup \{\texttt{True}, \texttt{False}\}$. Function symbols $\psi_\wedge, \psi_\vee, \psi_\neg$ denote the usual Boolean connectives (which, like f_p, ignore their first argument), $\sigma_{\max}$ denotes the max aggregation function for multisets and finally φ_{pr_3} denotes the projection function that returns its third argument.

Theorem 1. *Let $\mathcal{K} = (S, I, R, L)$ be a Kripke structure, let $\mathsf{G} = (S, R)$ be the corresponding graph, and let $\mathcal{M}$ be the function recursively translating CTL formulas to $\mu\mathcal{G}$ as in Table 2. Then for every state $s \in S$ we have that:*

$$s \in \llbracket \phi \rrbracket_\mathcal{K} \implies \llbracket \mathcal{M}(\phi) \rrbracket_\rho^{\mathsf{G},\xi}(L)(s) = \texttt{True}$$

$$s \notin \llbracket \phi \rrbracket_\mathcal{K} \implies \llbracket \mathcal{M}(\phi) \rrbracket_\rho^{\mathsf{G},\xi}(L)(s) = \texttt{False}$$

Proof. The proof is standard and follows the same structure used to prove the correctness of the translation from CTL to μ-calculus [13,20].

Table 3. Petri net models used for the experiments, for which we reported here the number of nodes and edges in the reachability graph (RG).

ID	Petri Net	#nodes in RG	#edges in RG
1	RobotManipulation-PT-00001	110	274
2	TokenRing-PT-005	166	365
3	Philosophers-PT-000005	243	945
4	RobotManipulation-PT-00002	1430	5 500
5	Dekker-PT-010	6144	171 530
6	BART-PT-002	17 424	53 328
7	ClientsAndServers-PT-N0001P0	27 576	113 316
8	Philosophers-PT-000010	59 049	459 270
9	Referendum-PT-0010	59 050	393 661
10	SatelliteMemory-PT-X00100Y0003	76 358	209 484
11	RobotManipulation-PT-00005	184 756	1 137 708
12	Dekker-PT-015	278 528	16 834 575
13	HouseConstruction-PT-00005	1 187 984	7 191 110

5.3 Evaluation

We compare the performance of the $\mu\mathcal{G}$ CTL model checker introduced in the previous section with two other existing tools: pyModelChecking[1], which implements a CTL model checker in Python, and the μCRL2 toolset [15], which is a well-known and broadly used model checker.

We consider the Petri net models from the Model Checking Contest 2022 (MCC2022) [1]. Among the available models, we selected those for which it was possible to generate the reachability graph (RG). These models are summarised in Table 3. For each model, there are 16 CTL formulas for which we have to compute the set of satisfying states.

Our experiment measured the total time it took to verify these 16 formulas for each Petri net model. It was performed on a Windows 11 machine with an Intel Core i7-10875H CPU, NVIDIA GeForce RTX 2070 Max-Q GPU with 6GiB of VRAM, and 16GiB of RAM.

We consider two execution setups for $\mu\mathcal{G}$. In the first setup, which we refer to as the "split" setup, we verify each of the 16 CTL formulas one by one by first generating the corresponding graph neural network model and then running it on the Kripke structure obtained from the Petri net. In the second setup, which we call the "full" setup, we model-check all 16 formulas at once, in parallel, by concatenating the expression corresponding to each formula with the parallel composition operator of $\mu\mathcal{G}$. This second approach can obtain considerable speedups compared to the first but is at risk of running out of memory. For both the setups, we also report the time spent to generate the *TensorFlow*

[1] https://github.com/albertocasagrande/pyModelChecking.

computation graph, an operation commonly referred to as "tracing". A computation graph defines the data flow of the computations to perform, with nodes representing operations and arrows representing the flow of data. This tracing phase has to be performed only once for each $\mu\mathcal{G}$ model, after which the model can be used without retracing the graph. The pyModelChecking Python library is used to verify each formula one by one on the Kripke structure, as in the case of the $\mu\mathcal{G}$ split setup. Finally, in the case of μCRL2, we use the Petri net's labeled transition system and convert the CTL formulas into the equivalent μ-calculus formulas. Then for each formula, we record the time needed to generate the corresponding *parametrized boolean equation system* (PBES) and the time it takes for μCRL2 to solve it. The PBES is generated using the lts2pbes command with the -p argument, which may lead to smaller PBESs. Then the PBES is solved using the pbessolve command with the -threads=8 argument to allow the best multi-threaded performance possible on our machine.

The experimental results are shown in Table 4. For each instantiated Petri net model, we report the computation graph generation and execution times. For $\mu\mathcal{G}$, we report the time for the *split* model, where the total time needed to model check all the formulas is shown, and for the *full* model. The last two columns in the table show the μCRL2 time for generating and solving the PBESs.

Table 4. Execution times for $\mu\mathcal{G}$ models, pyModelChecking and μCRL2.

Petri Net	Tracing (split)	Running (split)	Tracing (full)	Running (full)	pyMC	μCRL2 PBES gen.	μCRL2 PBES solv.
1	7.541 s	0.406 s	6.494 s	0.17 s	0.048 s	0.476 s	0.118 s
2	13.534 s	0.552 s	7.704 s	0.189 s	0.203 s	10.822 s	0.128 s
3	9.379 s	0.426 s	8.441 s	0.174 s	0.125 s	2.345 s	0.13 s
4	8.655 s	0.609 s	7.974 s	0.264 s	0.863 s	5.739 s	0.142 s
5	9.926 s	0.684 s	8.621 s	0.176 s	6.001 s	132.027 s	0.164 s
6	25.265 s	4.987 s	12.21 s	0.958 s	24.399 s	481.579 s	0.161 s
7	9.593 s	1.603 s	8.677 s	0.727 s	17.53 s	105.978 s	0.173 s
8	8.928 s	2.008 s	7.401 s	0.619 s	52.184 s	1031.431 s	0.219 s
9	10.404 s	1.79 s	9.491 s	0.476 s	51.117 s	610.559 s	0.237 s
10	8.515 s	3.942 s	7.826 s	1.359 s	28.542 s	214.721 s	0.209 s
11	8.727 s	4.940 s	8.094 s	1.492 s	136.821 s	1232.92 s	0.366
12	10.493 s	16.593 s	8.911 s	OOM	497.917 s	12551.7 s	4.227 s
13	9.008 s	61.964 s	8.445 s	25.003 s	936.875 s	7160.645 s	1.884 s

Except for the smallest graphs, both the full and split $\mu\mathcal{G}$ models are faster than pyModelChecking, even when taking into account the one-time cost of building the computation graph. The split $\mu\mathcal{G}$ model is also slightly slower than the full model, as expected, but it is able to successfully solve the Dekker-PT-015 task without running out of memory, which the full model could not. In comparison to μCRL2, we notice that the solution of PBESs with 8 threads is very fast, much faster than running the $\mu\mathcal{G}$ model. On the other hand, the generation of PBESs is a very time-consuming task that has to be performed for each combination of graphs and formulas: verifying the same formula on two different graphs requires two different PBESs. Therefore, if we consider the total time it takes for μCRL2 to generate and solve the PBESs, we conclude again that, except for the smallest instances, $\mu\mathcal{G}$ requires far less time to verify all the formulas. This is clearly exemplified by the already mentioned Dekker-PT-015 dataset, for which $\mu\mathcal{G}$ is able to verify all the formulas in under 30 s, while μCRL2 needs almost three hours and a half. Despite these positive results, a model checker based on $\mu\mathcal{G}$ has also a number of drawbacks. Not only can the $\mu\mathcal{G}$ model only be used if the full graph fits into the GPU memory, but it is further limited by the complexity of the CTL formula to verify: very "wide" formulas that require keeping in memory many different node-labeling functions of the graph at the same time are more likely to exhaust memory, even if the graph itself may not be very large. In contrast, other model-checking tools do not have memory limitations associated with the complexity of the formulas to verify.

6   Related Work

We surveyed the literature by looking at previous work on the topic of model checking tools that either use machine learning or are executed on GPUs.

The contributions of machine learning to model checking were, until recently, limited to helping classical model checkers to find invalidating runs more quickly or reducing the rate of spurious counterexamples [2]. More recently, at least two attempts have been made to implement a model checker using only machine learning models. Both attempts have in common that the requirement of providing an exact answer to all queries is relaxed, therefore changing the task to approximate model checking.

Neural Model Checking is the first such attempt [33]. The authors use neural networks to learn a graph-specific classifier trained on the graphs' execution traces. They focus on continuous and hybrid systems and only consider time-bounded reachability properties, but their method can be applied both online and offline and claims a prediction accuracy greater than 99%.

The second attempt [41] consists in predicting the output of a Linear Temporal Logic (LTL [34]) model checker given the encodings of an LTL formula and a Kripke structure. While the framework can boast very high prediction accuracy and claims to avoid the state explosion problem altogether, it cannot generalize to different sizes of input data. The authors note that the network is unable to generalize what it learned to Kripke structures of different sizes and formulae of different lengths.

A lot of work has been devoted in the past decade to developing GPU-accelerated model checkers. A commented list of these tools, none of which considers CTL model checking, is reported below. All these approaches rely on hand-crafting low-level code that can be executed on a GPU. In contrast, $\mu\mathcal{G}$ is a high-level language that completely abstracts from the underlying architecture: the same $\mu\mathcal{G}$ program can be run on a CPU, GPU, or TPU. The use of

TensorFlow, or any other high-level machine learning library, guarantees that executions will be optimized for the available hardware.

For LTL model checking, DiVinE-CUDA [4–6] is an explicit-state model checker that runs accepting cycle detection algorithms on possibly multiple GPUs. Cycles are detected using either the Maximal Accepting Predecessor algorithm (MAP) or the One-Way-Catch-Them-Young (OWCTY) algorithm, while a parallel algorithm on the CPU explicitly generates the state space. On-the-fly reachability checking was tackled by GPURC [40] using breadth-first search with dynamic load balancing. Another approach for GPU-accelerated LTL model checking is the work in [7], where the authors re-implement Holzmann's parallel BFS algorithm used by the multi-core SPIN model checker. Later, the same authors developed Grapple [19], an explicit-state swarm verification model checker.

Liveness properties have been first tackled in [37], which use Rabin automata and Breadth-First Search with piggybacking. The most recent work in the context of LTL safety property model checking on GPUs used the Forward-Backward algorithm [16].

Another GPU-accelerated model checker is GPUexplore [39], which can be used to check for deadlocks and verify safety properties on-the-fly [38]. GPU-explore works on networks of labeled transition systems, which are assumed to represent parallel processes, and the formulas are represented as LTSs too.

For the case of quantitative analysis, the first LTLC model checker for GPUs uses a mixed DFS-BFS algorithm for solving multiple feasibility checking problems in parallel [27]. A GPU-accelerated model checker for Probabilistic Computation Tree Logic (PCTL [25]) based on PRISM was developed and described by [10–12], which use a parallel implementation of the Jacobi method.

7   Conclusion

We have presented $\mu\mathcal{G}$, a formal language that allows programming GNNs. The latter can be seen as a higher-order function $\phi_{\mathsf{G},\xi} : H[T_1] \to H[T_2]$. An application of the language for the task of CTL model checking is shown and evaluated against other model-checking tools.

In the future, we plan to apply $\mu\mathcal{G}$ to other tasks: in the context of model checking, we would like to apply our approach for the model checking of probabilistic and stochastic logics such as PCTL and CSL [3].

The applications of $\mu\mathcal{G}$ are not limited to model checking. Indeed, we will investigate the use of $\mu\mathcal{G}$ on more standard GNN tasks. In particular, we will use our approach to solve typical data analysis problems. The starting point is the analysis of the CORA citation network dataset, which has already been performed with $\mu\mathcal{G}$ but is omitted here due to space constraints.

Finally, we will also study the integration of standard *learning techniques* that have been used with GNNs in our language. Note that, in this work, we have not considered functions that can be optimized. Nevertheless, one could consider parametric functions that can be learned in a supervised setting.

References

1. Amparore, E., et al.: Presentation of the 9th edition of the model checking contest. In: Beyer, D., Huisman, M., Kordon, F., Steffen, B. (eds.) TACAS 2019. LNCS, vol. 11429, pp. 50–68. Springer, Cham (2019). https://doi.org/10.1007/978-3-030-17502-3_4

2. Amrani, M., Lúcio, L., Bibal, A.: ML + FV = ♡? A Survey on the Application of Machine Learning to Formal Verification. arXiv:1806.03600 (2018). http://arxiv.org/abs/1806.03600

3. Aziz, A., Sanwal, K., Singhal, V., Brayton, R.: Verifying continuous time Markov chains. In: Alur, R., Henzinger, T.A. (eds.) CAV 1996. LNCS, vol. 1102, pp. 269–276. Springer, Heidelberg (1996). https://doi.org/10.1007/3-540-61474-5_75

4. Barnat, J., Brim, L., Ceška, M., Lamr, T.: CUDA accelerated LTL model checking. In: 2009 15th International Conference on Parallel and Distributed Systems, pp. 34–41 (2009). https://doi.org/10.1109/ICPADS.2009.50. ISSN 1521-9097

5. Barnat, J., Bauch, P., Brim, L., Češka, M.: Designing fast LTL model checking algorithms for many-core GPUs. J. Parallel Distrib. Comput. 72(9), 1083–1097 (2012). https://doi.org/10.1016/j.jpdc.2011.10.015. https://www.sciencedirect.com/science/article/pii/S0743731511002140

6. Barnat, J., Brim, L., Češka, M.: DiVinE-CUDA - a tool for GPU accelerated LTL model checking. Electron. Proc. Theor. Comput. Sci. 14, 107–111 (2009). https://doi.org/10.4204/EPTCS.14.8. http://arxiv.org/abs/0912.2555. http://arxiv.org/abs/0912.2555. arXiv:0912.2555

7. Bartocci, E., DeFrancisco, R., Smolka, S.A.: Towards a GPGPU-parallel SPIN model checker. In: Proceedings of the 2014 International SPIN Symposium on Model Checking of Software, San Jose CA USA, pp. 87–96. ACM (2014). https://doi.org/10.1145/2632362.2632379. https://dl.acm.org/doi/10.1145/2632362.2632379

8. Battaglia, P.W., et al.: Relational inductive biases, deep learning, and graph networks (2018). https://arxiv.org/abs/1806.01261v3. arXiv:1806.01261

9. Belenchia, M., Thórisson, K.R., Eberding, L.M., Sheikhlar, A.: Elements of task theory. In: Goertzel, B., Iklé, M., Potapov, A. (eds.) AGI 2021. LNCS (LNAI), vol. 13154, pp. 19–29. Springer, Cham (2022). https://doi.org/10.1007/978-3-030-93758-4_3

10. Bosnacki, D., Edelkamp, S., Sulewski, D., Wijs, A.: Parallel probabilistic model checking on general purpose graphics processors. Int. J. Softw. Tools Technol. Transfer 13, 21–35 (2011). https://doi.org/10.1007/s10009-010-0176-4

11. Bošnački, D., Edelkamp, S., Sulewski, D.: Efficient probabilistic model checking on general purpose graphics processors. In: Păsăreanu, C.S. (ed.) SPIN 2009. LNCS, vol. 5578, pp. 32–49. Springer, Heidelberg (2009). https://doi.org/10.1007/978-3-642-02652-2_7

12. Bošnački, D., Edelkamp, S., Sulewski, D., Wijs, A.: GPU-PRISM: an extension of PRISM for general purpose graphics processing units. In: 2010 Ninth International Workshop on Parallel and Distributed Methods in Verification, and Second International Workshop on High Performance Computational Systems Biology, pp. 17–19 (2010). https://doi.org/10.1109/PDMC-HiBi.2010.11

13. Bradfield, J., Walukiewicz, I.: The mu-calculus and model checking. In: Clarke, E., Henzinger, T., Veith, H., Bloem, R. (eds.) Handbook of Model Checking, pp. 871–919. Springer, Cham (2018). https://doi.org/10.1007/978-3-319-10575-8_26

14. Bronstein, M.M., Bruna, J., Cohen, T., Veličković, P.: Geometric Deep Learning: Grids, Groups, Graphs, Geodesics, and Gauges (2021). https://doi.org/10.48550/arXiv.2104.13478. http://arxiv.org/abs/2104.13478. http://arxiv.org/abs/2104.13478. arXiv:2104.13478

15. Bunte, O., et al.: The mCRL2 toolset for analysing concurrent systems. In: Vojnar, T., Zhang, L. (eds.) TACAS 2019. LNCS, vol. 11428, pp. 21–39. Springer, Cham (2019). https://doi.org/10.1007/978-3-030-17465-1_2

16. Chu, C., Luo, G., Zhang, M.: An optimized model checking parallel algorithm based on CUDA. In: 2019 IEEE 18th International Conference on Cognitive Informatics Cognitive Computing (ICCI*CC), pp. 446–452 (2019). https://doi.org/10.1109/ICCICC46617.2019.9146097

17. Clarke, E.M., Emerson, E.A.: Design and synthesis of synchronization skeletons using branching time temporal logic. In: Kozen, D. (ed.) Logic of Programs 1981. LNCS, vol. 131, pp. 52–71. Springer, Heidelberg (1982). https://doi.org/10.1007/BFb0025774

18. Dastres, R., Soori, M.: Artificial neural network systems. Int. J. Imaging Robot. (IJIR) 21(2), 13–25 (2021). https://hal.archives-ouvertes.fr/hal-03349542

19. DeFrancisco, R., Cho, S., Ferdman, M., Smolka, S.A.: Swarm model checking on the GPU. Int. J. Softw. Tools Technol. Transf. 22(5), 583–599 (2020). https://doi.org/10.1007/s10009-020-00576-x

20. Emerson, E.A.: Model checking and the mu-calculus. Descriptive Complex. Finite Models 31, 185–214 (1996)

21. Gilmer, J., Schoenholz, S.S., Riley, P.F., Vinyals, O., Dahl, G.E.: Neural Message Passing for Quantum Chemistry. arXiv:1704.01212 (2017). http://arxiv.org/abs/1704.01212. arXiv:1704.01212

22. Grattarola, D., Alippi, C.: Graph Neural Networks in TensorFlow and Keras with Spektral. arXiv:2006.12138 (2020). http://arxiv.org/abs/2006.12138. arXiv: 2006.12138

23. Grattarola, D., Zambon, D., Bianchi, F.M., Alippi, C.: Understanding pooling in graph neural networks. IEEE Trans. Neural Netw. Learn. Syst. 1–11 (2022). https://doi.org/10.1109/TNNLS.2022.3190922

24. Hamilton, W.L.: Graph representation learning. Synth. Lect. Artif. Intell. Mach. Learn. 14(3), 1–159 (2020)

25. Hansson, H., Jonsson, B.: A logic for reasoning about time and reliability. Form. Aspects Comput. 6(5), 512–535 (1994). https://doi.org/10.1007/BF01211866

26. Kozen, D.: Results on the propositional μ-calculus. In: Nielsen, M., Schmidt, E.M. (eds.) ICALP 1982. LNCS, vol. 140, pp. 348–359. Springer, Heidelberg (1982). https://doi.org/10.1007/BFb0012782

27. Kwon, Y.M., Kim, E.: A design of GPU-based quantitative model checking. In: Henglein, F., Shoham, S., Vizel, Y. (eds.) VMCAI 2021. LNCS, vol. 12597, pp. 441–463. Springer, Cham (2021). https://doi.org/10.1007/978-3-030-67067-2_20

28. Lamb, L.C., D'avila Garcez, A., Gori, M., Prates, M.O.R., Avelar, P.H.C., Vardi, M.Y.: Graph neural networks meet neural-symbolic computing: a survey and perspective. In: Proceedings of the Twenty-Ninth International Joint Conference on Artificial Intelligence (2020)

29. Marcus, G.: Deep learning: a critical appraisal (2018). https://arxiv.org/abs/1801.00631. arXiv:1801.00631

30. Marcus, G.: The Next Decade in AI: Four Steps Towards Robust Artificial Intelligence (2020). https://arxiv.org/abs/2002.06177v3. arXiv:2002.06177

31. Morris, C., Fey, M., Kriege, N.: The power of the Weisfeiler-Leman algorithm for machine learning with graphs. In: Proceedings of the Thirtieth International Joint Conference on Artificial Intelligence, pp. 4543–4550. International Joint Conferences on Artificial Intelligence Organization, Montreal, Canada (2021). https://doi.org/10.24963/ijcai.2021/618. https://www.ijcai.org/proceedings/2021/618

32. Nielson, H.R., Nielson, F.: Denotational semantics. In: Nielson, H.R., Nielson, F. (eds.) Semantics with Applications: An Appetizer, pp. 91–126. Springer, Heidelberg (2007). https://doi.org/10.1007/978-1-84628-692-6_5

33. Phan, D., Grosu, R., Paoletti, N., Smolka, S.A., Stoller, S.D.: How to Learn a Model Checker. arXiv:1712.01935 (2017). http://arxiv.org/abs/1712.01935. arXiv: 1712.01935

34. Pnueli, A.: The temporal logic of programs. In: 18th Annual Symposium on Foundations of Computer Science (SFCS 1977), pp. 46–57 (1977). https://doi.org/10.1109/SFCS.1977.32. ISSN 0272-5428

35. Scarselli, F., Gori, M., Tsoi, A.C., Hagenbuchner, M., Monfardini, G.: The graph neural network model. IEEE Trans. Neural Netw. **20**(1), 61–80 (2009). https://doi.org/10.1109/TNN.2008.2005605

36. Susskind, Z., Arden, B., John, L.K., Stockton, P., John, E.B.: Neuro-symbolic AI: an emerging class of AI workloads and their characterization. CoRR abs/2109.06133 (2021). https://arxiv.org/abs/2109.06133

37. Wijs, A.: BFS-based model checking of linear-time properties with an application on GPUs. In: Chaudhuri, S., Farzan, A. (eds.) CAV 2016. LNCS, vol. 9780, pp. 472–493. Springer, Cham (2016). https://doi.org/10.1007/978-3-319-41540-6_26

38. Wijs, A., Bošnački, D.: Many-core on-the-fly model checking of safety properties using GPUs. Int. J. Softw. Tools Technol. Transfer **18**(2), 169–185 (2015). https://doi.org/10.1007/s10009-015-0379-9

39. Wijs, A., Bošnački, D.: GPUexplore: many-core on-the-fly state space exploration using GPUs. In: Ábrahám, E., Havelund, K. (eds.) TACAS 2014. LNCS, vol. 8413, pp. 233–247. Springer, Heidelberg (2014). https://doi.org/10.1007/978-3-642-54862-8_16

40. Wu, Z., Liu, Y., Sun, J., Shi, J., Qin, S.: GPU accelerated on-the-fly reachability checking. In: 2015 20th International Conference on Engineering of Complex Computer Systems (ICECCS), pp. 100–109 (2015). https://doi.org/10.1109/ICECCS.2015.21

41. Zhu, W., Wu, H., Deng, M.: LTL model checking based on binary classification of machine learning. IEEE Access (2019). https://doi.org/10.1109/ACCESS.2019.2942762

Security

Branching Bisimulation Semantics Enables Noninterference Analysis of Reversible Systems

Andrea Esposito[✉], Alessandro Aldini, and Marco Bernardo

Dipartimento di Scienze Pure e Applicate, Università di Urbino, Urbino, Italy
`a.esposito30@campus.uniurb.it`

Abstract. The theory of noninterference supports the analysis and the execution of secure computations in multi-level security systems. Classical equivalence-based approaches to noninterference mainly rely on weak bisimulation semantics. We show that this approach is not sufficient to identify potential covert channels in the presence of reversible computations. As illustrated via a database management system example, the activation of backward computations may trigger information flows that are not observable when proceeding in the standard forward direction. To capture the effects of back and forth computations, it is necessary to move to a sufficiently expressive semantics that, in an interleaving framework, has been proven to be branching bisimilarity in a previous work by De Nicola, Montanari, and Vaandrager. In this paper we investigate a taxonomy of noninterference properties based on branching bisimilarity along with their preservation and compositionality features, then we compare it with the classical hierarchy based on weak bisimilarity.

1 Introduction

Noninterference was introduced by Goguen and Meseguer [22] to reason about the way in which illegitimate information flows can occur in multi-level security systems from high-level agents to low-level ones due to covert channels. Since the first definition conceived for deterministic state machines, in the last four decades a lot of work has been done that led to a variety of extensions (dealing with nondeterminism or quantitative domains) in multiple frameworks (from language-based security to concurrency theory); see, e.g., [15,2,32,24,25] and the references therein. Analogously, the techniques proposed to verify information-flow security properties based on noninterference have followed several different approaches, ranging from the application of type theory [44] and abstract interpretation [19] to control flow analysis and equivalence or model checking [16,33,3].

Noninterference guarantees that low-level agents can never infer from their observations what high-level agents are doing. Regardless of its specific definition, noninterference is closely tied to the notion of behavioral equivalence, because the idea is to compare the system behavior with high-level actions being prevented and the system behavior with those actions being hidden. Historically, one of the most established formal definitions of noninterference properties relies

© IFIP International Federation for Information Processing 2023
M. Huisman and A. Ravara (Eds.): FORTE 2023, LNCS 13910, pp. 57–74, 2023.
https://doi.org/10.1007/978-3-031-35355-0_5

on weak bisimilarity in a process algebraic framework [34], as it naturally lends itself to reason formally about covert channels and illegitimate information flows.

While the literature concentrated on weak bisimilarity so far [15], in this paper we claim that it is worth studying nondeterministic noninterference in a different setting, relying on branching bisimulation semantics. Branching bisimilarity was introduced in [21] as a refinement of weak bisimilarity to preserve the branching structure of processes also when abstracting from invisible actions. It features a complete axiomatization whose only τ-axiom is $a.(\tau.(y + z) + y) = a.(y + z)$, where a is an action, τ is an invisible action, and y and z are process terms. Moreover, while weak bisimilarity can be verified in $O(n^2 \cdot m \cdot \log n)$, where m is the number of transitions and n is the number of states of the labeled transition system underlying the process at hand, branching bisimilarity can be verified more efficiently. An $O(m \cdot n)$ algorithm has been provided in [23] and, more recently, an even faster $O(m \cdot \log n)$ algorithm has been developed in [26].

A clear motivation for passing to branching bisimilarity is provided by the setting of reversible computing – for which no information flow security approach exists to the best of our knowledge – where weak bisimilarity does not represent a proper tool for the comprehensive analysis of covert channels. In this setting, the model of computation features both forward and backward computations, i.e., computational processes are reversible [28,6]. This paradigm has turned out to have interesting applications in computational biology [38,39], parallel discrete-event simulation [36,41], robotics [31], control theory [42], fault tolerant systems [10,12,29,43], and concurrent program debugging [18,30].

Behavioral equivalences for reversible processes must take into account the fact that computations are allowed to proceed not only forward but also backward. To this aim, back-and-forth bisimilarity, introduced in [11], requires that two systems are able to mimic each other's behavior stepwise not only in performing actions that follow the arrows of the labeled transition systems, but also in undoing those actions when going backwards. Formally, back-and-forth bisimulations are defined on computation paths instead of states thus preserving not only causality but also history, as backward moves are constrained to take place along the same path followed in the forward direction even in the presence of concurrency. In [11] it was shown that strong back-and-forth bisimilarity coincides with the usual notion of strong bisimilarity, while weak back-and-forth bisimilarity is surprisingly finer than standard weak bisimilarity, and it coincides with branching bisimilarity. In particular, this latter result will allow us to investigate the nature of covert channels in reversible systems by using a standard process calculus, e.g., without having to decorate executed actions like in [37] or store them into stack-based memories like in [9].

Once established that branching bisimilarity enables noninterference analysis of reversible systems, the novel contribution of this paper is the study of noninterference security properties based on branching bisimilarity. In addition to investigating preservation and compositionality features, we compare the resulting properties with those based on weak bisimilarity [15] and we establish a taxonomy of the former that can be naturally applied to those based on weak back-and-forth bisimilarity for reversible systems. Moreover, we show that, in the setting of reversible systems, weak bisimilarity does not provide a proper framework for the identification of subtle covert channels, while branching bisimilarity does. This is carried out through a database management system example.

This paper is organized as follows. In Sect. 2, we recall background definitions and results for several bisimulation equivalences and information-flow security properties based on weak bisimilarity, along with a process language to formalize those properties. In Sect. 3, we introduce the database management system example. In Sect. 4, we recast the same information-flow security properties in terms of branching bisimilarity, then we present some results about preservation of those properties under branching bisimilarity and compositionality with respect to the operators of the considered language. Moreover, we show results about inclusion among all the previously discussed properties, which are summarized in a new taxonomy. In Sect. 5, we recall the notion of back-and-forth bisimulation and its relationship with the aforementioned bisimulations, emphasizing that weak back-and-forth bisimilarity coincides with branching bisimilarity, which allows us to apply our results to reversible systems. In Sect. 6, we add reversibility to the database management system example to illustrate the need of branching-bisimilarity-based noninterference. Finally, in Sect. 7 we provide some concluding remarks and discuss future work.

2 Background Definitions and Results

In this section, we recall bisimulation equivalences (Sect. 2.1) and introduce a basic process language (Sect. 2.2) through which we express bisimulation-based information-flow security properties (Sect. 2.3).

2.1 Bisimulation Equivalences

To represent the behavior of a process we use a labeled transition system [27], which is a state-transition graph whose transitions are labeled with actions.

Definition 1. *A* labeled transition system (LTS) *is a triple* $(S, A, \longrightarrow)$ *where* $S \neq \emptyset$ *is an at most countable set of states,* $A \neq \emptyset$ *is a countable set of actions, and* $\longrightarrow \subseteq S \times A \times S$ *is a transition relation.*   ∎

A transition (s, a, s') is written $s \xrightarrow{a} s'$, where s is the source state and s' is the target state. We say that s' is reachable from s, written $s' \in reach(s)$, iff $s' = s$ or there is a sequence of finitely many transitions such that the target state of each of them coincides with the source state of the subsequent one, with the source of the first one being s and the target of the last one being s'.

Strong bisimilarity [34,35] identifies processes that are able to mimic each other's behavior stepwise. This preserves the branching structure of processes.

Definition 2. *Let* $(S, A, \longrightarrow)$ *be an LTS and* $s_1, s_2 \in S$. *We say that* s_1 *and* s_2 *are* strongly bisimilar, *written* $s_1 \sim s_2$, *iff* $(s_1, s_2) \in \mathcal{B}$ *for some strong bisimulation* $\mathcal{B}$. *A symmetric binary relation* $\mathcal{B}$ *over* S *is a* strong bisimulation *iff,*

60   A. Esposito et al.

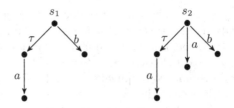

Fig. 1. States s_1 and s_2 are weakly bisimilar but not branching bisimilar

whenever $(s_1, s_2) \in \mathcal{B}$, then for all actions $a \in A$:

– whenever $s_1 \xrightarrow{a} s_1'$, then $s_2 \xrightarrow{a} s_2'$ with $(s_1', s_2') \in \mathcal{B}$. ∎

Weak bisimilarity [34] abstracts from unobservable actions, which are denoted by τ. Let $s \xRightarrow{\tau^*} s'$ means that $s' \in reach(s)$ and, whenever $s' \neq s$, there is a finite sequence of transitions from s to s' each of which is labeled with τ.

Definition 3. *Let $(S, A, \longrightarrow)$ be an LTS and $s_1, s_2 \in S$. We say that s_1 and s_2 are weakly bisimilar, written $s_1 \approx s_2$, iff $(s_1, s_2) \in \mathcal{B}$ for some weak bisimulation $\mathcal{B}$. A symmetric binary relation $\mathcal{B}$ over S is a weak bisimulation iff, whenever $(s_1, s_2) \in \mathcal{B}$, then:*

– whenever $s_1 \xrightarrow{\tau} s_1'$, then $s_2 \xRightarrow{\tau^*} s_2'$ with $(s_1', s_2') \in \mathcal{B}$;
– whenever $s_1 \xrightarrow{a} s_1'$ for $a \in A \setminus \{\tau\}$, then $s_2 \xRightarrow{\tau^*} \xrightarrow{a} \xRightarrow{\tau^*} s_2'$ with $(s_1', s_2') \in \mathcal{B}$. ∎

Branching bisimilarity [21] is finer than weak bisimilarity as it preserves the branching structure of the abstracted τ-actions.

Definition 4. *Let $(S, A, \longrightarrow)$ be an LTS and $s_1, s_2 \in S$. We say that s_1 and s_2 are branching bisimilar, written $s_1 \approx_b s_2$, iff $(s_1, s_2) \in \mathcal{B}$ for some branching bisimulation $\mathcal{B}$. A symmetric binary relation $\mathcal{B}$ over S is a branching bisimulation iff, whenever $(s_1, s_2) \in \mathcal{B}$, then for all actions $a \in A$:*

– whenever $s_1 \xrightarrow{a} s_1'$, then:
  • either $a = \tau$ and $(s_1', s_2) \in \mathcal{B}$;
  • or $s_2 \xRightarrow{\tau^*} \bar{s}_2 \xrightarrow{a} s_2'$ with $(s_1, \bar{s}_2) \in \mathcal{B}$ and $(s_1', s_2') \in \mathcal{B}$. ∎

An example that highlights the higher distinguishing power of branching bisimilarity is given in Fig. 1, where every LTS is depicted as a directed graph in which vertices represent states and action-labeled edges represent transitions. The initial states s_1 and s_2 of the LTSs are weakly bisimilar but not branching bisimilar. The only transition that distinguishes s_1 and s_2 is the a-transition of s_2, which can be mimicked by s_1 according to weak bisimilarity by performing the τ-transition followed by the a-transition. However, s_1 cannot respond in the same way according to branching bisimilarity. If s_1 performs the τ-transition followed by the a-transition, then the state reached after the τ-transition should be branching bisimilar to s_2, which is not the case because of the b-transition departing from s_2.

2.2   A Process Calculus with High and Low Actions

We now introduce a basic process calculus to formalize the security properties of interest. To address two security levels, actions are divided into high and low. We denote by $\mathcal{A} = \mathcal{A}_{\mathcal{H}} \cup \mathcal{A}_{\mathcal{L}}$ the set of visible actions, where $\mathcal{A}_{\mathcal{H}} \cap \mathcal{A}_{\mathcal{L}} = \emptyset$, with $\mathcal{A}_{\mathcal{H}}$ being the set of high-level actions, ranged over by h, and $\mathcal{A}_{\mathcal{L}}$ being the set of low-level actions, ranged over by l. Furthermore $\mathcal{A}_{\tau} = \mathcal{A} \cup \{\tau\}$, where $\tau \notin \mathcal{A}$ is the invisible or silent action.

The set $\mathbb{P}$ of process terms is obtained by considering typical operators from [34,8]. In particular, in addition to the usual operators for sequential, alternative, and parallel compositions, we include restriction and hiding as they are necessary to formalize noninterference properties. The syntax is:

$$P ::= \underline{0} \mid a . P \mid P + P \mid P \|_L P \mid P \setminus L \mid P / L$$

where:

- $\underline{0}$ is the terminated process.
- $a . \_$, for $a \in \mathcal{A}_{\tau}$, is the action prefix operator describing a process that initially performs action a.
- $\_ + \_$ is the alternative composition operator expressing a nondeterministic choice between two processes based on their executable actions.
- $\_ \|_L \_$, for $L \subseteq \mathcal{A}$, is the parallel composition operator that forces two processes to synchronize on any action in L.
- $\_ \setminus L$, for $L \subseteq \mathcal{A}$, is the restriction operator, which prevents the execution of actions in L.
- $\_ / L$, for $L \subseteq \mathcal{A}$, is the hiding operator, which turns all the executed actions in L into the invisible action τ.

The operational semantic rules for the process language are shown in Table 1 and produce the LTS $(\mathbb{P}, \mathcal{A}_{\tau}, \longrightarrow)$ where $\longrightarrow \subseteq \mathbb{P} \times \mathcal{A}_{\tau} \times \mathbb{P}$, to which the bisimulation equivalences defined in the previous section are applicable.

2.3   Weak-Bisimilarity-Based Information-Flow Security Properties

The intuition behind noninterference in a two-level security system is that, whenever a group of agents at the high security level performs some actions, the effect of those actions should not be seen by any agent at the low security level. Below is a representative selection of weak-bisimilarity-based noninterference properties – *Nondeterministic Non-Interference* (NNI) and *Non-Deducibility on Composition* (NDC) – followed by their relationships [15], which we then comment.

Definition 5. *Let* $P \in \mathbb{P}$:

- $P \in \text{BSNNI} \Longleftrightarrow P \setminus \mathcal{A}_{\mathcal{H}} \approx P / \mathcal{A}_{\mathcal{H}}$.
- $P \in \text{BNDC} \Longleftrightarrow$ *for all* $Q \in \mathbb{P}$ *such that every* $Q' \in reach(Q)$ *can execute only actions in* $\mathcal{A}_{\mathcal{H}}$ *and for all* $L \subseteq \mathcal{A}_{\mathcal{H}}$, $P \setminus \mathcal{A}_{\mathcal{H}} \approx ((P \|_L Q) / L) \setminus \mathcal{A}_{\mathcal{H}}$.
- $P \in \text{SBSNNI} \Longleftrightarrow P \in \text{BSNNI}$ *and for all* $P' \in reach(P)$, $P' \in \text{BSNNI}$.

Table 1. Operational semantic rules

Prefix		$a \cdot P \xrightarrow{a} P$
Choice	$\dfrac{P_1 \xrightarrow{a} P_1'}{P_1 + P_2 \xrightarrow{a} P_1'}$	$\dfrac{P_2 \xrightarrow{a} P_2'}{P_1 + P_2 \xrightarrow{a} P_2'}$
Synchronization	$\dfrac{P_1 \xrightarrow{a} P_1' \quad P_2 \xrightarrow{a} P_2' \quad a \in L}{P_1 \parallel_L P_2 \xrightarrow{a} P_1' \parallel_L P_2'}$	
Interleaving	$\dfrac{P_1 \xrightarrow{a} P_1' \quad a \notin L}{P_1 \parallel_L P_2 \xrightarrow{a} P_1' \parallel_L P_2}$	$\dfrac{P_2 \xrightarrow{a} P_2' \quad a \notin L}{P_1 \parallel_L P_2 \xrightarrow{a} P_1 \parallel_L P_2'}$
Restriction	$\dfrac{P \xrightarrow{a} P' \quad a \notin L}{P \setminus L \xrightarrow{a} P' \setminus L}$	
Hiding	$\dfrac{P \xrightarrow{a} P' \quad a \in L}{P/L \xrightarrow{\tau} P'/L}$	$\dfrac{P \xrightarrow{a} P' \quad a \notin L}{P/L \xrightarrow{a} P'/L}$

– $P \in$ SBNDC $\iff$ *for all $P' \in reach(P)$ and for all P'' such that $P' \xrightarrow{a} P''$ for some $a \in \mathcal{A}_\mathcal{H}$, $P' \setminus \mathcal{A}_\mathcal{H} \approx P'' \setminus \mathcal{A}_\mathcal{H}$.* ∎

Theorem 1. SBNDC $\subset$ SBSNNI $\subset$ BNDC $\subset$ BSNNI. ∎

Historically, one of the first and most intuitive proposals is the *Bisimulation-based Strong Nondeterministic Non-Interference* (BSNNI). Basically, it is satisfied by any process P that behaves the same when its high-level actions are prevented (as modeled by $P \setminus \mathcal{A}_\mathcal{H}$) or when they are considered as hidden, unobservable actions (as modeled by $P / \mathcal{A}_\mathcal{H}$). The equivalence between these two low-level views of P states that a low-level observer cannot distinguish the high-level behavior of the system. For instance, in $l \cdot \underline{0} + h \cdot l \cdot \underline{0}$ a low-level agent that observes the execution of l cannot infer anything about the execution of h. Indeed, $(l \cdot \underline{0} + h \cdot l \cdot \underline{0}) \setminus \{h\} \approx (l \cdot \underline{0} + h \cdot l \cdot \underline{0}) / \{h\}$ because $l \cdot \underline{0} \approx l \cdot \underline{0} + \tau \cdot l \cdot \underline{0}$.

BSNNI is not powerful enough to capture covert channels that derive from the behavior of the high-level agent interacting with the system. For instance, $l \cdot \underline{0} + h_1 \cdot h_2 \cdot l \cdot \underline{0}$ is BSNNI for the same reason discussed above. However, a high-level agent could decide to enable h_1 and then disable h_2, thus turning the low-level view of the system into $l \cdot \underline{0} + \tau \cdot \underline{0}$, which is clearly distinguishable from $l \cdot \underline{0}$, as only in the former the low-level observer may not observe l. To overcome such a limitation, the most obvious solution consists of checking explicitly the interaction between the system and every possible high-level agent Q. The resulting property is the *Bisimulation-based Non-Deducibility on Composition* (BNDC), which is characterized by a universal quantification over Q.

To circumvent the verification problems related to such a quantifier, several properties have been proposed that are stronger than BNDC. They all express some persistency conditions, stating that the security checks shall be somehow extended also to the derivatives of a secure process. Three of the most representative ones are the variant of BSNNI that requires every reachable state to satisfy BSNNI itself, called *Strong* BSNNI (SBSNNI), the variant of BNDC that requires every reachable state to satisfy BNDC, called *Persistent* BNDC

(P_BNDC), and the *Strong* BNDC (SBNDC), which requires the low-level view of every reachable state to be the same before and after the execution of any high-level action. Notice that the SBNDC condition states that the execution of high-level actions must be completely transparent to the low-level agents. The properties P_BNDC and SBSNNI have been proven to be equivalent in [17], hence we will focus only on SBSNNI.

3   Use Case: DBMS Transactions – Part I

Consider a multi-threaded system supporting the execution of concurrent transactions operating on a healthcare database. Authorized users can write data on such a database, which is then accessed by a dedicated module to feed the training set for a machine learning model built for data analysis purposes.

On the one hand, different authentication mechanisms can be employed to identify users and ensure data authenticity for each transaction. We address a simple password-based mechanism (*pwd*), a more sophisticated two-factor authentication system (*2fa*), and finally a scheme based on single sign on (*sso*) [7]. On the other hand, to protect the privacy of health data in the trained model, only data transmitted through a highly secure mechanism, i.e., *2fa* or *sso*, can be used to feed the training set. In any case, users must not be aware of which data are actually chosen to train the machine learning model [5]. To this aim, the database management system (DBMS) is enabled to internally and transparently decide not to consider for the training set some transactions.

A simplified model describing how a write transaction is handled by the considered DBMS is represented by the following process term, whose LTS is depicted in Fig. 2:

$$WT := l_{pwd}.\underline{0} + \tau.(\tau.l_{sso}.\underline{0} + \tau.l_{2fa}.\underline{0}) + (h.l_{sso}.\underline{0} + h.l_{2fa}.\underline{0})$$

The low-level actions of the form $l_\star$ express that the transaction is conducted under the authentication method represented by $\star$, while the high-level action h expresses a private interaction with the machine learning module intended to avoid the transfer of the transaction data to the training set.

The DBMS is ready to manage the transaction through the password-based mechanism, as described by subterm $l_{pwd}.\underline{0}$. Alternatively, it internally decides that the transaction data will be passed to the training set and, therefore, one of the two highly secure mechanisms must be chosen nondeterministically, as described by subterm $\tau.(\tau.l_{sso}.\underline{0} + \tau.l_{2fa}.\underline{0})$. Otherwise, it can interact with the machine learning module, while nondeterministically choosing one of the two highly secure mechanisms, as described by subterm $h.l_{sso}.\underline{0} + h.l_{2fa}.\underline{0}$. This interaction is intended to confuse the user, who should not infer whether the transaction data will be used for the training set or not by simply observing which kind of authentication is required by the DBMS. This privacy condition is ensured if the interaction with the machine learning module does not interfere with the low-level view of the system perceived by the user, which can be verified as a noninterference property.

64   A. Esposito et al.

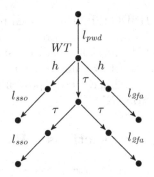

Fig. 2. LTS underlying WT

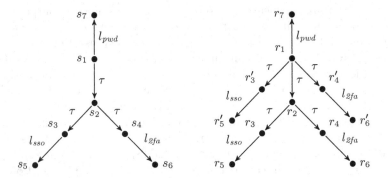

Fig. 3. LTSs of the low-level views of WT: $WT \setminus \mathcal{A}_{\mathcal{H}}$ (left) and $WT / \mathcal{A}_{\mathcal{H}}$ (right)

As far as $\approx$-based noninterference is concerned, WT does not leak any information from high level to low level. Indeed, the system is SBSNNI and hence also BNDC and BSNNI by virtue of Theorem 1. First, by observing Fig. 3, it is easy to see that $WT \setminus \mathcal{A}_{\mathcal{H}} \approx WT / \mathcal{A}_{\mathcal{H}}$. The weak bisimulation relating the two low-level views of WT is given by the following partition of the state space:

$$\{\{s_1, r_1\}, \{s_2, r_2\}, \{s_3, r_3, r_3'\}, \{s_4, r_4, r_4'\}, \{s_5, r_5, r_5', s_6, r_6, r_6', s_7, r_7\}\}$$

Then, by observing that the only high-level action is enabled at the initial state of WT, it follows that WT is SBSNNI.

4 Security Properties Based on Branching Bisimilarity

While the literature on noninterference mainly concentrates on weak bisimulation semantics, in this section we recast information-flow security definitions in terms of branching bisimilarity and investigate their characteristics as well as their relationships with the definitions based on weak bisimilarity.

The noninterference properties that reformulate the ones in Definition 5 by replacing the weak bisimilarity check with the branching bisimilarity check are termed, respectively, BrSNNI, BrNDC, SBrSNNI, and SBrNDC.

4.1 Preservation and Compositionality

All the $\approx_b$-based noninterference properties turn out to be preserved by $\approx_b$. This means that, whenever a process P_1 is secure under any of such properties, then every other branching bisimilar process P_2 is secure too. This is very useful for automated property verification, as it allows one to work with the process with the smallest state space among the equivalent ones.

Theorem 2. *Let $P_1, P_2 \in \mathbb{P}$ and $\mathcal{P} \in \{BrSNNI, BrNDC, SBrSNNI, SBrNDC\}$. If $P_1 \approx_b P_2$, then $P_1 \in \mathcal{P} \Longleftrightarrow P_2 \in \mathcal{P}$.* ∎

As far as modular verification is concerned, like in the weak bisimilarity case [15] only the local properties SBrSNNI and SBrNDC are compositional, i.e., are preserved by the operators of the calculus.

Theorem 3. *Let $P, P_1, P_2 \in \mathbb{P}$ and $\mathcal{P} \in \{SBrSNNI, SBrNDC\}$. Then:*

1. $P \in \mathcal{P} \Longrightarrow a \, . \, P \in \mathcal{P}$ *for all* $a \in \mathcal{A}_\tau \setminus \mathcal{A}_\mathcal{H}$.
2. $P_1, P_2 \in \mathcal{P} \Longrightarrow P_1 \|_L P_2 \in \mathcal{P}$ *for all* $L \subseteq \mathcal{A}$.
3. $P \in \mathcal{P} \Longrightarrow P \setminus L \in \mathcal{P}$ *for all* $L \subseteq \mathcal{A}_\mathcal{L}$ *if* $\mathcal{P} = SBrSNNI$, $L \subseteq \mathcal{A}$ *if* $\mathcal{P} = SBrNDC$.
4. $P \in \mathcal{P} \Longrightarrow P / L \in \mathcal{P}$ *for all* $L \subseteq \mathcal{A}_\mathcal{L}$. ∎

Note that, like for weak bisimilarity, no property based on branching bisimilarity is compositional with respect to alternative composition. As an example, let us consider processes $P_1 := l \, . \, \underline{0}$ and $P_2 := h \, . \, \underline{0}$. Both are BrSNNI, as $l \, . \, \underline{0} \setminus \{h\} \approx_b l \, . \, \underline{0} / \{h\}$ and $h \, . \, \underline{0} \setminus \{h\} \approx_b h \, . \, \underline{0} / \{h\}$, but $P_1 + P_2 \notin$ BrSNNI because $(l \, . \, \underline{0} + h \, . \, \underline{0}) \setminus \{h\} \approx_b l \, . \, \underline{0} \not\approx_b l \, . \, \underline{0} + \tau \, . \, \underline{0} \approx_b (l \, . \, \underline{0} + h \, . \, \underline{0}) / \{h\}$. It can be easily checked that $P_1 + P_2 \notin \mathcal{P}$ for $\mathcal{P} = \{BrNDC, SBrSNNI, SBrSNNI\}$.

We point out that compositionality with respect to action prefix and hiding, although limited to non-high actions and low actions respectively, is established by Theorem 3 but was not investigated in [15] under weak bisimilarity.

4.2 Taxonomy of Security Properties

First of all, the relationships among the $\approx_b$-based noninterference properties follow the same pattern as Theorem 1.

Theorem 4. *SBrNDC $\subset$ SBrSNNI $\subset$ BrNDC $\subset$ BrSNNI.* ∎

All the inclusions above are strict as we now show:

- The process $\tau \, . \, l \, . \, \underline{0} + l \, . \, l \, . \, \underline{0} + h \, . \, l \, . \, \underline{0}$ is SBrSNNI because $(\tau \, . \, l \, . \, \underline{0} + l \, . \, l \, . \, \underline{0} + h \, . \, l \, . \, \underline{0}) \setminus \{h\} \approx_b (\tau \, . \, l \, . \, \underline{0} + l \, . \, l \, . \, \underline{0} + h \, . \, l \, . \, \underline{0}) / \{h\}$ and action h is enabled only by the initial process so every derivative is BrSNNI. It is not SBrNDC because the low-level view of the process reached after action h, i.e., $(l \, . \, \underline{0}) \setminus \{h\}$, is not branching bisimilar to $(\tau \, . \, l \, . \, \underline{0} + l \, . \, l \, . \, \underline{0} + h \, . \, l \, . \, \underline{0}) \setminus \{h\}$.

- The process $l.\underline{0} + l.l.\underline{0} + l.h.l.\underline{0}$ is BrNDC because, whether there are synchronizations with high-level actions or not, the overall process can always perform either an l-action or a sequence of two l-actions without incurring any problematic branching. The process is not SBrSNNI because the reachable process $h.l.\underline{0}$ is not BrSNNI.
- The process $l.\underline{0} + h.h.l.\underline{0}$ is BrSNNI due to $(l.\underline{0} + h.h.l.\underline{0})\setminus\{h\} \approx_b (l.\underline{0} + h.h.l.\underline{0})/\{h\}$, but is not BrNDC due to $(((l.\underline{0} + h.h.l.\underline{0}) \parallel_{\{h\}} (h.\underline{0}))/\{h\})$ $\setminus\{h\} \not\approx_b (l.\underline{0} + h.h.l.\underline{0}) \setminus \{h\}$ as $(l.\underline{0} + h.h.l.\underline{0}) \setminus \{h\}$ behaves as $l.\underline{0}$.

Secondly, we observe that all the $\approx_b$-based noninterference properties listed in Theorem 4 imply the corresponding properties listed in Definition 5 due to the fact that $\approx_b$ is finer than $\approx$ [21].

Theorem 5. *The following properties hold:*

1. BrSNNI $\subset$ BSNNI.
2. BrNDC $\subset$ BNDC.
3. SBrSNNI $\subset$ SBSNNI.
4. SBrNDC $\subset$ SBNDC.   ∎

All the inclusions above are strict due to the following result.

Theorem 6. *Let $P_1, P_2 \in \mathbb{P}$ be such that $P_1 \approx P_2$ but $P_1 \not\approx_b P_2$. If P_1 and P_2 do not include high-level actions, then $Q \in \{P_1 + h.P_2, P_2 + h.P_1\}$ is such that:*

1. $Q \in$ BSNNI *but* $Q \notin$ BrSNNI.
2. $Q \in$ BNDC *but* $Q \notin$ BrNDC.
3. $Q \in$ SBSNNI *but* $Q \notin$ SBrSNNI.
4. $Q \in$ SBNDC *but* $Q \notin$ SBrNDC.   ∎

An alternative strategy to explore the differences between $\approx$ and $\approx_b$ with respect to B/BrSNNI and SB/BrSNNI is to consider the two τ-axioms $\tau.x+x = \tau.x$ and $a.(\tau.x+y)+a.x = a.(\tau.x+y)$ for $\approx$ [34]. The strategy is inspired by the initial remarks in [21], where it is noted that the two mentioned axioms are not valid for $\approx_b$ and are responsible for the lack of distinguishing power of $\approx$ over τ-branching processes. For each axiom, the strategy consists of constructing a pair of new processes from the ones equated in the axiom, such that they are weakly bisimilar by construction but not branching bisimilar. Then from this pair of processes we define a new process P such that $P \setminus \mathcal{A}_\mathcal{H}$ and $P / \mathcal{A}_\mathcal{H}$ are isomorphic to the constructed processes.

Theorem 7. *From $\tau.x + x = \tau.x$ it is possible to construct $P \in \mathbb{P}$ such that $P \in$ BSNNI but $P \notin$ BrSNNI and $P \in$ SBSNNI but $P \notin$ SBrSNNI.*   ∎

Theorem 8. *From $a.(\tau.x+y)+a.x = a.(\tau.x+y)$ it is possible to construct $P \in \mathbb{P}$ such that $P \in$ BSNNI but $P \notin$ BrSNNI and $P \in$ SBSNNI but $P \notin$ SBrSNNI.*   ∎

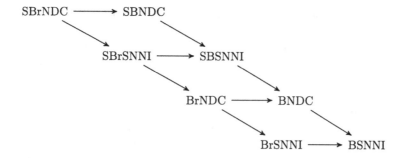

Fig. 4. Taxonomy of security properties based on weak and branching bisimilarities

Based on the results in Theorems 1, 4, and 5, the diagram in Fig. 4 summarizes the inclusions among the various noninterference properties, where $\mathcal{P} \to \mathcal{Q}$ means that $\mathcal{P}$ is strictly included in $\mathcal{Q}$. The missing arrows in the diagram, witnessing incomparability, are justified by the following counterexamples:

- SBNDC vs. SBrSNNI. The process $\tau.l.\underline{0} + l.l.\underline{0} + h.l.\underline{0}$ is BrSNNI as $\tau.l.\underline{0} + l.l.\underline{0} \approx_b \tau.l.\underline{0} + l.l.\underline{0} + \tau.l.\underline{0}$. It is also SBrSNNI because every reachable state does not enable any more high-level actions. However it is not SBNDC, because after the process has performed the high-level action h it can perform a single action l, while the original process with the restriction on high-level actions can go down a path where it performs two l-actions. On the other hand, the process Q mentioned in Theorem 6 is SBNDC but neither BrSNNI nor SBrSNNI.
- SBSNNI vs. BrNDC. The process $l.h.l.\underline{0} + l.\underline{0} + l.l.\underline{0}$ is BrSNNI as $l.\underline{0} + l.\underline{0} + l.l.\underline{0} \approx_b l.\tau.l.\underline{0} + l.\underline{0} + l.l.\underline{0}$. In particular, the subprocesses $l.\tau.l.\underline{0}$ and $l.l.\underline{0}$ are equated by virtue of the other axiom of weak bisimilarity, $a.\tau.x = a.x$, which holds also for branching bisimilarity. The same process is also BrNDC as it includes only one high-level action, hence the only possible high-level strategy coincides with the check conducted by BrSNNI. However, the process is not SBSNNI because of the reachable process $h.l.\underline{0}$, which is not BSNNI. On the other hand, the process Q mentioned in Theorem 6 is SBSNNI but not BrSNNI and, therefore, cannot be BrNDC.
- BNDC vs. BrSNNI. The process $l.\underline{0} + h_1.h_2.l.\underline{0}$ is not BNDC (see Sect. 2.3), but it is BrSNNI as $l.\underline{0} \approx_b l.\underline{0} + \tau.\tau.l.\underline{0}$. In contrast, the process Q mentioned in Theorem 6 is both BSNNI and BNDC, but not BrSNNI.

It is worth noting that the strongest property based on weak bisimilarity (SBNDC) and the weakest property based on branching bisimilarity (BrSNNI) are incomparable. The former is a very restrictive property because it requires a local check every time a high-level action is performed, while the latter requires a check only on the initial state. On the other hand, as shown in Theorem 6 it is very easy to construct processes that are secure under properties based on $\approx$ but not on $\approx_b$, due to the minimal number of high-level actions in Q.

5   Noninterference in Reversible Processes

As anticipated, we use reversible computing to motivate the study of branching-bisimilarity-based noninterference properties. To this aim, we now recall from [11] back-and-forth bisimilarity and its relationship with standard bisimilarity.

An LTS represents a reversible process if each of its transitions is seen as bidirectional. This means that any transition can be undone and that any undone transition can be redone. When going backward, it is of paramount importance to respect causality. While this is straightforward for sequential processes, it is not obvious for concurrent ones, because the last performed action is the first one to be undone but this action may not necessarily be identifiable uniquely in the presence of concurrency.

Consider for example a process that can perform action a in parallel with action b. This process can be represented as a diamond-like LTS where from the initial state an a-transition and a b-transition depart, which are respectively followed by a b-transition and an a-transition, both of which reach the final state. Suppose that action a completes before action b, so that the a-transition is executed before the b-transition. Once in the final state, either the b-transition is undone before the a-transition, or the a-transition is undone before the b-transition. Both options are causally consistent, as a and b are independent of each other, but only the former is history preserving too.

The history-preserving option is the one that was addressed in [11] in order to study reversible processes in an interleaving setting. To accomplish this, strong and weak bisimulations were redefined as binary relations between histories, formalized below as runs, instead of states. The resulting behavioral equivalences are respectively called strong and weak back-and-forth bisimilarities in [11].

Definition 6. *A sequence* $\xi = s_0 \xrightarrow{a_1} s_1 \xrightarrow{a_2} s_2 \ldots s_{n-1} \xrightarrow{a_n} s_n$ *is called a* path *from state* s_0 *of length* $n \in \mathbb{N}$. *We let first*$(\xi) = s_0$ *and last*$(\xi) = s_n$; *the empty path is indicated with* ε. *We denote by Path*(s) *the set of paths from state* s. ∎

Definition 7. *A pair* $\rho = (s, \xi)$ *is called a* run *from state* s *iff* $\xi \in Path(s)$, *in which case we let path*$(\rho) = \xi$, *first*$(\rho) = first(\xi)$, *last*$(\rho) = last(\xi)$, *with first*$(\rho) = last(\rho) = s$ *when* $\xi = \varepsilon$. *We denote by Run*(s) *the set of runs from state* s. ∎

Definition 8. *Let* $\rho = (s, \xi) \in Run(s)$ *and* $\rho' = (s', \xi') \in Run(s')$:

- *Their composition* $\rho\rho' = (s, \xi\xi') \in Run(s)$ *is defined iff last*$(\rho) = first(\rho')$.
- *We write* $\rho \xrightarrow{a} \rho'$ *iff there exists* $\rho'' = (s, s \xrightarrow{a} s')$ *with* $s = last(\rho)$ *such that* $\rho' = \rho\rho''$. ∎

In the behavioral equivalences of [11], for the LTS $(S, A, \longrightarrow)$ the set R of its runs is considered in lieu of the set S of its states.

Definition 9. *Let* $(S, A, \longrightarrow)$ *be an LTS and* $s_1, s_2 \in S$. *We say that* s_1 *and* s_2 *are* strongly back-and-forth bisimilar, *written* $s_1 \sim_{bf} s_2$, *iff* $((s_1, \varepsilon), (s_2, \varepsilon)) \in \mathcal{B}$

for some strong back-and-forth bisimulation $\mathcal{B}$. *A symmetric binary relation* $\mathcal{B}$ *over* R *is a* strong back-and-forth bisimulation *iff, whenever* $(\rho_1, \rho_2) \in \mathcal{B}$, *then for all actions* $a \in A$:

- *whenever* $\rho_1 \xrightarrow{a} \rho_1'$, *then* $\rho_2 \xrightarrow{a} \rho_2'$ *with* $(\rho_1', \rho_2') \in \mathcal{B}$;
- *whenever* $\rho_1' \xrightarrow{a} \rho_1$, *then* $\rho_2' \xrightarrow{a} \rho_2$ *with* $(\rho_1', \rho_2') \in \mathcal{B}$. ∎

Definition 10. *Let* $(S, A, \longrightarrow)$ *be an LTS and* $s_1, s_2 \in S$. *We say that* s_1 *and* s_2 *are* weakly back-and-forth bisimilar, *written* $s_1 \approx_{bf} s_2$, *iff* $((s_1, \varepsilon), (s_2, \varepsilon)) \in \mathcal{B}$ *for some weak back-and-forth bisimulation* $\mathcal{B}$. *A symmetric binary relation* $\mathcal{B}$ *over* R *is a* weak back-and-forth bisimulation *iff, whenever* $(\rho_1, \rho_2) \in \mathcal{B}$, *then:*

- *whenever* $\rho_1 \xrightarrow{\tau} \rho_1'$, *then* $\rho_2 \xRightarrow{\tau^*} \rho_2'$ *with* $(\rho_1', \rho_2') \in \mathcal{B}$;
- *whenever* $\rho_1' \xrightarrow{\tau} \rho_1$, *then* $\rho_2' \xRightarrow{\tau^*} \rho_2$ *with* $(\rho_1', \rho_2') \in \mathcal{B}$;
- *whenever* $\rho_1 \xrightarrow{a} \rho_1'$ *for* $a \in A \setminus \{\tau\}$, *then* $\rho_2 \xRightarrow{\tau^*} \xrightarrow{a} \xRightarrow{\tau^*} \rho_2'$ *with* $(\rho_1', \rho_2') \in \mathcal{B}$;
- *whenever* $\rho_1' \xrightarrow{a} \rho_1$ *for* $a \in A \setminus \{\tau\}$, *then* $\rho_2' \xRightarrow{\tau^*} \xrightarrow{a} \xRightarrow{\tau^*} \rho_2$ *with* $(\rho_1', \rho_2') \in \mathcal{B}$. ∎

In [11] it was shown that strong back-and-forth bisimilarity coincides with strong bisimilarity. Surprisingly, weak back-and-forth bisimilarity does not coincide with weak bisimilarity. Instead, it coincides with branching bisimilarity.

Theorem 9. *Let* $(S, A, \longrightarrow)$ *be an LTS and* $s_1, s_2 \in S$. *Then:*

- $s_1 \sim_{bf} s_2$ *iff* $s_1 \sim s_2$.
- $s_1 \approx_{bf} s_2$ *iff* $s_1 \approx_b s_2$. ∎

As a consequence, the properties BrSNNI, BrNDC, SBrSNNI, and SBrNDC do not change if $\approx_b$ is replaced by $\approx_{bf}$. This allows us to study noninterference properties for reversible systems by using $\approx_b$ in a standard process calculus like the one of Sect. 2.2, without having to decorate executed actions like in [37] or store them into stack-based memories like in [9].

6 Use Case: DBMS Transactions – Part II

The example provided in Sect. 3 is useful to illustrate the limitations of weak bisimilarity when investigating potential covert channels in reversible systems.

It turns out that $WT \setminus \mathcal{A}_\mathcal{H} \not\approx_b WT / \mathcal{A}_\mathcal{H}$, i.e., WT is not BrSNNI, and hence not even BrNDC, SBrSNNI, and SBrNDC by virtue of Theorem 4. As can be seen in Fig. 3, the reason is that, if $WT / \mathcal{A}_\mathcal{H}$ performs the leftmost τ-action and hence moves to state r_3', from which the only executable action is l_{sso}, then according to the definition of branching bisimilarity $WT \setminus \mathcal{A}_\mathcal{H}$ can either:

1. stay idle, but from that state $WT \setminus \mathcal{A}_\mathcal{H}$ can then perform actions other than l_{sso} that cannot be matched on the side of $WT / \mathcal{A}_\mathcal{H}$;
2. perform two τ-actions thereby reaching state s_3, but the traversed state s_2 is not branching bisimilar to the initial state of $WT / \mathcal{A}_\mathcal{H}$.

In a standard model of execution, where the computation can proceed only forward, the distinguishing power of branching bisimilarity may be considered too severe, as no practical covert channel actually occurs and the system can be considered noninterfering as shown in Sect. 3. Indeed, a low-level user has no possibility of distinguishing the internal move performed by $WT/\mathcal{A}_\mathcal{H}$ and leading to $l_{sso} \cdot \underline{0}$ from the sequence of internal moves performed by $WT \setminus \mathcal{A}_\mathcal{H}$ and leading to $l_{sso} \cdot \underline{0}$ as well. This motivates the fact that, historically, weak bisimilarity has been preferred in the setting of noninterference.

Now we know that, if we replace the branching bisimulation semantics with the weak back-and-forth bisimulation semantics, nothing changes about the outcome of noninterference verification. Assuming that the DBMS allows transactions to be reversed, it is instructive to discuss why BrSNNI is not satisfied by following the formalization of the weak back-and-forth bisimulation semantics provided in Sect. 5.

After $WT/\mathcal{A}_\mathcal{H}$ performs the run $(r_1, (r_1 \xrightarrow{\tau} r_3' \xrightarrow{l_{sso}} r_5'))$, process $WT \setminus \mathcal{A}_\mathcal{H}$ can respond by performing the run $(s_1, (s_1 \xrightarrow{\tau} s_2 \xrightarrow{\tau} s_3 \xrightarrow{l_{sso}} s_5))$. If either process goes back by undoing l_{sso}, then the other one can undo l_{sso} as well and the states r_3' and s_3 are reached. However, if $WT \setminus \mathcal{A}_\mathcal{H}$ goes further back by undoing $s_2 \xrightarrow{\tau} s_3$, then $WT/\mathcal{A}_\mathcal{H}$ can either:

- undo $r_1 \xrightarrow{\tau} r_3'$, but in this case r_1 enables action l_{pwd} while s_2 does not;
- stay idle, but in this case r_3' enables only l_{sso}, while s_2 can go down the path $s_2 \xrightarrow{\tau} s_4 \xrightarrow{l_{2fa}} s_6$ as well.

This line of reasoning immediately allows us to reveal a potential covert channel under reversible computing. In fact, let us assume that the transaction modeled by WT is not only executed forward, but also enables backward computations triggered, e.g., whenever debugging mode is activated. This may happen in response to some user-level malfunctioning, which may be due, for instance, to the authentication operation or to the transaction execution. As formally shown above, if the action l_{sso} performed just after the high-level interaction is undone, then the system enables again the execution of the action l_{pwd}. This is motivated in our example by the fact that, in any case, the transaction data will not be transferred to the training set, so that any kind of authentication is admissible. On the other hand, this is not possible by undoing the action l_{sso} departing from state r_3 in $WT/\mathcal{A}_\mathcal{H}$, because in such a case the transaction data must be protected through a highly secure mechanism. In other words, by reversing the computation the low-level user can become aware of the fact that the transaction data are feeding the training set or not.

In the literature, there are several reverse debuggers working in this way like, e.g., UndoDB [13], a Linux-based interactive time-travel debugger that can handle multiple threads and their backward execution. For instance, it is integrated within the DBMS SAP HANA [1] in order to reduce time-to-resolution of software failures. In our example, by virtue of the observations conducted above, if the system is executed backward just after performing l_{sso}, a low-level user can decide whether a high-level action had occurred before or not, thus revealing a covert channel. Such a covert channel is completely concealed during the forward execution of the system and is detected only when the system is executed backward. More in general, this may happen when the reverse debugger is activated by virtue of some unexpected event (e.g., segmentation faults, stack overflow errors, memory corruption) caused intentionally or not, and by virtue of which some undesired information flow emerges towards the low-level users.

7   Conclusions

Our study of branching-bisimilarity-based noninterference properties has established a connection with reversible computing in the sense that those properties, which we have investigated in a standard process calculus, are directly applicable to reversible systems. To the best of our knowledge, this is the first attempt of defining noninterference properties relying on branching bisimilarity and of reasoning about covert channels in reversible systems.

Firstly, we have rephrased in the setting of branching bisimilarity the classical taxonomy of nondeterministic noninterference properties based on weak bisimilarity. This generates an extended taxonomy that is conservative with respect to the classical one and emphasizes the strictness of certain inclusions as well as the incomparability of certain properties. In addition, we have studied preservation and compositionality features of the new noninterference properties.

Secondly, we have shown that potential covert channels arising in reversible systems cannot be revealed by employing weak bisimulation semantics. Indeed, the higher discriminating power of branching bisimilarity is necessary to capture information flows emerging whenever backward computations are admitted. The correspondence discovered in [11] between branching bisimilarity and weak backand-forth bisimilarity confirms the adequacy of our approach.

As for future work, we are planning to further extend the noninterference taxonomy to include more expressive properties taking into account quantitative aspects of processes [4,25]. Moreover, unlike the corresponding results for weak-bisimilarity-based noninterference properties, whose proofs rely on the use of an up-to technique for weak bisimilarity [40], in Theorems 3 and 4 we have proceeded by induction on the depth of the tree-like LTS underlying the considered process term, because the up-to techniques for branching bisimilarity [20,14] seem to be too restrictive with respect to the conditions required by the noninterference checks. Thus, we would like to study whether there exist suitable relaxations of the latter techniques so as to be able to reformulate the proofs of Theorems 3 and 4 accordingly, which would open the way to including recursion in the language.

Acknowledgment. This research has been supported by the PRIN project *NiRvAna – Noninterference and Reversibility Analysis in Private Blockchains*.

References

1. UndoDB case studies. https://undo.io/resources/type/case-studies/. Accessed Mar 2023
2. Aldini, A.: Classification of security properties in a Linda-like process algebra. Sci. Comput. Program. **63**(1), 16–38 (2006)
3. Aldini, A., Bernardo, M.: Component-oriented verification of noninterference. J. Syst. Architect. **57**(3), 282–293 (2011)
4. Aldini, A., Bernardo, M., Corradini, F.: A Process Algebraic Approach to Software Architecture Design. Springer, London (2010). https://doi.org/10.1007/978-1-84800-223-4
5. Bai, Y., Fan, M., Li, Y., Xie, C.: Privacy risk assessment of training data in machine learning. In: Proceedings of the 34th IEEE International Conference on Communications (ICC 2022), p. 1015. IEEE-CS Press (2022)
6. Bennett, C.H.: Logical reversibility of computation. IBM J. Res. Dev. **17**(6), 525–532 (1973)
7. Boonkrong, S.: Authentication and Access Control. Apress, Berkeley (2020)
8. Brookes, S.D., Hoare, C.A.R., Roscoe, A.W.: A theory of communicating sequential processes. J. ACM **31**, 560–599 (1984)
9. Danos, V., Krivine, J.: Reversible communicating systems. In: Gardner, P., Yoshida, N. (eds.) CONCUR 2004. LNCS, vol. 3170, pp. 292–307. Springer, Heidelberg (2004). https://doi.org/10.1007/978-3-540-28644-8_19
10. Danos, V., Krivine, J.: Transactions in RCCS. In: Abadi, M., de Alfaro, L. (eds.) CONCUR 2005. LNCS, vol. 3653, pp. 398–412. Springer, Heidelberg (2005). https://doi.org/10.1007/11539452_31
11. De Nicola, R., Montanari, U., Vaandrager, F.: Back and forth bisimulations. In: Baeten, J.C.M., Klop, J.W. (eds.) CONCUR 1990. LNCS, vol. 458, pp. 152–165. Springer, Heidelberg (1990). https://doi.org/10.1007/BFb0039058
12. de Vries, E., Koutavas, V., Hennessy, M.: Communicating transactions. In: Gastin, P., Laroussinie, F. (eds.) CONCUR 2010. LNCS, vol. 6269, pp. 569–583. Springer, Heidelberg (2010). https://doi.org/10.1007/978-3-642-15375-4_39
13. Engblom, J.: A review of reverse debugging. In: Proceedings of the 4th System, Software, SoC and Silicon Debug Conference (S4D 2012), pp. 1–6. IEEE-CS Press (2012)
14. Erkens, R., Rot, J., Luttik, B.: Up-to techniques for branching bisimilarity. In: Chatzigeorgiou, A., et al. (eds.) SOFSEM 2020. LNCS, vol. 12011, pp. 285–297. Springer, Cham (2020). https://doi.org/10.1007/978-3-030-38919-2_24
15. Focardi, R., Gorrieri, R.: Classification of security properties. In: Focardi, R., Gorrieri, R. (eds.) FOSAD 2000. LNCS, vol. 2171, pp. 331–396. Springer, Heidelberg (2001). https://doi.org/10.1007/3-540-45608-2_6
16. Focardi, R., Piazza, C., Rossi, S.: Proofs methods for bisimulation based information flow security. In: Cortesi, A. (ed.) VMCAI 2002. LNCS, vol. 2294, pp. 16–31. Springer, Heidelberg (2002). https://doi.org/10.1007/3-540-47813-2_2
17. Focardi, R., Rossi, S.: Information flow security in dynamic contexts. J. Comput. Secur. **14**(1), 65–110 (2006)
18. Giachino, E., Lanese, I., Mezzina, C.A.: Causal-consistent reversible debugging. In: Gnesi, S., Rensink, A. (eds.) FASE 2014. LNCS, vol. 8411, pp. 370–384. Springer, Heidelberg (2014). https://doi.org/10.1007/978-3-642-54804-8_26
19. Giacobazzi, R., Mastroeni, I.: Abstract non-interference: a unifying framework for weakening information-flow. ACM Trans. Privacy Secur. **21**(2) (2018)

20. Glabbeek, R.J.: A complete axiomatization for branching bisimulation congruence of finite-state behaviours. In: Borzyszkowski, A.M., Sokołowski, S. (eds.) MFCS 1993. LNCS, vol. 711, pp. 473–484. Springer, Heidelberg (1993). https://doi.org/10.1007/3-540-57182-5_39
21. van Glabbeek, R.J., Weijland, W.P.: Branching time and abstraction in bisimulation semantics. J. ACM **43**, 555–600 (1996)
22. Goguen, J.A., Meseguer, J.: Security policies and security models. In: Proceedings of the 2nd IEEE Symposium on Security and Privacy (SSP 1982), pp. 11–20. IEEE-CS Press (1982)
23. Groote, J.F., Vaandrager, F.: An efficient algorithm for branching bisimulation and stuttering equivalence. In: Paterson, M.S. (ed.) ICALP 1990. LNCS, vol. 443, pp. 626–638. Springer, Heidelberg (1990). https://doi.org/10.1007/BFb0032063
24. Hedin, D., Sabelfeld, A.: A perspective on information-flow control. In: Software Safety and Security - Tools for Analysis and Verification, vol. 33, pp. 319–347 (2012)
25. Hillston, J., et al.: Persistent stochastic non-interference. Fund. Inform. **181**(1), 1–35 (2021)
26. Jansen, D.N., Groote, J.F., Keiren, J.J.A., Wijs, A.: An $O(m \log n)$ algorithm for branching bisimilarity on labelled transition systems. In: TACAS 2020. LNCS, vol. 12079, pp. 3–20. Springer, Cham (2020). https://doi.org/10.1007/978-3-030-45237-7_1
27. Keller, R.M.: Formal verification of parallel programs. Commun. ACM **19**, 371–384 (1976)
28. Landauer, R.: Irreversibility and heat generated in the computing process. IBM J. Res. Dev. **5**, 183–191 (1961)
29. Lanese, I., Lienhardt, M., Mezzina, C.A., Schmitt, A., Stefani, J.-B.: Concurrent flexible reversibility. In: Felleisen, M., Gardner, P. (eds.) ESOP 2013. LNCS, vol. 7792, pp. 370–390. Springer, Heidelberg (2013). https://doi.org/10.1007/978-3-642-37036-6_21
30. Lanese, I., Nishida, N., Palacios, A., Vidal, G.: CauDEr: a causal-consistent reversible debugger for erlang. In: Gallagher, J.P., Sulzmann, M. (eds.) FLOPS 2018. LNCS, vol. 10818, pp. 247–263. Springer, Cham (2018). https://doi.org/10.1007/978-3-319-90686-7_16
31. Laursen, J.S., Ellekilde, L.P., Schultz, U.P.: Modelling reversible execution of robotic assembly. Robotica **36**, 625–654 (2018)
32. Mantel, H.: Information flow and noninterference. In: van Tilborg, H.C.A., Jajodia, S. (eds.) Encyclopedia of Cryptography and Security, pp. 605–607. Springer, Boston (2011). https://doi.org/10.1007/978-1-4419-5906-5_874
33. Martinelli, F.: Analysis of security protocols as open systems. Theoret. Comput. Sci. **290**(1), 1057–1106 (2003)
34. Milner, R.: Communication and Concurrency. Prentice Hall, Hoboken (1989)
35. Park, D.: Concurrency and automata on infinite sequences. In: Deussen, P. (ed.) GI-TCS 1981. LNCS, vol. 104, pp. 167–183. Springer, Heidelberg (1981). https://doi.org/10.1007/BFb0017309
36. Perumalla, K.S., Park, A.J.: Reverse computation for rollback-based fault tolerance in large parallel systems - evaluating the potential gains and systems effects. Clust. Comput. **17**, 303–313 (2014)
37. Phillips, I., Ulidowski, I.: Reversing algebraic process calculi. J. Log. Algebraic Program. **73**, 70–96 (2007)

38. Phillips, I., Ulidowski, I., Yuen, S.: A reversible process calculus and the modelling of the ERK signalling pathway. In: Glück, R., Yokoyama, T. (eds.) RC 2012. LNCS, vol. 7581, pp. 218–232. Springer, Heidelberg (2013). https://doi.org/10.1007/978-3-642-36315-3_18

39. Michele Pinna, G.: Reversing steps in membrane systems computations. In: Gheorghe, M., Rozenberg, G., Salomaa, A., Zandron, C. (eds.) CMC 2017. LNCS, vol. 10725, pp. 245–261. Springer, Cham (2018). https://doi.org/10.1007/978-3-319-73359-3_16

40. Sangiorgi, D., Milner, R.: The problem of "weak bisimulation up to". In: Cleaveland, W.R. (ed.) CONCUR 1992. LNCS, vol. 630, pp. 32–46. Springer, Heidelberg (1992). https://doi.org/10.1007/BFb0084781

41. Schordan, M., Oppelstrup, T., Jefferson, D.R., Barnes, P.D., Jr.: Generation of reversible C++ code for optimistic parallel discrete event simulation. N. Gener. Comput. **36**, 257–280 (2018)

42. Siljak, H., Psara, K., Philippou, A.: Distributed antenna selection for massive MIMO using reversing Petri nets. IEEE Wirel. Commun. Lett. **8**, 1427–1430 (2019)

43. Vassor, M., Stefani, J.-B.: Checkpoint/rollback vs causally-consistent reversibility. In: Kari, J., Ulidowski, I. (eds.) RC 2018. LNCS, vol. 11106, pp. 286–303. Springer, Cham (2018). https://doi.org/10.1007/978-3-319-99498-7_20

44. Zheng, L., Myers, A.C.: Dynamic security labels and noninterference (extended abstract). In: Dimitrakos, T., Martinelli, F. (eds.) Formal Aspects in Security and Trust. IIFIP, vol. 173, pp. 27–40. Springer, Boston, MA (2005). https://doi.org/10.1007/0-387-24098-5_3

Impact Analysis of Coordinated Cyber-Physical Attacks via Statistical Model Checking: A Case Study

Ruggero Lanotte[1], Massimo Merro[2(✉)], and Nicola Zannone[3]

[1] Università dell'Insubria, Como, Italy
ruggero.lanotte@uninsubria.it
[2] Università degli Studi di Verona, Verona, Italy
massimo.merro@univr.it.it
[3] Eindhoven University of Technology, Eindhoven, The Netherlands

Abstract. *Cyber-Physical Systems* are exposed to *cyber-physical attacks*, *i.e.*, security breaches in cyberspace that alter the underlying physical processes.

We use UPPAAL SMC to analyze a non-trivial coordinated multi-engine system equipped with both a tamperproof distributed intrusion detection system (IDS) and a tamperproof supervisor component to mitigate eventual loss of performance. We rely on *statistical model checking* to evaluate the impact of three *coordinated cyber-physical attacks* injecting malicious code in all controllers of the multi-engine system to compromise the performance of the whole system. Here, the coordination of the attackers is a necessary requirement to achieve the desired malicious goals. Our security analysis provides an estimate of both the *physical impact* of the attacks on the physical process of the system and the *effectiveness* of the IDS. We believe that by assessing the impact of attacks, system engineers may understand whether they have to develop more accurate impact metrics or focus on different invariants to enhance their IDSs in order to detect such attacks.

Keywords: Cyber-physical attack · Security analysis · Statistical model checking

1   Introduction

Cyber-Physical Systems (CPSs) integrate networking and distributed computing systems with physical processes. Applications include automation, smart cities, medical systems, agriculture, and in particular safety-critical applications such as electric power generation and distribution, nuclear power production, and water supply.

As industrial organizations are increasingly connecting their operational technology (OT) network with the corporate networks to improve business and operational efficiency, CPSs are more and more exposed to *cyber-physical attacks* [16], *i.e.*, security threats in cyberspace that adversely affect the physical processes.

© IFIP International Federation for Information Processing 2023
M. Huisman and A. Ravara (Eds.): FORTE 2023, LNCS 13910, pp. 75–94, 2023.
https://doi.org/10.1007/978-3-031-35355-0_6

According to Gollmann et al. [10], the possible *goals* of cyber-physical attacks can be classified into three main groups: (i) *equipment damage*, such as over-stress of equipment, to reduce their expected life cycle, or violation of safety limits; (ii) *production damage*, in order to compromise product quality, product rate or operating costs; (iii) *compliance violations*, such as increasing of environmental pollution. To achieve these goals, cyber-physical attacks can tamper with both the physical and the cyber layer to bring the system into a state desired by the attacker. In particular, they may manipulate *sensor measurements* and/or *actuator commands*.

Recent years have seen the emergence of *coordinated cyber-physical attacks*, i.e., attacks that need to coordinate and possibly collaborate with each other via some (possibly) covert channel to achieve the desired malicious goals, involving different components of the target CPS. These attacks can cause more severe consequences than single cyber-physical attacks, such as disruption of the plant and cascading failures, and can mask manipulations of physical processes. Although a large body of research has investigated defense mechanisms to protect CPSs against (coordinated) cyber-physical attacks [13,35], there is still little understanding of the potential impact of such kind of attacks on the physical processes. In general, we believe that by assessing the impact of attacks on the physical process, system engineers may better understand whether they have to develop more accurate impact metrics [22,24,30,32] or focus on different invariants to enhance their IDSs in order to detect such attacks, possibly at an early stage.

To perform a systematic impact assessment of cyber-physical attacks on CPSs, we need tool-supported methods for the safety verification of CPSs. One of the central problems in the *safety verification* of CPSs is the *reachability problem*: can an unsafe state be reached by an execution of the system (possibly under attack) starting from a given initial state? In general, the reachability problem for *hybrid systems* (and CPSs) is stubbornly undecidable; although decidability has been proven for specific classes of systems (see, *e.g.*, [1,14,20]). However, even when decidable, the exhaustive verification of hybrid systems based on *model checking* techniques often relies on non-polynomial algorithms, leading to the well-known state explosion problem.

Statistical Model Checking (SMC) [25] is a technique combining *model checking* [7] with the classical *Monte Carlo simulation* [12], aiming at providing support for quantitative analysis, as well as addressing the size barrier, to allow the analysis of large models such as CPSs [8]. Unlike model checking, statistical model checking does not guarantee a 100% correct analysis but allows us to bind the error of the analysis. In this work, we apply UPPAAL SMC [9], the statistical extension of the UPPAAL model checker [3], to support the composition of timed and/or probabilistic automata.

In UPPAAL SMC, two statistical parameters α and ϵ, lying in the real interval $[0, 1]$, must be specified by the user to fix the maximum probability of *false negatives* and probabilistic *uncertainty*, respectively. The number of runs that the simulator must perform to guarantee the level of required precision depends on both α and ϵ, and it is computed using ad-hoc statistical techniques [25]. UPPAAL SMC returns a confidence interval $[p-\epsilon, p+\epsilon]$, in which p is the probability to satisfy the checked property.

Contribution: This work aims to investigate formal methodologies to statically analyze the impact of *coordinated cyber-physical attacks* on both the underlying physical process and invariant-based intrusion detection systems. In particular, we use UPPAAL SMC to analyze the *robustness* of a proposed non-trivial *coordinated multi-engine* system equipped with both a tamperproof distributed intrusion detection system (IDS) and a tamperproof supervisor component to mitigate the eventual loss of performance via load balancing. Each engine of the system is equipped with a cooling system to maintain the working temperature of the engine within a specific range. Each engine is also equipped with a local IDS that checks whether the activity of the cooling system is consistent with the engine temperature. Eventual violations of these safety invariants are notified to a central IDS, which tries to detect coordinated cyber-physical attacks targeting more engines at the same time.

We rely on *statistical model checking* as a methodology for achieving a security analysis of our coordinated multi-engine system. We have evaluated the *physical impact* [24,31] of three carefully chosen *coordinated cyber-physical attacks* injecting malicious code in all controllers of our multi-engine system to achieve *production damage* and/or *equipment damage*. We actually verified two families of *system invariants* of the system under attack: one focused on the runtime evolution of the physical-components of the CPS, and a second one focused on the effectiveness of the IDS in detecting the proposed attacks.

The verification of our multi-engine system under attack, i.e., the effectiveness of the distributed IDS and the physical impact of the attacks, was performed within a reasonable time, showing the potential for our analysis to handle the analysis of larger systems.

Outline: The remainder of the paper is structured as follows. Next section introduces our coordinated multi-engine system. Section 3 presents its implementation and verification in UPPAAL SMC, and Sect. 4 presents its security analysis. Finally, Sect. 5 discusses related work and concludes the paper by providing directions for future work.

2 A Coordinated and Refrigerated Multi-engine System

As a case study, we propose a *coordinated multi-engine system* consisting of n refrigerated engines, Eng^i, interacting with both a supervisory component and a distributed IDS. The supervisory component aims to optimize the performance of the whole engine system, whereas the distributed IDS is devoted to detecting *coordinated attacks*, i.e., attacks that tamper with more than one component of the multi-engine system at the same time.

Each engine comprises a cooling system and is characterized by three system variables: (i) a physical variable *temp* recording the temperature of the engine, with initial value 95; (ii) a control variable *cool* indicating whether the cooling system is on or off, with initial value off; (iii) a control variable *speed* indicating the engine speed, with values ranging in the set {slow, half, full}; in normal conditions all engines run at half speed.

The runtime evolution of the temperature of each engine depends on the current state of the two control variables. When the cooling system is active ($cool = $ on), the temperature decreases according to the differential equation $temp' = -r$, where r is uniformly chosen in one of the following real intervals: (a) $[0.8, 1]$, if $speed = $ slow; (b) $[0.4, 0.5]$, if $speed = $ half; (c) $[0.2, 0.4]$, if $speed = $ full. When the cooling system is inactive ($cool = $ off), the temperature increases according to the differential equation $temp' = r$, where r is uniformly chosen in one of the following real intervals: (a) $[0.1, 0.2]$, if $speed = $ slow; (b) $[0.3, 0.5]$, if $speed = $ half; (c) $[0.8, 1]$, if $speed = $ full.

Each engine also comprises two *logical components*: a controller, *Ctrl*, and a *local intrusion detection system*, *L-IDS*. The controller maintains the temperature within a specific range by means of a cooling system. At each scan cycle, *Ctrl* checks the temperature of its engine. When the sensed temperature is above 100 degrees, the controller activates the cooling system; the cooling activity is maintained for 20 consecutive time instants. If the temperature is not above 100 degrees, the controller turns off the cooling system. In both cases, before restarting its scan cycle, the controller waits for instructions from the supervisor to change the speed of the engine.

The local IDS, *L-IDS*, is in charge of checking specific *system invariants* representing system anomalies. Specifically, the *L-IDS* checks whether: (i) the cooling system is active when the temperature is above 101 degrees and (ii) the cooling system is off when the temperature is below 80 degrees. If these invariants are violated, it triggers a warning signaling overheating or under-heating at its engine. Note that, for the sake of simplicity, the intrusion detection system employed is quite basic; it is straightforward to extend it to support more informative tests on process variables and/or on control variables.

The multi-engine system comprises two centralized logical components: a *central IDS* (*C-IDS*) and a *Supervisor*. The *C-IDS* rises an alarm when at least two different *L-IDSs* signal the violation of their invariants. The Supervisor tries to *mitigate* the effects of system anomalies as follows: when an engine is overheating (resp. under-heating), it asks the associated controller to slow down the engine speed (resp. to run at FULL speed); then, the Supervisor requires an adjacent engine to run at FULL (resp. SLOW) speed to compensate the performance of the whole multi-engine system. When the overheating/under-heating anomaly is resolved, it asks the involved controllers to reset its engine at half power. Note that system engineers may require engines not involved in the compensation process (i.e., they are running at half speed) to run at FULL/LOW speed. However, requests for work compensation or speed changes may be accepted or not, depending on whether the engine receiving the request is in condition to run at the required speed; in particular, mitigation activities have priority over system engineers' requests. The pseudocode of all logical components is provided in Fig. 1 and Fig. 2.

A simulation of the temperature evolution of a multi-engine system composed by three engines is given in Fig. 3. Note that the different behavior of one engine in the first part of the graph is due to a LOW request of the system engineer. In

Ctrl: if (*cooling* == false)
    {read *temp*(x);
      if ($x > 100$)
        {*cooling* := true;
         cnt := 0;
         write *cool*⟨on⟩}
        else {write *cool*⟨off⟩}
    }
  else
    {*cnt* := *cnt* + 1;
     write *cool*⟨on⟩;
     if (*cnt* == 5) {*cooling* := false}
    };
  receive *instruction*(z);
  write *speed*⟨z⟩;
  goto *Ctrl*

L-IDS: read *temp*(t);
    read *cool*(*cooling*);
    if ($t > 101$ and *cooling* = off)
      {send *status_hot*} //overheating warning
    elseif($t < 90$ and *cooling* = on)
      {send *status_cold*} //under-heating warning
    else
      {send *status_ok*}; //temperature okay
    goto *L-IDS*

Fig. 1. Local logical components

Sup: for each local IDS
    {receive *status* of the associated controller};
  read system engineers' requests for controllers;
  for each controller *c*
    {compute its speed, $speed_c$, according to
     its status and engineers' requests };
  for each controller *c*
    {send *instruction*⟨$speed_c$⟩};
  goto *Sup*

C-IDS: for each local IDS
    {receive *status* of the associated controller};
    if (there are at least 2 engines with warnings)
      {snd *alarm*}
    elseif (there is only 1 warning)
      {snd *warning*}
    else
      {snd *okay*};
    goto *C-IDS*

Fig. 2. Centralized logical components: Supervisor and central IDS

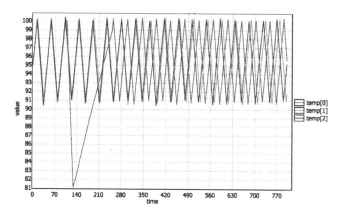

Fig. 3. Runtime evolution of the temperatures of the multi-engine system with three engines

that time window the engine slows down, its temperatures grows more slowly, and, as a consequence, its cooling system becomes more effective in cooling down the temperature.

3   An Implementation in UPPAAL SMC

In this section, we model and verify in UPPAAL SMC [9] the coordinated multi-engine system, presented in Sect. 2, consisting of three engines. The UPPAAL SMC models of our system and the attacks discussed in the next section are available at the repository https://github.com/ruggerolanotte/multi-engine_system.

UPPAAL **Representation.** As other cyber-physical use cases presented in the literature (see related work in Sect. 5), we modeled the coordinated multi-engine system by making a clear distinction between *physical components* (physical process, sensors and actuators), *logical components* (controllers and IDSs), and *communication channels* between logical components and between logical components and physical devices (sensors and actuators). In particular, we modeled both the physical components and the logical components in terms of *parallel timed automata*.

The physical component, also called plant, consists of three automata parameterized on the *id* of the corresponding engine: (i) the _Engine_ automaton, shown in Fig. 4, governs the runtime evolution of the temperature, variable *temp[id]*,

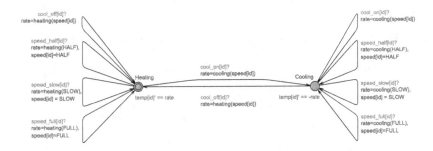

Fig. 4. UPPAAL model of the engine

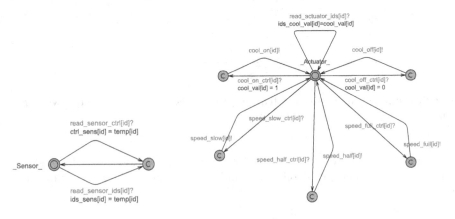

Fig. 5. UPPAAL models of the physical devices (sensors and actuators)

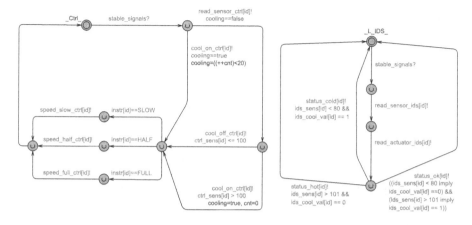

Fig. 6. UPPAAL models of the local logical components (*Ctrl* and *L-IDS*).

by means of a function *heating()*; similarly, a *cooling()* function models the presence of the cooling system; (ii) the *_Sensor_* automaton (see the left-hand-side of Fig. 5) updates the temperature measurements used by the controller and the local IDS; (iii) the *_Actuator_* automaton (see the right-hand-side of Fig. 5) handles the two actuators associated with the cooling system and the engine speed, respectively. The physical component also includes a small automaton to synchronize both the controllers and the local IDSs with measurements coming from *_Sensor_* (via a synchronization channel stable_signals).

The logical component of our model is given in Fig. 6. It consists of two automata, *_Ctrl_* and *_L_IDS_*, modeling the controller and the local intrusion detection system, respectively (again, they are parametric on the *id* of the associated engine). *_Ctrl_* waits for stable measurements, via a synchronization channel stable_signals, that are recorded in the local variables (*ctrl_sens[id]* and *ids_sens[id]*, respectively). On the other hand, *_L_IDS_* determines the status of the cooling system (hot, cold, okay) and sends it to both centralized logical components, the *Supervisor* and the *C-IDS*.

The two centralized logical components *C-IDS* and *Supervisor* are modeled by the automata *_C_IDS_* and *_Supervisor_*, respectively (see Fig. 7 and Fig. 8). Both automata wait for information on the status of each engine from the local intrusion detection systems. Then: (i) *_C_IDS_* does intrusion detection against coordinated attackers; (ii) *_Supervisor_* writes the instructions to the controllers, according to the performance policy described before, using the function *decide_speed_instr()*.

We simulate system engineers' activities through an additional automaton modeling their requests to change the speed of the engines. An engineer can randomly choose one of the three engines and demand it to run in either FULL or SLOW speed (both cases with a 50% probability). Each request has a duration of 150 time units. The first request occurs in a time instant uniformly chosen in the interval [50, 100]. The other requests start after the end of the previous one in a time instant uniformly chosen in the interval [2500, 3000].

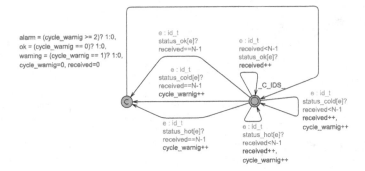

Fig. 7. UPPAAL model of the centralized IDS (*C-IDS*).

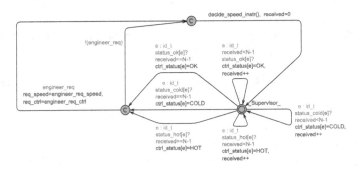

Fig. 8. UPPAAL model of the Supervisor.

Verification of Our Multi-engine System. As we are interested in studying the impact of cyber-physical attacks on our multi-engine system, our verification aims at ensuring the correct behavior of the IDS in the absence of attacks. Moreover, we are interested in characterizing the physical runtime behavior of the system. This information will be used in Sect. 4 as a baseline to study the physical impact of three different attacks.

Settings. We conducted our impact evaluation using a notebook with the following set-up: (i) 2.8 GHz Intel i7 7700 HQ, with 16 GB memory, and Linux Ubuntu 20.04 LTS OS; (ii) UPPAAL SMC model-checker 64-bit, version 4.1.26-2. The statistical parameters of false negatives (α) and probabilistic uncertainty (ϵ) are both set to 0.01, leading to a 99% accuracy. Note that these parameters only affect the accuracy of the results and the consequent time required for the analyses. Considering a lower accuracy would result in faster analyses. For our analysis, we simulate runs of our system that are 10,000 time units long. As the system consists of periodic sub-components (the single engines), the length of the run has been chosen long enough to observe several cycles of the system.

System Analysis. To verify the proper functioning of the IDS employed in our multi-engine system in the absence of attacks, we use UPPAAL SMC and model the system behavior of interest as *probability estimation* queries of formulas of the form $\lozenge_{\leq t}\, e_{prop}$, where t is a *time bound* (in our case 10,000) and e_{prop} is a side-effect free expression over variables. In practice, given a formula $\lozenge_{\leq t} e_{prop}$, UPPAAL SMC returns a probability interval $[p_1, p_2]$ in which the property e_{prop} holds in at least one time instant in $0..t$. In the following, as we work with a 99% accuracy, we write that a property *holds with high probability* when UPPAAL SMC says that the property holds with a probability in the interval $[0.980005, 1]$. Similarly, we write that a property *does not hold with high probability* when UPPAAL SMC says that the property holds with a probability laying in the interval $[0, 0.0199955]$.

In normal conditions, the intrusion detection system should not trigger any warning or alarm, i.e., it should not generate false positives. We formalize these properties in terms of probability estimation queries as follows:

P1: $\lozenge_{\leq t}\, (warning == 1)$
P2: $\lozenge_{\leq t}\, (alarm == 1)$

Intuitively, **P1** and **P2** returns the probabilities that a warning or an alert is triggered within time t, respectively. The analysis shows that our multi-engine system does yield neither warnings nor alarms. In particular, we verified that neither **P1** nor **P2** hold, with high probability, on runs of at most 10000 time instants. The verification of each property required approximately 40 minutes.

To study the *physical impact* of cyber-physical attacks on our multi-engine system, we focus on two specific physical target for attackers: (i) the increased activity of the cooling system with the consequent increase in coolant consumption, and (ii) modifications of the average temperatures of the engines. To derive this information, we use UPPAAL's *value estimation* queries $E[t; N](max : total\_var)$ by introducing two auxiliary variables: $total\_cooling[i]$ and $total\_temp[i]$, for $i \in \{0, 1, 2\}$. The integer variable $total\_cooling[i]$ counts the time instants in a run in which the cooling system of the engine i is active, whereas the double variable $total\_temp[i]$ returns the summation of the temperatures reached by the engine i in all time instants of a run. We use these variables to compute the average cooling time and temperature for a run.

By running 2000 execution traces, each consisting of 10000 time instants, we obtain the following information: (1) each engine spends, on average, around 47% of its time in cooling down the temperature; (2) the temperature of the three engines is, on average, around 95.5 degrees. Formally, these results are obtained using the following value estimations in UPPAAL SMC:

E1: $E[<= 10000; 2000](max : \sum_{\in \{0,1,2\}} total\_cooling[i]/3) = 4700.9 \pm 1.37$.
E2: $E[<= 10000; 2000](max : total\_temp[i]/10000) = 95.4554 \pm 0.0028$, for $i \in \{0, 1, 2\}$.

Here, "$max : expr$" returns for all 2000 simulation runs, the maximum value reached by the expression $expr$. The verification of each value estimation requires around 4 hours.

It is worth noting that value estimations are not associated with an accuracy but only provide an average of the estimated values over the tested runs along with a graphical representation of the distribution of the real values computed for each run. Thus, to assess the quality of the estimated value with respect to all runs, we leveraged this information to verify a lower and an upper bound of the estimated value (extracted from its distribution of **E1** and **E2**) with an accuracy of 99%. To this end, we define the following two properties:

P3: $\Diamond_{\leq 10000}$ (*time*==10000 and $\exists i \in \{0,1,2\}$. not(4500 $\leq$ *total_cooling*[i] $\leq$ 4900))

P4: $\Diamond_{\leq 10000}$ (*time*==10000 and $\exists i \in \{0,1,2\}$. not(95 $\leq$ *total_temp*[i]/10000 $\leq$ 96))

The simulation of the multi-engine system for 10,000 runs shows that both properties do not hold with a high priority. Accordingly: (1) in each run, each engine spends at least 45% and at most 49% of its time in cooling down the temperature; (2) the temperature of each engine lays, on average, between 95 and 96 degrees. The verification of each of the queries above requires around 40 minutes.

4   An SMC-Based Security Analysis

In this section, we use UPPAAL SMC to perform a security analysis of the system under investigation when exposed to three different cyber-physical attacks aiming to cause *equipment* and/or *production damage* (cf. the attack goals seen in the Introduction). In particular, we implement three coordinated attacks consisting of (three) distinct distributed attackers, injecting malicious code in each controller of our multi-engine system. The distributed attackers coordinate with each other via a *covert channel* without introducing extra, possibly suspicious, communications between engines' controllers. Notice that we focus on attacks that compromise the controllers only (the automaton _Ctrl_ in our implementation), that is, we assume that the other logical components of the systems (local and central IDSs and Supervisor) have been secured against malicious attacks, and their runtime behavior cannot be altered by the attacker. To this end, we modeled the three attacks by replacing the automaton _Ctrl_ of each engine with a compromised version resulting from the attacker's injection. All attacks go through four phases: *waiting, starting, active* and *ended*. We assume that the attack duration is established a priori by the attacker, and that the exact time when the attack begins depends on some specific request of system engineers to change the speed of one or more engines.

We verify the system under attack in runs of 10000 time units. The time instant when the attack is triggered by the request of a system engineer is stored in a variable *start* whose value is randomly chosen in the time interval [50, 100]. Given the periodicity of our system, we chose an attack window of 9000 time units, covering several cycles. This choice provides us the possibility to observe eventual anomalies after the attack. Note that these attack time parameters, such as beginning of the attack and its duration, do not influence the outcome of the specific attacks and, thus, they are the same for all three attacks. The verification of each probabilistic estimation required at most 40 minutes and the computation of each value estimation around 4 h.

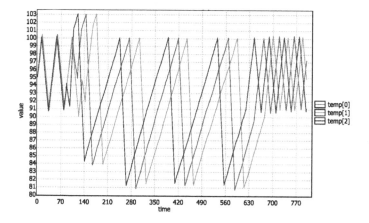

Fig. 9. Simulation of the multi-engine system exposed to Attack 1.

Attack 1: Degrading System Performance

Objective. The goal of the attacker is to compromise the performance of the multi-engine system by forcing the three engines to run at SLOW speed whenever a system engineer asks for higher performance by demanding an engine to switch from HALF to FULL speed. Accordingly, it can be seen as an attack aiming at *production damage*.

Description. Initially, the compromised multi-engine system behaves normally (the three attackers are in the *waiting phase*) until the system engineer demands a specific engine to run at FULL speed via the Supervisor. Upon receiving such a request, the associated attacker steps in the *starting phase* and performs a flooding/integrity attack on the *cool* actuator to induce an overheating for a few time instants. Thus, an overheating warning is transmitted by the local IDS to the Supervisor which sends instructions to the compromised engine controller to run at SLOW speed. At the same time, the attacker maintains that speed for the whole attack window via a flooding/integrity attack on the *speed* actuator (*active phase*). Furthermore, the Supervisor sends a request for compensation (FULL request) to the adjacent engine controller. This triggers the corresponding attacker to force the engine at SLOW speed. Note that Supervisor's requests are used as *covert channel* to propagate the attack to the whole multi-engine system.

In Fig. 9, we reports the temperature behavior of the three engines under attack. For the sake of visualization, the figure plots runs of 800 time units where the attack lasts 500 time units; note that the reported behavior is similar to the one that can be observed in the simulations used for our analysis. We can observe that in the time interval [90, 110], the three engines experience an overheating due to the beginning of the attack. Then, during the attack window, as the engines run at the SLOW speed, their temperatures grow more slowly. At the same time, their cooling systems are more effective in dropping their temperatures.

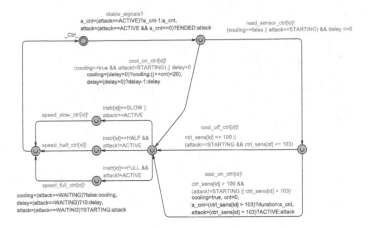

Fig. 10. UPPAAL automaton _Ctrl_ compromised by Attack 1.

Therefore, when under attack, the engines exhibit a different (actually wider) periodic behavior.

The compromised controller of each engine is modeled by the automaton of Fig. 10. This automaton extends the one in Fig. 6 (left-hand side) by adding a variable *attack* to denote the different phases of the attack. In the *waiting phase*, the compromised controller behaves as the one in Fig. 6 while waiting for a trigger coming from system engineers or the Supervisor (bottom-left of Fig. 10). In the *starting phase* (top-right of Fig. 10), the flooding on the actuator *cool* is modeled by manipulating the communication between the controller and the actuator (via channel *cool_off_ctrl[id]*) until the temperature exceeds the threshold of 103 °C, which triggers the intervention of the Supervisor (bottom-right of Fig. 10). Then, in the *active phase* the engine is maintained at SLOW speed via a similar flooding on the actuator *speed* (this time via channel *speed_slow_ctrl[id]*) for the duration of the attack (bottom-left of Fig. 10). Finally, at the end of the attack window (top-left of Fig. 10), the controller restores its genuine behavior.

Security Analysis. We assessed the impact of the attack on the multi-engine system. First, we verified if the attack is successful in forcing the three engines to run at SLOW speed during the attack window, up to a short transitory initial phase necessary to propagate the attack to the three engines. To this end, we defined the following property:

$\Diamond_{\leq 10000} (start + 150 \leq time \leq start + 90000$ and $\exists i \in \{0, 1, 2\}. speed[i]! = SLOW)$ Intuitively, this property checks whether any of the three engines does not run at SLOW speed during the attack window. Our analysis shows that the property does not hold with high probability; thus, we can conclude that the attack was successful with high probability. Note that the attack propagation time is derived from an empirical observation of the attacked system's simulation graph, where 150 time units is a (safe) upper bound of the real propagation time.

To verify the stealthiness of the attack, we verified if properties **P1** and **P2** (cf. Sect. 3) hold when the system is under attack. Our verification shows that the *central IDS* does not fire any alarm (i.e., **P2** does not hold with high probability). However, some warnings were triggered by the *local IDS* as we observe that **P1** holds with high probability. An in-depth investigation showed that the warnings only happen in the initial transitory phase when the attack propagates throughout the multi-engine system. Formally, we verified that:

- $\Diamond_{\leq 10000} (start \leq time < start + 150$ and $warning == 1)$ holds with high probability.
- $\Diamond_{\leq 10000} (time < start$ and $time \geq start + 150$ and $warning == 1)$ does not hold with high probability.

We also verified properties **P3** and **P4** to study the attack's impact on system performance. We observed that the average cooling time decreases to 17.5% (compared to 47% in the regular situation) and that the average temperature decreases to 91 (compared to 95.5 in the regular situation), showing that this attack has a limited impact on system performance.

Attack 2: Putting the Multi-engine System Under Stress

Objective. The attacker aims to stress the multi-engine system by forcing the three engines to run at FULL speed whenever a system engineer asks an engine to switch from HALF to SLOW speed. Thus, the main goal is *equipment damage* as engines under stress are prone to ruptures in the long run; the attack also achieves *production damage* because running all engines at FULL power results in extra coolant consumption.

Description. Initially, the compromised multi-engine system behaves normally (the three attackers are in the *waiting phase*) until the system engineer demands a specific engine to run at SLOW speed via the Supervisor. Upon receiving such a request, the associated attacker steps in the *starting phase* and performs a flooding/integrity attack on the *cool* actuator to induce an under-heating for a few time instants. This results in a warning of the local IDS that triggers the Supervisor to instruct the engine to run at FULL speed. At the same time, the attacker maintains that speed for the whole attack window via a flooding/integrity attack on the *speed* actuator (*active phase*). Furthermore, the Supervisor sends a request for compensation (request for SLOW speed) to the adjacent controller. This triggers the corresponding attacker to force the engine at FULL speed. Again, the Supervisor's requests are used as covert channel to propagate the attack.

Figure 11 reports the evolution of the temperature for the three engines. Similarly to the previous attack, we illustrate the system behavior for a run of 800 time units where the system engineering randomly chose the SLOW (triggering) request in the interval [50, 100]; the attack lasts 500 units of time. We can observe that in the time interval [70, 180], the three engines experience an under-heating

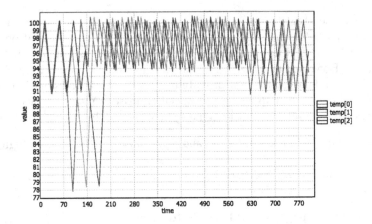

Fig. 11. Simulation of the multi-engine system exposed to Attack 2.

due to the beginning of the attack. Then, during the attack window, as the engines run at the FULL speed; thus, their temperatures grow more quickly and decrease more slowly. Again, when under attack, the engines exhibit a different (actually shorter) periodic behavior.

Security Analysis. We assessed the impact of the attack on the multi-engine system. First, we verified if the attack is successful in forcing the three engines to run at FULL speed during the attack, up to a short transitory initial phase (150 time units) necessary to propagate the attack to three engines. To this end, we defined the following property:

$\Diamond_{\leq 10000}$ ($start + 150 \leq time \leq start + 90000$ and $\exists i \in \{0, 1, 2\}. speed[i]! = FULL$) Intuitively, this property checks whether any of the three engines does not run at FULL speed during the attack window. Our analysis shows that this property does not hold with high probability; thus, we can conclude that the attack was successful: all engines run at FULL speed during the attack window.

To verify the level of stealthiness of the attack, we verified if properties **P1** and **P2** (cf. Sect. 3) hold when the system is under attack. Our verification shows that the *central IDS* does not fire any alarm (i.e., **P2** does not hold with high probability). However, **P1** holds with high probability, indicating that the *local IDS* triggers some warnings. Further investigation showed that the warnings only happen in the initial transitory phase when the attack propagates throughout the multi-engine system. This insight is obtained by verifying the following properties:

- $\Diamond_{\leq 10000}$ ($start \leq time < start + 150$ and $warning == 1$) holds with high probability.
- $\Diamond_{\leq 10000}$ ($time < start$ and $time \geq start + 150$ and $warning == 1$) does not hold with high probability.

We also studied the attack's impact on system performance using properties **P3** and **P4**. We observed that, on average, each engine spends 72% of its time cooling down the temperature (compared to 47% in the regular situation). Formally:

$$E[<= 10000; 2000](max : \sum_{i \in \{i=0,1,2\}} total\_cooling[i]/3) = 7221.45 \pm 0.264.$$

From this estimation, we can derive quantitative information on the increase of coolant consumption due to the attack: every engine spends *at least* 71% and *at most* 73% of its time in cooling down the temperature. We obtained this by observing that the following property does not hold with high probability:

$$\Diamond_{\leq 10000} (time == 10000 \text{ and } \exists i \in \{0, 1, 2\} . not(7100 \leq total\_cooling[i] \leq 7300))$$

A similar analysis for the temperature shows the average temperature at each engine increased to 97 degrees (compared to 95.5 degrees obtained in the regular situation).

Attack 3: Pushing the Multi-engine System to the Temperature Threshold

Objective. The attacker aims to keep the temperature of the engines close to the threshold, 100 degrees, when a system engineer asks for slowing down an engine. This is achieved by tampering with the cooling systems of all engines. Thus, the main goal of the attack is *equipment damage* as the engines work for a long period at a temperature very close to the threshold, with obvious consequences on its physical components in the long run.

Description. The attack proceeds as in Attack 2. The only difference is in the *active phase*, where each attacker, injected in the controller, reduces the duration of the cooling activity by deactivating the cooling system as soon as the temperature reaches 100 degrees.

Figure 12 shows a simulation of the system under attack. As for the previous attacks, we show a run of 800 time units where the system engineering randomly chose the SLOW (triggering) request in the interval $[50, 100]$ and the attack lasts 500 time units. We can observe that in the time interval $[60, 140]$, the three engines experience an under-heating due to the beginning of the attack. Then, during the attack window, as the engines run at the HALF (normal) speed; However, when under attack, the three engines all work at a temperature very close to the threshold of 100 °C.

Security Analysis. We assessed the impact of the attack on the multi-engine system. To verify if the attack is successful, we computed the value estimation of the temperature of each engine for the system under attack. These value estimations show that the temperature of the three engines is, on average, 99.25 degrees. Formally,

$$E[<= 10000; 2000](max : total\_temp[i]/10000) = 99.23 \pm 0.0002.$$

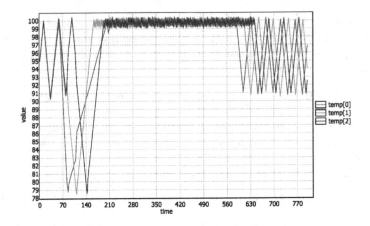

Fig. 12. Simulation of the multi-engine system exposed to Attack 3.

From this estimation, we can determine that the attack is successful in increasing the average temperature of all engines. In particular, we observed that the following property does not hold with high probability:

$$\Diamond_{\leq 10000} \, (time == 10000 \text{ and } \exists i \in \{0, 1, 2\}. \, not(98.8 \leq total\_temp[i]/10000 \leq 99.8)) \, .$$

Therefore, the temperature of each engine lays, on average, between 98.8 and 99.8 degrees (instead of 95 and 96 degrees as in normal situations).

To verify the level of stealthiness of the attack, we verified if properties **P1** and **P2** (cf. Sect. 3) hold when the system is under attack. Similarly to the previous attacks, our verification shows that the *central IDS* does not fire any alarm (i.e., **P2** does not hold with high probability), but *local IDS* triggers some warnings (i.e., **P1** holds with high probability). As in the previous cases, the warnings only happen in the initial transitory phase when the attack propagates throughout the multi-engine system, as demonstrated by the following properties:

- $\Diamond_{\leq 10000} \, (start \leq time < start + 150 \text{ and } warning == 1)$ holds with high probability.
- $\Diamond_{\leq 10000} \, (time < start \text{ and } time \geq start + 150 \text{ and } warning == 1)$ does not hold with high probability.

In this attack, the consumption of coolant remains unaffected, with the engine spending 47% of its time in cooling down the temperature.

5   Conclusions, Related and Future Work

We have used UPPAAL SMC [9] to perform *statistical model checking* of a coordinated and refrigerated multi-engine system enriched with a distributed intrusion detection system. As discussed in Lanotte *et al.* [23], SMC allows to better scale on the dimension of the CPS under security analysis, when compared to the classical model checking tools. In particular, in prior unpublished work we implemented the refrigerated engine system at the core of our coordinated multi-engine system, using different model-checking tools, such as PRISM [19], UPPAAL [2], Real-Time Maude [27], and prohver, i.e., the safety model checker within the MODEST TOOLSET [11]. All these model-checking tools, however, suffer from the classical state explosion problem, even for relatively small systems. SMC enables a considerable step forward in the size of the CPSs we can verify.

Following this research line, the goal of this work was to test UPPAAL SMC as a tool for achieving a security analysis of a non-trivial CPS under attack. We have evaluated the physical impact of three carefully chosen *coordinated cyber-physical attacks* aiming at achieving *production damages* and/or *equipment damages*. In particular, we verified two families of *system invariants* of the system under attack: one focused on the runtime evolution of the physical-component of the CPS, and a second one focused on the effectiveness of the IDS (logical component) in detecting the proposed attacks. Here, the physical impact was measured in terms of changes in the average engine temperatures and the coolant consumption of the entire system. Many other physical invariants of our multi-engine could be checked similarly (number of activations/deactivations of the cooling system, efficiency of the engines, number of switches of the speed of each engine, etc.). Thus, we believe that our methodology can be easily generalized to any CPS under attack.

Our analysis provided us with insights into the effectiveness of the proposed distributed IDS and the impact of the attacks on the physical behavior of the system. In particular, we observed that the studied attacks are *stealthy*, as the IDS yields only some warning and no alarms, and are effective in achieving their goals. By assessing the impact of attacks on the physical process, system engineers may better understand whether they have to develop more accurate metrics or focus on different invariants to enhance their IDSs in order to detect such attacks, possibly at an early stage.

The modeling language provided by UPPAAL SMC has demonstrated to be effective in specifying realistic cyber-physical systems in terms of parallel timed automata. Such automata scale well and allowed us to represent cyber-physical attacks by focusing on specific compromised components. The time required for the analyses, with a 99% accuracy, was very reasonable: at most 40 min for each probabilistic estimation and around 4 h for each value estimation. To the best of our knowledge, this work is the first that studies the viability of UPPAAL SMC to perform security analyses of non-trivial CPSs exposed to coordinated cyber-physical attacks.

Related Work. Pedroza et al. [28] proposed a UML-based environment to model critical embedded systems. The verification of safety properties relies on UPPAAL, whereas the verification of security properties (*e.g.*, confidentiality and integrity) relies on ProVerif [5]. Wardell et al. [33] proposed an approach for identifying security vulnerabilities of industrial control systems by modeling malicious attacks as PROMELA models. Kumar et al. [18] introduced an attack-fault tree formalism to describe attack scenarios; they conduct formal analyses using

UPPAAL SMC to obtain quantitative estimations on the impact of both system failures and security threats. Cheh *et al.* [6] used UPPAAL SMC to perform statistical model checking on a railway system to assess the safety of the system under attack. Similar to our work, they tied safety analyses to security analyses and considered an attack that manipulates the communication messages exchanged between the signaling components of the railway system (this affects the speed of the trains and the routes they take). More precisely, their attack can remove, insert, modify, or delay those network packets, akin to a Dolev-Yao attacker. Huang *et al.* [15] analyzed the impact of attacks compromising the safety of automotive systems. In particular, they considered attacks affecting vehicle communication: forgery of fake data, replay of old data, and spoofing of vehicle IDs. Both safety and security properties are verified in UPPAAL SMC. Taormina *et al.* [29] modeled the interaction between the physical and cyber layer of water distribution systems in epanetCPA, an open-source MATLAB toolbox allowing users to design custom cyber-physical attacks and simulate the hydraulic response of water networks. epanetCPA features a wide range of cyber-physical attacks: physical attacks on sensors and actuators, deception attacks, DoS on communication channels, replay attacks, and alteration of PLC and SCADA control statements. Although this tool can deal with several cyber-physical attacks, its analysis is based on single simulations. Lanotte *et al.* [21] used the safety checker prohver within the MODEST TOOLSET for the security analysis of a simple engine system with one physical variable, one sensor, and one actuator. Munteanu *et al.* [26] tested the effectiveness of the statistical model checker modes of the same toolset when doing a security and safety analysis of a significantly larger CPS. Jahandideh *et al.* [17] propose the Hybrid Rebeca language (an extension of the actor-based language Rebeca) to support the modeling of cyber-physical systems. The SpaceEx framework is used for reachability analysis. In particular, the authors show that event-based asynchronous models in Hybrid Rebeca improve the analysis by reducing the number of real variables and increase modularity. More recently, Zarneshan *et al.* [34] use Timed Rebecca to validate the interactions among the timing properties of components in interoperable medical systems. More recently, Bernardeschi *et al.* [4] have proposed a formal methodology to validate the design of drone co-operative systems based on co-simulation and formal verification. The methodology relies on the Prototype Verification System, an interactive theorem prover based on a higher-order logic language, and the Functional Mock-up Interface.

Future Work. As future work, we aim to stress the scalability of our SMC analysis by increasing the number of engines involved in our multi-engine system. Moreover, we plan to replicate and test more complex coordinated cyber-physical attacks targeting CPS controllers [13,35]. We believe that our work poses the basis for the design and development of detection mechanisms that leverage an understanding of the impact of cyber-physical attacks. We plan to investigate how our methodology can be extended to assist system engineers in devising tailored impact metrics and in identifying system invariants to enhance IDSs to detect cyber-physical attacks, possibly at their early stage.

Acknowledgments. We thank the reviewers for their insightful feedback.

References

1. Alur, R., Dill, D.L.: A theory of timed automata. Theor. Comput. Sci. **126**(2), 183–235 (1994)
2. Behrmann, G., David, A., Larsen, K.G., Håkansson, J., Pettersson, P., Yi, W., Hendriks, M.: UPPAAL 4.0. In: QEST 2006, pp. 125–126. IEEE Computer Society (2006)
3. Behrmann, G., David, A., Larsen, K.G.: A tutorial on UPPAAL. In: Bernardo, M., Corradini, F. (eds.) SFM-RT 2004. LNCS, vol. 3185, pp. 200–236. Springer, Heidelberg (2004). https://doi.org/10.1007/978-3-540-30080-9_7
4. Bernardeschi, C., Domenici, A., Fagiolini, A., Palmieri, M.: Co-simulation and formal verification of co-operative drone control with logic-based specifications. Comput. J. **66**(2), 295–317 (2023)
5. Blanchet, B.: Automatic verification of correspondences for security protocols. J. Comput. Secur. **17**(4), 363–434 (2009)
6. Cheh, C., Fawaz, A., Noureddine, M.A., Chen, B., Temple, W.G., Sanders, W.H.: Determining tolerable attack surfaces that preserves safety of cyber-physical systems. In: PRDC, pp. 125–134. IEEE Computer Society (2018)
7. Clarke, E.M., Grumberg, O., Peled, D.A.: Model Checking. MIT Press, Cambridge (2001)
8. Clarke, E.M., Zuliani, P.: Statistical model checking for cyber-physical systems. In: Bultan, T., Hsiung, P.-A. (eds.) ATVA 2011. LNCS, vol. 6996, pp. 1–12. Springer, Heidelberg (2011). https://doi.org/10.1007/978-3-642-24372-1_1
9. David, A., Larsen, K.G., Legay, A., Mikuăionis, M., Poulsen, D.B.: Uppaal SMC tutorial. STTT **17**(4), 397–415 (2015)
10. Gollmann, D., Gurikov, P., Isakov, A., Krotofil, M., Larsen, J., Winnicki, A.: Cyber-physical systems security: experimental analysis of a vinyl acetate monomer plant. In: ACM CCPS, pp. 1–12 (2015)
11. Hartmanns, A., Hermanns, H.: The modest toolset: an integrated environment for quantitative modelling and verification. In: Ábrahám, E., Havelund, K. (eds.) TACAS 2014. LNCS, vol. 8413, pp. 593–598. Springer, Heidelberg (2014). https://doi.org/10.1007/978-3-642-54862-8_51
12. Hastings, W.K.: Monte carlo sampling methods using markov chains and their applications. Biometrika **57**(1), 97–109 (1970)
13. He, H., Yan, J.: Cyber-physical attacks and defences in the smart grid: a survey. IET Cyber-Phys. Syst. Theor. Appl. **1**(1), 13–27 (2016)
14. Henzinger, T.A., Kopke, P.W., Puri, A., Varaiya, P.: What's decidable about hybrid automata? J. Comput. Syst. Sci. **57**(1), 94–124 (1998)
15. Huang, L., Kang, E.-Y.: Formal verification of safety & security related timing constraints for a cooperative automotive system. In: Hähnle, R., van der Aalst, W. (eds.) FASE 2019. LNCS, vol. 11424, pp. 210–227. Springer, Cham (2019). https://doi.org/10.1007/978-3-030-16722-6_12
16. Huang, Y., Cárdenas, A.A., Amin, S., Lin, Z., Tsai, H., Sastry, S.: Understanding the physical and economic consequences of attacks on control systems. Int. J. Crit. Infrastructure Prot. **2**(3), 73–83 (2009)
17. Jahandideh, I., Ghassemi, F., Sirjani, M.: An actor-based framework for asynchronous event-based cyber-physical systems. Softw. Syst. Model. **20**(3), 641–665 (2021). https://doi.org/10.1007/s10270-021-00877-y

18. Kumar, R., Stoelinga, M.: Quantitative security and safety analysis with attack-fault trees. In: HASE, pp. 25–32. IEEE Computer Society (2017)

19. Kwiatkowska, M., Norman, G., Parker, D.: PRISM 4.0: verification of probabilistic real-time systems. In: Gopalakrishnan, G., Qadeer, S. (eds.) CAV 2011. LNCS, vol. 6806, pp. 585–591. Springer, Heidelberg (2011). https://doi.org/10.1007/978-3-642-22110-1_47

20. Lanotte, R., Merro, M., Mogavero, F.: On the decidability of linear bounded periodic cyber-physical systems. In: HSCC, pp. 87–98. ACM (2019)

21. Lanotte, R., Merro, M., Munteanu, A.: A modest security analysis of cyber-physical systems: a case study. In: Baier, C., Caires, L. (eds.) FORTE 2018. LNCS, vol. 10854, pp. 58–78. Springer, Cham (2018). https://doi.org/10.1007/978-3-319-92612-4_4

22. Lanotte, R., Merro, M., Munteanu, A., Tini, S.: Formal impact metrics for cyber-physical attacks. In: CSF, pp. 1–16. IEEE (2021)

23. Lanotte, R., Merro, M., Munteanu, A., Viganò, L.: A formal approach to physics-based attacks in cyber-physical systems. ACM Trans. Priv. Secur. **23**(1), 3:1–3:41 (2020)

24. Lanotte, R., Merro, M., Tini, S.: Towards a formal notion of impact metric for cyber-physical attacks. In: Furia, C.A., Winter, K. (eds.) IFM 2018. LNCS, vol. 11023, pp. 296–315. Springer, Cham (2018). https://doi.org/10.1007/978-3-319-98938-9_17

25. Legay, A., Delahaye, B., Bensalem, S.: Statistical model checking: an overview. In: Barringer, H., Barringer, H., et al. (eds.) RV 2010. LNCS, vol. 6418, pp. 122–135. Springer, Heidelberg (2010). https://doi.org/10.1007/978-3-642-16612-9_11

26. Munteanu, A., Pasqua, M., Merro, M.: Impact analysis of cyber-physical attacks on a water tank system via statistical model checking. In: FormaliSE@ICSE 2020, pp. 34–43. ACM (2020)

27. Ölveczky, P.C., Meseguer, J.: Semantics and pragmatics of real-time maude. Higher-Order Symbolic Comput. **20**(1–2), 161–196 (2007)

28. Pedroza, G., Apvrille, L., Knorreck, D.: AVATAR: a SysML environment for the formal verification of safety and security properties. In: NOTERE, pp. 1–10. IEEE (2011)

29. Taormina, R., Galelli, S., Douglas, H., Tippenhauer, N., Salomons, E., Ostfeld, A.: A toolbox for assessing the impacts of cyber-physical attacks on water distribution systems. Environ. Model. Softw. **112**, 46–51 (2019)

30. Umsonst, D., Sandberg, H., Cárdenas, A.A.: Security analysis of control system anomaly detectors. In: ACC, pp. 5500–5506. IEEE (2017)

31. Urbina, D.I., et al.: Limiting the impact of stealthy attacks on industrial control systems. In: ACM CCS, pp. 1092–1105. ACM (2016)

32. Urbina, D.I., et al.: Limiting the impact of stealthy attacks on industrial control systems. In: CCS, pp. 1092–1105. ACM (2016). https://doi.org/10.1145/2976749.2978388

33. Wardell, D.C., Mills, R.F., Peterson, G.L., Oxley, M.E.: A method for revealing and addressing security vulnerabilities in cyber-physical systems by modeling malicious agent interactions with formal verification. Procedia Com. Sc. **95**, 24–31 (2016)

34. Zarneshan, M., Ghassemi, F., Khamespanah, E., Sirjani, M., Hatcliff, J.: Specification and verification of timing properties in interoperable medical systems. Log. Methods Comput. Sci. **18**(2), 13:1–13:37 (2022)

35. Zhang, H., Liu, B., Wu, H.: Smart grid cyber-physical attack and defense: a review. IEEE Access **9**, 29641–29659 (2021)

Probabilities, Time and other Resources

Operations on Timed Scenarios

Neda Saeedloei[1]([⊠]) and Feliks Kluźniak[2]

[1] Towson University, Towson, USA
nsaeedloei@towson.edu
[2] RelationalAI, Berkeley, USA
feliks.kluzniak@relational.ai

Abstract. We introduce three operations for timed scenarios: subsumption, intersection and union. They have constructive definitions based on the syntactic properties of the constituent scenarios. We show that they have the desired semantic properties. These results expand the theory of timed scenarios, but their development was inspired by practical considerations: they are directly relevant to the problem of synthesizing a timed automaton with a minimal number of clocks from a set of scenarios.

1 Introduction

Using scenarios for specification and implementation of complex systems (including real time systems and distributed systems [1,2]), and synthesizing formal models of systems from scenarios have been active areas of research for several decades [3–10].

In our earlier work [11] we developed, from first principles, a formal, yet simple notation for timed scenarios. Intuitively, a scenario is a sequence of events along with a set of constraints between the times of these events. It can be used to specify the partial behaviours of a system or a component of a system. Our scenarios can be used as a general formalism for modeling the behaviours of a variety of complex systems, including distributed systems.

We defined the semantics of a timed scenario as the set of all *behaviours* (a.k.a timed words [12]) that are allowed by the scenario.

One of our objectives is to use our scenarios to automatically synthesize formal models in the form of timed automata [12] with a *minimal number of clocks*. This is important, since the number of clocks crucially affects the cost of verification of timed automata [13].

As part of our earlier work [11] we obtained a canonical representation (a "stable distance table") for the entire class of scenarios that are equivalent to a given one. We used stable distance tables as a linchpin of various algorithms for determining the consistency and equivalency of scenarios, as well as for optimizing scenarios [14,15].

In the current paper we use our stable distance tables once more to develop the notions of intersection, union and subsumption for timed scenarios. We introduce appropriate operations with well-defined semantics for computing the intersection and union of two consistent scenarios, as well as for determining

© IFIP International Federation for Information Processing 2023
M. Huisman and A. Ravara (Eds.): FORTE 2023, LNCS 13910, pp. 97–114, 2023.
https://doi.org/10.1007/978-3-031-35355-0_7

whether a scenario is subsumed by another one.

Intuitively, given two consistent scenarios, their intersection is a scenario that expresses all those behaviours that are allowed by both, while their union is a scenario that captures all the behaviours that are allowed by either of them or both. A scenario is subsumed by another one if its set of behaviours is subsumed by that of the other one.

Having defined these operations, we develop some interesting relationships between them. In particular, we study the conditions under which the union of the behaviours allowed by two scenarios can be represented by a single scenario.

These operations are directly relevant to the problem of synthesizing timed automata from a set of scenarios, which is not addressed in the current paper.

2   Preliminaries

2.1   Timed Automata

A *timed automaton* [12] is a tuple $\mathcal{A} = \langle \Sigma, Q, q_0, Q_f, C, T \rangle$, where Σ is a finite alphabet, Q is the (*finite*) set of locations, $q_0 \in Q$ is the initial location, $Q_f \subseteq Q$ is the set of final locations, C is a finite set of *clock* variables (clocks for short), and $T \subseteq Q \times Q \times \Sigma \times 2^C \times 2^{\Phi(C)}$ is the set of transitions. In each transition $(q, q', e, \lambda, \phi)$, λ is the set of clocks to be reset with the transition and $\phi \subset \Phi(C)$ is a set of clock constraints over C of the form $c \sim a$ (where $\sim \in \{\leq, <, \geq, >, =\}$, $c \in C$ and a is a constant in the set of rational numbers, $\mathbb{Q}$). A *clock valuation* ν for C is a mapping from C to $\mathbb{R}^{\geq 0}$. Clock valuation ν *satisfies* a set of clock constraints ϕ over C iff every clock constraint in ϕ evaluates to true after each clock c is replaced with $\nu(c)$. For $\tau \in \mathbb{R}, \nu + \tau$ denotes the clock valuation which maps every clock c to the value $\nu(c) + \tau$. For $Y \subseteq C$, $[Y \mapsto \tau]\nu$ is the valuation which assigns τ to each $c \in Y$ and agrees with ν over the rest of the clocks.

A *timed word* over an alphabet Σ is a pair (σ, τ) where $\sigma = \sigma_1\sigma_2...$ is a finite [16,17] or infinite [12] word over Σ and $\tau = \tau_1\tau_2...$ is a finite or infinite sequence of (time) values such that (i) $\tau_i \in \mathbb{R}^{\geq 0}$, (ii) $\tau_i \leq \tau_{i+1}$ for all $i \geq 1$, and (iii) if the word is infinite, then for every $t \in \mathbb{R}^{\geq 0}$ there is some $i \geq 1$ such that $\tau_i > t$.

A run ρ of $\mathcal{A}$ over a timed word (σ, τ) is a finite or infinite sequence of the form $\langle q_0, \nu_0 \rangle \xrightarrow[\tau_1]{\sigma_1} \langle q_1, \nu_1 \rangle \xrightarrow[\tau_2]{\sigma_2} \langle q_2, \nu_2 \rangle \xrightarrow[\tau_3]{\sigma_3} \dots$, where for all $i \geq 0$, $q_i \in Q$ and ν_i is a clock valuation such that (i) $\nu_0(c) = 0$ for all clocks $c \in C$ and (ii) for every $i > 1$ there is a transition in T of the form $(q_{i-1}, q_i, \sigma_i, \lambda_i, \phi_i)$, such that $(\nu_{i-1} + \tau_i - \tau_{i-1})$ satisfies ϕ_i, and ν_i equals $[\lambda_i \mapsto 0](\nu_{i-1} + \tau_i - \tau_{i-1})$.

A run over a finite timed word is *accepting* if it ends in a final location [17]. The *language* of $\mathcal{A}$, $L(\mathcal{A})$, is the set $\{(\sigma, \tau) \mid \mathcal{A}$ has an accepting run[1] over $(\sigma, \tau)\}$.

2.2   Timed Scenarios

(This subsection briefly recounts our earlier work [11,14].)

---

[1] In this work we only consider finite runs.

γ
0 : a ; 1 : b \{$\tau_{0,1} \leq 1$\} ; 2 : c ; 3 : d \{$\tau_{0,3} = 5, \tau_{2,3} \leq 2$\} .

η
0 : a ; 1 : b \{$\tau_{0,1} \leq 1$\} ; 2 : c \{$\tau_{0,2} \geq 3$\} ; 3 : d \{$\tau_{0,3} = 5$\} .

	1	2	3
0	$(0, 1)$	$(0, \infty)$	$(5,5)$
1		$(0, \infty)$	$(0, \infty)$
2			$(0, 2)$

	1	2	3
0	$(0, 1)$	$(3, 5)$	$(5, 5)$
1		$(2, 5)$	$(4, 5)$
2			$(0, 2)$

Fig. 1. Two equivalent scenarios   **Fig. 2.** γ's initial table and its stable form

Let Σ be a finite set of symbols called *events*. A *behaviour* over Σ is a sequence $(e_0, t_0)(e_1, t_1)(e_2, t_2) \ldots$, such that $e_i \in \Sigma$, $t_i \in \mathbb{R}^{\geq 0}$ and $t_{i-1} \leq t_i$ for $i \in \{1, 2 \ldots\}$. For a finite behaviour $\mathcal{B} = (e_0, t_0)(e_1, t_1) \ldots (e_{n-1}, t_{n-1})$ of length n, and for any $0 \leq i < j < n$, the *distance*, in time units, of event j from event i in $\mathcal{B}$ is denoted by $t_{ij}^{\mathcal{B}}$. That is, $t_{ij}^{\mathcal{B}} = t_j - t_i$.

A *timed scenario* (*scenario* for short) of length $n \in \mathbb{N}$ over Σ is a pair $(\mathcal{E}, \mathcal{C})$, where $\mathcal{E} = e_0 e_1 \ldots e_{n-1}$ is a sequence of events, and $\mathcal{C} \subset \Phi(n)$ is a finite set of constraints. Each constraint in $\Phi(n)$ is of the form $b \sim a$, where b is the symbol $\tau_{i,j}$ (for some integers $0 \leq i < j < n$), $\sim \in \{\leq, \geq\}$ [2] and a is a constant in the set of rational numbers, $\mathbb{Q}$. The intended interpretation is that $\tau_{i,j}$ is the time distance between the i-th and the j-th events in the behaviours described by a timed scenario.

A scenario will be written as a sequence of events, separated by semicolons and terminated by a period. If the scenario contains a constraint such as $\tau_{i,j} \sim a$, then event j in the sequence will be accompanied by the constraint. Equality will be expressed directly using $=$, rather than in terms of $\leq$ and $\geq$. We refer to this as the external representation of the scenario. Scenario γ in Fig. 1 is the external representation of scenario $(abcd, \{\tau_{0,1} \leq 1, \tau_{0,3} \geq 5, \tau_{0,3} \leq 5, \tau_{2,3} \leq 2\})$.

A behaviour $\mathcal{B} = (e_0, t_0)(e_1, t_1) \ldots (e_{n-1}, t_{n-1})$ over Σ is *allowed* by scenario $\xi = (\mathcal{E}, \mathcal{C})$ iff $\mathcal{E} = e_0 \ldots e_{n-1}$ and every $\tau_{i,j} \sim a$ in $\mathcal{C}$ evaluates to true after $\tau_{i,j}$ is replaced by $t_{ij}^{\mathcal{B}}$. If $\mathcal{B}$ is allowed by ξ, then we say $\mathcal{B}$ satisfies all constraints of ξ.

The constraints $\tau_{i,j} \geq 0$ and $\tau_{i,j} \leq \infty$, which always evaluate to true after we replace them with some $t_{ij}^{\mathcal{B}}$, will be called *default constraints*.

The *semantics* of scenario ξ, denoted by $[\![\xi]\!]$, is the set of behaviours that are allowed by ξ. For scenario γ in Fig. 1 $[\![\gamma]\!] = \{(a, t_0)(b, t_1)(c, t_2)(d, t_3) \mid t_3 \geq t_2 \geq t_1 \geq t_0 \wedge t_1 - t_0 \leq 1 \wedge t_3 - t_0 = 5 \wedge t_3 - t_2 \leq 2\}$.

A scenario ξ is *consistent* iff $[\![\xi]\!] \neq \emptyset$. It is *inconsistent* iff $[\![\xi]\!] = \emptyset$.

Two scenarios $\xi = (\mathcal{E}, \mathcal{C}_1)$ and $\eta = (\mathcal{E}, \mathcal{C}_2)$ are *equivalent* iff $[\![\xi]\!] = [\![\eta]\!]$. For example, γ and η of Fig. 1 are equivalent.

For a consistent scenario ξ of length n, and for $0 \leq i < j < n$, $m_{ij}^{\xi} = min\{t_{ij}^{\mathcal{B}} \mid \mathcal{B} \in [\![\xi]\!]\}$ and $M_{ij}^{\xi} = max\{t_{ij}^{\mathcal{B}} \mid \mathcal{B} \in [\![\xi]\!]\}$. The absence of an upper bound for some i and j will be denoted by $M_{ij}^{\xi} = \infty$. We will write just m_{ij} and M_{ij} when ξ is understood. For any behaviour in $[\![\xi]\!]$, $0 \leq m_{ij} \leq t_{ij} \leq M_{ij} \leq \infty$.

---

[2] To keep the presentation compact, sharp inequalities are not allowed [11]. Equality is expressed in terms of $\leq$ and $\geq$.

For a consistent scenario ξ of length n, and for any $0 \leq i < j < k < n$ the following inequations hold [11]:

$$m_{ij} + m_{jk} \leq m_{ik} \leq \left\{ \begin{array}{l} m_{ij} + M_{jk} \\ M_{ij} + m_{jk} \end{array} \right\} \leq M_{ik} \leq M_{ij} + M_{jk} \qquad (1)$$

Let $\xi = (\mathcal{E}, \mathcal{C})$ be a scenario of length n, such that, for any $0 \leq i < j < n$, $\mathcal{C}$ contains at most one constraint of the form $\tau_{i,j} \geq c$ and at most one of the form $\tau_{i,j} \leq c$. A *distance table* for ξ is a representation of $\mathcal{C}$ in the form of a triangular matrix $\mathcal{D}^\xi$. For $0 \leq i < j < n$, $\mathcal{D}^\xi[i,j] = (l_{ij}^\xi, h_{ij}^\xi)$, where l_{ij}^ξ and h_{ij}^ξ are rational numbers. If $\tau_{i,j} \geq c \in \mathcal{C}$ then $l_{ij}^\xi = c$, otherwise $l_{ij}^\xi = 0$; if $\tau_{i,j} \leq c \in \mathcal{C}$ then $h_{ij}^\xi = c$, otherwise $h_{ij}^\xi = \infty$. We will write just l_{ij} and h_{ij} when ξ is understood. The distance table corresponding to γ of Fig. 1 is shown on the left of Fig. 2.

A distance table of size n is *valid* iff $l_{ij} \leq h_{ij}$, for all $0 \leq i < j < n$. A table that is not valid is *invalid*. If $\mathcal{D}^\xi$ is invalid, then ξ is obviously inconsistent.

A valid distance table of size n is *stable* iff, for all $0 \leq i < j < k < n$, the inequations in (1) hold when m_{ij}, m_{jk}, m_{ik} are replaced by l_{ij}, l_{jk}, l_{ik} and M_{ij}, M_{jk}, M_{ik} are replaced by h_{ij}, h_{jk}, h_{ik}. If $\mathcal{D}^\xi$ is stable then ξ is consistent.

To *stabilize* $\mathcal{D}^\xi$ the following six rules are repeatedly applied until the table becomes either invalid or stable[3] [11]. The stabilized table is denoted by $\mathcal{D}_s^\xi$.

$$l_{ij} + l_{jk} > l_{ik} \longrightarrow l_{ik} := l_{ij} + l_{jk} \qquad l_{ik} > l_{ij} + h_{jk} \longrightarrow l_{ij} := l_{ik} - h_{jk}$$

$$l_{ik} > h_{ij} + l_{jk} \longrightarrow l_{jk} := l_{ik} - h_{ij} \qquad l_{ij} + h_{jk} > h_{ik} \longrightarrow h_{jk} := h_{ik} - l_{ij}$$

$$h_{ij} + l_{jk} > h_{ik} \longrightarrow h_{ij} := h_{ik} - l_{jk} \qquad h_{ik} > h_{ij} + h_{jk} \longrightarrow h_{ik} := h_{ij} + h_{jk}$$

At least one of these rules is applicable if and only if some inequation in (1) does not hold. The purpose of each rule is to tighten a constraint just enough to establish a particular inequation. A stable distance table[4] has two properties. First, as a result of applying the rules above, the table includes all the constraints that are implied (see definitions 1 and 2) by the initial set of constraints. Second, all the constraints represented by the table are as *tight* as possible:

Observation 1. *Let ξ be a scenario of length n. If $\mathcal{D}_s^\xi$ is its stable table, then for every $0 \leq i < j < n$, $l_{ij} = m_{ij}$ and $h_{ij} = M_{ij}$, that is, $\mathcal{D}_s^\xi[i,j] = (m_{ij}^\xi, M_{ij}^\xi)$.*

$\mathcal{D}_s^\xi[i,j]$ specifies the set of all the possible values of t_{ij} that can appear in the behaviours allowed by the corresponding scenario.

Two scenarios ξ and η are equivalent iff $\mathcal{D}_s^\xi = \mathcal{D}_s^\eta$. The table on the right-hand side of Fig. 2 is the stable distance table obtained from the constraints of either γ or η (which shows that they are equivalent: $[\![\gamma]\!] = [\![\eta]\!]$).

---

[3] The cost is $O(n^3)$, where n is the length of the scenario [11].

[4] The stable distance tables, though derived in a very different fashion, turned out to be essentially equivalent to Dill's Difference Bounds Matrices (DBMs) [18]. However, when applied to the particular case of scenarios, the constraint reduction technique for DBMs [19] is weaker than our optimisation algorithms [14,15]. A detailed comparison can be found in our earlier work [14].

Given a scenario ξ with its stable distance table $\mathcal{D}_s^\xi$, we use $\mathcal{C}(\mathcal{D}_s^\xi)$ to denote the set of constraints represented by $\mathcal{D}_s^\xi$.

Definition 1. *Let ξ be a scenario of length n, $\mathcal{D}_s^\xi$ be its stable table, $c \in \mathcal{C}(\mathcal{D}_s^\xi)$ be a non-default constraint, $S \subset \mathcal{C}(\mathcal{D}_s^\xi)$, and $0 \le i < j < k < n$. Constraint c is directly supported by S, denoted by $S \rightsquigarrow c$, iff c and S satisfy one of the following six conditions:*

1. $c = \tau_{i,k} \ge u$, $S = \{\tau_{i,j} \ge v, \tau_{j,k} \ge w\}$, and $u = v + w$.
2. $c = \tau_{i,j} \ge u$, $S = \{\tau_{i,k} \ge v, \tau_{j,k} \le w\}$, and $u = v - w$.
3. $c = \tau_{j,k} \ge u$, $S = \{\tau_{i,k} \ge v, \tau_{i,j} \le w\}$, and $u = v - w$.
4. $c = \tau_{j,k} \le u$, $S = \{\tau_{i,k} \le v, \tau_{i,j} \ge w\}$, and $u = v - w$.
5. $c = \tau_{i,j} \le u$, $S = \{\tau_{i,k} \le v, \tau_{j,k} \ge w\}$, and $u = v - w$.
6. $c = \tau_{i,k} \le u$, $S = \{\tau_{i,j} \le v, \tau_{j,k} \le w\}$, and $u = v + w$.

Each of the cases in Definition 1 corresponds to one of the six rules of stabilization mentioned before. For example, if $m_{13} = 3$, $M_{36} = 4$ and $m_{16} = 0$ (i.e., the corresponding constraint is missing), then the first rule will force m_{16} to be 7: the constraint $m_{16} = 7$ is directly supported by the other two.

Definition 2. *(quasi-transitivity) Let $\mathcal{D}_s^\xi$ be a stable table. $\rightsquigarrow^+ \subset 2^{\mathcal{C}(\mathcal{D}_s^\xi)} \times \mathcal{C}(\mathcal{D}_s^\xi)$ is the smallest relation that satisfies the following two conditions:*

1. *If $S \rightsquigarrow c$ then $S \rightsquigarrow^+ c$;*
2. *If $S \rightsquigarrow^+ c$ and there is a constraint $d \in S$ such that, for some $S' \in \mathcal{C}(\mathcal{D}_s^\xi)$, $S' \rightsquigarrow^+ d$ and $c \notin S'$, then $(S \setminus \{d\}) \cup S' \rightsquigarrow^+ c$.*

Constraint c is supported by S when $S \rightsquigarrow^+ c$. S is then called a support of c.

If $S \rightsquigarrow^+ c$, then we say that c is implied by S.

Intuitively, if a constraint d has a support, then d can be removed from the scenario. The removed d can be a member of the supports of other constraints, e.g., d can appear in a set S that supports c. As long as d has a support S' that does not include c, S can be updated by replacing d with S'. The relation $\rightsquigarrow^+$ captures all the possible supports for the constraints in $\mathcal{C}(\mathcal{D}_s^\xi)$.

Observation 2. *If $S \rightsquigarrow^+ c$, then $c \notin S$.*

Observation 3. *Let $S \rightsquigarrow^+ c$. If behaviour $\mathcal{B}$ satisfies all the constraints in S, then it also satisfies c.*

2.3   Timed Scenarios and Timed Automata

If $\xi = (\mathcal{E}, \mathcal{C})$ is a scenario of length n, and $\mathcal{C}$ contains a constraint $\tau_{i,j} \sim a$ for some $0 \le i < j < n$, and some $a \in \mathbb{Q}$, then the index i is an *anchor*. For an anchor i, if $0 < j < n$ is the largest number such that $\tau_{i,j} \sim a$ is a constraint in $\mathcal{C}$, then $[i, j)$ is the *range* of anchor i. If i_1 and i_2 are two anchors with ranges $[i_1, j_1)$ and $[i_2, j_2)$ in ξ, then the two ranges *overlap* iff $i_1 < i_2 < j_1$ or $i_2 < i_1 < j_2$.

For example, in scenario γ of Fig. 1, the range of anchor 0 is $[0, 3)$ and the range of anchor 2 is $[2, 3)$: these are overlapping.

Fig. 3. Equivalent timed automata corresponding to the scenarios of Fig. 1

$Anch_\xi$ is used to denote the set of anchors of ξ. If X is a set of clock variables, then the relation $alloc_\xi \subset Anch_\xi \times X$ is a clock allocation for ξ. $alloc_\xi$ is *complete* iff for every anchor $i \in Anch_\xi$ there is a clock $x \in X$ such that $(i,x) \in alloc_\xi$. $alloc_\xi$ is *incorrect* iff there exist two different anchors i and j in $Anch_\xi$ whose ranges overlap, such that $(i,x) \in alloc_\xi$ and $(j,x) \in alloc_\xi$ for some $x \in X$. $alloc_\xi$ is *correct* iff it is not incorrect. A correct and complete clock allocation is *optimal* if there is no other correct and complete allocation that uses fewer clocks. $\{(0,x),(2,y)\}$ is an optimal clock allocation for scenario γ of Fig. 1.

A scenario ξ can be trivially converted to a simple timed automaton $\mathcal{A}_\xi$: the language of $\mathcal{A}_\xi$ is equivalent to the set of behaviours allowed by ξ: $L(\mathcal{A}_\xi) = [\![\xi]\!]$.

A scenario ξ, can be transformed to an equivalent scenario η, by optimizing its set of constraints [15], so that (i) η has a minimal set of constraints[5], and (ii) $\mathcal{A}_\eta$ has the *minimal* number of clocks in the entire class of timed automata obtained from all scenarios equivalent to ξ. We call η the *optimized* form of ξ.

For example, scenario η of Fig. 1 is the optimized form of γ in that figure. Their corresponding language-equivalent timed automata are shown in Fig. 3. Notice that $\mathcal{A}_\eta$ has only one clock, while $\mathcal{A}_\gamma$ requires two clocks.

3   Operations on Scenarios and the Synthesis Problem

In this section we briefly present the motivation behind developing the notions of *subsumption*, *intersection*, and *union* for timed scenarios.

Given a finite set $\varXi$ of scenarios, our ultimate goal is to synthesize a timed automaton $\mathcal{A}_\varXi$ whose language would be $\bigcup_{\xi \in \varXi}[\![\xi]\!]$[6]. We want $\mathcal{A}_\varXi$ to have the minimal number of clocks in the entire class of language-equivalent timed automata.

Let $\varXi_o$ be the set of optimized scenarios obtained from the members of $\varXi$. Let $\varGamma_\mathcal{E} = \{(\mathcal{E},\mathcal{C}^0),(\mathcal{E},\mathcal{C}^1),...\} \subseteq \varXi_o$, i.e., the set of those members of $\varXi_o$ that have $\mathcal{E}$ as their sequence of events. The members of $\varGamma_\mathcal{E}$ may be involved in interesting relationships that may have a bearing on the best way to reach our goal.

Subsumption. If $\varGamma_\mathcal{E}$ contains two scenarios ξ and η, such that $[\![\xi]\!] \subseteq [\![\eta]\!]$, then ξ can be removed from $\varXi$. This cannot increase the number of clocks in $\mathcal{A}_\varXi$, but may decrease it, so such subsumed scenarios should always be removed.

For example, consider scenarios ξ and γ of Fig. 4. Notice that $[\![\xi]\!] \subseteq [\![\gamma]\!]$, that is, ξ is subsumed by γ (see Definition 4 in Sec. 4). So ξ can be removed from $\varXi$.

---

[5] That is, a constraint cannot be removed without changing the semantics.

[6] The complete account of the synthesis problem is addressed in a forthcoming paper.

$$\xi \quad \begin{array}{|l|} \hline 0:a\;; \\ 1:b\;; \\ 2:c\,\{\tau_{1,2}\le 5\}\;; \\ 3:d\,\{\tau_{0,3}\ge 7\}\;. \\ \hline \end{array} \qquad \eta \quad \begin{array}{|l|} \hline 0:a\;; \\ 1:b\;; \\ 2:c\,\{\tau_{1,2}\ge 5\}\;; \\ 3:d\,\{\tau_{0,3}\ge 7\}\;. \\ \hline \end{array} \qquad \gamma \quad \begin{array}{|l|} \hline 0:a\;; \\ 1:b\;; \\ 2:c\;; \\ 3:d\,\{\tau_{0,3}\ge 7\}\;. \\ \hline \end{array}$$

Fig. 4. Two scenarios ξ and η with complementary constraints, and their combination

This removal will result in a reduction in the number of clocks in the synthesized automaton: the two anchors in ξ have overlapping ranges, so $\mathcal{A}_\xi$ would require two clocks, but $\mathcal{A}_\gamma$ would only require one clock.

Union. The set $\Gamma_\mathcal{E}$ may contain a subset S, such that $|S| > 1$, but all its members can be replaced by a single scenario. More precisely, there may exist a scenario η such that $[\![\eta]\!] = \bigcup_{\xi \in S}[\![\xi]\!]$. We then say that the members of S can be *combined*. Combining scenarios can, in general, result in a reduction in the number of clocks in the synthesized automaton. We discuss this for a very simple case.

Let $\xi = (\mathcal{E}, \mathcal{C}^\xi)$ and $\eta = (\mathcal{E}, \mathcal{C}^\eta)$ in $\Gamma_\mathcal{E}$ be such that they can be combined into one scenario. Let the scenarios contain a pair of explicit constraints that are complementary, i.e., for some i, j and a we have $\tau_{i,j} \le a \in \mathcal{C}^\xi$ and $\tau_{i,j} \ge a \in \mathcal{C}^\eta$. Then in the combined scenario (see Definition 6 in Sec. 4) the only constraints on $\tau_{i,j}$ will be implicit default constraints.

As an example consider scenarios ξ and η of Fig. 4. These two scenarios can be combined: $[\![\xi]\!] \cup [\![\eta]\!]$ is captured by scenario γ in that figure. That is, ξ and η can be replaced by γ in Ξ. Notice that ξ and η each have two anchors 0 and 1 whose ranges overlap. Therefore $\mathcal{A}_\xi$ and $\mathcal{A}_\eta$ each would require two clocks. So the number of clocks in the automaton synthesized from ξ and η cannot be smaller than 2. However, a language-equivalent automaton synthesized from γ would require only one clock: by combining ξ and η we got rid of the pair of complementary constraints, (i.e., $\tau_{1,2} \le 5$ and $\tau_{1,2} \ge 5$) and thus of anchor 1.

In general, there are two situations where combining scenarios results in a reduction in the number of clocks in a synthesized automaton. One is when an anchor i disapears entirely, and another when the number of ranges that overlap with the range of i decreases.

So before we begin the synthesis process we should try to combine scenarios with identical sequences of events.

Intersection. $\Gamma_\mathcal{E}$ might contain two scenarios ξ and η, such that $[\![\xi]\!] \cap [\![\eta]\!] \ne \emptyset$. In that case, the intersection can be expressed by a timed scenario.

Computing the intersection of a set of scenarios is not directly relevant to our task, but will be useful in computing their union (see Sec. 4 for details).

Next, we formally define these three operations.

4 Subsumption, Intersection and Union

For a given scenario $\xi = (\mathcal{E}, \mathcal{C})$ the members of $\mathcal{C}$ will be referred to as *explicit constraints*. We know that in the stable distance table, $\mathcal{D}_s^\xi$, there are also *implicit* constraints: default constraints and constraints that are implied by $\mathcal{C}$.

Definition 3. *Let ξ be a scenario of length n and let $\mathcal{D}_s^\xi$ be its stable distance table. Then, for any $0 \le i < j < n$, the interval I_{ij}^ξ is $\{a \in \mathbb{Q} \mid m_{ij}^\xi \le a \le M_{ij}^\xi\}$ where $\mathcal{D}_s^\xi[i,j] = (m_{ij}^\xi, M_{ij}^\xi)$.*

Intuitively, I_{ij}^ξ corresponds to a pair of constraints: the time distance between events i and j in every behaviour in $[\![\xi]\!]$ must be at least m_{ij}^ξ and at most M_{ij}^ξ.

Definition 4. *Let ξ and η be two consistent scenarios with the same sequence of events. We say ξ is subsumed by η, denoted by $\xi \sqsubseteq \eta$, when $[\![\xi]\!] \subseteq [\![\eta]\!]$.*

Observation 4. *Let ξ and η be two consistent scenarios of length n with the same sequence of events. Then $\xi \sqsubseteq \eta$ iff $\forall_{0 \le i < j < n} I_{ij}^\xi \subseteq I_{ij}^\eta$.*

Thanks to Observation 4, it can be easily checked, in quadratic time, whether a scenario is subsumed by another one.

Definition 5. *Let ξ and η be two consistent scenarios of length n with the same sequence of events, $\mathcal{E}$, such that $\forall_{0 \le i < j < n} I_{ij}^\xi \cap I_{ij}^\eta \ne \emptyset$. The intersection of ξ and η, denoted by $\xi \cap \eta$, is a scenario whose sequence of events is $\mathcal{E}$ and whose constraints are given by $\mathcal{D}^{\xi \cap \eta}$, where $\mathcal{D}^{\xi \cap \eta}[i,j] = (\max(m_{ij}^\xi, m_{ij}^\eta), \min(M_{ij}^\xi, M_{ij}^\eta))$.*

If $\exists_{0 \le k < l < n} I_{kl}^\xi \cap I_{kl}^\eta = \emptyset$, then $\xi \cap \eta$ is not defined.

Assume $\mathcal{D}_s^\xi[i,j] = (a_1, b_1)$, $\mathcal{D}_s^\eta[i,j] = (a_2, b_2)$, and $\xi \cap \eta$ is defined. Then $\mathcal{D}^{\xi \cap \eta}[i,j] = (l_{ij}^{\xi \cap \eta}, h_{ij}^{\xi \cap \eta}) = (\max(a_1, a_2), \min(b_1, b_2))$. Since $I_{ij}^\xi \cap I_{ij}^\eta \ne \emptyset$, we have $\max(a_1, a_2) \le \min(b_1, b_2)$. So the initial table is always valid. But it might not be stable, so we must stabilise it to check whether $\xi \cap \eta$ is consistent. In the resulting stable table $l_{ij}^{\xi \cap \eta} \le m_{ij}^{\xi \cap \eta} \le M_{ij}^{\xi \cap \eta} \le h_{ij}^\xi$ for every $0 \le i < j < n$, because stabilisation only tightens the constraints.

Figures 5 and 6 show two scenarios, ξ and η, along with their stable distance tables. Observe that $I_{ij}^\xi \cap I_{ij}^\eta \ne \emptyset$, for $0 \le i < j \le 2$. Figure 7 shows the initial table corresponding to their intersection and its stabilized form.

Lemma 1. *Let ξ and η be two consistent scenarios such that $[\![\xi]\!] \cap [\![\eta]\!] \ne \emptyset$. Then the scenario $\xi \cap \eta$ is defined and consistent. Moreover, $[\![\xi]\!] \cap [\![\eta]\!] \subseteq [\![\xi \cap \eta]\!]$.*

Proof. Let $\mathcal{B} \in [\![\xi]\!] \cap [\![\eta]\!]$. Then

$\forall_{0 \le i < j < n} t_{ij}^{\mathcal{B}} \le M_{ij}^\xi \wedge t_{ij}^{\mathcal{B}} \le M_{ij}^\eta$. So $t_{ij}^{\mathcal{B}} \le \min(M_{ij}^\xi, M_{ij}^\eta)$.

$\forall_{0 \le i < j < n} t_{ij}^{\mathcal{B}} \ge m_{ij}^\xi \wedge t_{ij}^{\mathcal{B}} \ge m_{ij}^\eta$. So $t_{ij}^{\mathcal{B}} \ge \max(m_{ij}^\xi, m_{ij}^\eta)$.

Therefore $\forall_{0 \le i < j < n} \max(m_{ij}^\xi, m_{ij}^\eta) \le \min(M_{ij}^\xi, M_{ij}^\eta)$. So $\xi \cap \eta$ is defined.

Behaviour $\mathcal{B}$ satisfies all the constraints represented by the initial table of $\xi \cap \eta$, i.e., $\mathcal{D}^{\xi \cap \eta}$ (see Definition 5). Stabilization does not remove any behaviour, so $\mathcal{B}$ satisfies also all the constraints represented by $\mathcal{D}_s^{\xi \cap \eta}$. That is, $\mathcal{B} \in [\![\xi \cap \eta]\!]$. Therefore $[\![\xi \cap \eta]\!] \ne \emptyset$, and hence $\xi \cap \eta$ is consistent. Moreover, $[\![\xi]\!] \cap [\![\eta]\!] \subseteq [\![\xi \cap \eta]\!]$. $\qquad \square$

$0 : a$;
$1 : b \ \{\tau_{0,1} \leq 2\}$;
$2 : c \ \{\tau_{0,2} \geq 5\}$.

	1	2
0	$(0,2)$	$(5,\infty)$
1		$(3,\infty)$

Fig. 5. ξ and its stable distance table

$0 : a$;
$1 : b$;
$2 : c \ \{\tau_{1,2} =< 3\}$.

	1	2
0	$(0,\infty)$	$(0,\infty)$
1		$(0,3)$

Fig. 6. η and its stable distance table

	1	2
0	$(0,2)$	$(5,\infty)$
1		$(3,3)$

	1	2
0	$(2,2)$	$(5,5)$
1		$(3,3)$

Fig. 7. The initial table and its stabilized form for $\xi \cap \eta$

$0 : a$;
$1 : b \ \{\tau_{0,1} = 2\}$;
$2 : c \ \{\tau_{1,2} = 3\}$.

Fig. 8. $\xi \cap \eta$

Theorem 1. *Let ξ and η be two consistent scenarios such that $\xi \cap \eta$ is defined and consistent. Then $[\![\xi \cap \eta]\!] = [\![\xi]\!] \cap [\![\eta]\!]$.*

Proof. Assume the length of ξ and η is n, and let $\mathcal{B} \in [\![\xi \cap \eta]\!]$. Then
$$\forall_{0 \leq i < j < n} \ t_{ij}^{\mathcal{B}} \geq m_{ij}^{\xi \cap \eta} \geq l_{ij}^{\xi \cap \eta} = \max(m_{ij}^{\xi}, m_{ij}^{\eta}). \text{ So } t_{ij}^{\mathcal{B}} \geq m_{ij}^{\xi} \text{ and } t_{ij}^{\mathcal{B}} \geq m_{ij}^{\eta}.$$
$$\forall_{0 \leq i < j < n} \ t_{ij}^{\mathcal{B}} \leq M_{ij}^{\xi \cap \eta} \leq h_{ij}^{\xi \cap \eta} = \min(M_{ij}^{\xi}, M_{ij}^{\eta}). \text{ So } t_{ij}^{\mathcal{B}} \leq M_{ij}^{\xi} \text{ and } t_{ij}^{\mathcal{B}} \leq M_{ij}^{\eta}.$$
Therefore $\mathcal{B} \in [\![\xi]\!]$ and $\mathcal{B} \in [\![\eta]\!]$, that is, $\mathcal{B} \in [\![\xi]\!] \cap [\![\eta]\!]$. So $[\![\xi \cap \eta]\!] \subseteq [\![\xi]\!] \cap [\![\eta]\!]$.

Since $[\![\xi \cap \eta]\!] \neq \emptyset$, it follows that $[\![\xi]\!] \cap [\![\eta]\!] \neq \emptyset$ and, by Lemma 1, $[\![\xi]\!] \cap [\![\eta]\!] \subseteq [\![\xi \cap \eta]\!]$. So $[\![\xi \cap \eta]\!] = [\![\xi]\!] \cap [\![\eta]\!]$. □

Consider ξ and η of Figs. 5 and 6 once more. A simple analysis shows that in the set of behaviours that are allowed by both ξ and η the time distance between a and b, and between b and c must be exactly 2 and 3, respectively. Indeed, this is captured by scenario $\xi \cap \eta$, shown in Fig. 8, which is obtained from the stabilized table of Fig. 7.

Definition 6. *Let ξ and η be two consistent scenarios of length n with the same sequence of events, $\mathcal{E}$, such that $\forall_{0 \leq i < j < n} \ I_{ij}^{\xi} \cap I_{ij}^{\eta} \neq \emptyset$. The combination of ξ and η, denoted by $\xi \uplus \eta$, is a scenario whose sequence of events is $\mathcal{E}$ and whose constraints are given by $\mathcal{D}^{\xi \uplus \eta}$, where $\mathcal{D}^{\xi \uplus \eta}[i,j] = (\min(m_{ij}^{\xi}, m_{ij}^{\eta}), \max(M_{ij}^{\xi}, M_{ij}^{\eta}))$.*

If $\exists_{0 \leq i < j < n} \ I_{ij}^{\xi} \cap I_{ij}^{\eta} = \emptyset$, then $I_{ij}^{\xi} \cup I_{ij}^{\eta}$ does not constitute a single interval. In that case ξ and η cannot be combined, and so $\xi \uplus \eta$ is not defined.

Let $\mathcal{D}_s^{\xi}[i,j] = (a_1, b_1)$, $\mathcal{D}_s^{\eta}[i,j] = (a_2, b_2)$, and assume $\xi \uplus \eta$ is defined. Then $\mathcal{D}^{\xi \uplus \eta}[i,j] = (l_{ij}^{\xi \uplus \eta}, h_{ij}^{\xi \uplus \eta}) = (\min(a_1, a_2), \max(b_1, b_2))$. Clearly, $\mathcal{D}^{\xi \uplus \eta}$ is stable, since all the inequations in 1 are satisfied by its contents:

Observation 5. *If $\xi \uplus \eta$ is defined, then $\mathcal{D}^{\xi \uplus \eta} = \mathcal{D}_s^{\xi \uplus \eta}$. So $\xi \uplus \eta$ is consistent.*

Lemma 2. *Let ξ and η be two consistent scenarios such that $\xi \uplus \eta$ is defined. Then $[\![\xi]\!] \cup [\![\eta]\!] \subseteq [\![\xi \uplus \eta]\!]$.*

Proof. ξ is consistent, so $[\![\xi]\!] \neq \emptyset$. Let $\mathcal{B} \in [\![\xi]\!]$. Then
$$\forall_{0 \leq i < j < n} \ t_{ij}^{\mathcal{B}} \geq m_{ij}^{\xi} \geq \min(m_{ij}^{\xi}, m_{ij}^{\eta}) = l_{ij}^{\xi \uplus \eta}, \text{ and}$$

ξ	0 : a ; 1 : b $\{\tau_{0,1} \leq 4\}$; 2 : c .		1	2
		0	(0, 4)	(0, ∞)
		1		(0, ∞)

η	0 : a ; 1 : b ; 2 : c $\{\tau_{0,2} \geq 7\}$.		1	2
		0	(0, ∞)	(7, ∞)
		1		(0, ∞)

Fig. 9. Two scenarios, ξ and η, and their stable tables

γ	0 : a ; 1 : b ; 2 : c .		1	2
		0	(0, ∞)	(0, ∞)
		1		(0, ∞)

ζ	0 : a ; 1 : b $\{\tau_{0,1} = 5\}$; 2 : c $\{\tau_{0,2} = 6\}$.		1	2
		0	(5, 5)	(6, 6)
		1		(1, 1)

Fig. 10. The combination of ξ and η of Fig. 9, and scenario ζ with its stabilized table

$$\forall_{0 \leq i < j < n} \ t^{\mathcal{B}}_{ij} \leq M^{\xi}_{ij} \leq \max(M^{\xi}_{ij}, M^{\eta}_{ij}) = h^{\xi \uplus \eta}_{ij}.$$

Then $t^{\mathcal{B}}_{ij} \in I^{\xi \uplus \eta}_{ij}$. Therefore $\mathcal{B}$ satisfies all the constraints represented by $\mathcal{D}^{\xi \uplus \eta}$, which is stable by Observation 5. So $\mathcal{B} \in [\![\xi \uplus \eta]\!]$. Therefore $[\![\xi]\!] \cup [\![\eta]\!] \subseteq [\![\xi \uplus \eta]\!]$.

A similar argument can be made if $\mathcal{B} \in [\![\eta]\!]$. $\qquad\square$

Table $\mathcal{D}^{\xi \uplus \eta}_s$ allows all the behaviours in $[\![\xi]\!] \cup [\![\eta]\!]$. But there is a possibility that it may also allow some extra behaviours, namely those that satisfy all the constraints of the combination, but do not satisfy some of the constraints in ξ and some of the constraints in η.

Observation 6. Let ξ and η be two consistent scenarios such that $\xi \uplus \eta$ is defined. Then $[\![\xi \uplus \eta]\!] = [\![\xi]\!] \cup [\![\eta]\!] \cup \mathcal{Z}(\xi, \eta)$, where $[\![\xi]\!] \cap \mathcal{Z}(\xi, \eta) = \emptyset$ and $[\![\eta]\!] \cap \mathcal{Z}(\xi, \eta) = \emptyset$.

Observation 6 effectively defines $\mathcal{Z}(\xi, \eta)$. We call members of $\mathcal{Z}(\xi, \eta)$ *zigzagging* behaviours. Our goal is to charcterize the conditions under which $\mathcal{Z}(\xi, \eta) = \emptyset$.

It is not too difficult to find such zigzagging behaviours, if they exist. We discuss this for the case of combining two scenarios ξ and η into a scenario γ.

We identify a value $\alpha \in I^{\xi}_{ij}$ such that $\alpha \notin I^{\eta}_{ij}$, and a value $\beta \in I^{\eta}_{kl}$ ($i \neq k$ or $j \neq l$) such that $\beta \notin I^{\xi}_{kl}$. We then construct a scenario ζ with the same sequence of events as ξ and η, and the constraints $\{\tau_{i,j} = \alpha, \tau_{k,l} = \beta\}$. If ζ is consistent, we compute its intersection with γ. If the intersection is not empty, then γ is too permissive, since none of the behaviours allowed by ζ is allowed by ξ or η.

As an example consider two scenarios, ξ and η, of Fig. 9 along with their stable tables. Scenario γ of Fig. 10 shows the combined scenario along with its stable table. Scenario ζ of Fig. 10 represents a set of behaviours in which the time distance between events a and b is exactly 5, and between events a and c is exactly 6 units of time. There is no behaviour in the semantics of ζ that is allowed by either ξ or η of Fig. 9. Yet its intersection with γ (the combination of ξ and η) is not empty. *This indicates that the union of the sets of behaviours allowed by ξ and η cannot be represented by a single scenario.*

$0 : a$; $1 : b$; $2 : c \{\tau_{0,2} \geq 1, \tau_{0,2} \leq 6\}$; $3 : d$; $4 : e \{\tau_{1,4} \leq 8\}$.

ξ

$0 : a$; $1 : b$; $2 : c \{\tau_{0,2} \geq 4, \tau_{0,2} \leq 9\}$; $3 : d$; $4 : e \{\tau_{1,4} \leq 8\}$.

η

$0 : a$; $1 : b$; $2 : c \{\tau_{0,2} \geq 1, \tau_{0,2} \leq 9\}$; $3 : d$; $4 : e \{\tau_{1,4} \leq 8\}$.

$\xi \uplus \eta$

Fig. 11. Two scenarios that can be combined

As another example consider ξ and η of Fig. 11 where the union of behaviours allowed by ξ and η *can be* represented by a single scenario, namely their combination (see the scenario on the right). That is, no zigzagging behaviour is allowed by $\xi \uplus \eta$: every behaviour in $[\![\xi \uplus \eta]\!]$ is in $[\![\xi]\!]$ or in $[\![\eta]\!]$ or in both.

The union of two scenarios ξ and η can be expressed by a single scenario, namely their combination, if there are no zigzagging behaviours possible between ξ and η, i.e., $\mathcal{Z}(\xi, \eta) = \emptyset$.

Theorem 2. *Let ξ and η be two consistent scenarios of length n with the same sequence of events, $\mathcal{E}$, such that $\xi \uplus \eta$ is defined. Behaviour $\mathcal{B}^z$ with the sequence of events $\mathcal{E}$ belongs to $\mathcal{Z}(\xi, \eta)$ iff*

1. *For every $0 \leq i < j < n$, $t_{ij}^{\mathcal{B}^z} \in I_{ij}^{\xi \uplus \eta}$,*
2. *There exist $0 \leq i < j < n$ and $0 \leq k < l < n$ such that*
   (a) *$i \neq k$ or $j \neq l$, and*
   (b) *$t_{ij}^{\mathcal{B}^z} \notin I_{ij}^{\xi}$, $t_{ij}^{\mathcal{B}^z} \in I_{ij}^{\eta}$, and*
   (c) *$t_{kl}^{\mathcal{B}^z} \in I_{kl}^{\xi}$, $t_{kl}^{\mathcal{B}^z} \notin I_{kl}^{\eta}$.*

Proof. Let $\mathcal{B}^z \in Z(\xi, \eta)$. Then, by Observation 6, $\mathcal{B}^z \in [\![\xi \uplus \eta]\!]$. Therefore, for every $0 \leq i < j < n$, $t_{ij}^{\mathcal{B}^z} \in I_{ij}^{\xi \uplus \eta}$.

$\mathcal{B}^z \in Z(\xi, \eta)$, so, by Observation 6, $\mathcal{B}^z \notin [\![\xi]\!]$. Therefore there must be some constraint in ξ that is not satisfied by $\mathcal{B}^z$. So there exist some $0 \leq i < j < n$ such that $t_{ij}^{\mathcal{B}^z} \notin I_{ij}^{\xi}$. Therefore $t_{ij}^{\mathcal{B}^z} \in I_{ij}^{\eta}$.

$\mathcal{B}^z \notin [\![\eta]\!]$, so by a similar argument it can be shown that there exist some $0 \leq k < l < n$ such that $t_{kl}^{\mathcal{B}^z} \notin I_{kl}^{\eta}$ and $t_{kl}^{\mathcal{B}^z} \in I_{kl}^{\xi}$.

If $i = k$ and $j = l$, then $t_{ij}^{\mathcal{B}^z} \notin I_{ij}^{\xi}$ and $t_{kl}^{\mathcal{B}^z} \in I_{kl}^{\xi}$, which is a contradiction.

For the other direction, let $\mathcal{B}^z$ be a behaviour that satisfies conditions 1 and 2. Then $\mathcal{B}^z \in [\![\xi \uplus \eta]\!]$, but $\mathcal{B}^z \notin [\![\xi]\!]$ and $\mathcal{B}^z \notin [\![\xi]\!]$. So, by Observation 6, $\mathcal{B}^z \in \mathcal{Z}(\xi, \eta)$. □

In the rest of the paper when we write $ij \neq kl$, we mean $i \neq k \vee j \neq l$.

Observation 7. *Let ξ and η be two consistent scenarios. $\xi \subseteq \eta$ iff $\xi \uplus \eta = \eta$.*

Definition 7. *A scenario $\xi = (\mathcal{E}, \mathcal{C})$ is trivial if $\mathcal{C} = \emptyset$. ξ is non-trivial if it is not trivial.*

Intuitively, all the constraints of a trivial scenario are default constraints. For instance, scenario γ of Fig. 10 is trivial.

Observation 8. *Let ξ and η be two consistent scenarios with the same sequence of events. If ξ is trivial, then $\xi \cap \eta = \eta$ and $\xi \uplus \eta = \xi$.*

Lemma 3. *Let ξ and η be two consistent scenarios. If $\mathcal{Z}(\xi, \eta) \neq \emptyset$, then neither ξ nor η is trivial.*

Proof. Assume ξ is trivial. Then, by Observation 8, $\xi \uplus \eta = \xi$.

Let $\mathcal{B}^z \in \mathcal{Z}(\xi, \eta)$. By Observation 6, $\mathcal{B}^z \notin [\![\xi]\!]$. So $\mathcal{B}^z \notin [\![\xi \uplus \eta]\!]$. But this is contradictory to Observation 6.

By a similar argument it can be shown that η is not trivial.

$\square$

The consequence of Lemma 3 is that if $\mathcal{Z}(\xi, \eta)$ is not empty, then ξ and η must each have at least one *explicit* constraint.

Lemma 4. *Let ξ and η be two consistent scenarios. If $\mathcal{Z}(\xi, \eta) \neq \emptyset$, then $\xi \not\subseteq \eta$ and $\eta \not\subseteq \xi$.*

Proof. Assume $\xi \subseteq \eta$ or $\eta \subseteq \xi$.

Let $\mathcal{B}^z$ be a behaviour in $\mathcal{Z}(\xi, \eta)$. By Observation 6, $\mathcal{B}^z \notin [\![\xi]\!]$, and $\mathcal{B}^z \notin [\![\eta]\!]$.

If $\eta \subseteq \xi$, then by Observation 7, $\xi \uplus \eta = \xi$. So $\mathcal{B}^z \notin [\![\xi \uplus \eta]\!]$: a contradiction.

If $\xi \subseteq \eta$, then we can show a contradiction by a similar argument. $\square$

We will now examine ways of determining whether $\mathcal{Z}(\xi, \eta) \neq \emptyset$. This will be important for Observation 10 at the end of this section.

Lemma 5. *Let $\xi = (\mathcal{E}, \mathcal{C}_1)$ and $\eta = (\mathcal{E}, \mathcal{C}_2)$ be two optimized (see Sec. 2) scenarios. If $\mathcal{Z}(\xi, \eta) \neq \emptyset$, then there must be $c_1 \in \mathcal{C}_1$ and $c_2 \in \mathcal{C}_2$, such that $c_1 \notin \mathcal{C}_2$ and $c_2 \notin \mathcal{C}_1$.*

Proof. By Lemma 3, ξ and η are not trivial. That is, $\mathcal{C}_1 \neq \emptyset$ and $\mathcal{C}_2 \neq \emptyset$. Assume that every constraint in $\mathcal{C}_1$ is also in $\mathcal{C}_2$, or every constraint in $\mathcal{C}_2$ is also in $\mathcal{C}_1$. Then $\eta \subseteq \xi$ or $\xi \subseteq \eta$. Then, by Lemma 4, $\mathcal{Z}(\xi, \eta) = \emptyset$. But this is a contradiction. $\square$

Lemma 6. *Let $\xi = (\mathcal{E}, \mathcal{C}_1)$ and $\eta = (\mathcal{E}, \mathcal{C}_2)$ be two optimized scenarios of length n, such that $\xi \uplus \eta$ is defined and $\mathcal{Z}(\xi, \eta) \neq \emptyset$.*

If $\forall_{c_1 = \tau_{i,j} \sim a \in \mathcal{C}_1} \forall_{c_2 = \tau_{k,l} \sim b \in \mathcal{C}_2} (c_1 \in \mathcal{C}_2 \ \lor \ c_2 \in \mathcal{C}_1 \ \lor \ (i = k \land j = l))$, then there exists $0 \leq u < v < n$ such that every constraint in $\mathcal{C}_1 \setminus \mathcal{C}_2$ and every constraint in $\mathcal{C}_2 \setminus \mathcal{C}_1$ is between u and v (i.e., it is of the form $\tau_{u,v} \sim d$).

Proof. By Lemma 5, $\mathcal{C}_1 \setminus \mathcal{C}_2 \neq \emptyset$ and $\mathcal{C}_2 \setminus \mathcal{C}_1 \neq \emptyset$. Let c_1 be a constraint for some $\tau_{p,q}$ $(0 \leq p < q < n)$ in $\mathcal{C}_1 \setminus \mathcal{C}_2$. Then, by the assumption, every constraint in $\mathcal{C}_2$ is between events p and q, or is also in $\mathcal{C}_1$. So every constraint in $\mathcal{C}_2 \setminus \mathcal{C}_1$ must be between p and q. Similarly, every constraint in $\mathcal{C}_1$ is in $\mathcal{C}_2$ or between events p and q. So all the other constraints in $\mathcal{C}_1 \setminus \mathcal{C}_2$ (if any) must also be between events p and q. $\square$

Intuitively, if two optimized scenarios $\xi = (\mathcal{E}, \mathcal{C}_1)$ and $\eta = (\mathcal{E}, \mathcal{C}_2)$ are such that $\mathcal{Z}(\xi, \eta) \neq \emptyset$, and $\mathcal{C}_1$ and $\mathcal{C}_2$ differ only on constraints between a pair of events, say u and v, then *both* $\mathcal{C}_1$ and $\mathcal{C}_2$ must contain explicit constraints between u and v: if the constraint of, say, ξ were implicit, then that would imply $\eta \subseteq \xi$.

Theorem 3. *Let* $\xi = (\mathcal{E}, \mathcal{C}_1)$ *and* $\eta = (\mathcal{E}, \mathcal{C}_2)$ *be two optimized scenarios of length* n *such that* $\xi \uplus \eta$ *is defined. If* $\mathcal{Z}(\xi, \eta) \neq \emptyset$*, then there exist a constraint* $\alpha \in \mathcal{C}_1$ *of the form* $\tau_{i,j} \sim a$ $(0 \leq i < j < n, a \in \mathbb{Q})$*, and a constraint* $\beta \in \mathcal{C}_2$ *of the form* $\tau_{k,l} \sim b$ $(0 \leq k < l < n, ij \neq kl, b \in \mathbb{Q})$*, such that* $\alpha \notin \mathcal{C}_2$ *and* $\beta \notin \mathcal{C}_1$*.*

Proof. Assume the negation of the conclusion, that is,
$$\forall_{c_1 = \tau_{i,j} \sim a \in \mathcal{C}_1} \forall_{c_2 = \tau_{k,l} \sim b \in \mathcal{C}_2} (c_1 \in \mathcal{C}_2 \vee c_2 \in \mathcal{C}_1 \vee (i = k \wedge j = l)).$$

By Lemma 6, the explicit constraints of ξ and η must be identical, except for those that are between a single pair of event numbers, say p and q.

In that case, for every $0 \leq i < j < n$, the intervals I_{ij}^{ξ} and I_{ij}^{η} both correspond to explicit constraints or both correspond to implicit constraints in ξ and η.

$\mathcal{Z}(\xi, \eta) \neq \emptyset$, so there exists some behaviour $\mathcal{B}^z$ in $\mathcal{Z}(\xi, \eta)$. By Theorem 2, there must exist $0 \leq u < v < n$ and $0 \leq w < z < n$, where $uv \neq wz$, such that $t_{uv}^{\mathcal{B}^z} \notin I_{uv}^{\xi}$, $t_{uv}^{\mathcal{B}^z} \in I_{uv}^{\eta}$, and $t_{wz}^{\mathcal{B}^z} \in I_{wz}^{\xi}$, $t_{wz}^{\mathcal{B}^z} \notin I_{wz}^{\eta}$. So $I_{uv}^{\xi} \neq I_{uv}^{\eta}$ and $I_{wz}^{\xi} \neq I_{wz}^{\eta}$.

At least one of the intervals between u and v and between w and z must correspond to implicit constraints in *both* ξ and η. This is because there is only one pair of event numbers, p and q, that correspond to different explicit constraints in ξ and η. We consider three cases:

1. Both I_{uv}^{ξ} and I_{wz}^{η} correspond to implicit constraints in ξ and η.
   Assume I_{uv}^{ξ} corresponds to some constraint d in ξ. Because $t_{uv}^{\mathcal{B}^z} \notin I_{uv}^{\xi}$, d is not satisfied by $\mathcal{B}^z$. But then, by Observation 3, at least one explicit constraint $\alpha \in \mathcal{C}_1$ that is in the support of d must also not be satisfied by $\mathcal{B}^z$.
   Similarly, assume I_{wz}^{ξ} corresponds to some implicit constraint e in η. Because $t_{wz}^{\mathcal{B}^z} \notin I_{wz}^{\eta}$, constraint e is not satisfied by behaviour $\mathcal{B}^z$. By Observation 3 at least one explicit constraint $\beta \in \mathcal{C}_2$ $(\beta \neq \alpha)$ that is in the support of e must also not be satisfied by $\mathcal{B}^z$. But in that case, there are two possibilities:
   (a) α is of the form $\tau_{p,q} \sim a$ and β is of the form $\tau_{p,q} \sim b$.
       Neither α nor β are satisfied by $\mathcal{B}^z$, so $t_{pq}^{\mathcal{B}^z} \notin I_{pq}^{\xi}$ and $t_{pq}^{\mathcal{B}^z} \notin I_{pq}^{\eta}$. But then, $t_{pq}^{\mathcal{B}^z} \notin I_{pq}^{\xi \uplus \eta}$, which is in contradiction to pt. 1. of Theorem 2.
   (b) Only one of α or β corresponds to $\tau_{p,q}$.
       Let α be of the form $\tau_{p,q} \sim a$ and β be of the form $\tau_{r,s} \sim b$, where $rs \neq pq$. Then β must also belong to $\mathcal{C}_1$. Therefore, β in $\mathcal{C}_1$ is also not satisfied by $\mathcal{B}^z$. So, $t_{rs}^{\mathcal{B}^z} \notin I_{rs}^{\xi}$, and $t_{rs}^{\mathcal{B}^z} \notin I_{rs}^{\eta}$. But then, $t_{rs}^{\mathcal{B}^z} \notin I_{rs}^{\xi \uplus \eta}$, which is a contradiction. If β is of the form $\tau_{p,q} \sim a$, we can show a contradiction by a similar argument.
2. I_{uv}^{ξ} corresponds to an explicit constraint in both ξ and η, while I_{wz}^{ξ} corresponds to an implicit constraint in both ξ and η. Then $uv = pq$.
   Let I_{pq}^{ξ} and I_{pq}^{η} correspond to explicit constraints d and d' in ξ and η, respectively. $t_{uv}^{\mathcal{B}^z} \notin I_{uv}^{\xi}$ and $uv = pq$, so $t_{pq}^{\mathcal{B}^z} \notin I_{pq}^{\xi}$. Therefore, constraint d is not satisfied by $\mathcal{B}^z$. But because $t_{uv}^{\mathcal{B}^z} \in I_{uv}^{\eta}$ and $uv = pq$, $t_{pq}^{\mathcal{B}^z} \in I_{pq}^{\eta}$, and therefore constraint d' is satisfied by $\mathcal{B}^z$.

ξ	0 : a ; 1 : b ; 2 : c $\{\tau_{0,2} \geq 7\}$.		1	2
		0	$(0, \infty)$	$(7, \infty)$
		1		$(0, \infty)$

η	0 : a ; 1 : b $\{\tau_{0,1} \leq 8\}$; 2 : c $\{\tau_{0,2} \leq 10\}$.		1	2
		0	$(0, 8)$	$(0, 10)$
		1		$(0, 10)$

Fig. 12. Two scenarios, ξ and η, and their stable tables

Let I_{wz}^{ξ} and I_{wz}^{η} correspond to implicit constraints e and e' in ξ and η respectively. Since $t_{wz}^{\mathcal{B}^z} \in I_{wz}^{\xi}$, constraint e is satisfied by $\mathcal{B}^z$, but e' is not satisfied by $\mathcal{B}^z$, because $t_{wz}^{\mathcal{B}^z} \notin I_{wz}^{\eta}$. So e' is not a default constraint, and $e \neq e'$.

By Observation 3 at least one explicit constraint $\beta \in \mathcal{C}_2$ that is in the support of e' must also not be satisfied by $\mathcal{B}^z$. β cannot be equal to d', because d' is satisfied by $\mathcal{B}^z$.

Then β must also belong to $\mathcal{C}_1$. Therefore, β in $\mathcal{C}_1$ is also not satisfied by $\mathcal{B}^z$. Let β correspond to some constraint between r and s. Then, $t_{rs}^{\mathcal{B}^z} \notin I_{rs}^{\xi}$, and $t_{rs}^{\mathcal{B}^z} \notin I_{rs}^{\eta}$. But then, $t_{rs}^{\mathcal{B}^z} \notin I_{rs}^{\xi \uplus \eta}$, which is a contradiction.

3. I_{uv}^{ξ} corresponds to an implicit constraint in both ξ and η, while I_{wz}^{ξ} corresponds to an explicit constraint in both ξ and η. The argument is very similar to the one above.

□

Theorem 3 provides a sufficient condition for the non-existence of zigzagging behaviours: if $\xi = (\mathcal{E}, \mathcal{C}_1)$ and $\eta = (\mathcal{E}, \mathcal{C}_2)$ do not contain such an α and β, then $\mathcal{Z}(\xi, \eta) = \emptyset$. But the condition is not necessary, in general: if ξ and η contain such an α and β, there might still be no ζ in $\mathcal{Z}(\xi, \eta)$. As an example consider scenarios ξ and η of Fig. 12: ξ has an explicit constraint between events 0 and 2 (which is not in η), and η has an explicit constraint between events 0 and 1 (which is not in ξ), however, there is no behaviour in $\mathcal{Z}(\xi, \eta)$. If we take, say, $t_{12} = 11$ from $I_{12}^{\xi} \setminus I_{12}^{\eta}$ and $t_{02} = 6$ from $I_{02}^{\eta} \setminus I_{02}^{\xi}$, then $t_{02} < t_{12}$, which is impossible. Any other attempt at creating a zigzagging behaviour would fail for similar reasons.

To find out whether $\mathcal{Z}(\xi, \eta)$ is empty, we perform the following steps:

1. Let $\alpha = \tau_{i,j} \sim a \in \mathcal{C}_1 \setminus \mathcal{C}_2$, and $\beta = \tau_{k,l} \sim b \in \mathcal{C}_2 \setminus \mathcal{C}_1$ ($ij \neq kl$).
2. We construct scenarios (at most four[7]) that constrain t_{ij} to be in $I_{ij}^{\xi} \setminus I_{ij}^{\eta}$ and t_{kl} to be in $I_{kl}^{\eta} \setminus I_{kl}^{\xi}$.
3. Let ζ be one of these scenarios.
4. We stabilize ζ's initial table, i.e., $\mathcal{D}^{\zeta}$. If the resulting table is valid, and $\zeta \cap (\xi \uplus \eta)$ is defined and consistent, then there exists at least one zigzagging behaviour in $[\![\zeta]\!]$: $\mathcal{Z}(\xi, \eta) \neq \emptyset$.

---

[7] I_{ij}^{ξ} might be a subset of I_{ij}^{η}, and vice versa. Similarly, I_{kl}^{ξ} might be a subset of I_{kl}^{η}, and vice versa.

If no zigzagging behaviour can be found for any such pair of constraints α and β, then $\mathcal{Z}(\xi,\eta) = \emptyset$.

As an example consider scenarios ξ and η of Fig. 9 along with their stable distance tables once more. Observe that ξ and η are optimized. By comparing the corresponding intervals of the distance tables, it is easy to see that ξ and η are not subsets of each other. Moreover, $\xi \uplus \eta$ (shown on the left of Fig. 10) is defined (and therefore consistent).

As we mentioned before the union of the behaviours in $[\![\xi]\!]$ and $[\![\eta]\!]$ *cannot* be captured by their combination: $\mathcal{Z}(\xi,\eta) \neq \emptyset$. Scenario ζ, shown on the right of Fig. 10, is constructed following the steps above. Obviously, ζ is consistent: it allows all behaviours in which the time distance between a and b is at least 5, and between a and c is at most 6. Clearly, these behaviours are in $\xi \uplus \eta$, but are neither in $[\![\xi]\!]$, nor in $[\![\eta]\!]$. So in accordance with Theorem 3 there must be a pair of explicit constraints, one in ξ but not in η, and another one in η, but not in ξ, that are *not* between the same events. Indeed, the only explicit constraint of ξ (which is not in η) is between events 0 and 1, while η's only explicit constraint (which is not in ξ) is between events 0 and 2.

As another example consider the scenarios of Fig. 11 once more. The explicit constraints of ξ and η differ only on the constraints between one pair of events, namely, events 0 and 2, so by Theorem 3, $\mathcal{Z}(\xi,\eta) = \emptyset$.

Observation 9. *If $\mathcal{Z}(\xi,\eta) = \emptyset$, then every behaviour in $[\![\xi \uplus \eta]\!]$ must satisfy all the constraints in ξ, or all the constraints in η, or all the constraints in both ξ and η.*

Observation 10. *Let ξ and η be two consistent scenarios with the same sequence of events, such that $\xi \uplus \eta$ is defined. Then $[\![\xi \uplus \eta]\!] = [\![\xi]\!] \cup [\![\eta]\!]$ iff $\mathcal{Z}(\xi,\eta) = \emptyset$.*

Intuitively, the union of two scenarios ξ and η exists only when $\mathcal{Z}(\xi,\eta) = \emptyset$. In that case, their combination, i.e., $\xi \uplus \eta$ (Definition 6) becomes their union.

5   Conclusions and Related Work

We introduce subsumption, intersection and union operations for timed scenarios. We formally define these operations and their semantics.

Given two consistent scenarios ξ and η, ξ is subsumed by η, i.e., $\xi \sqsubseteq \eta$, iff $[\![\xi]\!] \subseteq [\![\eta]\!]$, that is, the set of behaviours allowed by ξ is a subset of that for η. We provide a constructive way of verifying whether that is the case (Definition 4 and Observation 4).

Next, we show that for two consistent scenarios ξ and η, if the set of behaviours allowed by both ξ and η is not empty, then the set can be captured by a single scenario, namely the intersection of ξ and η, i.e., $\xi \cap \eta$. Definition 5 shows how to construct $\xi \cap \eta$ and Theorem 1 describes its semantic properties.

Then we turn our attention to the union of scenarios. Given two consistent scenarios ξ and η, we want to know whether there exists a single scenario that would express the set of behaviours that are allowed by ξ or η, i.e., the union of the behaviours allowed by ξ and η. We constructively define $\xi \uplus \eta$ (Definition 6) and show that it captures the expected properties of union only under certain conditions: in particular, when it does not contain "zigzagging" behaviours (Observation 10). Intuitively, zigzagging behaviours belong neither to $[\![\xi]\!]$, nor to $[\![\eta]\!]$, even though they belong to $[\![\xi \uplus \eta]\!]$. We formalize zigzagging behaviours, and show that such behaviours are possible *only* when there is a certain relationship between the constraints of ξ and η (Theorem 3). This provides us with a *syntactic* criterion for determining whether $\xi \uplus \eta$ does indeed have the required semantic properties of union.

To the best of our knowledge this is the first attempt at developing such operations for timed scenarios. These operations are directly relevant to the problem of synthesizing timed automata with minimal number of clocks from a set of scenarios (see Sec. 3 for a brief discussion), which we will address in a forthcoming paper.

A detailed comparison of timed scenarios with other related work, in particular with Difference Bounds Matrices (DBMs), can be found in our earlier work [10, 14].

Inclusion and intersection operations have been defined for DBMs [20]. However, our subsumption and intersection operations, developed from first principles for timed scenarios, are naturally different.

Union of DBMs has been handled by convex hulls, leading to an approximation algorithm [21] and a safe abstraction [22]: the union of two zones (represented by DBMs) is generally a non-convex set, and therefore cannot be represented by a zone, i.e., a DBM.

Another method for checking whether the union of two DBMs is itself a DBM has been developed using convex hulls together with Clock Difference Diagrams (CDDs) [23].

Our union operation, with well-defined semantics, is defined in a different and straightforward way using the stable distance tables. An interesting property of our union is that no approximation is required, thanks to our syntactic criterion used for the existence of union.

References

1. Salah, A., Mizouni, R., Dssouli, R., Parreaux, B.: Formal composition of distributed scenarios. In: de Frutos-Escrig, D., Núñez, M. (eds.) FORTE 2004. LNCS, vol. 3235, pp. 213–228. Springer, Heidelberg (2004). https://doi.org/10.1007/978-3-540-30232-2_14
2. Greenyer, J.: Scenario-based modeling and programming of distributed systems. In: M. Köhler-Bussmeier, E. Kindler, H. Rölke (Eds.), Proceedings of the International Workshop on Petri Nets and Software Engineering 2021 co-located with the 42nd International Conference on Application and Theory of Petri Nets and Concurrency (PETRI NETS 2021), Paris, France, June 25th, 2021 (due to COVID-19: virtual conference), Vol. 2907 of CEUR Workshop Proceedings, CEUR-WS.org, pp. 241–252 (2021)

3. Somé, S., Dssouli, R., Vaucher, J.: From scenarios to timed automata: building specifications from users requirements. In: Proceedings of the Second Asia Pacific Software Engineering Conference, APSEC 1995, IEEE Computer Society, pp. 48–57 (1995)
4. Chandrasekaran, P., Mukund, M.: Matching scenarios with timing constraints. In: Asarin, E., Bouyer, P. (eds.) FORMATS 2006. LNCS, vol. 4202, pp. 98–112. Springer, Heidelberg (2006). https://doi.org/10.1007/11867340_8
5. Harel, D., Kugler, H., Pnueli, A.: Synthesis revisited: generating statechart models from scenario-based requirements. In: Kreowski, H.-J., Montanari, U., Orejas, F., Rozenberg, G., Taentzer, G. (eds.) Formal Methods in Software and Systems Modeling. LNCS, vol. 3393, pp. 309–324. Springer, Heidelberg (2005). https://doi.org/10.1007/978-3-540-31847-7_18
6. Uchitel, S., Kramer, J., Magee, J.: Synthesis of Behavioral Models from Scenarios. IEEE Trans. Softw. Eng. **29**(2), 99–115 (2003)
7. Akshay, S., Mukund, M., Kumar, K.N.: Checking coverage for infinite collections of timed scenarios. In: CONCUR 2007 - Concurrency Theory, 18th International Conference, CONCUR 2007, Proceedings, pp. 181–196 (2007)
8. Bollig, B., Katoen, J., Kern, C., Leucker, M.: Replaying play in and play out: synthesis of design models from scenarios by learning. In: Proceedings of the 13th International Conference on Tools and Algorithms for the Construction and Analysis of Systems, TACAS, 2007, pp. 435–450 (2007)
9. Alur, R., Martin, M., Raghothaman, M., Stergiou, C., Tripakis, S., Udupa, A.: Synthesizing finite-state protocols from scenarios and requirements. In: Yahav, E. (ed.) HVC 2014. LNCS, vol. 8855, pp. 75–91. Springer, Cham (2014). https://doi.org/10.1007/978-3-319-13338-6_7
10. Saeedloei, N., Kluźniak, F.: From scenarios to timed automata. In: Formal Methods: Foundations and Applications - 20th Brazilian Symposium, SBMF 2017, Proceedings, pp. 33–51 (2017)
11. Saeedloei, N., Kluźniak, F.: Timed scenarios: consistency, equivalence and optimization. In: Formal Methods: Foundations and Applications - 21st Brazilian Symposium, SBMF 2018, Proceedings, pp. 215–233 (2018)
12. Alur, R., Dill, D.L.: A theory of timed automata. Theor. Comput. Sci. **126**(2), 183–235 (1994)
13. Alur, R., Madhusudan, P.: Decision problems for timed automata: a survey. In: Formal Methods for the Design of Real-Time Systems, International School on Formal Methods for the Design of Computer, Communication and Software Systems, SFM-RT, Revised Lectures, pp. 1–24 (2004)
14. Saeedloei, N., Kluźniak, F.: Optimization of timed scenarios. In: Carvalho, G., Stolz, V. (eds.) SBMF 2020. LNCS, vol. 12475, pp. 119–136. Springer, Cham (2020). https://doi.org/10.1007/978-3-030-63882-5_8
15. Saeedloei, N., Kluźniak, F.: Minimization of the number of clocks for timed scenarios. In: Campos, S., Minea, M. (eds.) SBMF 2021. LNCS, vol. 13130, pp. 122–139. Springer, Cham (2021). https://doi.org/10.1007/978-3-030-92137-8_8
16. Abdulla, P.A., Deneux, J., Ouaknine, J., Worrell, J.: Decidability and complexity results for timed automata via channel machines. In: Caires, L., Italiano, G.F., Monteiro, L., Palamidessi, C., Yung, M. (eds.) ICALP 2005. LNCS, vol. 3580, pp. 1089–1101. Springer, Heidelberg (2005). https://doi.org/10.1007/11523468_88
17. Baier, C., Bertrand, N., Bouyer, P., Brihaye, T.: When are timed automata determinizable? In: Albers, S., Marchetti-Spaccamela, A., Matias, Y., Nikoletseas, S., Thomas, W. (eds.) ICALP 2009. LNCS, vol. 5556, pp. 43–54. Springer, Heidelberg (2009). https://doi.org/10.1007/978-3-642-02930-1_4

18. Dill, D.L.: Timing assumptions and verification of finite-state concurrent systems. In: Sifakis, J. (ed.) CAV 1989. LNCS, vol. 407, pp. 197–212. Springer, Heidelberg (1990). https://doi.org/10.1007/3-540-52148-8_17
19. Larsen, K.G., Larsson, F., Pettersson, P., Yi, W.: Efficient verification of real-time systems: compact data structure and state-space reduction. In: 18th IEEE Real-Time Systems Symposium, pp. 14–24 (1997)
20. Bengtsson, J., Yi, W.: Timed automata: semantics, algorithms and tools. In: Desel, J., Reisig, W., Rozenberg, G. (eds.) ACPN 2003. LNCS, vol. 3098, pp. 87–124. Springer, Heidelberg (2004). https://doi.org/10.1007/978-3-540-27755-2_3
21. Balarin, F.: Approximate reachability analysis of timed automata. In: 17th IEEE Real-Time Systems Symposium, pp. 52–61 (1996). https://doi.org/10.1109/REAL.1996.563700
22. Daws, C., Tripakis, S.: Model checking of real-time reachability properties using abstractions. In: Steffen, B. (ed.) TACAS 1998. LNCS, vol. 1384, pp. 313–329. Springer, Heidelberg (1998). https://doi.org/10.1007/BFb0054180
23. Behrmann, G., Larsen, K.G., Pearson, J., Weise, C., Yi, W.: Efficient Timed Reachability Analysis Using Clock Difference Diagrams. In: Halbwachs, N., Peled, D. (eds.) CAV 1999. LNCS, vol. 1633, pp. 341–353. Springer, Heidelberg (1999). https://doi.org/10.1007/3-540-48683-6_30

On the Use of Model and Logical Embeddings for Model Checking of Probabilistic Systems

Susmoy Das[(✉)] and Arpit Sharma

Department of Electrical Engineering and Computer Science,
Indian Institute of Science Education and Research Bhopal, Bhopal, India
{susmoy18,arpit}@iiserb.ac.in

Abstract. Logics for probabilistic process algebraic models are either not very expressive or cannot be intuitively used for specifying interesting performance and reliability properties due to the presence of fixed-point operators. Moreover, the model checking machinery for these logics is very limited and is not as efficient as their state-based counterparts. Recently, new probabilistic logics and a formal framework of embeddings has been proposed which enables one to seamlessly move between state and action-based probabilistic logics. Similarly, this framework also bridges the gap between these two modeling communities by relating the state and action-based probabilistic models. We focus on implementing this framework and studying the effect of applying it on several interesting case studies from the process algebraic domain. Our results show that it enables one to efficiently verify probabilistic process algebraic models using tools and methods developed in the state-based setting. Additionally, it also enables analyzing and model checking interesting reward-based properties.

Keywords: Markov chain · Verification · Logic · Probabilistic · Model checking · Embedding · Process algebra

1 Introduction

Action-labeled discrete-time Markov chains (ADTMCs) are widely used as semantic model for amongst others probabilistic variants of ACP [6], CCS [16], CSP [23], LOTOS [26] and Petri nets [24]. Similarly, probabilistic variants of Hennessy-Milner logic, e.g. [19,30] and modal μ-calculus [21,22,27,28] can be used for specifying performance and reliability properties that need to be verified. An issue with these logical formalisms is that they are either not very expressive, e.g. prHML [19,30] or cannot be easily (and intuitively) used for specifying interesting probabilistic properties due to the presence of fixed-point operators, e.g. [21,22,27,28]. Moreover, due to the limited tool support, e.g. mCRL2 [9,15] and CADP [14], probabilistic model checking of these logics is either not possible or is not as efficient as their state-based counterparts like

M. Huisman and A. Ravara (Eds.): FORTE 2023, LNCS 13910, pp. 115–131, 2023.
https://doi.org/10.1007/978-3-031-35355-0_8

PRISM [20] and Storm [13,18]. For example, the mCRL2 toolset allows modeling and minimization of probabilistic systems but does not provide support for the verification or model checking of these systems and the same remains a challenge. This has also been highlighted in [9] where developers of the mCRL2 have mentioned that *"the semantic and axiomatic underpinning of the process theory for probabilities is demanding"*. Additionally, existing tools in the probabilistic process algebraic setting also do not provide support for the verification of interesting reward-based properties [3], e.g. the expected cumulative cost.

Recently, in [11,12], we have defined a theoretical framework of model and logical embeddings which can be used to bridge the gap between these two modeling and verification communities. These model embeddings can be used to construct an ADTMC from a state-labeled discrete-time Markov chain (SDTMC) [7] and an SDTMC from an ADTMC, respectively. The inverse of these embeddings have also been defined [11] which can reverse the effects of their application. Our model embeddings also support model minimization by preserving forward bisimulation, backward bisimulation and trace equivalence relations. Additionally, in order to enable these model embeddings to support probabilistic model checking of randomized systems, we have proposed the syntax and semantics of an action-based Probabilistic Computation Tree Logic (APCTL) and an action-based PCTL* (APCTL*) both of which are interpreted over ADTMCs [12]. These logics are strictly more expressive than the probabilistic variant of Hennessy-Milner logic (prHML) [12] and the property specification becomes more intuitive as compared to the variants of probabilistic modal μ-calculus. Finally, we have defined the logical embeddings between APCTL↔PCTL, APCTL*↔PCTL*, and proved that these logical embeddings combined with the model embeddings can be used for analyzing and verifying models of one domain using the tools and techniques developed for the other domain.

This paper aims to validate the efficacy and usefulness of this theoretical framework by first implementing the model embeddings and then applying it on several interesting case studies. More specifically, our implementation accepts an ADTMC model encoded in mCRL2 [9] and transforms it to an equivalent SDTMC model used by the PRISM model checker [20]. This is achieved by preprocessing and scanning the lts file generated by the mCRL2 toolset and applying the model embeddings defined in [12] to obtain the PRISM machine readable files (MRFs) which contain information about the states, their labels, transitions and their associated probabilities. These files can be directly used for building the SDTMC models in PRISM. Additionally, we also provide the option of generating a human readable source code file in PRISM which can be opened using its graphical user interface (GUI) to inspect, parse and build the small-sized models. In order to model check the behavior, properties can be specified using the newly defined APCTL logic which are subsequently transformed into PCTL [7,17] formulae by applying our logical embeddings [12]. In the last step, the SDTMC model can be verified using PRISM model checker. Our experimental results show that this framework enables one to efficiently model check ADTMC models which otherwise cannot be verified using the mCRL2 toolset. Moreover, this framework also enables analyzing and model checking interesting reward-based properties on probabilistic models. These observations combined with the fact that property specification in the action-based setting has become very intuitive (thanks to APCTL and APCTL*) would encourage the researchers working in the process algebraic setting to model the probabilistic behavior using mCRL2 and verify it using the state-of-the-art machinery provided by the PRISM toolset.

We believe this paper is an important step forward in the direction of seamlessly connecting the state-based and action-based probabilistic modeling and verification tools, e.g. PRISM↔mCRL2, and Storm↔mCRL2. This is possible as our theoretical framework also allows moving from SDTMCs to ADTMCs and PCTL (PCTL* [5], resp.) to APCTL (APCTL*, resp.). Our long-term goal is to enable these two important modeling and verification communities which as of now have independently developed their methods and tools to leverage the advancements made by the other community. For example, using our framework, PRISM models can be minimized by applying the bisimulation minimization algorithms of mCRL2. In the last step, inverse embeddings can be applied to obtain the reduced model in PRISM.

Organization of the paper. The rest of this paper is organized as follows: Sect. 2 recalls the basic concepts of DTMCs and probabilistic logics. Section 3 presents the model and logical embeddings. Section 4 presents the overall architecture of our approach followed by Sect. 5 which presents and analyzes the experimental results. Finally, Sect. 6 concludes the paper and provides pointers for future research.

2   Preliminaries

This section recalls the basic concepts of discrete-time Markov chains with finite state space and probabilistic logics used for specifying properties over these models.

Definition 1. *An ADTMC is a tuple $\mathcal{D} = (S, Act, \mathcal{P}, s_0)$ where: (a) S is a countable, nonempty set of states; (b) Act is a set of actions which contains the special action τ; (c) $\mathcal{P} : S \times Act \times S \to [0,1]$ is the transition probability function satisfying $\sum_{s' \in S, a \in Act} \mathcal{P}(s,a,s') = 1 \; \forall s \in S$; and (d) s_0 is the initial state.*

$\mathcal{D}$ is called finite if S and Act are finite. τ is a special action used to denote an invisible computation. Let $\to = \{(s,a;p,s') \mid \mathcal{P}(s,a,s') = p > 0\}$ denote the set of all the transitions for an ADTMC $\mathcal{D}$. We denote $s \xrightarrow{a,p} s'$ if $(s,a;p,s') \in \to$. An alternating sequence of states and actions $s_0\alpha_1, s_1\alpha_2, s_2\alpha_3, \ldots$ s.t. $\mathcal{P}(s_i, \alpha_{i+1}, s_{i+1}) > 0 \; \forall i$ is an infinite run in an ADTMC. We denote a run by ρ. A finite run is of the form : $s_0\alpha_1, s_1\alpha_2, s_2\alpha_3, \ldots, s_{n-1}\alpha_n, s_n$ where $\mathcal{P}(s_i, \alpha_{i+1}, s_{i+1}) > 0$ for $0 \le i < n$. The length of a finite run, denoted by $len(\rho)$ is given by the number of transitions along that run. Length of the finite run given above is $len(\rho) = n$. For an infinite run ρ, we have, $len(\rho) = \infty$. We denote the n-th state along a run ρ by $\rho[n-1]$ ($\rho[0]$ denotes the first state from which the run starts) and the n-th action along the run by $\rho_\alpha[n]$ ($\rho_\alpha[1]$ denotes the first transition label of the run). Let $Runs(s)$ denote the set of all infinite runs starting in s. Let $Runs_{fin}(s)$ denote the set of all finite runs starting in s.

Definition 2 (Cylinder set [11]). *Let* $s_0, \ldots, s_k \in S$ *with* $\mathcal{P}(s_i, a_{i+1}, s_{i+1}) > 0$ *for* $0 \leq i < k$. $Cyl(s_0 a_1, \ldots, s_{k-1} a_k, s_k)$ *denotes the* cylinder set *consisting of all runs* $\rho \in Runs(s_0)$ *s.t.* $\rho[i] = s_i$ *for* $0 \leq i \leq k$ *and* $\rho_\alpha[i] = a_i$ *for* $1 \leq i \leq k$.

Let $\mathcal{F}(Runs(s_0))$ denote the smallest σ-algebra on $Runs(s_0)$ which contains all sets of the form $Cyl(s_0 a_1, \ldots, s_{k-1} a_k, s_k)$ s.t. $s_0 a_1, \ldots, s_{k-1} a_k, s_k$ is an alternating sequence of states and actions with $\mathcal{P}(s_i, a_{i+1}, s_{i+1}) > 0$, $(0 \leq i < k)$. The probability measure $\Pr$ on $\mathcal{F}(Runs(s_0))$ is the unique measure defined by induction on k in the following way. Let $\Pr(Cyl(s_0)) = 1$ and for $k > 0 : \Pr(Cyl(s_0 a_1, \ldots, s_{k-1} a_k, s')) = \Pr(Cyl(s_0 a_1, \ldots, s_{k-2} a_{k-1}, s_{k-1})) \cdot \mathcal{P}(s_{k-1}, a_k, s')$. Next, we present the necessary definitions and basic concepts related to state-labeled discrete-time Markov chains (SDTMCs).

Definition 3. *An SDTMC is a tuple* $\mathcal{D} = (S, AP, \mathcal{P}, s_0, L)$ *where: (a) S is a countable, nonempty set of states; (b) AP is the set of atomic propositions; (c) $\mathcal{P}$ is the transition probability function satisfying* $\mathcal{P} : S \times S \to [0, 1]$ *s.t.* $\forall s \in S$: $\sum_{s' \in S} \mathcal{P}(s, s') = 1$; *(d) s_0 is the initial state; and (d) $L : S \to 2^{AP}$ is a labeling function.*

$\mathcal{D}$ is called finite if S and AP are finite. Let $\to = \{(s, p, s') \mid \mathcal{P}(s, s') = p > 0\}$ denote the set of all transitions for an SDTMC $\mathcal{D}$. We denote $s \xrightarrow{p} s'$ if $(s, p, s') \in \to$. A sequence of states $s_0, s_1, s_2, \ldots$ where $\mathcal{P}(s_i, s_{i+1}) > 0$ $\forall i$ is an infinite path in an SDTMC. We denote a path by π. A finite path is of the form $: s_0, s_1, s_2, \ldots, s_n$ where $\mathcal{P}(s_i, s_{i+1}) > 0$ for $0 \leq i < n$. The length of a finite path, denoted by $len(\pi)$ is given by the number of transitions along that path. Length of the finite path given above is $len(\pi) = n$. For an infinite path π, we have, $len(\pi) = \infty$. We denote the n-th state along a path π by $\pi[n-1]$ ($\pi[0]$ denotes the first state from which the path starts). Let $Paths(s)$ denote the set of all infinite paths starting in s. Let $Paths_{fin}(s)$ denote the set of all finite paths starting in s.

Definition 4 (Cylinder set [7,31]). *Let* $s_0, \ldots, s_k \in S$ *with* $\mathcal{P}(s_i, s_{i+1}) > 0$ *for* $0 \leq i < k$. $Cyl(s_0, \ldots, s_k)$ *denotes the* cylinder set *consisting of all paths* $\pi \in Paths(s_0)$ *s.t.* $\pi[i] = s_i$ *for* $0 \leq i \leq k$.

Let $\mathcal{F}(Paths(s_0))$ be the smallest σ-algebra on $Paths(s_0)$ which contains all sets $Cyl(s_0, \ldots, s_k)$ s.t. $s_0, \ldots, s_k$ is a state sequence with $\mathcal{P}(s_i, s_{i+1}) > 0$, $(0 \leq i < k)$. The probability measure $\Pr$ on $\mathcal{F}(Path(s_0))$ is the unique measure defined by induction on k in the following way. Let $\Pr(Cyl(s_0)) = 1$ and for $k > 0 :$ $\Pr(Cyl(s_0, \ldots, s_k, s')) = \Pr(Cyl(s_0, \ldots, s_k)) \cdot \mathcal{P}(s_k, s')$.

Next, we recall the definition of an auxiliary logic of actions $ActFor$ [12,29] which will be subsequently used for defining APCTL. The collection $ActFor$ of action formulae is defined as:

$$\chi ::= a \mid \neg\chi \mid \chi_1 \vee \chi_2 \text{ where } a \in Act \setminus \{\tau\}$$

where χ, χ_1, χ_2 range over action formulae. We write **true** as $a \vee \neg a$, where a is some arbitrarily chosen action, and **false** as $\neg$**true**. An action formula allows us to express constraints on actions that are visible (along a run or after the next step), e.g. $a \vee b$ implies that only actions a or b are allowed in the run. Here, **true** stands for 'all the visible actions are allowed'. The satisfaction relation for *ActFor* is given by : (a) $a \models_A b \Leftrightarrow a = b$; (b) $a \models_A \neg\chi \Leftrightarrow a \not\models_A \chi$; and (c) $a \models_A \chi_1 \vee \chi_2 \Leftrightarrow a \models_A \chi_1$ or $a \models_A \chi_2$. The syntax of APCTL is defined by the state formulae generated by the following grammar, where $\Phi, \Phi', \ldots$ range over state formulae, Ψ over run formulae and χ and χ' are action formulae (generated by *ActFor*):

- State Formulae: $\Phi ::== \mathbf{true} \mid \neg\Phi \mid \Phi \wedge \Phi' \mid \mathcal{P}_J(\Psi)$
- Run Formulae: $\Psi ::== \mathbf{X}_\chi\Phi \mid \mathbf{X}_\tau\Phi \mid \Phi_\chi\mathbf{U}\Phi' \mid \Phi_\chi\mathbf{U}_{\chi'}\Phi'$

where $J \subseteq [0,1] \subset \mathbb{R}$ is an interval. Satisfaction of a APCTL state formula Φ by a state s or a run formula Ψ by a run ρ, notation, $\mathcal{D}, s \models_A \Phi$ ($\mathcal{D}, \rho \models_A \Psi$, resp.) or just $s \models_A \Phi$ ($\rho \models_A \Psi$, resp.) is defined inductively by :

$s \models_A \mathbf{true}$	always;
$s \models_A \neg\Phi$	iff $s \not\models_A \Phi$;
$s \models_A \Phi \wedge \Phi'$	iff $s \models_A \Phi$ and $s \models_A \Phi'$;
$s \models_A \mathcal{P}_J(\Psi)$	iff $\displaystyle\sum_{\rho \in Runs(s), \rho \models_A \Psi} Pr(\rho) \in J$;
$\rho \models_A \mathbf{X}_\chi\Phi$	iff $\rho_\alpha[1] \models_A \chi$ and $\rho[1] \models_A \Phi$;
$\rho \models_A \mathbf{X}_\tau\Phi$	iff $\rho_\alpha[1] = \tau$ and $\rho[1] \models_A \Phi$;
$\rho \models_A \Phi_\chi\mathbf{U}\Phi'$	iff $\exists k \geq 0$, s.t. $\rho[k] \models_A \Phi'$ and $\forall 0 \leq i < k, \rho[i] \models_A \Phi$ and $\forall 1 \leq j \leq k, \rho_\alpha[j] \models_A \chi$ or $\rho_\alpha[j] = \tau$; and
$\rho \models_A \Phi_\chi\mathbf{U}_{\chi'}\Phi'$	iff $\exists k > 0$, s.t. $\rho[k] \models_A \Phi'$ and $\rho_\alpha[k] \models_A \chi'$, and $\forall 0 \leq i < k$, $\rho[i] \models_A \Phi$ and $\forall 1 \leq j < k, \rho_\alpha[j] \models_A \chi$ or $\rho_\alpha[j] = \tau$.

Next, we present the syntax and semantics of Probabilistic Computation Tree Logic (PCTL) [7,17]. PCTL is a probabilistic branching-time temporal logic that allows one to express the probability measures of satisfaction for a temporal property by a state in an SDTMC. The syntax is given by the following grammar where $\Phi, \Phi', \ldots$ range over PCTL state formulae and $\Psi, \Psi', \ldots$ range over path formulae:

- State Formulae: $\Phi ::== \mathbf{true} \mid a \mid \neg\,\Phi \mid \Phi \wedge \Phi' \mid \mathcal{P}_J(\Psi)$, for some $a \in$ AP
- Path Formulae : $\Psi ::== \mathbf{X}\Phi \mid \Phi\mathbf{U}\Phi'$

where $J \subseteq [0,1] \subset \mathbb{R}$ is an interval. Satisfaction of a PCTL state formula Φ by a state s or a path formula Ψ by a path π, notation, $s \models_S \Phi$ or $\pi \models_S \Psi$ is defined inductively by :

$$s \models_S \textbf{true} \qquad \text{always;}$$
$$s \models_S a \qquad \text{iff } a \in L(s);$$
$$s \models_S \neg\varPhi \qquad \text{iff } s \not\models_S \varPhi;$$
$$s \models_S \varPhi \wedge \varPhi' \qquad \text{iff } s \models_S \varPhi \text{ and } s \models_S \varPhi';$$
$$s \models_S \mathcal{P}_J(\varPsi) \qquad \text{iff} \qquad \sum_{\pi \in Paths(s), \pi \models_S \varPsi} Pr(\pi) \in J;$$
$$\pi \models_S \mathbf{X}\varPhi \qquad \text{iff } \pi[1] \models_S \varPhi; \text{ and}$$
$$\pi \models_S \varPhi\mathbf{U}\varPhi' \qquad \text{iff } \exists k \geq 0, \text{ s.t. } \pi[k] \models_S \varPhi' \text{ and } \forall 0 \leq i < k, \pi[i] \models_S \varPhi.$$

Proposition 1. *[12] The logic APCTL is strictly more expressive than prHML.*

Theorem 1. *[12] PCTL and APCTL are equally expressive.*

3   Model and Logical Embeddings

This section presents the model embeddings [12] which can be used to construct an SDTMC from an ADTMC. Note that these embeddings preserve strong forward, strong backward bisimulation and trace equivalence relations [11,12]. Additionally, we also present the logical embeddings which allows one to construct an equivalent PCTL property from an APCTL formula.

Definition 5 (sld). *Let* $\mathcal{D} = (S, Act, \mathcal{P}, s_0)$ *be an ADTMC. The embedding* $sld : ADTMC \to SDTMC$ *is formally defined as* $sld(\mathcal{D}) = (S', AP', \mathcal{P}', s_0', L')$ *s.t.*

- $S' = S \cup \{(a, t) \mid \mathcal{P}(s, a, t) > 0 \text{ for some } s, t \in S \text{ and } a \neq \tau\},$
- $AP' = (Act \setminus \{\tau\}) \cup \{\bot\}$ *where* $\bot \notin Act,$
- *The rate function* $\mathcal{P}'$ *is defined by:*

$$\mathcal{P}'(s, (a, t)) = \mathcal{P}(s, a, t) \quad \text{for all } s, t \in S \text{ s.t. } \mathcal{P}(s, a, t) > 0 \text{ and } a \neq \tau,$$
$$\mathcal{P}'(s, t) = \mathcal{P}(s, \tau, t) \quad \text{for all } s, t \in S \text{ s.t. } \mathcal{P}(s, \tau, t) > 0, \text{ and}$$
$$\mathcal{P}'((a, t), t) = 1 \qquad\qquad\qquad \text{for all } (a, t) \in S' \setminus S,$$

- $s_0' = s_0,$ *and*
- $L'(s) = \{\bot\} \ \forall s \in S \text{ and } L'((a, t)) = \{a\}.$

Given an ADTMC $\mathcal{D}$ and an APCTL formula $\varPhi$, the logical embedding $sldl'$ constructs an equivalent PCTL property which can be interpreted over the embedded SDTMC, i.e. $sld(\mathcal{D})$. We define the embedding $sldl' : APCTL \to PCTL$ inductively as follows :

$$sldl'(\mathbf{true}) \qquad\qquad =\mathbf{true};$$
$$sldl'(\neg\varPhi) \qquad\qquad\quad =\neg sldl'(\varPhi);$$
$$sldl'(\varPhi\wedge\varPhi') \qquad\quad =sldl'(\varPhi)\wedge sldl'(\varPhi');$$
$$sldl'(\mathcal{P}_J(\mathbf{X}_\chi\varPhi)) \quad\;\; =\mathcal{P}_J(\mathbf{X}(\neg\bot\wedge\chi\wedge\mathcal{P}_{[1,1]}(\mathbf{X}(\bot\wedge sldl'(\varPhi)))));$$
$$sldl'(\mathcal{P}_J(\mathbf{X}_\tau\varPhi)) \quad\;\; =(\bot\wedge\mathcal{P}_J(\mathbf{X}(\bot\wedge sldl'(\varPhi))));$$
$$sldl'(\mathcal{P}_J(\varPhi_\chi\mathbf{U}\varPhi')) \;\; =\mathcal{P}_J(((\bot\wedge sldl'(\varPhi))\vee(\neg\bot\wedge\chi))\mathbf{U}(\bot\wedge sldl'(\varPhi'))); \text{ and}$$
$$sldl'(\mathcal{P}_J(\varPhi_\chi\mathbf{U}_{\chi'}\varPhi')) =\mathcal{P}_J(((\bot\wedge sldl'(\varPhi))\vee(\neg\bot\wedge\chi))\mathbf{U}((\neg\bot\wedge\chi')\wedge$$
$$\mathcal{P}_{[1,1]}(\mathbf{X}(\bot\wedge sldl'(\varPhi'))))).$$

4 Implementation

Fig. 1 shows the overall architecture of our approach. We have automated the process of converting an ADTMC model encoded in mCRL2 [1,9] to an SDTMC model of PRISM [2,20] by applying the model embeddings defined in Def. 5. The code has been written in the Python programming language. For a model encoded in mCRL2, we first construct its corresponding LPS using the 'mcrl22lps' tool supported by the mCRL2. Next, we use the 'lps' file to construct an 'lts' file using the 'lps2lts' tool also supported by the mCRL2 toolset. For both these cases, we assume that the user is going to work with the default parameters and no other additional options of the toolset would be selected while making these conversions. We use the .aut extension (Aldebaran format) as the output choice for the lts file generated by the mCRL2. The lts file contains the information about the state space and the transitions of the ADTMC model. Our implementation (automated encoder shown in Fig. 1) takes this machine-readable lts file in the .aut extension as its input, and then pre-processes it to obtain the information regarding the number of states, transitions, and initial states. This is followed by the creation of new states and transitions according to

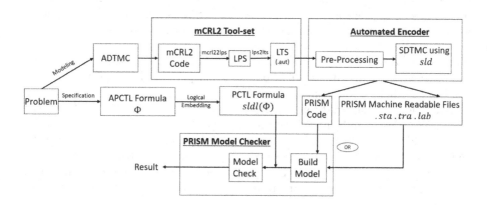

Fig. 1. Framework Overview

the definition of the model embedding given in Def. 5. This is done by scanning the lts file where each line of this file has to be in one of the following forms :

```
(origin_state,action,destination_state)
(origin_state,action,destination_distribution)
```

Here, destination_distribution[1] is of the form $[d_1\ p_1\ d_2\ p_2\ \ldots\ p_{n-1}\ d_n]$ which means origin_state reaches state d_i ($1 \leq i \leq n - 1$) via action action with probability p_i and quoteorigin_state reaches d_n via action with probability $1 - \sum_{i=1}^{n-1} p_i$. Lines of the form (origin_state,action,destination_state) refers to a transition from the origin_state to the destination_state via action and with probability 1. We consider the pair (action, destination) for every transition and check if the action is τ (invisible) or not. If it is a τ transition, we add the transition origin_state to destination_state directly in the embedded model, copy the original probability and label both the states with the atomic proposition $\perp$. If the action$\neq \tau$, we check if the pair (action, destination) has already been generated or not. If not, then we add it as a new state in the model and label it with action. Subsequently, we add two new transitions to the embedded model. The first transition goes from the origin_state to the new state with the original probability and the second transition goes from the new state to the destination_state with the probability 1. We also label the origin_state and the destination_state with the atomic proposition $\perp$. In a similar vein, we scan all the lines of the lts file and apply the above mentioned transformations.

Finally, these transformations are encoded into a set of MRFs, viz., a states file (.sta) containing information about the states of the model, a transitions file (.tra) containing information about all the transitions of the model and their associated probabilities, and a labels file (.lab) which contains all the information about the state labels. These three MRFs can be used to build the required PRISM model directly. Additionally, we also provide the option of generating a human readable source code file in PRISM which can be opened using its GUI to inspect, parse and build the model. Note that it is advisable to build the models directly using the machine-readable files of PRISM as this step is much quicker as compared to the model building step which uses the source code files.

Time Complexity. In the worst case, every state of the model can reach all the other states including itself in one step (as per the design of the lts file). This means that the outer loop would be executed $|S|$ times and the inner loop searching for the destination_state will also be executed $|S|$ times. Hence, the worst-case time complexity of the encoding presented in this paper would be of the order of $|S|^2$. Note that this is not a limitation as our encoding can be considered as a one-time investment where the embedded PRISM model can be used for verifying multiple probabilistic and reward-based properties. Moreover, as our experiments would demonstrate (e.g. see Table 1, Table 2 and Table 3), in

---

[1] Note that every distribution is internally represented as a single transition in the mCRL2.

practice the time required for transforming an lts file to the set of MRFs grows linearly with the size of the ADTMC model.

5 Case Studies

In order to validate the efficacy and usefulness of our approach, we have conducted detailed experiments with multiple case studies involving randomized systems. We have only selected those case studies which have already been modeled in the mCRL2 toolset. All the experiments were conducted on a workstation having 2.2 GHz 'Intel(R) Xeon(R) CPU E5-2650 v4' processor with 64 GB System Memory (4 × 16 GB DDR4) running Ubuntu 20.04 LTS. We have used the default settings of the PRISM toolset for evaluating our models. All reported times are in seconds and are obtained by taking the average of running the experiment 10 times. We report the encoding time for both the source code files and MRFs. Note that the source code files are only suitable for small-sized models as the time required for building PRISM models using these files is much higher as compared to the MRFs. Similarly, the time required for transforming an lts file to the source code files is also much higher as compared to the transformation from an lts to the MRFs. For this reason, we have used the MRFs for building the probabilistic models and for verifying them in PRISM. The detailed report of our experiments including the replication package (artefact) can be found in this repository[2].

5.1 Monty Hall TV Show Problem

In the Monty Hall problem, there are three doors, behind one of which lies a prize. The game begins when the player selects a door with probability $\frac{1}{3}$. Next, the host of the game opens one of the remaining doors showing that it does not hide the prize. Now, the player can decide to either stick to the original choice or switch doors. If the player decides to switch doors and select the third door, the probability of winning the prize is $\frac{2}{3}$. In the mCRL2 model of this problem, the player switches his choice once the first door has been opened. It has two actions, the action prize-true indicates that the prize is won and the action prize-false has the obvious complement interpretation. Hence, the prize can be won if the door selected initially did not contain the prize. The ADTMC modeled in mCRL2 has 10 states and 9 transitions. This property can be specified in APCTL as follows:

$$\mathcal{P} =?[(\mathbf{true})_{\mathbf{true}}\mathbf{U}_{prize-true}(\mathbf{true})]$$

The corresponding PCTL formula obtained by applying our logical embeddings is as follows :

$$\mathcal{P} =?[((\bot \wedge \mathbf{true}) \vee (\neg\bot \wedge \mathbf{true}))\mathbf{U}((\neg\bot \wedge \; prize - true) \wedge \mathcal{P}_{[1,1]}[\mathbf{X}(\bot \wedge \mathbf{true})])]$$

---

[2] https://doi.org/10.5281/zenodo.7813997.

This ADTMC can be transformed to an SDTMC using our model embeddings where the time required for generating MRFs is 0.00093 seconds. Similarly, the time required for generating the PRISM source code file is 0.00075 seconds. The SDTMC model was built in 0.0155 seconds and the time required for model checking this query was 0.0005 seconds. We also calculated the probability of not getting the prize which is $\frac{1}{3}$. This property was also verified in 0.0005 seconds.

5.2   Simulating a Dice Using Fair Coins

This problem aims to simulate the behavior of a 6-sided dice using a fair coin. In every step of the algorithm, a coin is tossed and there is 50% chance of taking each of the two possible choices. The algorithm terminates when you reach one of the values in the die. The mCRL2 model of this problem has 26 states and 26 transitions. By applying our model embeddings, the PRISM code file was generated in 0.00142 seconds and the MRFs were generated in 0.00188 seconds. The corresponding SDTMC has 63 states and 90 transitions. To show the correctness of this model, we need to ensure that each value from 1 to 6 should appear on the dice with a probability of $\frac{1}{6}$. This property can be specified in APCTL as follows :

$$\mathcal{P} = ?[(\mathbf{true})_{flip-true \vee flip-false} \mathbf{U}_{dice-i}(\mathbf{true})]$$

where $i = 1 \ldots 6$. The corresponding PCTL formula is as follows :

$$\mathcal{P} = ?[((\bot \wedge \mathbf{true}) \vee (\neg\bot \wedge (flip - true \vee flip - false))) \mathbf{U}((\neg\bot \wedge dice - i) \wedge \mathcal{P}_{[1,1]}[\mathbf{X}(\bot \wedge \mathbf{true})])]$$

PRISM took 0.022 seconds to build the model and the time required for model checking each of these properties was 0.00072 seconds. The case studies section of the PRISM model checking toolset discusses an additional important property, viz., 'What are the expected number of coin tosses required for an output of the dice throw?'. The answer to this query is $\frac{11}{3}$. This is a reward-based property and it cannot be specified and verified using mCRL2. In our embedded model, we have added a reward 'Flip' with value 1 for all the states which were labeled 'flip-true' or 'flip-false' as these states indicate that a coin toss has happened in the original model. Accordingly, we calculated the following formula :

$$R\{Flip\} = ?[F(dice - 1|dice - 2|dice - 3|dice - 4|dice - 5|dice - 6)] = \frac{11}{3}$$

The result of this query was obtained in 0.00165 seconds.

5.3   Ant on a Grid

Richard Chatwin's famous 'Ant on a Grid' puzzle appeared in The New York Times [4] and the puzzle has also been modeled in mCRL2. The puzzle is as follows: an ant is sitting on an 8×8 2-D grid board. Initially, the ant is at the intersection of the third horizontal line and the fifth vertical line (see Fig. 2).

The ant can move to an adjacent intersection along the grid lines, and it is equally likely to move in any one of the four directions. If the ant manages to reach the horizontal boundary, it survives; if the ant reaches the vertical boundary, it dies. What is the probability that the ant survives? The state-space of the corresponding model encoded in mCRL2 has 240 states and 240 transitions. The actions 'step', 'live', and 'dead' model that the ant takes a step, survives or dies, respectively. Using the model embeddings, we converted the ADTMC model to an SDTMC

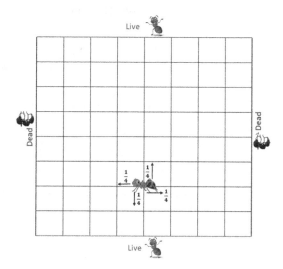

Fig. 2. Ant on a Grid

model where 0.0133 and 0.0165 seconds were required for generating the source code file and the set of MRFs, respectively. The embedded model has 577 states and 1300 transitions. The query 'What is the probability that the ant survives?' and its complement can be written in APCTL as follows:

$$\mathcal{P} =?[(\mathbf{true})_{step}\mathbf{U}_{live}(\mathbf{true})] \text{ and } \mathcal{P} =?[(\mathbf{true})_{step}\mathbf{U}_{dead}(\mathbf{true})]$$

Another interesting query that has emerged from the discussion forum for this puzzle is : 'What is the probability that the ant keeps moving inside the grid, never going to any of the edges?'. The complement of this property in APCTL is as follows :

$$\mathcal{P} =?[(\mathbf{true})_{\mathbf{true}}\mathbf{U}_{(live \vee dead)}(\mathbf{true})]$$

Let p be the probability of satisfying this property. Then the probability that the ant keeps moving inside the grid never going to any of the edges is $1 - p$. After applying the logical embeddings, the corresponding PCTL properties are as follows :

$$P_1 : \quad \mathcal{P} =?[((\bot \wedge \mathbf{true}) \vee (\neg\bot \wedge step))\mathbf{U}((\neg\bot \wedge live) \wedge \mathcal{P}_{[1,1]}[\mathbf{X}(\bot \wedge \mathbf{true})])]$$
$$P_2 : \quad \mathcal{P} =?[((\bot \wedge \mathbf{true}) \vee (\neg\bot \wedge step))\mathbf{U}((\neg\bot \wedge dead) \wedge \mathcal{P}_{[1,1]}[\mathbf{X}(\bot \wedge \mathbf{true})])]$$
$$P_3 : \quad \mathcal{P} =?[((\bot) \vee (\neg\bot))\mathbf{U}((\neg\bot \wedge (live \vee dead)) \wedge \mathcal{P}_{[1,1]}[\mathbf{X}(\bot \wedge \mathbf{true})])]$$

The probability of satisfying these PCTL properties and the time required for encoding, model building and model checking for different grid sizes has been shown in Table 1. Note that as we change the grid size, we have also changed the initial position of the ant by multiplying it with the same factor by which the grid size was increased. It can be observed that no matter what the grid is and what is

Table 1. Results for Ant on a Grid

Grid Size	Initial Position	ADTMC $|S| = |T|$	Encoding Time Code	MRF	SDTMC $|S'|$	$|T'|$	Build Time	Property	Value	Time
8 × 8	(5,3)	240	0.0133	0.0165	577	1300	0.066	P_1	0.5862	0.009
								P_2	0.4138	0.011
								P_3	1.0	0.006
16 × 16	(10,6)	1008	0.0664	0.069	2241	5268	0.195	P_1	0.5387	0.043
								P_2	0.4613	0.044
								P_3	1.00	0.015
64 × 64	(40,24)	16368	15.27	0.9998	33729	82836	3.375	P_1	0.508	4.503
								P_2	0.4908	4.511
								P_3	1.0	0.113
256 × 256	(160,96)	262128	5134.615	16.8762	528321	1314708	76.745	P_1	0.4967	1157.645
								P_2	0.4923	1165.757
								P_3	1.0	2.955

the initial position of the ant, the probability that the ant is stuck inside the grid and never arrives at any of the edges is $1 - p = 0$, where p is the probability of satisfying P_3. We also see that as the grid size increases, the probability that the ant is going to survive decreases and goes close to a 50–50 scenario. An additional interesting query that has emerged from the discussions of the New York Times column is 'What are the expected number of steps required by the ant to hit the boundary (dead/alive)?'. As mentioned earlier, such properties cannot be specified or analyzed using mCRL2. By adding rewards to our embedded model, we can analyze this property in PRISM. We have associated a reward structure that gives a reward of 1 to all states where 'step' was true. Next, we computed the following PRISM query :

```
R{"step"}=?[F ("dead"|"alive")]
```

The result of this query was 11.724 and the verification time was 0.008 seconds. The result of our query matches the value obtained via other techniques reported in [4].

5.4 Lost Boarding Pass Problem

There is a plane with N seats. The first passenger boarding the plane lost his boarding ticket and selects a random seat. Each subsequent passenger will use his own seat unless it is already occupied. In that case, he also selects a random seat. The question is 'What is the probability that the last passenger entering the plane will sit in his own seat?'. The mCRL2 model of this problem has actions 'enter', 'enter-plane', and 'last-passenger-has-his-own-seat' which refer to entering the plane, picking a seat, and whether the last person boarding is sitting on his own seat, respectively. The APCTL formula for this property is as follows :

$$\mathcal{P} =?[(\mathbf{true})_{enter\vee enter-plane} \mathbf{U}_{last-passenger-has-his-own-seat-true}(\mathbf{true})]$$

The corresponding embedded formula in PCTL is :

$$\mathcal{P} =?[((\bot \wedge \mathbf{true}) \vee (\neg\bot \wedge (enter \vee enter - plane)))\mathbf{U}((\neg\bot \wedge last -$$
$$passenger - has - his - own - seat - true) \wedge \mathcal{P}_{[1,1]}[\mathbf{X}(\bot \wedge \mathbf{true})])]$$

Table 2. Results for Lost Boarding Pass Problem

10^N	ADTMC $|S| = |T| + 1$	Encoding Time Code	MRF	SDTMC $|S'|$	$|T'|$	Build Time	Value	Time
1	71	0.0032	0.0041	158	191	0.0295	0.5	0.006
2	791	0.036	0.0412	1778	2171	0.133	0.5	0.039
3	7991	1.351	0.3685	17978	21971	1.525	0.5	1.195
4	79991	262.2	3.8421	179978	219971	20.736	0.5	93.031
5	799991	50460.889	39.7816	1799978	2199971	303.93	0.5	38752.431

The time required for model encoding, model building, and model checking for different values of N has been shown in Table 2. A reward query for the given problem is: 'what is the expected value of "enter" at the instance when the last passenger chooses his/her seat?'. For a plane with N seats, this should always be $N - 1$. We have verified this reward property in PRISM using the following query :

```
R{"enter"}=?[F "last-passenger-has-his-own-seat-true"|
"last-passenger-has-his-own-seat-false"]
```

The time required for verifying this query in PRISM for $N = 10$, 100, and 1000 is 0.0007, 0.025, and 1.416 seconds, respectively.

5.5 Bounded Re-transmission Protocol (BRP)

BRP is a data link protocol for transmitting partitioned files over unreliable channels [10]. It sends a file in a number of chunks, but allows only a bounded number of re-transmissions of each chunk. Let N denote the number of chunks and MAX be the maximum allowed number of re-transmissions of each chunk. There is a channel (K) which facilitates this send and receive process of each chunk but the channel has a failure rate of 10%. As a result, we need another channel (L) which sends an acknowledgment to the sender when the sent chunk has been received successfully. Let the failure rate of L be 20%. Whenever a failure occurs, the sender re-attempts to send the chunk. As mentioned earlier, the number of re-attempts is bounded by MAX and after this the process is considered to have failed and needs to be restarted.

A ADTMC which models this protocol has been given as one of the example case studies in the mCRL2 toolset. The model hides a number of actions by labeling them as τ transitions. Here, action 'c-aF' denote that the sender is starting an attempt to send a chunk; 'success-frame' models that a chunk was acknowledged successfully; 'c-success-file' models that all parts of the file were sent and acknowledged (transmission complete) ; and 'fail-transmission' models that maximum attempts have been made and the process needs to be restarted. We will check the following queries on this model: (a) 'What is the probability that the file will be sent successfully without losing a chunk more than MAX times?', (b) 'What is the probability that the file will be sent successfully after starting over a finite number of times?'. These queries can be encoded in APCTL as follows:

$$P_1 : \mathcal{P} =?[(\mathbf{true})_{(c-aF \vee success-frame)} \mathbf{U}_{c-success-file}(\mathbf{true})]$$
$$P_2 : \mathcal{P} =?[(\mathbf{true})_{(c-aF \vee success-frame \vee fail-transmission)} \mathbf{U}_{c-success-file}(\mathbf{true})]$$

Table 3. 'Results for BRP Problem

(N,MAX)	ADTMC	Encoding Time		SDTMC		Build	Prpoerty	Value	Time
	$|S| = |T|$	Code	MRF	$|S'|$	$|T'|$	Time			
(16,2)	387	0.0101	0.0122	516	612	0.051	P_1	0.952	0.016
							P_2	1.0	0.005
(16,3)	499	0.0129	0.015	660	788	0.063	P_1	0.993	0.024
							P_2	1.0	0.008
(16,4)	611	0.0187	0.0187	804	964	0.067	P_1	0.999	0.025
							P_2	1.0	0.01
(16,5)	723	0.0187	0.0222	948	1140	0.084	P_1	1.0	0.031
							P_2	1.0	0.015
(32,2)	771	0.0201	0.0236	1028	1220	0.085	P_1	0.907	0.021
							P_2	1.0	0.01
(32,3)	995	0.0261	0.0299	1316	1572	0.101	P_1	0.986	0.049
							P_2	1.0	0.029
(32,4)	1219	0.0327	0.0374	1604	1924	0.125	P_1	0.998	0.046
							P_2	1.0	0.029
(32,5)	1443	0.0398	0.0442	1892	2276	0.164	P_1	1.0	0.049
							P_2	1.0	0.023
(64,2)	1539	0.0430	0.0474	2052	2436	0.218	P_1	0.822	0.101
							P_2	1.0	0.071
(64,3)	1987	0.0599	0.0613	2628	3140	0.217	P_1	0.972	0.105
							P_2	1.0	0.071
(64,4)	2435	0.0790	0.0740	3204	3844	0.225	P_1	0.996	0.112
							P_2	1.0	0.065
(64,5)	2883	0.0956	0.0876	3780	4548	0.305	P_1	1.0	0.152
							P_2	1.0	0.111

The embedded PCTL formulas can be constructed by applying the logical embeddings. We report the time required for encoding, building the model, and model checking for different values of N and MAX in Table 3. An interesting reward-based property is: What are the expected number of attempts made by the sender before all the chunks of the file were sent and acknowledged, i.e. reaching a state labeled 'c-success-file'?. We define a reward 'caF' and associate a reward of 1 with all the states whose label is 'c-aF'. Next, we can formulate the query in PRISM as follows :

$$R\{"caF"\}=?[F\ "c\text{-}success\text{-}file"]$$

For $N = 16, MAX = 2$, this query is verified in 0.005 seconds and the answer is 19.148. Similarly, for $N = 32, MAX = 2$ and $N = 64, MAX = 2$, the values are 39.254, and 82.53, respectively. The time required for verifying these properties is : 0.014 seconds and 0.056 seconds, respectively.

6   Conclusion

This paper studies the effect of applying model and logical embeddings to probabilistic process algebraic models. Our approach accepts ADTMC models encoded in mCRL2 and transforms it to an SDTMC model which can be used by the PRISM toolset for verification. The user has the flexibility to either generate the set of machine readable files (MRFs) or human readable source code files both of which can be used for building the PRISM models. Our approach enables verifying the probabilistic behavior modeled using mCRL2 by transforming the APCTL properties to the PCTL formulae and checking them on the embedded SDTMC using PRISM. Note that mCRL2 does not provide support for the verification of probabilistic models, and therefore our approach would be very useful for the performance and reliability evaluation of such systems. In a similar vein, our approach can also be used to verify interesting reward-based properties which cannot be specified using mCRL2. This research work can be extended in several interesting directions which are as follows: 1) Implement a prototypical tool that allows converting PRISM models to mCRL2 models and vice versa. This tool should also provide support for the automatic translation of logical specifications, e.g. PCTL (PCTL*, resp.) to APCTL (APCTL*, resp.) and vice versa. For example, such a tool would enable minimizing PRISM models using bisimulation algorithms implemented in mCRL2. 2) Investigate the possibility of developing similar toolsets for connecting other probabilistic model checkers, e.g. one can try to develop a tool which would allow verifying CADP models [25] using PRISM toolset and vice versa. 3) Motivated by the fact that our embeddings can also be used for analyzing reward-based properties, we also plan to extend APCTL and APCTL* with rewards and accordingly modify the logical embeddings. Finally, it would also be interesting to investigate if these model embeddings preserve weighted probabilistic equivalence [31,32] and weak equivalence relations, e.g. weak forward bisimulation [8].

References

1. https://www.mcrl2.org/web/user_manual/index.html#
2. https://www.prismmodelchecker.org/
3. Andova, S., Hermanns, H., Katoen, J.-P.: Discrete-time rewards model-checked. In: Larsen, K.G., Niebert, P. (eds.) FORMATS 2003. LNCS, vol. 2791, pp. 88–104. Springer, Heidelberg (2004). https://doi.org/10.1007/978-3-540-40903-8_8
4. Antonick, G.: Ant on a grid. Wordplay : the crossword blog of the New York Times (2013). https://archive.nytimes.com/wordplay.blogs.nytimes.com/2013/08/12/ants-2/
5. Aziz, A., Singhal, V., Balarin, F.: It usually works: the temporal logic of stochastic systems. In: Computer Aided Verification, 7th International Conference, Liège, Belgium, 3–5 July 1995, Proceedings, pp. 155–165 (1995)
6. Baeten, J.C.M., Bergstra, J.A., Smolka, S.A.: Axiomatizing probabilistic processes: ACP with generative probabilities. Inf. Comput. **121**(2), 234–255 (1995)
7. Baier, C., Katoen, J.P.: Principles of Model Checking. MIT Press, Cambridge (2008)
8. Baier, C., Katoen, J.P., Hermanns, H., Wolf, V.: Comparative branching-time semantics for Markov chains. Inf. Comput. **200**(2), 149–214 (2005)
9. Bunte, O., et al.: The mCRL2 toolset for analysing concurrent systems. In: Vojnar, T., Zhang, L. (eds.) TACAS 2019. LNCS, vol. 11428, pp. 21–39. Springer, Cham (2019). https://doi.org/10.1007/978-3-030-17465-1_2
10. D'Argenio, P.R., Jeannet, B., Jensen, H.E., Larsen, K.G.: Reachability analysis of probabilistic systems by successive refinements. In: de Alfaro, L., Gilmore, S. (eds.) PAPM-PROBMIV 2001. LNCS, vol. 2165, pp. 39–56. Springer, Heidelberg (2001). https://doi.org/10.1007/3-540-44804-7_3
11. Das, S., Sharma, A.: Embeddings between state and action labeled probabilistic systems. In: SAC 2021: The 36th ACM/SIGAPP Symposium on Applied Computing, Virtual Event, Republic of Korea, 22–26 March 2021, pp. 1759–1767 (2021)
12. Das, S., Sharma, A.: Embeddings between state and action based probabilistic logics. In: Formal Aspects of Component Software - 18th International Conference, FACS 2022, Virtual Event, 10–11 November 2022, Proceedings, pp. 121–140 (2022)
13. Dehnert, C., Junges, S., Katoen, J.-P., Volk, M.: A s coming: a modern probabilistic model checker. In: Majumdar, R., Kunčak, V. (eds.) CAV 2017. LNCS, vol. 10427, pp. 592–600. Springer, Cham (2017). https://doi.org/10.1007/978-3-319-63390-9_31
14. Garavel, H., Lang, F., Mateescu, R., Serwe, W.: CADP 2010: a toolbox for the construction and analysis of distributed processes. In: Tools and Algorithms for the Construction and Analysis of Systems - 17th International Conference, TACAS 2011, Held as Part of the Joint European Conferences on Theory and Practice of Software, ETAPS 2011, Saarbrücken, Germany, 26–April 3 March 2011, Proceedings, pp. 372–387 (2011)
15. Groote, J.F., Keiren, J.J.A., Luttik, B., de Vink, E.P., Willemse, T.A.C.: Modelling and analysing software in mCRL2. In: Arbab, F., Jongmans, S.-S. (eds.) FACS 2019. LNCS, vol. 12018, pp. 25–48. Springer, Cham (2020). https://doi.org/10.1007/978-3-030-40914-2_2
16. Hansson, H., Jonsson, B.: A calculus for communicating systems with time and probabitilies. In: RTSS, pp. 278–287. IEEE Computer Society (1990)
17. Hansson, H., Jonsson, B.: A logic for reasoning about time and reliability. Formal Asp. Comput. **6**(5), 512–535 (1994)

18. Hensel, C., Junges, S., Katoen, J., Quatmann, T., Volk, M.: The probabilistic model checker storm. Int. J. Softw. Tools Technol. Transf. **24**(4), 589–610 (2022)
19. Hermanns, H., Parma, A., Segala, R., Wachter, B., Zhang, L.: Probabilistic logical characterization. Inf. Comput. **209**(2), 154–172 (2011)
20. Kwiatkowska, M., Norman, G., Parker, D.: PRISM 4.0: verification of probabilistic real-time systems. In: Gopalakrishnan, G., Qadeer, S. (eds.) CAV 2011. LNCS, vol. 6806, pp. 585–591. Springer, Heidelberg (2011). https://doi.org/10.1007/978-3-642-22110-1_47
21. Larsen, K.G., Mardare, R., Xue, B.: Probabilistic mu-calculus: decidability and complete axiomatization. In: 36th IARCS Annual Conference on Foundations of Software Technology and Theoretical Computer Science, FSTTCS 2016, 13–15 December 2016, Chennai, India. LIPIcs, vol. 65, pp. 25:1–25:18. Schloss Dagstuhl - Leibniz-Zentrum für Informatik (2016)
22. Liu, W., Song, L., Wang, J., Zhang, L.: A simple probabilistic extension of modal mu-calculus. In: Proceedings of the Twenty-Fourth International Joint Conference on Artificial Intelligence, IJCAI 2015, Buenos Aires, Argentina, 25–31 July 2015, pp. 882–888 (2015)
23. Lowe, G.: Probabilistic and prioritized models of timed CSP. Theor. Comput. Sci. **138**(2), 315–352 (1995)
24. Marsan, M.A., Conte, G., Balbo, G.: A class of generalized stochastic Petri nets for the performance evaluation of multiprocessor systems. ACM Trans. Comput. Syst. **2**(2), 93–122 (1984)
25. Mateescu, R., Requeno, J.I.: On-the-fly model checking for extended action-based probabilistic operators. Int. J. Softw. Tools Technol. Transf. **20**(5), 563–587 (2018)
26. Miguel, C., Fernández, A., Vidaller, L.: LOTOS extended with probablistic behaviours. Formal Asp. Comput. **5**(3), 253–281 (1993)
27. Mio, M.: Game semantics for probabilistic modal μ-calculi. The University of Edinburgh, Edinburgh (2012)
28. Mio, M.: Probabilistic modal mu-calculus with independent product. Log. Methods Comput. Sci. **8**(4) (2012)
29. De Nicola, R., Vaandrager, F.: Action versus state based logics for transition systems. In: Guessarian, I. (ed.) LITP 1990. LNCS, vol. 469, pp. 407–419. Springer, Heidelberg (1990). https://doi.org/10.1007/3-540-53479-2_17
30. Parma, A., Segala, R.: Logical characterizations of bisimulations for discrete probabilistic systems. In: Foundations of Software Science and Computational Structures, 10th International Conference, FOSSACS 2007, Held as Part of the Joint European Conferences on Theory and Practice of Software, ETAPS 2007, Braga, Portugal, March 24-April 1, 2007, Proceedings, pp. 287–301 (2007)
31. Sharma, A.: Weighted probabilistic equivalence preserves ω-regular properties. In: Schmitt, J.B. (ed.) MMB&DFT 2012. LNCS, vol. 7201, pp. 121–135. Springer, Heidelberg (2012). https://doi.org/10.1007/978-3-642-28540-0_9
32. Sharma, A.: Reduction Techniques for Nondeterministic and Probabilistic Systems. Ph.D. thesis, RWTH Aachen University, Germany (2015)

On Bisimilarity for Polyhedral Models and SLCS

Vincenzo Ciancia[1]([✉])[ID], David Gabelaia[2][ID], Diego Latella[1][ID], Mieke Massink[1][ID], and Erik P. de Vink[3][ID]

[1] Consiglio Nazionale delle Ricerche - ISTI, Pisa, Italy
{Vincenzo.Ciancia,Diego.Latella,Mieke.Massink}@cnr.it
[2] TSU Razmadze Mathematical Institute, Tbilisi, Georgia
[3] Eindhoven University of Technology, Eindhoven, The Netherlands
evink@win.tue.nl

Abstract. The notion of bisimilarity plays an important role in concurrency theory. It provides formal support to the idea of processes having "equivalent behaviour" and is a powerful tool for model reduction. Furthermore, bisimilarity typically coincides with logical equivalence of an appropriate modal logic enabling model checking to be applied on reduced models. Recently, notions of bisimilarity have been proposed also for models of space, including those based on polyhedra. The latter are central in many domains of application that exploit mesh processing and typically consist of millions of cells, the basic components of face-poset models, discrete representations of polyhedral models. This paper builds on the *polyhedral semantics* of the Spatial Logic for Closure Spaces (SLCS) for which the geometric spatial model checker `PolyLogicA` has been developed, that is based on face-poset models. We propose a novel notion of spatial bisimilarity for face-poset models, called $\pm$-bisimilarity. We show that it coincides with logical equivalence induced by SLCS on such models. The latter corresponds to logical equivalence with respect to SLCS on polyhedra which, in turn, coincides with simplicial bisimilarity, a notion of bisimilarity for continuous spaces.

Keywords: Bisimulation relations · Spatial bisimilarity · Spatial logics · Logical equivalence · Spatial model checking · Polyhedral models

1 Introduction

In concurrency theory, the notion of bisimilarity plays an important role. It provides formal support to the idea of processes having "equivalent behaviour"

Research partially supported by MUR projects PRIN 2017FTXR7S, "IT-MaTTerS", PRIN 2020TL3X8X "T-LADIES", bilateral project between CNR (Italy) and SRNSFG (Georgia) "Model Checking for Polyhedral Logic" (#CNR-22-010), and European Union - Next Generation EU - Italian MUR project PNRR PRI ECS00000017 PRR.AP008.003 "THE - Tuscany Health Ecosystem". The authors are listed in alphabetical order, as they equally contributed to the work presented in this paper.

M. Huisman and A. Ravara (Eds.): FORTE 2023, LNCS 13910, pp. 132–151, 2023.
https://doi.org/10.1007/978-3-031-35355-0_9

and is a powerful tool for model reduction. Furthermore, bisimilarity often coincides with logical equivalence of appropriate modal logics enabling techniques for enhancing model checking [32,33,43]. Recently, notions of bisimilarity have been proposed also for models of space [11,19], including polyhedral models [12].

In this work we are following a *topological* approach to spatial logic. This approach has its origin in the early ideas by McKinsey and Tarski [42], who gave a topological interpretation of the "necessarily" operator of the **S4** modal logic. The approach was extended to consider *Closure Spaces* (CS) [50], a generalisation of topological spaces, covering also discrete spaces such as general graphs, following work by Galton [29,30] and Smyth and Webster [47], among others. Recent work by Ciancia et al. (see [24,25]) builds on these theoretical developments using CSs, or better, *Closure Models* (CMs), as the underlying framework for the *Spatial Logic for Closure Spaces* (SLCS). A closure model is composed of a CS together with a valuation function mapping every atomic proposition letter p of a given set into the set of points in the space satisfying p. A spatio-temporal model checker, topochecker [22], has been developed for the subclass of finite closure spaces. Spatial and spatio-temporal logics and related model checking tools have been used in several application domains such as collective and distributed systems [5, 20,26,41,45,48]. Moreover, the spatial model-checker VoxLogicA[1] [10] has been developed, that is optimised for digital 2D and 3D images, interpreted as a special case of finite closure spaces, and has been applied successfully in the area of medical imaging [7–10].

However, for the 2D and 3D visualisation of continuous spatial objects, both in medical imaging and virtual reality, polyhedral models of *continuous* space are often used. Such spatial models consist of a suitable splitting of the image of an object into areas of different size, known as *meshes*. These include triangular surface meshes or tetrahedral volume meshes (see for example [37]). In [12], an interpretation of SLCS on polyhedral models has been defined along with a novel notion of bisimilarity for such models, namely *simplicial bisimilarity*. Moreover, the theoretical foundations have been developed for polyhedral model checking, including a global model checking algorithm for SLCS and its implementation in the PolyLogicA (see footnote 1) tool. A visualiser for models and model checking results has been developed as well. Figure 1 provides an example of the use of polyhedral model checking to visualise some part of interest in a 3D tetrahedral volume mesh of a maze composed of 147,245 cells. A cell (see Fig. 2) is the basic element of the face-poset model, a discrete representation of a polyhedral model. In [12], also a relational interpretation of SLCS on face-poset models has been proposed and it has been shown that the mapping of polyhedral models to face-poset models preserves and reflects the logic. Figure 1b highlights the result of polyhedral SLCS model checking for a set of spatial reachability properties, for the maze in Fig. 1a, characterising those white rooms and their connecting gray corridors, from which both a red and a green room can be reached, without passing by black rooms. For details on the property specification and model checking experiments see [12].

---

[1] Available from the VoxLogicA repository at https://github.com/vincenzoml/VoxLogicA.

It should be pointed out that, often, images consist of a very large number of cells—much larger than in the example mentioned above—typically several millions or more.

Contribution. The main contribution of the present paper is the development of a novel notion of spatial bisimulation, namely ±-bisimilarity on face-poset models representing polyhedral models. We show that two cells are logically equivalent according to the relational interpretation of SLCS (see [12]) if and only if they are ±-bisimilar. A direct consequence of this result is that two points in a polyhedral model are logically equivalent if and only if the unique cells they belong to are ±-bisimilar in the face-poset model. This result paves the way to face-poset model reduction based on ±-bisimilarity, while preserving the SLCS properties of the polyhedral models they represent. We illustrate this by means of a running example of a polyhedral model and the reduction of its discrete representation modulo ±-bisimilarity (see Figs. 3, 4, 5 and 8). As a corollary, we note that two points in a polyhedral model are simplicial bisimilar if and only if their corresponding cells in the face-poset are ±-bisimilar. These results also show how suitable adaptations of notions and results that constitute a flourishing area of research in the field of concurrency theory can be exploited in other domains as well, including theories of space and spatially distributed systems. All in all, our results allow for model-checking of SLCS formulas on a continuous spatial model by conducting actual computations on the minimal face-poset representation.

Further Related Work. In the domain of geographic information systems (GIS) simplicial complexes are used as an efficient data structure to store large geospatial data sets [14] in 2D or 3D. They also form the core of several important tools in this domain such as the GeoToolKit [6]. Polyhedral model checking techniques

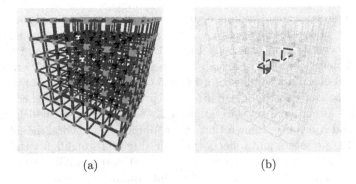

(a)   (b)

Fig. 1. (a) 3D maze with green, white and black rooms, and one red room somewhere in the middle. (b) Polyhedral model checking result highlighting white rooms and their connecting grey corridors from which both a red and a green room can be reached without passing by black rooms. Source [12]. (Color figure online)

could potentially enrich the spatial query languages that are currently used in this database-oriented domain.

Polyhedra are also used in the theoretical foundations of real-time and hybrid model checking (see for example [3,4,13,35,36] and references therein). In that context polyhedra, and their related notions such as template polyhedra [13,46] and zonotopes [31], are obtained from sets of linear inequalities involving real-time constraints on system behaviour and are a natural representation of sets of states of such systems. However, in the present paper we focus on *spatial* properties of continuous space rather than on behavioural properties of systems.

In [34], coalgebraic bisimilarity has been developed for a general kind of models, generalising the topological ones, known as Neighbourhood Frames. To the best of our knowledge, the notions of path and reachability are not part of that framework (that is, bisimilarity in neighbourhood semantics is based on a one-step relation rather than on paths), thus the results therein, although more general than the theory of CSs, cannot be directly reused in the setting of our current work. In [38,39] the spatial logic SLCS is studied from a model-theoretic perspective. In particular, in [38] the authors focus on issues of expressivity of SLCS in relation to topological connectedness and separation. In [39] it is shown that the logic admits finite models for quasi-discrete neighbourhood models, but it does not do it for general neighbourhood models. The work in [40] introduces bisimulation relations that characterise spatial logics with reachability in simplicial complexes. It uses SLCS, but with different simplex semantics.

Spatial logics have also been proposed to describe situations in which modal operators are interpreted syntactically against the structure of agents in a process calculus. Some classical examples can be found in [16,17]. A recent example following such an approach is given in [49]. It concerns model checking of security aspects in cyber-physical systems, in a spatial context based on the idea of bigraphical reactive systems introduced by Milner [44].

The work on *spatial model checking* for logics with reachability originated in [24] and was further developed in [25], which includes also a comparison to the work of Aiello on spatial *until* operators (see e.g. [1]). In [2], Aiello envisaged practical applications of topological logics with an *until* operator to minimisation of images. Recent work in [19,27] builds on—and extends—that vision, taking CoPa-bisimilarity as a suitable equivalence for spatial minimisation.

2 Background and Notation

We first introduce some background concepts and related notation. For a function $f : X \to Y$, and subsets $A \subseteq X$ and $B \subseteq Y$, we define $f(A)$ and $f^{-1}(B)$ as $\{f(a) \mid a \in A\}$ and $\{a \mid f(a) \in B\}$, respectively. The *restriction* of f on A is denoted by $f|A$. The set of natural numbers and that of real numbers are denoted by $\mathbb{N}$ and $\mathbb{R}$, respectively. We use the standard interval notation: for $x, y \in \mathbb{R}$ we let $[x, y]$ be the set $\{r \in \mathbb{R} \mid x \leq r \leq y\}$, $[x, y) = \{r \in \mathbb{R} \mid x \leq r < y\}$ and so on, where $[x, y]$ is equipped with the Euclidean topology inherited from $\mathbb{R}$. We use a similar notation for intervals over $\mathbb{N}$: for $n, m \in \mathbb{N}$ $[m; n]$ denotes

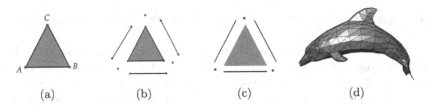

Fig. 2. (a) A simplicial complex (actually a simplex itself). (b) Decomposed into its simplexes as faces. (c) Partitioned into its cells. (d) A triangular surface mesh of a dolphin [18].

the set $\{i \in \mathbb{N} \mid m \leq i \leq n\}$, $[m; n)$ denotes the set $\{i \in \mathbb{N} \mid m \leq i < n\}$, and similarly for $(m; n]$ and $(m; n)$.

In the remainder of this section, we recall the main results concerning the interpretation of SLCS on polyhedral models. The interested reader is referred to [12] for a detailed treatment of the subject. Section 2.1 below recalls the basic notions of simplex, simplicial complex and polyhedral model. Then, in Sect. 2.2 simplicial bisimilarity and the SLCS interpretation on polyhedral models are briefly reviewed as well as their relationship. The discrete representation of polyhedral models in terms of face-poset models and the SLCS interpretation on the latter is recalled in Sect. 2.3 where their formal relationship is also shown.

2.1 Simplex, Simplicial Complexes and Polyhedra

The notions of simplex, simplicial complex and polyhedron form the basis for geometrical reasoning in a finite setting, amenable to polyhedral model-checking and related techniques. A *simplex* is the convex hull of a set of affinely independent points[2], namely the vertices of the simplex.

Definition 1 (Simplex). *A simplex σ of dimension d is the convex hull of a finite set $\{\mathbf{v_0}, \dots, \mathbf{v_d}\} \subseteq \mathbb{R}^m$ of $d + 1$ affinely independent points, i.e. $\sigma = \{\lambda_0 \mathbf{v_0} + \dots + \lambda_d \mathbf{v_d} \mid \lambda_0, \dots, \lambda_d \in [0, 1] \text{ and } \sum_{i=0}^{d} \lambda_i = 1\}$.* •

Note that a simplex is a subset of the ambient space $\mathbb{R}^m$ and so it inherits its topological structure. Given a simplex σ with vertices $\mathbf{v_0}, \dots, \mathbf{v_d}$, any subset of $\{\mathbf{v_0}, \dots, \mathbf{v_d}\}$ spans a simplex σ' in turn: we say that σ' is a *face* of σ, written $\sigma' \sqsubseteq \sigma$. Clearly, $\sqsubseteq$ is a partial order relation.

The *relative interior* of a simplex plays a similar role as the notion of "interior" in topology and is defined as follows:

Definition 2 (Relative Interior of a Simplex). *Given a simplex σ with vertices $\{\mathbf{v_0}, \dots, \mathbf{v_d}\}$ the relative interior $\tilde{\sigma}$ of σ is the set $\{\lambda_0 \mathbf{v_0} + \dots + \lambda_d \mathbf{v_d} \mid \lambda_0, \dots, \lambda_d \in (0, 1] \text{ and } \sum_{i=0}^{d} \lambda_i = 1\}$.* •

---

[2] $\mathbf{v_0}, \dots, \mathbf{v_d}$ are affinely independent if $\mathbf{v_1} - \mathbf{v_0}, \dots, \mathbf{v_d} - \mathbf{v_0}$ are linearly independent. In particular, this condition implies that $d \leq m$.

We write $\widetilde{\sigma}' \preceq \widetilde{\sigma}$ whenever $\sigma' \sqsubseteq \sigma$, noting that $\preceq$ is a partial order as well and that $\widetilde{\sigma}' \preceq \widetilde{\sigma}$ if and only if $\widetilde{\sigma}'$ is included in the topological closure of $\widetilde{\sigma}$.

The notion of *simplicial complex* builds upon that of simplex and is the fundamental tool for constructing complex geometrical objects as sets of points in $\mathbb{R}^m$, namely polyhedra, out of simplexes.

Definition 3 (Simplicial Complex and Polyhedron). *A simplicial complex K is a finite collection of simplexes of $\mathbb{R}^m$ such that: (i) if $\sigma \in K$ and $\sigma' \sqsubseteq \sigma$ then also $\sigma' \in K$; (ii) if $\sigma, \sigma' \in K$ then $\sigma \cap \sigma' \sqsubseteq \sigma$ and $\sigma \cap \sigma' \sqsubseteq \sigma'$. The* polyhedron $|K|$ *of K is the set-theoretic union of the simplexes in K.*   •

Relations $\sqsubseteq$ and $\preceq$ on simplexes are inherited by simplicial complexes: relation $\sqsubseteq$ on simplicial complex K is the union of the face relations on the simplexes composing K, and similarly for $\preceq$. Note that different simplicial complexes can give rise to the same polyhedron and that the set $\widetilde{K} = \{\widetilde{\sigma} \mid \sigma \in K \setminus \{\emptyset\}\}$ of non-empty relative interiors of the simplexes of a simplicial complex K forms a partition of polyhedron $|K|$. The elements of $\widetilde{K}$ are called *cells* and $(\widetilde{K}, \preceq)$ is the face-poset of K. Note that, by definition of partition, each $x \in |K|$ belongs to a unique cell in the face-poset. We recall that the polyhedron $|K|$ is a subset of the ambient space $\mathbb{R}^m$ and so inherits its topological structure.

Example. Figure 2 shows a triangle as an example of a simplicial complex, and its simplexes in the face relation. The triangle can be partitioned into 7 cells (see Fig. 2c): its interior (ABC, an open triangle), three open segments (AB, BC, AC, the sides without endpoints) and the three vertices (A, B, C). Each vertex is a face of two open segments (and of the open triangle itself), and each open segment is a face of the open triangle. The figure shows also a small example of a triangular surface mesh of a dolphin (Fig. 2d).

Paths play a fundamental role in the definition of SLCS and are defined below:

Definition 4 (Topological and Simplicial Path). *A topological path in a topological space P is a total, continuous function $\pi : [0,1] \to P$. Given a polyhedron $|K|$, a topological path $\pi : [0,1] \to |K|$ is simplicial if and only if there is a finite sequence $r_0 = 0 < \ldots < r_n = 1$ of values in $[0,1]$ and cells $\widetilde{\sigma}_1, \ldots, \widetilde{\sigma}_n \in \widetilde{K}$ such that, for all $i = 1, \ldots, n$, we have $\pi((r_{i-1}, r_i)) \subseteq \widetilde{\sigma}_i$.*   •

In the polyhedral semantics of SLCS proposed in [12], all the points of a polyhedral model that belong to the same cell are required to satisfy the same set of atomic proposition letters. This is reflected in the definition below:

Definition 5 (Polyhedral Model). *For simplicial complex K and set of proposition letters AP, a* polyhedral model *is a pair $(|K|, V)$ where $V : AP \to \mathcal{P}(|K|)$ is a valuation function such that, for all $p \in AP$, $V(p)$ is a union of cells in $\widetilde{K}$.*   •

2.2   Simplicial Bisimulation and SLCS on Polyhedral Models

The notion of simplicial bisimilarity for polyhedra is central in the theory of the polyhedral interpretation of SLCS, together with Theorem 1 below [12]. Simplicial

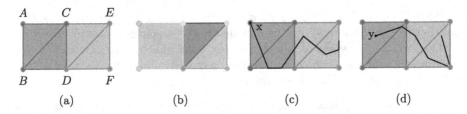

Fig. 3. An example of simplicial bisimilarity. Adapted from [12]. (Color figure online)

bisimilarity is based on the notion of topological paths and is recalled below as well. The use of paths is reminiscent to the definition of stuttering equivalence for Kripke structures or branching bisimilarity for process calculi [15,28,33]. However, here, the notion is cast in the setting of continuous space.

Definition 6 (Simplicial Bisimulation). *Given a Polyhedral Model* $\mathcal{X} = (|K|, V)$, *a symmetric binary relation* $B \subseteq |K| \times |K|$ *is a* simplicial bisimulation *if, for all* $x_1, x_2 \in |K|$, $B(x_1, x_2)$ *implies the following:*

1. $V^{-1}(\{x_1\}) = V^{-1}(\{x_2\})$;
2. *for each simplicial path* π_1 *with* $\pi_1(0) = x_1$ *there is a simplicial path* π_2 *with* $\pi_2(0) = x_2$ *such that* $B(\pi_1(t), \pi_2(t))$ *for all* $t \in [0, 1]$;   •

In [12] it has been shown that, for any given polyhedral model the largest simplicial bisimulation exists. We call it *Simplicial Bisimilarity* and we write $x_1 \sim x_2$ whenever x_1 and x_2 are simplicial bisimilar.

Example. Figure 3 illustrates simplicial bisimilarity. Figure 3a shows a polyhedral model composed of four triangles forming two adjacent squares. Atomic proposition letters are represented by colours (e.g. red points satisfy red, green points satisfy green etc.). Figure 3b shows the nine equivalence classes induced by simplicial bisimilarity in the polyhedral model of Fig. 3a. Different classes are shown using different colours.[3] From the figure it is clear that, for instance, no point, call it x_1, in the yellow class (i.e. open segment CD) is bisimilar to any point, call it x_2, in the cyan class. This is because there are simplicial paths π_1 starting from x_1 that *immediately* enter the green area of Fig. 3a (i.e. $V^{-1}(\pi_1(\varepsilon)) = $ green for any small $\varepsilon > 0$) whereas this is impossible for any simplicial path π_2 starting from x_2 ($V^{-1}(\pi_2(\varepsilon)) = $ red for any small $\varepsilon > 0$ and every such path π_2). This implies that $B(x_1, x_2)$ for no simplicial bisimulation B. In fact, the second condition of Definition 6 would be violated since $B(\pi_1(\varepsilon), \pi_2(\varepsilon))$ cannot hold for ε as above. Similarly, a simplicial path starting from point D (i.e. the only point in the orange) can *immediately* enter the red area of Fig. 3a. On the other hand, no simplicial path starting from any other point satisfying gray can do that.

---

[3] Note that the colours of the classes have only an illustrative purpose; in particular they have nothing to do with the colours expressing the evaluation function of atomic proposition letters.

Note, in particular, that any point in the gray segment CE can reach the red area via a simplicial path, but any such path must first go through part of CE itself and/or the green area CDE. So, also in this case, the second condition of Definition 6 would be violated. Figures 3c and 3d show an example of pairs of simplicial paths that witness $x \sim y$.

The following definition introduces the variant of SLCS for polyhedral models proposed in [12]. In the present paper, we denote it by SLCS$_\gamma$.

Definition 7 (SLCS on polyhedral models - SLCS$_\gamma$). *The abstract language of SLCS$_\gamma$ is the following:* $\Phi ::= p \mid \neg\Phi \mid \Phi_1 \wedge \Phi_2 \mid \gamma(\Phi_1, \Phi_2)$.

The satisfaction relation of SLCS$_\gamma$ with respect to a given polyhedral model $\mathcal{X} = (|K|, V)$, *SLCS$_\gamma$ formula* Φ, *and* $x \in |K|$ *is defined recursively on the structure of* Φ *as follows:*

$$\mathcal{X}, x \models p \quad \Leftrightarrow x \in V(p);$$
$$\mathcal{X}, x \models \neg\Phi \quad \Leftrightarrow \mathcal{X}, x \models \Phi \text{ does not hold;}$$
$$\mathcal{X}, x \models \Phi_1 \wedge \Phi_2 \quad \Leftrightarrow \mathcal{X}, x \models \Phi_1 \text{ and } \mathcal{X}, x \models \Phi_2;$$
$$\mathcal{X}, x \models \gamma(\Phi_1, \Phi_2) \Leftrightarrow \text{ a topological path } \pi : [0,1] \to |K| \text{ exists such that } \pi(0) = x,$$
$$\mathcal{X}, \pi(1) \models \Phi_2, \text{ and } \mathcal{X}, \pi(r) \models \Phi_1 \text{ for all } r \in (0,1).$$

Note that the above definition generalises the classical topological interpretation of the $\square$ modality as interior. In fact, $\square\Phi$ is equivalent to $\neg\gamma(\neg\Phi, \mathtt{true})$ (see [12]).

Example. Again with reference to model $\mathcal{X}$ of Fig. 3a, it is easy to see that any point in the yellow class satisfies, for instance, $\gamma(\mathtt{green}, \mathtt{true})$, and also $\gamma(\mathtt{green}, \mathtt{red})$ and $\mathtt{red} \wedge \gamma(\mathtt{green}, \mathtt{red})$.

Definition 8 (SLCS$_\gamma$ Logical Equivalence). *Given Polyhedral Model* $\mathcal{X} = (|K|, V)$ *and* $x_1, x_2 \in |K|$ *we say that* x_1 *and* x_2 *are logically equivalent with respect to SLCS$_\gamma$, written* $x_1 \simeq_{\mathrm{SLCS}_\gamma} x_2$, *if and only if, for all SLCS$_\gamma$ formulas* Φ *the following holds:* $\mathcal{M}(\mathcal{X}), x_1 \models \Phi$ *if and only if* $\mathcal{M}(\mathcal{X}), x_2 \models \Phi$.

Logical equivalence coincides with simplicial bisimilarity [12]:

Theorem 1 (Corollary 6.5 of [12]). *Given Polyhedral Model* $\mathcal{X} = (|K|, V)$, $x_1, x_2 \in |K|$ *the following holds:* $x_1 \simeq_{\mathrm{SLCS}_\gamma} x_2$ *if and only if* $x_1 \sim x_2$. □

2.3 Face-Poset Models and SLCS

The following definition characterises the discrete representation of polyhedral models we will use in the rest of the paper (see Fig. 4).

Definition 9 (face-poset model). *Given Polyhedral Model* $\mathcal{X} = (|K|, V)$, *the face-poset model* $\mathcal{M}(\mathcal{X})$ *is the Kripke model* $(W, \preceq, \mathcal{V})$ *where* $(W, \preceq) = (\tilde{K}, \preceq)$ *is the face-poset of K and* $\tilde{\sigma} \in \mathcal{V}(p)$ *if and only if* $\tilde{\sigma} \subseteq V(p)$.

Below, we recall the definition of ±-paths introduced in [12]. They faithfully represent, in the face-poset model, topological paths in the polyhedral one. Consider, for instance, the polyhedron consisting of a segment from a given point P to a point Q and its related face-poset. A path starting from, say, point P can "immediately enter" the open segment PQ, whereas a path starting from a point within the open segment cannot "immediately proceed" to P (nor to Q); it *has* to first traverse a fraction of the open segment PQ, then ending in P (or Q). This is reflected in the face-poset by requiring that a path therein, i.e. a ±-path, cannot perform a *first* step going against the partial order (going "down"), whereas in its *last* step it cannot follow strictly the partial order (going "up").

Definition 10 (±-path). *Let* $\mathcal{M}(\mathcal{X}) = (W, \preceq, \mathcal{V})$ *be a finite face-poset model and let* $\preceq^{\pm}$ *be the relation* $\preceq \cup \succeq$. *We say that, for* $\ell \in \mathbb{N}$, *sequence* $\pi : [0; \ell] \to W$ *is a* ±-path *(and we indicate it by* $\pi : [0; \ell] \xrightarrow{\pm} W$*) if* $\ell \geq 2$ *and the following holds:* $\pi(0) \preceq \pi(1) \preceq^{\pm} \pi(2) \preceq^{\pm} \ldots \preceq^{\pm} \pi(\ell - 1) \succeq \pi(\ell)$. •

The following definition re-interprets SLCS on finite face-posets and is based on ±-paths [12]. In order to avoid confusion, in the sequel, we will call the resulting logic SLCS$_{\pm}$.

Definition 11 (SLCS on finite face-posets - SLCS$_{\pm}$). *The satisfaction relation of* SLCS$_{\pm}$ *with respect to a given finite face-poset model* $\mathcal{M}(\mathcal{X}) = (W, \preceq, \mathcal{V})$, SLCS$_{\pm}$ *formula* Φ, *and* $w \in W$ *is defined recursively on the structure of* Φ:

$$\mathcal{M}(\mathcal{X}), w \models p \quad \Leftrightarrow w \in \mathcal{V}(p);$$
$$\mathcal{M}(\mathcal{X}), w \models \neg\Phi \quad \Leftrightarrow \mathcal{M}(\mathcal{X}), w \models \Phi \text{ does not hold};$$
$$\mathcal{M}(\mathcal{X}), w \models \Phi_1 \wedge \Phi_2 \quad \Leftrightarrow \mathcal{M}(\mathcal{X}), w \models \Phi_1 \text{ and } \mathcal{M}(\mathcal{X}), w \models \Phi_2;$$
$$\mathcal{M}(\mathcal{X}), w \models \gamma(\Phi_1, \Phi_2) \Leftrightarrow a \text{ ±-path } \pi : [0; \ell] \xrightarrow{\pm} W \text{ exists such that } \pi(0) = w,$$
$$\mathcal{M}(\mathcal{X}), \pi(\ell) \models \Phi_2, \text{ and}$$
$$\mathcal{M}(\mathcal{X}), \pi(i) \models \Phi_1 \text{ for all } i \in (0; \ell).$$

Definition 12 (Logical Equivalence). *Given finite face-poset model* $\mathcal{M}(\mathcal{X}) = (W, \preceq, \mathcal{V})$ *and* $w_1, w_2 \in W$ *we say that* w_1 *and* w_2 *are* logically equivalent *with respect to* SLCS$_{\pm}$, *written* $w_1 \simeq_{\text{SLCS}_{\pm}} w_2$ *if and only if, for all* SLCS$_{\pm}$ *formulas* Φ *the following holds:* $\mathcal{M}(\mathcal{X}), w_1 \models \Phi$ *if and only if* $\mathcal{M}(\mathcal{X}), w_2 \models \Phi$. •

A fundamental result, see [12], follows, where with slight overloading, for $x \in |K|$, we let $\mathcal{M}(x)$ denote the unique cell $\tilde{\sigma} \in \tilde{K}$ such that $x \in \tilde{\sigma}$ (see Fig. 4 for an illustration).

Example. With reference to the face-poset model $\mathcal{M}(\mathcal{X})$ of Fig. 4b for polyhedral model $\mathcal{X}$ of Fig. 3a, it is easy to see that cells C and CD satisfy $\gamma(\text{green}, \text{true})$, and also $\gamma(\text{green}, \text{red})$ and $\text{red} \wedge \gamma(\text{green}, \text{red})$.

Theorem 2 (Theorem 4.4 of [12]). *Let* $\mathcal{X} = (|K|, V)$ *a polyhedral model and* $\mathcal{M}(\mathcal{X})$ *the associated face-poset model as by Definition 9. For all* $x \in |K|$ *and formula* Φ *the following holds:* $\mathcal{X}, x \models \Phi$ *if and only if* $\mathcal{M}(\mathcal{X}), \mathcal{M}(x) \models \Phi$. □

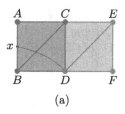
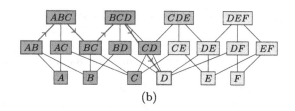

Fig. 4. (a) A polyhedral model $\mathcal{X}$ with atomic propositions **red**, **green** and **gray**, and a path from a point x to vertex D. (b) Hasse diagram of face-poset model $\mathcal{M}(\mathcal{X})$ and a path (in blue) corresponding to the path in $\mathcal{X}$. (Color figure online)

We close this section with the definition of some notation for *sequences*, which ±-paths are a particular case of, and that will be useful in the rest of the paper.

Definition 13 (Sequences). *Given a set X, a sequence over X from x, of length $\ell \in \mathbb{N}$, is a total function $s : [0; \ell] \to X$ such that $s(0) = x$. For sequence s of length ℓ, we often use the notation $(x_i)_{i=0}^{\ell}$ where $x_i = s(i)$ for $i \in [0; \ell]$. Given sequences $s' = (x_i')_{i=0}^{\ell'}$ and $s'' = (x_i'')_{i=0}^{\ell''}$, with $x_{\ell'}' = x_0''$, the* sequentialisation *$s' \cdot s'' : [0; \ell' + \ell''] \to X$ of s' with s'' is the sequence from x_0' defined as follows:*

$$(s' \cdot s'')(i) = \begin{cases} s'(i), & \text{if } i \in [0; \ell'], \\ s''(i - \ell'), & \text{if } i \in [\ell'; \ell' + \ell'']. \end{cases}$$

For sequence $s = (x_i)_{i=0}^{n}$ and $k \in [0; n]$ we define the k-shift operator $\_ \uparrow k$ as follows: $s \uparrow k = (x_{j+k})_{j=0}^{n-k}$ and, for $0 < m \leq n$, we let $s \leftarrow m$ denote the sequence obtained from s by inserting a copy of $s(m)$ immediately before $s(m)$ itself, i.e. $s \leftarrow m = (s[0; m]) \cdot ((s(m), s(m)), (s \uparrow m))$. Finally, a (non-empty) prefix *of s is a sequence $s|[0; k]$, for some $k \in [0; n]$.* •

For example, for sequence (a, b, c) of length 2 and sequence (c, d) of length 1, we have $(a, b, c) \cdot (c, d) = (a, b, c, d)$, of length 3, $(a) \cdot (a, b) = (a, b)$, $(a) \cdot (a) = (a)$. Note the difference between sequentialisation and concatenation '++': for instance, $(a, b) ++ (c) = (a, b, c)$ whereas $(a, b) \cdot (c)$ is undefined since $b \neq c$, $(a) ++ (a)$ is (a, a) whereas $(a) \cdot (a) = (a)$. We have $(a, b, c) \uparrow 1 = (b, c)$ and $(a, b, c) \uparrow 2 = (c)$ while $(a, b, c) \leftarrow 1 = (a, b, b, c)$. Sequences $(a), (a, b), (a, b, c)$ are all the (non-empty) prefixes of (a, b, c).

3 ±-Bisimilarity and the Coincidence Result

In this section, we present the novel notion of ±-bisimulation, that is based on the notion of ±-path *compatibility*, inspired by compatibility of paths in quasi-discrete closure models introduced in [27]. We additionally show that ±-bisimilarity coincides with logical equivalence for SLCS$_\pm$.

Definition 14 (±-path compatibility). *Given face-poset model $\mathcal{M}(\mathcal{X}) = (W, \preceq, \mathcal{V})$ and binary relation $B \subseteq W \times W$, two ±-paths $\pi_1 = (w_i)_{i=0}^{k_1}$, $\pi_2 = $*

$(w_j'')_{j=0}^{k_2}$ *are called* compatible *with respect to B in* $\mathcal{M}(\mathcal{X})$ *if, for some* $N > 0$, *two total monotone non-decreasing surjections* $z_1 : [0; k_1] \to [1; N]$ *and* $z_2 : [0; k_2] \to [1; N]$ *exist such that* $z_1(1) = z_2(1)$, $z_1(k_1 - 1) = z_2(k_2 - 1)$ *and* $B(w_i', w_j'')$ *for all indices* $i \in [0; k_1]$ *and* $j \in [0; k_2]$ *satisfying* $z_1(i) = z_2(j)$. •

The functions z_1 and z_2 are referred to as *matching functions*. Note that both the number N and functions z_1 and z_2 need not be unique. The minimal number $N > 0$ for which matching functions exist is defined to be the *number of zones* of the two ±-paths π_1 and π_2. It is easy to see that, whenever two ±-paths are compatible, for any pair of matching function z_1 and z_2 the following holds, by virtue of monotonicity and surjectivity: $z_1(0) = z_2(0) = 1$ and $z_1(k_1) = z_2(k_2) = N$. Hence $B(w_0', w_0'')$ and $B(w_{k_1}', w_{k_2}'')$, and of course $B(w_1', w_1'')$ and $B(w_{k_1-1}', w_{k_2-1}'')$.

Given binary relation $B \subseteq W \times W$, compatibility of ±-paths with respect to B is a binary relation over ±-paths. We write $\pi_1 \, \mathsf{comp}^B \pi_2$ whenever ±-paths π_1 and π_2 are compatible with respect to B. Lemma 1 below, proved in [21], states some properties of ±-paths compatibility that turn useful in the sequel.

Lemma 1. *Let* $\mathcal{M}(\mathcal{X}) = (W, \preceq, \mathcal{V})$ *be a face-poset,* $B \subseteq W \times W$ *a relation,* π, π_1, π_2 ±-paths *with* π *of length* $\ell > 0$, $s_1 : [0; \ell_1] \to W, s_2 : [0; \ell_2] \to W$ *sequences of length* $\ell_1, \ell_2 \in \mathbb{N}$ *respectively,* $m \in (0; \ell)$. *The following holds:*

1. $\pi \, \mathsf{comp}^B (\pi \leftarrow m)$.
2. *If B is an equivalence relation, then:*
   (a) *so is* comp^B, *and*
   (b) *the sequentialisation of two sequences of equivalent elements, and non-decreasing first step, with two compatible ±-paths results in compatible ±-paths. Formally: if* $\pi_1 \, \mathsf{comp}^B \pi_2$, $s_h(0) \preceq s_h(1)$ *and* $s_h(\ell_h) = \pi_h(0)$ *for* $h \in [1; 2]$, *with* $B(s_1(i), s_2(j))$ *for all* $i \in [0; \ell_1)$ *and* $j \in [0; \ell_2)$, *then* $s_1 \cdot \pi_1$ *and* $s_2 \cdot \pi_2$ *are ±-paths that are compatible with respect to B.*

Definition 15. (±-bisimulation). *Let* $\mathcal{M}(\mathcal{X}) = (W, R, \mathcal{V})$ *be a finite face-poset model. A symmetric binary relation* $B \subseteq W \times W$ *is a poset ±-bisimulation if, for all* $w_1, w_2 \in W$, *if* $B(w_1, w_2)$ *then the following holds:*

1. $\mathcal{V}^{-1}(\{w_1\}) = \mathcal{V}^{-1}(\{w_2\})$;
2. *for each ±-path π_1 from w_1 there is a ±-path π_2 from w_2 such that* $\pi_1 \, \mathsf{comp}^B \pi_2$.

We say that w_1 and w_2 are ±-bisimilar, written $w_1 \rightleftharpoons_\pm w_2$, if there is a ±-bisimulation B such that $B(w_1, w_2)$. •

Example. With reference to the polyhedral model $\mathcal{X}$ of Fig. 3a, in Fig. 5b the ±-bisimilarity equivalence classes are shown in different colours for $\mathcal{M}(\mathcal{X})$. In Fig. 5a we recall the simplicial bisimilarity quotient of model $\mathcal{X}$. There is no ±-path starting from any of the cells in the cyan class that is compatible with ±-path $\pi_{CD} = (CD, CDE, CDE)$ from cell CD in the yellow class as it is easy to see in Fig. 4b. The same applies for ±-path $\pi_C = (C, CDE, CDE)$ from cell

C.[4] Similarly, let us consider cell D. We have already seen that there is no other point in the polyhedral model that is simplicial bisimilar to point D. Let us consider $\pm$-path $\pi_D = (D, CD, CD)$. In the sequel we show there cannot be any $\pm$-path from any other cell satisfying **gray** that is compatible with π_D. In fact, any other such a $\pm$-path π should be such that $\pi(1)$ satisfies **red** (this is required by the fact that $z_D(1) = z(1)$ for any pair of matching functions for π_D and π) and $\pi(j)$ should not satisfy **green** for any j (since no element of π_D satisfies **green**). On the other hand, any $\pm$-path π' starting from any other cell satisfying **gray** and reaching a cell satisfying **red** is such that $\pi'(1)$ does *not* satisfy **red**. Furthermore, many such $\pm$-paths have an element that satisfies **green**. Thus, there is no $\pm$-path starting from any other **gray** cell that is compatible with (D, CD, CD) and D is in fact in a different class than any other **gray** cell.

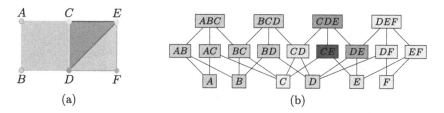

(a)   (b)

Fig. 5. Equivalence classes of the polyhedral model of Fig. 3a w.r.t. simplicial bisimilarity (a) and those of its face-poset model w.r.t. $\pm$-bisimilarity (b).

We are now in a position to state and prove the two main technical results of this paper, viz. soundness of $\pm$-bisimilarity—Theorem 3—and the fact that logical equivalence is a $\pm$-bisimulation—Theorem 4.

Theorem 3. *For w_1, w_2 in finite face-poset model $\mathcal{M}(\mathcal{X})$, the following holds: if $w_1 \rightleftharpoons_\pm w_2$ then $w_1 \simeq_{\text{SLCS}_\pm} w_2$.*

Proof. Let $\mathcal{M}(\mathcal{X}) = (W, \preceq, \mathcal{V})$ be a face-poset model. We proceed by induction on the structure of Φ in $\text{SLCS}_\pm$. We only cover the case $\gamma(\Phi_1, \Phi_2)$ since the others are straightforward. Let w_1 and w_2 be two points of $\mathcal{M}(\mathcal{X})$ such that $w_1 \rightleftharpoons_\pm w_2$. Suppose $w_1 \models \gamma(\Phi_1, \Phi_2)$. Let $\pi_1 = (w_i')_{i=0}^{k_1}$ be a $\pm$-path from w_1 satisfying $\pi_1(k_1) \models \Phi_2$ and $\pi_1(i) \models \Phi_1$ for all $i \in (0; k_1)$. Since $w_1 \rightleftharpoons_\pm w_2$, a $\pm$-path $\pi_2 = (w_i'')_{i=0}^{k_2}$ from w_2 exists that is compatible with π_1 with respect to $\rightleftharpoons_\pm$. Let, for appropriate $N > 0$, $z_1 : [0; k_1] \to [1; N]$ and $z_2 : [0; k_2] \to [1; N]$ be matching functions for π_1 and π_2. Without loss of generality, $z_2^{-1}(\{N\}) = \{k_2\}$.

Since $z_1(k_1) = z_2(k_2) = N$, we have $\pi_1(k_1) \rightleftharpoons_\pm \pi_2(k_2)$. Thus $\pi_2(k_2) \models \Phi_2$ by Induction Hypothesis. Moreover, if $j \in (0; k_2)$, then $z_2(j) < N$ by assumption and there is $i \in (0; k_1)$ such that $z_1(i) = z_2(j)$, that is $\pi_1(i) \rightleftharpoons_\pm \pi_2(j)$.

---

[4] Recall that partial orders are transitive and reflexive.

Since $\pi_1(i) \models \Phi_1$, it follows that $\pi_2(j) \models \Phi_1$ by Induction Hypothesis. Therefore $\pm$-path π_2 witnesses $w_2 \models \gamma(\Phi_1, \Phi_2)$. $\qquad\square$

Theorem 4. *For finite face-poset model $\mathcal{M}(\mathcal{X})$, $\simeq_{\mathrm{SLCS}_\pm}$ is a $\pm$-bisimulation.*

Proof. Let $\mathcal{M}(\mathcal{X}) = (W, \preceq, \mathcal{V})$ be a finite face-poset model. We check that $\simeq_{\mathrm{SLCS}_\pm}$ satisfies requirement (2) of Definition 15. Requirement (1) is immediate. Let, for points $x, y \in W$, the $\mathrm{SLCS}_\pm$-formula $\delta_{x,y}$ be such that $\delta_{x,y}$ is $\mathbf{true}$ if $x \simeq_{\mathrm{SLCS}_\pm} y$, and $x \models \delta_{x,y}$ and $y \models \neg\delta_{x,y}$ if $x \not\simeq_{\mathrm{SLCS}_\pm} y$. Put $\chi(x) = \bigwedge_{y \in W} \delta_{x,y}$. It is easy to see that, for $x, y \in W$, it holds that

$$y \models \chi(x) \text{ if and only if } x \simeq_{\mathrm{SLCS}_\pm} y. \tag{1}$$

Let Π be the set of all finite sequences $(x_i)_{i=0}^n$ over $\mathcal{M}(\mathcal{X})$. Note that such sequences might not be $\pm$-paths. Furthermore, let function $\mathbf{zones} : \Pi \to \mathbb{N}$ be such that, for sequence $s = (x_i)_{i=0}^n$,

$$\begin{aligned} \mathbf{zones}(s) &= 1 & &\text{if } n = 0 \\ \mathbf{zones}(s) &= \mathbf{zones}(s{\uparrow}1) & &\text{if } n > 0 \text{ and } x_0 \simeq_{\mathrm{SLCS}_\pm} x_1 \\ \mathbf{zones}(s) &= \mathbf{zones}(s{\uparrow}1) + 1 & &\text{if } n > 0 \text{ and } x_0 \not\simeq_{\mathrm{SLCS}_\pm} x_1 \end{aligned}$$

A sequence s is said to have k zones, if $\mathbf{zones}(s) = k$.

Claim. For all $k \geqslant 1$, for all $x_1, x_2 \in W$, if $x_1 \simeq_{\mathrm{SLCS}_\pm} x_2$ and π_1 is a $\pm$-path from x_1 and π_1 has k zones, then a $\pm$-path π_2 from x_2 exists such that π_2 is compatible with π_1 with respect to $\simeq_{\mathrm{SLCS}_\pm}$. The claim is proven by induction on k.

Base case, $k = 1$: If $x_1 \simeq_{\mathrm{SLCS}_\pm} x_2$ and $\pi_1 = (x_i')_{i=0}^n$ is a $\pm$-path from x_1 that has 1 zone only, then $x_1 \simeq_{\mathrm{SLCS}_\pm} x_i'$ for all $i \in [0; n]$. Let π_2 be the $\pm$-path (x_2, x_2, x_2). Since $x_1 \simeq_{\mathrm{SLCS}_\pm} x_2$, also $x_2 \simeq_{\mathrm{SLCS}_\pm} x_i'$ for all $i \in [0; n]$. Hence, π_2 is compatible with π_1 with respect to $\simeq_{\mathrm{SLCS}_\pm}$ with matching functions $z_1(i) = 1$ for all $i \in [0; n]$ and $z_2(j) = 1$ for all $j \in [0; 2]$.

Induction step, $k{+}1$: Suppose $x_1 \simeq_{\mathrm{SLCS}_\pm} x_2$ and $\pi_1 = (x_i')_{i=0}^n$ is a $\pm$-path from x_1 of $k{+}1$ zones. Let $m > 0$ be such that $x_1 \simeq_{\mathrm{SLCS}_\pm} x_i'$ for all $i \in [0; m)$ and $x_1 \not\simeq_{\mathrm{SLCS}_\pm} x_m'$. We distinguish two cases:

Case A: $m = 1$ (Fig. 6 shows an example for $m = 1$ and length $n = 3$). In this case, it holds that $x_1 \models \gamma(\chi(x_1'), \mathbf{true})$. Since $x_2 \simeq_{\mathrm{SLCS}_\pm} x_1$, we also have $x_2 \models \gamma(\chi(x_1'), \mathbf{true})$. Therefore, a $\pm$-path π' exists from x_2 such that $\pi'(1) \models \chi(x_1')$, i.e. $\pi'(1) \simeq_{\mathrm{SLCS}_\pm} x_1'$ by Eq. 1 (Fig. 6a). Let us, first of all, consider the sequence $\pi_1' = (x_1', x_1') \cdot (\pi_1{\uparrow}1)$, obtained by inserting a copy of x_1' before $(\pi_1{\uparrow}1)$ (Fig. 6b and Fig. 6c). Note that π_1' is a $\pm$-path of length n. In fact, $\pi_1'(0) \preceq \pi_1'(1)$, since $\pi_1'(0) = \pi_1'(1)$ by construction. Furthermore, $\pi_1'(n-1) = \pi_1(n-1) \succeq \pi_1(n) = \pi_1'(n)$, where $\pi_1(n-1) \succeq \pi_1(n)$ because π_1 is a $\pm$-path. Finally, all the subsequent intermediate elements of π_1' are in the $\preceq^\pm$ relation by construction. Moreover, note that π_1' has the same number of zones as $\pi_1{\uparrow}1$, that is k. So, by the Induction Hypothesis, since $\pi'(1) \simeq_{\mathrm{SLCS}_\pm} x_1'$, there is a $\pm$-path π'' from $\pi'(1)$ such that $\pi'' \, \mathbf{comp}^{\simeq_{\mathrm{SLCS}_\pm}} \pi_1'$ (see Fig. 6c). Now, using Lemma 1.2b,

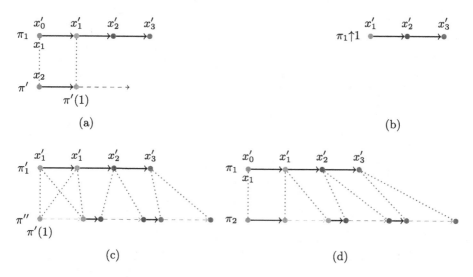

Fig. 6. Example illustrating the proof of Theorem 4, for $n = 3$, **Case A:** $m = 1$. In the figure, different zones are shown by using different colours, and we assume **zones**$(\pi_1) = 4$. Dotted lines in magenta indicate pairs belonging to $\simeq_{\text{SLCS}\pm}$. (Color figure online)

for sequences $\pi'|[0;1]$ and $\pi_1|[0;1]$ and $\pm$-paths π'' and π_1' respectively, we get $(\pi'|[0;1]\cdot\pi'') \text{ comp}^{\simeq_{\text{SLCS}\pm}} (\pi_1|[0;1])\cdot\pi_1'$. Finally, noting that $(\pi_1|[0;1])\cdot\pi_1'$ is exactly $\pi_1{\leftarrow}1$ and using Lemma 1.1, we get $(\pi_1|[0;1])\cdot\pi_1' \text{ comp}^{\simeq_{\text{SLCS}\pm}} \pi_1$. Since $\simeq_{\text{SLCS}\pm}$ is an equivalence relation, we finally get, using Lemma 1.2a, $(\pi'|[0;1]\cdot\pi'') \text{ comp}^{\simeq_{\text{SLCS}\pm}} \pi_1$ and we choose $\pi_2 = \pi'|[0;1] \cdot \pi''$ (see Fig. 6d).

Case B: $m > 1$. If $m > 1$ then it holds that $x_1 \models \gamma(\chi(x_1), \chi(x_m'))$. Since, by hypothesis, $x_2 \simeq_{\text{SLCS}\pm} x_1$ also $x_2 \models \gamma(\chi(x_1), \chi(x_m'))$. Thus, a $\pm$-path π', of some length $\ell \geq 2$, from x_2 exists, such that $\pi'(\ell) \models \chi(x_m')$ and $\pi'(j) \models \chi(x_1)$ for all $j \in (0;\ell)$. We have that $x_m' \simeq_{\text{SLCS}\pm} \pi'(\ell)$ and $x_1 \simeq_{\text{SLCS}\pm} \pi'(j)$ for all $j \in (0;\ell)$, by Eq. 1. In the sequel, we focus on the case $1 < m < n$. The proof for the case $1 < m = n$ is straightforward and is shown in [21].

Suppose $m > 1$ and $m < n$ (Fig. 7 shows an example for $m = 2$ and $n = 3$). In a similar way as before, we first consider the sequence $\pi_1' = (x_m', x_m') \cdot (\pi_1{\uparrow}m)$ and let h be the length of π_1'. Note that π_1' is a $\pm$-path. In fact $(\pi_1{\uparrow}m) = (\dots x_{n-1}', x_n')$ has length at least 1—it has at least two elements, because $m < n$ and the length of (x_m', x_m') is 1. So, by definition of sequentialisation π_1' has length at least 2—it has at least three elements. Moreover $\pi_1'(0) = \pi_1'(1)$ by construction, so $\pi_1'(0) \preceq \pi_1'(1)$ and $\pi_1'(h-1) = \pi_1(n-1) \succeq \pi_1(n) = \pi_1'(h)$, since π_1 is a $\pm$-path. Finally, all the subsequent intermediate elements of π_1' are in the $\preceq^{\pm}$ relation by construction. Note, furthermore, that π_1' has the same number of zones as $(\pi_1{\uparrow}m)$, namely k. So, by the Induction Hypothesis, since $\pi'(\ell) \simeq_{\text{SLCS}\pm} x_m'$ we know that there is a $\pm$-path π'' from $\pi'(\ell)$ such that $\pi'' \text{ comp}^{\simeq_{\text{SLCS}\pm}} \pi_1'$ (see

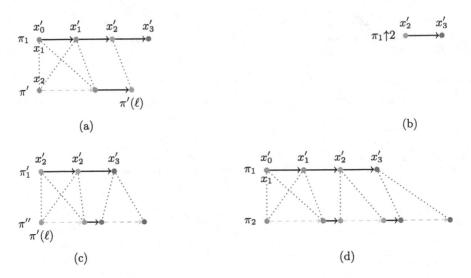

Fig. 7. Example illustrating the proof of Theorem 4, for $n = 3$, **Case B** and $1 < m < n$. In the figure, different zones are shown by using different colours, and we assume $\mathbf{zones}(\pi_1) = 3$. Dotted lines in magenta indicate pairs that belong to $\simeq_{\text{SLCS}_\pm}$. (Color figure online)

Fig. 7c). Now, using Lemma 1.2b, for sequences π' and $\pi_1|[0;m]$ and $\pm$-paths π'' and π_1' respectively, we get $(\pi' \cdot \pi'') \, \mathbf{comp}^{\simeq_{\text{SLCS}_\pm}} (\pi_1|[0;m]) \cdot \pi_1'$. Finally, noting that $(\pi_1|[0;m]) \cdot \pi_1'$ is exactly $\pi_1{\leftarrow}m$ and using Lemma 1.1, we get $(\pi_1|[0;m]) \cdot \pi_1' \, \mathbf{comp}^{\simeq_{\text{SLCS}_\pm}} \pi_1$. Since $\simeq_{\text{SLCS}_\pm}$ is an equivalence relation, we finally get, using Lemma 1.2a, $\pi' \cdot \pi'' \, \mathbf{comp}^{\simeq_{\text{SLCS}_\pm}} \pi_1$ and we choose $\pi_2 = \pi' \cdot \pi''$ (see Fig. 7d).

This proves the claim. From the claim it follows immediately that $\simeq_{\text{SLCS}_\pm}$ satisfies the second condition of Definition 15. □

On the basis of Theorem 3 and Theorem 4, we have that the largest $\pm$-bisimulation exists, it is a $\pm$-bisimilarity, it is an equivalence relation, and it coincides with logical equivalence in the face-poset induced by $\text{SLCS}_\pm$:

Corollary 1. *For every finite face-poset* $\mathcal{M}(\mathcal{X}) = (W, \preceq, \mathcal{V})$, $w_1, w_2 \in W$, *the following holds:* $w_1 \rightleftharpoons_\pm w_2$ *if and only if* $w_1 \simeq_{\text{SLCS}_\pm} w_2$. □

In conclusion, recalling that for all $x \in \mathcal{X}$ and SLCS_γ formula $\varPhi$, we have that $\mathcal{X}, x \models \varPhi$ if and only if $\mathcal{M}(\mathcal{X}), \mathcal{M}(x) \models \varPhi$, we get the following final result:

Corollary 2. *For all polyhedral models* $\mathcal{X}$, $x_1, x_2 \in \mathcal{X}$: $x_1 \sim x_2$ *if and only if* $x_1 \simeq_{\text{SLCS}_\gamma} x_2$ *if and only if* $\mathcal{M}(x_1) \rightleftharpoons_\pm \mathcal{M}(x_2)$ *if and only if* $\mathcal{M}(x_1) \simeq_{\text{SLCS}_\pm} \mathcal{M}(x_2)$. □

Example. Figure 8 shows the minimal model $\min(\mathcal{M}(\mathcal{X}))$, modulo $\pm$-bisimilarity, of $\mathcal{M}(\mathcal{X})$ (see Fig. 4b). Model $\min(\mathcal{M}(\mathcal{X}))$ has been obtained in a similar way

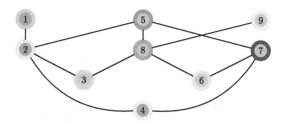

Fig. 8. Hasse diagram of the minimal model, modulo ±-bisimilarity, of the model of Fig. 4b.

as described in Proposition 1 of [23]. Note that the model is transitive and reflexive, because of Corollary 1 above, and the reflexivity and idempotency axioms of topological modal logic. Thus, in Fig. 8 the model is represented by its Hasse diagram. Each element of $\min(\mathcal{M}(\mathcal{X}))$ is coloured according to the atomic proposition satisfied by the members of the corresponding ±-bisimilarity class and its border has the colour of the class (see Fig. 5b). The ±-path $(1, 1, 1, 1, 3)$ in the minimal model corresponds to (AB, ABC, BC, BCD, D) shown in Fig. 4b and $(2, 5, 2)$ witnesses formula **red** $\wedge$ $\gamma(\textbf{green}, \textbf{red})$ in the minimal model.

4 Conclusions and Future Work

We have introduced a novel notion of spatial bisimilarity, namely ±-bisimilarity on face-poset models representing polyhedral models. We have shown that it coincides with logical equivalence based on the variant of **SLCS** proposed in [12]. Consequently, two points in a polyhedral model are simplicial bisimilar if and only if their corresponding cells in the face-poset are ±-bisimilar.

Part of future work will be to investigate the relationship between bisimilarity notions developed for face-poset models, and those developed in the context of closure models, e.g. those studied in [19,27]. Furthermore, we plan to develop slightly weaker notions of ±-bisimilarity, together with their associated spatial logics. Such coarser equivalences are of interest for further model reduction. We will investigate approaches along the lines of the work in [23] for CMs. Finally, the issue of the impact of adding a "converse" operator for γ to the logic—in a similar vein as for other reachability operators, in e.g. [8,19,27]—on the associated bisimilarity and its geometrical interpretation is another subject for future study.

Acknowledgements. We thank Nick Bezhanishvili, Gianluca Grilletti and Jan Friso Groote for interesting discussions concerning various aspects of polyhedral model-checking, bisimulations and model reduction techniques.

References

1. Aiello, M.: Spatial reasoning: theory and practice. Ph.D. thesis, Institute of Logic, Language and Computation, University of Amsterdam (2002)
2. Aiello, M.: The topo-approach to spatial representation and reasoning. AIIA NOTIZIE (4) (2003)
3. Alur, R.: Formal verification of hybrid systems. In: Proceedings of the 11th International Conference on Embedded Software, EMSOFT 2011, part of the Seventh Embedded Systems Week, ESWeek 2011, Taipei, Taiwan, 9–14 October 2011, pp. 273–278. ACM (2011). https://doi.org/10.1145/2038642.2038685
4. Alur, R., Giacobbe, M., Henzinger, T.A., Larsen, K.G., Mikučionis, M.: Continuous-time models for system design and analysis. In: Steffen, B., Woeginger, G. (eds.) Computing and Software Science. LNCS, vol. 10000, pp. 452–477. Springer, Cham (2019). https://doi.org/10.1007/978-3-319-91908-9_22
5. Audrito, G., Casadei, R., Damiani, F., Stolz, V., Viroli, M.: Adaptive distributed monitors of spatial properties for cyber-physical systems. J. Syst. Softw. **175**, 110908 (2021). https://doi.org/10.1016/j.jss.2021.110908
6. Balovnev, O.T., et al.: The story of the GeoToolKit - an object-oriented geodatabase kernel system. GeoInformatica **8**(1), 5–47 (2004). https://doi.org/10.1023/B:GEIN.0000007723.77851.8f
7. Banci Buonamici, F., Belmonte, G., Ciancia, V., Latella, D., Massink, M.: Spatial logics and model checking for medical imaging. Int. J. Softw. Tools Technol. Transfer **22**(2), 195–217 (2019). https://doi.org/10.1007/s10009-019-00511-9
8. Belmonte, G., Broccia, G., Ciancia, V., Latella, D., Massink, M.: Feasibility of spatial model checking for nevus segmentation. In: Bliudze, S., Gnesi, S., Plat, N., Semini, L. (eds.) 9th IEEE/ACM International Conference on Formal Methods in Software Engineering, FormaliSE@ICSE 2021, Madrid, Spain, 17–21 May 2021, pp. 1–12. IEEE (2021). https://doi.org/10.1109/FormaliSE52586.2021.00007
9. Belmonte, G., Ciancia, V., Latella, D., Massink, M.: Innovating medical image analysis via spatial logics. In: ter Beek, M.H., Fantechi, A., Semini, L. (eds.) From Software Engineering to Formal Methods and Tools, and Back. LNCS, vol. 11865, pp. 85–109. Springer, Cham (2019). https://doi.org/10.1007/978-3-030-30985-5_7
10. Belmonte, G., Ciancia, V., Latella, D., Massink, M.: VoxLogicA: a spatial model checker for declarative image analysis. In: Vojnar, T., Zhang, L. (eds.) TACAS 2019. LNCS, vol. 11427, pp. 281–298. Springer, Cham (2019). https://doi.org/10.1007/978-3-030-17462-0_16
11. van Benthem, J., Bezhanishvili, G.: Modal logics of space. In: Aiello, M., Pratt-Hartmann, I., Benthem, J.V. (eds.) Handbook of Spatial Logics, pp. 217–298. Springer, Dordrecht (2007). https://doi.org/10.1007/978-1-4020-5587-4_5
12. Bezhanishvili, N., Ciancia, V., Gabelaia, D., Grilletti, G., Latella, D., Massink, M.: Geometric Model checking of continuous space. Log. Methods Comput. Sci. **18**(4), 7:1–7:38 (2022). https://lmcs.episciences.org/10348. https://doi.org/10.46298/LMCS-18(4:7)2022. ISSN 1860-5974
13. Bogomolov, S., Frehse, G., Giacobbe, M., Henzinger, T.A.: Counterexample-guided refinement of template polyhedra. In: Legay, A., Margaria, T. (eds.) TACAS 2017. LNCS, vol. 10205, pp. 589–606. Springer, Heidelberg (2017). https://doi.org/10.1007/978-3-662-54577-5_34
14. Breunig, M., et al.: Geospatial data management research: Progress and future directions. ISPRS Int. J. Geo Inf. **9**(2), 95 (2020). https://doi.org/10.3390/ijgi9020095

15. Browne, M.C., Clarke, E.M., Grumberg, O.: Characterizing finite Kripke structures in propositional temporal logic. Theor. Comput. Sci. **59**, 115–131 (1988). https://doi.org/10.1016/0304-3975(88)90098-9
16. Caires, L., Cardelli, L.: A spatial logic for concurrency (part I). Inf. Comput. **186**(2), 194–235 (2003). https://doi.org/10.1016/S0890-5401(03)00137-8
17. Cardelli, L., Gordon, A.D.: Anytime, anywhere: modal logics for mobile ambients. In: Wegman, M.N., Reps, T.W. (eds.) POPL 2000, Proceedings of the 27th ACM SIGPLAN-SIGACT Symposium on Principles of Programming Languages, Boston, Massachusetts, USA, 19–21 January 2000, pp. 365–377. ACM (2000). https://doi.org/10.1145/325694.325742
18. Chrschn: A triangle mesh of dolphin (2007). https://en.wikipedia.org/wiki/File:Dolphin_triangle_mesh.png. Accessed 7 Feb 2023
19. Ciancia, V., Latella, D., Massink, M., de Vink, E.P.: Back-and-forth in space: on logics and bisimilarity in closure spaces. In: Jansen, N., Stoelinga, M., van den Bos, P. (eds.) A Journey From Process Algebra via Timed Automata to Model Learning. LNCS, vol. 13560, pp. 98–115. Springer, Cham (2022). https://doi.org/10.1007/978-3-031-15629-8_6
20. Ciancia, V., Latella, D., Massink, M., Paškauskas, R., Vandin, A.: A tool-chain for statistical spatio-temporal model checking of bike sharing systems. In: Margaria, T., Steffen, B. (eds.) ISoLA 2016. LNCS, vol. 9952, pp. 657–673. Springer, Cham (2016). https://doi.org/10.1007/978-3-319-47166-2_46
21. Ciancia, V., Gabelaia, D., Latella, D., Massink, M., de Vink, E.P.: On bisimilarity for polyhedral models and SLCS - preliminary version. Technical report. ISTI-TR-2022/018, CNR-ISTI (2023). https://doi.org/10.32079/ISTI-TR-2023/003
22. Ciancia, V., Gilmore, S., Grilletti, G., Latella, D., Loreti, M., Massink, M.: Spatio-temporal model checking of vehicular movement in public transport systems. Int. J. Softw. Tools Technol. Transfer **20**(3), 289–311 (2018). https://doi.org/10.1007/s10009-018-0483-8
23. Ciancia, V., Groote, J., Latella, D., Massink, M., de Vink, E.: Minimisation of spatial models using branching bisimilarity. In: Chechik, M., Katoen, J.P., Leucker, M. (eds.) FM 2023. LNCS, vol. 14000, pp. 263–281. Springer, Cham (2023). https://doi.org/10.1007/978-3-031-27481-7_16
24. Ciancia, V., Latella, D., Loreti, M., Massink, M.: Specifying and verifying properties of space. In: Diaz, J., Lanese, I., Sangiorgi, D. (eds.) TCS 2014. LNCS, vol. 8705, pp. 222–235. Springer, Heidelberg (2014). https://doi.org/10.1007/978-3-662-44602-7_18
25. Ciancia, V., Latella, D., Loreti, M., Massink, M.: Model checking spatial logics for closure spaces. Log. Methods Comput. Sci. **12**(4) (2016). https://doi.org/10.2168/LMCS-12(4:2)2016
26. Ciancia, V., Latella, D., Massink, M., Paškauskas, R.: Exploring spatio-temporal properties of bike-sharing systems. In: 2015 IEEE International Conference on Self-Adaptive and Self-Organizing Systems Workshops, SASO Workshops 2015, Cambridge, MA, USA, 21–25 September 2015, pp. 74–79. IEEE Computer Society (2015). https://doi.org/10.1109/SASOW.2015.17
27. Ciancia, V., Latella, D., Massink, M., de Vink, E.P.: On bisimilarity for quasi-discrete closure spaces (2023). https://arxiv.org/abs/2301.11634
28. De Nicola, R., Vaandrager, F.W.: Three logics for branching bisimulation. J. ACM **42**(2), 458–487 (1995). https://doi.org/10.1145/201019.201032
29. Galton, A.: The mereotopology of discrete space. In: Freksa, C., Mark, D.M. (eds.) COSIT 1999. LNCS, vol. 1661, pp. 251–266. Springer, Heidelberg (1999). https://doi.org/10.1007/3-540-48384-5_17

30. Galton, A.: Discrete mereotopology. In: Calosi, C., Graziani, P. (eds.) Mereology and the Sciences. SL, vol. 371, pp. 293–321. Springer, Cham (2014). https://doi.org/10.1007/978-3-319-05356-1_11

31. Girard, A., Le Guernic, C.: Zonotope/hyperplane intersection for hybrid systems reachability analysis. In: Egerstedt, M., Mishra, B. (eds.) HSCC 2008. LNCS, vol. 4981, pp. 215–228. Springer, Heidelberg (2008). https://doi.org/10.1007/978-3-540-78929-1_16

32. van Glabbeek, R.J., Weijland, W.P.: Branching time and abstraction in bisimulation semantics. J. ACM **43**(3), 555–600 (1996). https://doi.org/10.1145/233551.233556

33. Groote, J.F., Jansen, D.N., Keiren, J.J.A., Wijs, A.: An O(mlogn) algorithm for computing stuttering equivalence and branching bisimulation. ACM Trans. Comput. Log. **18**(2), 13:1–13:34 (2017). https://doi.org/10.1145/3060140

34. Hansen, H., Kupke, C., Pacuit, E.: Neighbourhood structures: bisimilarity and basic model theory. Log. Methods Comput. Sci. **5**(2) (2009). https://lmcs.episciences.org/1167

35. Henzinger, T.A.: The theory of hybrid automata. In: Inan, M.K., Kurshan, R.P. (eds.) Verification of Digital and Hybrid Systems, pp. 265–292. Springer, Heidelberg (2000). https://doi.org/10.1007/978-3-642-59615-5_13

36. Henzinger, T.A., Ho, P.-H.: HyTech: the cornell hybrid technology tool. In: Antsaklis, P., Kohn, W., Nerode, A., Sastry, S. (eds.) HS 1994. LNCS, vol. 999, pp. 265–293. Springer, Heidelberg (1995). https://doi.org/10.1007/3-540-60472-3_14

37. Levine, J.A., Paulsen, R.R., Zhang, Y.: Mesh processing in medical-image analysis - a tutorial. IEEE Comput. Graphics Appl. **32**(5), 22–28 (2012). https://doi.org/10.1109/MCG.2012.91

38. Linker, S., Papacchini, F., Sevegnani, M.: Analysing spatial properties on neighbourhood spaces. In: Esparza, J., Král', D. (eds.) 45th International Symposium on Mathematical Foundations of Computer Science, MFCS 2020, 24–28 August 2020, Prague, Czech Republic. LIPIcs, vol. 170, pp. 66:1–66:14. Schloss Dagstuhl - Leibniz-Zentrum für Informatik (2020). https://doi.org/10.4230/LIPIcs.MFCS.2020.66

39. Linker, S., Papacchini, F., Sevegnani, M.: Finite models for a spatial logic with discrete and topological path operators. In: Bonchi, F., Puglisi, S.J. (eds.) 46th International Symposium on Mathematical Foundations of Computer Science, MFCS 2021, 23–27 August 2021, Tallinn, Estonia. LIPIcs, vol. 202, pp. 72:1–72:16. Schloss Dagstuhl - Leibniz-Zentrum für Informatik (2021). https://doi.org/10.4230/LIPIcs.MFCS.2021.72

40. Loreti, M., Quadrini, M.: A spatial logic for a simplicial complex model. CoRR (2021). https://arxiv.org/abs/2105.08708

41. Massink, M., Paškauskas, R.: Model-based assessment of aspects of user-satisfaction in bicycle sharing systems. In: IEEE 18th International Conference on Intelligent Transportation Systems, ITSC 2015, Gran Canaria, Spain, 15–18 September 2015, pp. 1363–1370. IEEE (2015). https://doi.org/10.1109/ITSC.2015.224

42. McKinsey, J., Tarski, A.: The algebra of topology. Ann. Math. **45**, 141–191 (1944). https://doi.org/10.2307/1969080

43. Milner, R.: Communication and Concurrency. PHI Series in Computer Science. Prentice Hall (1989)

44. Milner, R.: The Space and Motion of Communicating Agents. Cambridge University Press, Cambridge (2009)

45. Nenzi, L., Bortolussi, L., Ciancia, V., Loreti, M., Massink, M.: Qualitative and quantitative monitoring of spatio-temporal properties with SSTL. Log. Methods Comput. Sci. **14**(4) (2018). https://doi.org/10.23638/LMCS-14(4:2)2018
46. Sankaranarayanan, S., Dang, T., Ivančić, F.: Symbolic model checking of hybrid systems using template polyhedra. In: Ramakrishnan, C.R., Rehof, J. (eds.) TACAS 2008. LNCS, vol. 4963, pp. 188–202. Springer, Heidelberg (2008). https://doi.org/10.1007/978-3-540-78800-3_14
47. Smyth, M.B., Webster, J.: Discrete spatial models. In: Aiello, M., Pratt-Hartmann, I., van Benthem, J. (eds.) Handbook of Spatial Logics, pp. 713–798. Springer, Dordrecht (2007). https://doi.org/10.1007/978-1-4020-5587-4_12
48. Tsigkanos, C., Nenzi, L., Loreti, M., Garriga, M., Dustdar, S., Ghezzi, C.: Inferring analyzable models from trajectories of spatially-distributed internet of things. In: 2019 IEEE/ACM 14th International Symposium on Software Engineering for Adaptive and Self-Managing Systems (SEAMS), pp. 100–106 (2019). https://doi.org/10.1109/SEAMS.2019.00021
49. Tsigkanos, C., Pasquale, L., Ghezzi, C., Nuseibeh, B.: Ariadne: topology aware adaptive security for cyber-physical systems. In: Bertolino, A., Canfora, G., Elbaum, S.G. (eds.) 37th IEEE/ACM International Conference on Software Engineering, ICSE 2015, Florence, Italy, 16–24 May 2015, vol. 2, pp. 729–732. IEEE Computer Society (2015). https://doi.org/10.1109/ICSE.2015.234
50. Čech, E.: Topological spaces. In: Pták, V. (ed.) Topological Spaces, chap. III, pp. 233–394. Publishing House of the Czechoslovak Academy of Sciences/Interscience Publishers, John Wiley & Sons, Prague/London-New York-Sydney (1966). Revised edition by Zdeněk Frolíc and Miroslav Katětov. Scientific editor, Vlastimil Pták. Editor of the English translation, Charles O. Junge. MR0211373

Model-Based Testing and Petri Nets

With a Little Help from Your Friends: Semi-cooperative Games via Joker Moves

Petra van den Bos[1][(✉)] and Marielle Stoelinga[1,2]

[1] Formal Methods and Tools, University of Twente, Enschede, The Netherlands
p.vandenbos@utwente.nl
[2] Department of Software Science, Radboud University, Nijmegen, The Netherlands

Abstract. This paper coins the notion of Joker games where Player 2 is not strictly adversarial: Player 1 gets help from Player 2 by playing a Joker. We formalize these games as cost games, and study their theoretical properties. Finally, we illustrate their use in model-based testing.

1 Introduction

Winning Strategies. We study 2 player concurrent games played on a game graph with reachability objectives, i.e., the goal for Player 1 is to reach a set of goal states R. A central notion in such games is the concept of a *winning strategy*, which assigns—in states where this is possible—moves to Player 1 so that she always reaches the goal R, no matter how Player 2 plays.

Concurrent reachability games have abundant applications, e.g. controller synthesis [3], assume/guarantee reasoning [11], interface theory [16], security [25] and test case optimization [14,20]. However, it is also widely acknowledged [4,11,17] that the concept of a winning strategy is often too strong in these applications: unlike games like chess, the opponent does not try to make Player 1's life as hard as possible, but rather, the behaviour of Player 2 is unknown. Moreover, winning strategies do not prescribe any move in states where Player 1 cannot win. This is a major drawback: even if Player 1 cannot win, some strategies are better than others.

Several solutions have been proposed to remedy this problem, via *best effort strategies*, i.e. strategies that determine which move to play in losing states. For example, Berwanger [4] coins the notion of strategy dominance, where one strategy is better than another if it wins against more opponent strategies. The maximal elements in the lattice of Player-1 strategies, called *admissible* strategies, are proposed as best strategies in losing states. Further, specific solutions have been proposed to refine the notion of winning in specific areas, especially in controller synthesis: [11] refines the synthesis problem into a co-synthesis problem, where components compete conditionally: their first aim is to satisfy their own specification, and their second aim is to violate the other component's specification. In [5], a hierarchy of collaboration levels is defined, formalizing how cooperative a controller for an LTL specification can be.

M. Huisman and A. Ravara (Eds.): FORTE 2023, LNCS 13910, pp. 155–172, 2023.
https://doi.org/10.1007/978-3-031-35355-0_10

Our Approach: Joker Games. The above notions are all qualitative, i.e., they refine the notion of winning strategy, but do not quantify how much collaboration from the opponent is needed. To fill this gap, we introduce *Joker games*.

By fruitfully building upon robust strategy synthesis results by Neider et al. [13,23], a *Joker strategy* provides a best effort strategy in cases where Player 1 cannot win. Concretely, we allow Player 1, in addition to her own moves, to play a so-called *Joker move*. With such a Joker move, Player 1 can choose her own move *and* the opponent's move, so that Player 2 helps Player 1 reaching the goal. Then, we minimize the number of Jokers needed to win the game, thereby minimizing the help needed from Player 2 Player to win. We formalize such Joker-minimal strategies as cost-minimal strategies in a priced game.

While the construction for Joker strategies closely follows the construction in [13,23] (and later in [2]), our games extend these results in several ways: First, the games in [2,13,23] are turn-based and deterministic, whereas ours are concurrent and nondeterministic. That is, outcome of the moves may lead to several next states. Nondeterminism is essential in game-based testing, to model a faithful interaction between the tester and the system-under-test [6].

An important difference is that Neider et al. focus on finding optimal strategies in the form of attractor strategies, while we present our Joker strategies as general cost-minimal strategies. In fact, we show that all attractor strategies are cost-minimal, but not all cost minimal strategies are attractor strategies. In particular, non-attractor strategies may outperform attractor strategies with respect to other objectives like the number of moves needed to reach the goal.

Furthermore, we establish several new results for Joker games: (1) While concurrent games require randomized strategies to win a game, this is not true for the specific Joker moves: these can be played deterministically. (2) If we play a strategy with n Jokers, each play contains exactly n Joker moves. (3) Even with deterministic strategies, Joker games are determined. (4) The classes of Joker strategies and admissible strategies do not coincide.

Finally, we illustrate how Joker strategies can be applied in practice, by extracting test cases from Joker strategies. Here we use techniques from previous work [6], to translate game strategies to test cases. We refer to [6] for related work on game-based approaches for testing. In the experiments of this paper we show on four classes of case studies that obtained test cases outperform the standard testing approach of random testing. Specifically, Joker-inspired test cases reach the goal more often than random ones, and require fewer steps to do so.

Contributions. Summarizing, the main contributions of this paper are:

- We formalize the minimum help Player 1 needs from Player 2 to win as cost-minimal strategies in a Joker game.
- We establish several properties: the minimum number of Jokers equals minimum cost, each play of a Joker strategy uses n Jokers, Joker game determinacy, Jokers can be played deterministically, in randomized setting, and admissible strategies do not coincide with cost-minimal strategies.
- We refine our Joker approach with second objective of the number of moves.
- We illustrate the benefits of our approach for test case generation.

Paper Organization. Section 2 recapitulates concurrent games. Section 3 introduces Joker games, and Sect. 4 investigates their properties. In Sect. 6 we study multi-objective Joker strategies, and in Sect. 6 admissible strategies. In Sect. 7 we apply Joker strategies to test case generation. Section 8 concludes the paper. Proofs for the theorems of this paper are given in [7], and the artefact of our experimental results of Sect. 7 is provided in [1].

2   Concurrent Games

We consider concurrent games played by two players on a game graph. In each state, Player 1 and 2 *concurrently* choose an action, leading the game in one of the (nondeterministically chosen) next states.

Definition 1. *A concurrent game is a tuple $G = (Q, q^0, Act_1, Act_2, \Gamma_1, \Gamma_2, Moves)$ where:*

- *Q is a finite set of states,*
- *$q^0 \in Q$ is the initial state,*
- *For $i \in \{1,2\}$, Act_i is a finite and non-empty set of Player i actions,*
- *For $i \in \{1,2\}$, $\Gamma_i : Q \to 2^{Act_i} \setminus \emptyset$ is an enabling condition, which assigns to each state q a non-empty set $\Gamma_i(q)$ of actions available to Player i in q,*
- *Moves $: Q \times Act_1 \times Act_2 \to 2^Q$ is a function that given the actions of Player 1 and 2 determines the set of next states $Q' \subseteq Q$ the game can be in. We require that $Moves(q, a, x) = \emptyset$ iff $a \notin \Gamma_1(q) \lor x \notin \Gamma_2(q)$.*

For the rest of the paper, we fix concurrent game $G = (Q, q^0, Act_1, Act_2, \Gamma_1, \Gamma_2, Moves)$. Next, we define a *play* as a sequence of states and actions.

Definition 2. *An* infinite play *is an infinite sequence*
$\pi = q_0\langle a_0, x_0\rangle q_1\langle a_1, x_1\rangle q_2 \ldots$ *with $a_j \in \Gamma_1(q_j)$, $x_j \in \Gamma_2(q_j)$, and $q_{j+1} \in Moves(q_j, a_j, x_j)$ for all $j \in \mathbb{N}$. We write $\pi_j^q = q_j$, $\pi_j^a = a_j$, and $\pi_j^x = x_j$ for the j-th state, Player 1 action, and Player 2 action respectively. The set of infinite plays with $\pi_0^q = q$ is denoted $\Pi^\infty(q)$. We define $\Pi^\infty(G) = \Pi^\infty(q^0)$.*

A play $\pi_{0:j} = q_0\langle a_0, x_0\rangle q_1 \ldots \langle a_{j-1}, x_{j-1}\rangle q_j$ is a (finite) play prefix of infinite play π. We write $\pi_{end}^a = a_{j-1}$, $\pi_{end}^x = x_{j-1}$, and $\pi_{end}^q = q_j$ for the last Player 1 action, last Player 2 action and last state of a finite play π. All states in $\pi_{0:j}$ are collected in $States(\pi_{0:j}) = \{\pi_k^q \mid 0 \le k \le j\}$. The set of all (finite) plays of a set of infinite plays $P \subseteq \Pi^\infty(q)$ is denoted $Pref(P) = \{\pi_{0:j} \mid \pi \in P, j \in \mathbb{N}\}$. We define $\Pi(G) = Pref(\Pi^\infty(G))$, and for any $q \in Q$: $\Pi(q) = Pref(\Pi^\infty(q))$.

We consider plays where Player 1 wins, i.e. reaches a state in $R \subseteq Q$.

Definition 3. *A play $\pi \in \Pi^\infty(q) \cup \Pi(q)$ for $q \in Q$ is* winning *for reachability goal R, if there exist a $j \in \mathbb{N}$ such that $\pi_j^q \in R$. The* winning index *of a play $\pi \in \Pi^\infty(q) \cup \Pi(G)$ is: $WinInd(\pi, R) = \min\{j \in \mathbb{N} \mid \pi_j^q \in R\}$, where $\min \emptyset = \infty$.*

Given a play prefix, players choose their actions according to a strategy. A strategy is positional, if the choice for an action only depends on the last state of the play. The game outcomes are the possible plays of the game when using the strategy. We define deterministic strategies here; see Sect. 4 for randomization.

Definition 4. *A strategy for Player $i \in \{1,2\}$ starting in state $q \in Q$ is a function $\sigma_i : \Pi(q) \to Act_i$, such that $\sigma_i(\pi) \in \Gamma_i(\pi_{end}^q)$ for any $\pi \in \Pi(q)$. We write $\Sigma_i(q)$ for the set of all Player i strategies starting in q, and set $\Sigma_i(G) = \Sigma_i(q_0)$. A strategy $\sigma_i \in \Sigma_i(q)$ is* positional *if for all plays $\forall \pi, \tau \in \Pi(q)$ we have $\pi_{end}^q = \tau_{end}^q \implies \sigma_i(\pi) = \sigma_i(\tau)$. The* outcome *of a Player 1 strategy $\sigma_1 \in \Sigma_1(q)$ is the set of infinite plays that occur if Player 1 plays according to σ_1:*

$$Outc(\sigma_1) = \{\pi \in \Pi^\infty(q) \mid \forall j \in \mathbb{N} : \sigma_1(\pi_{0:j}) = \pi_{j+1}^a\}$$

A Player 1 strategy is winning if all its game outcomes are winning. Player 1 can win the game by using a winning strategy from a state of its winning region.

Definition 5. *Let $q \in Q$ be a game state. A Player 1 strategy $\sigma_1 \in \Sigma(q)$ is* winning, *if all plays from $Outc(\sigma_1)$ are winning. The Player 1* winning region $WinReg(G, R)$ *for game G and goal R is the set of all states $Q' \subseteq Q$ such that for each $q \in Q'$, Player 1 has a winning strategy $\sigma_1 \in \Sigma_1(q)$.*

3 Joker Games

We formalize the notion of help by Player 2 by associating to each concurrent game G a Joker game $G^\diamond$. In $G^\diamond$, Player 1 can always get control, i.e. choose any enabled move, at the cost of using a Joker. Thus, in any state q of the game, Player 1 may either choose a regular Player 1 action $a \in \Gamma_1(q)$, or a Joker action $(a, x, q') \in \Gamma_1(q) \times \Gamma_2(q) \times Q$ with $q' \in Moves(q, a, x)$. In this way, a Joker action encodes getting help from Player 2 and 'the system' (the nondeterministic choice of a state from $Moves(q, a, x)$).

We are interested in strategies using the minimum number of Jokers that Player 1 needs to win, because we will use this later in model-based testing settings, where the test execution is neither cooperative nor adversarial. Thus, we set up a cost game where Joker actions have cost 1 and regular Player 1 actions cost 0. We use $\diamond$ to define the parts of a Joker game that differ from those of a regular game. With $\spadesuit$, we specifically refer to states, moves, etc. where Jokers are actually played.

Definition 6. *We associate to each concurrent game G a Joker game $G^\diamond = (Q, q^0, Act_1 \cup (Act_1 \times Act_2 \times Q), Act_2, \Gamma_1^\diamond, \Gamma_2, Moves^\diamond, Cost(G^\diamond, R))$ where:*

$$\Gamma_1^\spadesuit(q) = \{(a, x, q') \in \Gamma_1(q) \times \Gamma_2(q) \times Q \mid q' \in Moves(q, a, x)\}$$

$$\Gamma_1^\diamond(q) = \Gamma_1(q) \cup \Gamma_1^\spadesuit(q)$$

$$Moves^\diamond(q, a, x) = \begin{cases} \{q'\} & \text{if } a = (a', x', q') \in \Gamma_1^\spadesuit(q) \\ Moves(q, a, x) & \text{otherwise} \end{cases}$$

$$Cost(G^\diamond, R)(q, a) = \begin{cases} 1 & \text{if } a \in \Gamma_1^\spadesuit(q) \\ 0 & \text{otherwise} \end{cases}$$

For the rest of the paper we fix Joker game $G^\diamond$. We will write $\Sigma_1^\diamond(q)$ for the set of strategies in $G^\diamond$ starting at state q. Note that the states of both games are the same, and that all plays of G are also plays of $G^\diamond$.

Definition 7 defines the cost of plays, strategies, and states. The cost of a play π arises by adding the costs of all moves until the goal R is reached. If R is never reached, the cost of π is ∞. The cost of a strategy σ_1 considers the worst case resolution of Player 2 actions and nondeterministic choices. The cost of a state q is the cost of Player 1's cost-minimal strategy from q.

Definition 7. *Let $q \in Q$ be a state, $\pi \in \Pi^\infty(q) \cup \Pi(q)$ a play, and $\sigma_1 \in \Sigma_1^\diamond(q)$ a strategy in Joker game $G^\diamond$. For goal states R, define their cost as follows:*

$$Cost(G^\diamond, R)(\pi) = \begin{cases} \sum_{j=0}^{WinInd(\pi,R)-1} Cost(G^\diamond, R)(q_j, a_j) & \text{if } \pi \text{ is winning} \\ \infty & \text{otherwise} \end{cases}$$

$$Cost(G^\diamond, R)(\sigma_1) = \sup_{\pi \in Outc(\sigma_1)} Cost(G^\diamond, R)(\pi)$$

$$Cost(G^\diamond, R)(q) = \inf_{\sigma_1 \in \Sigma_1^\diamond(q)} Cost(G^\diamond, R)(\sigma_1)$$

A strategy $\sigma \in \Sigma_1^\diamond(q)$ is cost-minimal *if $\sigma \in \underset{\sigma_1 \in \Sigma_1^\diamond(q)}{\arginf} \{Cost(G^\diamond, R)(\sigma_1)\}$*

Winning States in Joker Games. Normally, the value of a cost game is computed by a fixed point computation.

$$v_0(q) = 0 \text{ if } q \in R$$
$$v_0(q) = \infty \text{ if } q \notin R$$
$$v_{k+1}(q) = \min_{a \in \Gamma_1(q)} \max_{x \in \Gamma_2(q)} \max_{q' \in Moves(q,a,x)} Cost(G^\diamond, R)(q, a) + v_k(q')$$

Joker games allow this computation to be simplified, by exploiting their specific structure with cost 0 for competitive and cost 1 for cooperative moves. We adapt the classical attractor construction (see e.g., [26]) on the original game G. The construction relies on two concepts: the predecessor $Pre(Q')$ contains all states with some move into Q'; the controllable predecessor contains those states where Player 1 can force the game into Q', no matter how Player 2 plays and how the nondeterminism is resolved. We note that $Pre(Q')$ can be equivalently defined as the states $q \in Q$ with $(a, x, q') \in \Gamma_1^\diamond(q)$ (for $q' \in Q'$).

Definition 8. *Let $Q' \subseteq Q$ be a set of states. The* predecessor $Pre(Q')$ *of Q', and the* controllable predecessor $CPre_1(Q')$ *of Q' are:*

$$Pre(Q') = \{q \in Q \mid \exists a \in \Gamma_1(q), \exists x \in \Gamma_2(q), \exists q' \in Moves(q, a, x) : q' \in Q'\}$$
$$CPre_1(Q') = \{q \in Q \mid \exists a \in \Gamma_1(q), \forall x \in \Gamma_2(q) : Moves(q, a, x) \subseteq Q'\}$$

The classical *attractor* is the set of states from which Player 1 can force the game to reach R, winning the game. It is constructed by expanding the goal states via $CPre_1$, until a fixed point is reached [15]; the rank k indicates in which computation step a state was added [26]. Thus, the lower k, the fewer moves Player 1 needs to reach its goal.

Definition 9. *The Player 1 attractor is* $Attr(G, R)$, *where:*

$$Attr^0(G, R) = R$$
$$Attr^{k+1}(G, R) = Attr^k(G, R) \cup CPre_1(Attr^k(G, R))$$
$$Attr(G, R) = \bigcup_{k \in \mathbb{N}} Attr^k(G, R)$$

The function $ARank(G, R) : Q \rightarrow \mathbb{N}$ *associates to each state* $q \in Q$ *a rank* $ARank(G, R)(q) = \min\{k \in \mathbb{N} \mid q \in Attr^k(G, R)\}$. *Recall that* $\min \emptyset = \infty$.

The cost of state q in $G^\diamond$ is obtained by interleaving the attractor and predecessor operators, computing sets of states that we call the *Joker attractor*. See Fig. 1 for an illustration of the computation. Since *Attr* and *Pre* only use elements from G, the computation is performed in G. We will see that for defining the Joker attractor strategy (Definition 12) we do need Joker game $G^\diamond$. In states of set $JAttr^k(G, R)$, the game can be won with at most k Jokers, i.e., with cost k. Clearly, states that can be won by Player 1 in G have cost 0, so these fall into $JAttr^0(G, R)$. Similarly, if all states in Q' can be won with at most k jokers, then so can states in $Attr(Q')$. In Joker states, Player 1 can only win from any opponent if she uses a Joker. By playing a Joker, the game moves to a state in $JAttr^k(G, R)$. Joker states are the predecessors of $JAttr^k(G, R)$.

Definition 10. *The Player 1 Joker attractor is* $JAttr(G, R)$, *where:*

$$JAttr^0(G, R) = Attr(G, R)$$
$$JAttr^{k+1}_\diamond(G, R) = Pre(JAttr^k(G, R))$$
$$JAttr^{k+1}(G, R) = JAttr^k(G, R) \cup Attr(G, JAttr^{k+1}_\diamond(G, R))$$
$$JAttr(G, R) = \bigcup_{k \in \mathbb{N}} JAttr^k(G, R)$$

We call $JAttr(G, R)$ *the Joker attractor of* G. *The Joker states are* $JAttr_\spadesuit(G, R) = \bigcup_{k \in \mathbb{N}} JAttr^{k+1}_\diamond(G, R) \setminus JAttr^k(G, R)$. *To each Joker attractor* $JAttr(G, R)$ *we associate a Joker rank function* $JRank(G, R) : Q \rightarrow \mathbb{N}$, *where for each state* $q \in Q$ *we define* $JRank(G, R)(q) = \min\{k \in \mathbb{N} \mid q \in JAttr^k(G, R)\}$.

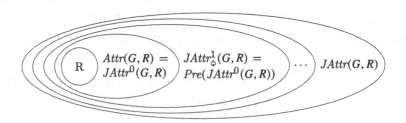

Fig. 1. Illustration of the Joker attractor computation: it starts with states in R initially and then adds states using the attractor and Joker attractor operations, until a fixpoint is reached.

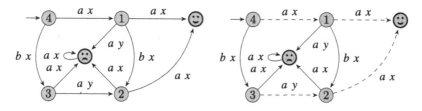

Fig. 2. Left: concurrent game $G_{a\vee b}$ with goal state ☺ and initial state 4. Right: same game, with dashed edges for moves of a Joker attractor strategy.

Example 1. We compute the Joker attractor for goal ☺ in for concurrent game $G_{a\vee b}$ of Fig. 2, together with the $JRank(G, R)$. We indicate whether the state is a Joker state or not, i.e., whether Player 1 plays a Joker.

$$JAttr^0(G_{a\vee b}, ☺) = \{☺\}$$

$$JAttr^1_☼(G, R)(G_{a\vee b}, ☺) = \{1, 2, ☺\}$$

$$JAttr^1(G_{a\vee b}, ☺) = \{1, 2, 4, ☺\}$$

$$JAttr^2_☼(G, R)(G_{a\vee b}, ☺) =$$

$$JAttr^2(G_{a\vee b}, ☺) = JAttr^3(G_{a\vee b}, ☺) = \{1, 2, 3, 4, ☺\}$$

$q \in Q$	$JRank$	Joker state
1	1	yes
2	1	yes
3	2	yes
4	1	no
☺	0	no
☺	∞	no

Theorem 1 states the correctness of equations in Definition 10: the number of Jokers needed to reach R, i.e. $JRank(G, R)(q)$, equals $Cost(G^◊, R)(q)$.

Theorem 1. *For all $q \in Q$, we have $JRank(G, R)(q) = Cost(G^◊, R)(q)$.*

Winning Strategies in Joker Games. The attractor construction cannot only be used to compute the states of the Joker attractor, but also to construct the corresponding winning strategy. To do so, we need to update the definitions of the (controllable) predecessor. This requires some extra administration, recording which actions used in *Pre* and $CPre_1$ are *witnesses* for moving to states Q'.

$$wPre(Q') = \{(q, a, x) \in Q \times Act_1 \times Act_2 \mid a \in \Gamma_1(q) \wedge x \in \Gamma_2(q)$$
$$\wedge (\exists q' \in Moves(q, a, x) : q' \in Q')\}$$
$$wCPre_1(Q') = \{(q, a) \in Q \times Act_1 \mid a \in \Gamma_1(q) \wedge (\forall x \in \Gamma_2(q) : Moves(q, a, x) \subseteq Q')\}$$

Now, we obtain the sets of winning actions, by replacing, in the construction of $JAttr(G, R)$, *Pre* and *CPre* by *wPre* and $wCPre_1$, respectively. With *wPre* and $wCPre_1$ we select actions for moving from the states that are newly added to the $k + 1$-th attractor, or the $k + 1$-th Joker attractor set, respectively, to move to states of the k-th attractor, or k-th Joker attractor set, respectively.

Definition 11. *We define the* witnessed *attractor $wAttr(G, R)$ and Joker attractor $wJAttr(G, R)$:*

$$wAttr^0(G,R) = \emptyset$$

$$wAttr^{k+1}(G,R) = wAttr^k(G,R) \cup \{(q,a) \in wCPre_1(Attr^k(G,R)) \mid q \notin Attr^k(G,R)\}$$

$$wAttr(G,R) = \bigcup_{k \in \mathbb{N}} wAttr^k(G,R)$$

$$wJAttr^0(G,R) = \emptyset$$

$$wJAttr^{k+1}(G,R) = wJAttr^k(G,R) \cup \{(q,a,x) \in wPre(JAttr^k(G,R)) \mid q \notin JAttr^k(G,R)\}$$

$$wJAttr(G,R) = \bigcup_{k \in \mathbb{N}} wJAttr^k(G,R)$$

A *Joker attractor strategy* in $G^\diamond$ is a strategy that plays according to the witnesses: in Joker states, a Joker action from $wJAttr^k(G,R)$ is played. In non-Joker states q, the strategy takes its action from $wAttr(G,R)$ if the state has $JRank(G,R)(q){=}0$, and from $wAttr(JAttr^k_\diamond(G,R))$ if the state has $JRank(G,R)(q) = k$ for some $k > 0$.

Definition 12. *A strategy* $\sigma_1 \in \Sigma_1^\diamond(q)$ *in* $G^\diamond$ *is a Joker attractor strategy, if for any* $\pi \in \Pi(G^\diamond)$ *with* $\pi_{end}^q \in JAttr(G,R)$ *and* $JRank(G,R)(\pi_{end}^q) = k$ *we have:*

$$(\pi_{end}^q \in JAttr_\bullet(G,R) \implies \sigma_1(\pi) \in wJAttr(G,R)) \qquad \wedge$$

$$(k = 0 \wedge \pi_{end}^q \notin R \implies (\pi_{end}^q, \sigma_1(\pi)) \in wAttr(G,R)) \qquad \wedge$$

$$(k > 0 \wedge \pi_{end}^q \notin JAttr_\bullet(G,R) \implies (\pi_{end}^q, \sigma_1(\pi)) \in wAttr(JAttr^k_\diamond(G,R)))$$

4   Properties of Joker Games

We establish five fundamental properties of Joker games.

1. All outcomes use same number of Jokers. A first, and perhaps surprising result is that, all outcomes in Joker attractor strategy σ, use exactly the same number of Joker actions, namely $JRank(G,R)(q)$ Jokers, if σ starts in state q. This follows from the union-like computation illustrated in Fig. 1. This is unlike cost-minimal strategies in general cost games, where some outcomes may use lower costs. This is also unlike cost-minimal strategies in $JAttr(G,R)$ that are not obtained via the attactor construction, see Fig. 3.

Theorem 2. *Let* $q \in JAttr(G,R)$. *Then:*

1. *Let* $\sigma_1^J \in \Sigma_1^\diamond(q)$ *be a Joker attractor strategy in* $G^\diamond$. *Then any play* $\pi \in Outc(\sigma_1^J)$ *has exactly* $JRank(G,R)(q)$ *Joker actions in winning prefix* $\pi_{0:WinInd(\pi)}$.
2. *Let* $\sigma_1 \in \Sigma_1^\diamond(q)$ *be a cost-minimal strategy in* $G^\diamond$. *Then any play* $\pi \in Outc(\sigma_1)$ *has at most* $JRank(G,R)(q)$ *Joker actions in the winning prefix* $\pi_{0:WinInd(\pi)}$.

The intuition of the proof of Theorem 2 can be derived from Fig. 3: a Joker is always played in a Joker state. By construction of the Joker attractor strategy, the Joker action moves the game from q to a state q' with $JRank(G,R)(q')+1 = JRank(G,R)(q)$. In non-Joker states no Joker is used to reach a next Joker state.

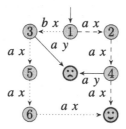

Fig. 3. A cost-minimal strategy is depicted by the dashed edges. It plays a cost-0 a action in state 1, and hopes Player 2 plays x to arrive in ☺ with cost 0. If Player 2 plays y, the strategy plays a Joker in state 2 to win nevertheless. The computation of the Joker attractor yields that state 1 and 2 both have $JRank$ 1. Since state 1 is reached first, the Joker attractor strategy (dotted) plays a Joker in this state immediately, and reaches ☺ directly from state 1. This example shows that cost-minimal strategies from state 1 may use less than $JRank(G, R)(1)$ Jokers, and Joker attractor strategies from 1 always use $JRank(G, R)(1)$ Jokers.

Fig. 4. This game G_{cost} has a cost-minimal strategy (dashed; cost 1 for the Joker used in state 4) that is not a Joker attractor strategy. The unique Joker attractor strategy (dotted) selects Player 1 action b from state 1 (to Joker state 3), since $1, 2 \in Attr^1(G_{cost}, JAttr^1_\bullet(G_{cost}, \{☺\}))$. The dashed strategy requires fewer moves to reach ☺ (3 vs 4).

2. Characterization of winning states.

For the set of states $JAttr(G, R)$, we establish that: (1) for every goal R, the winning region in Joker game $G^\lozenge$ (i.e., states where Player 1 can win with any strategy, not necessarily cost-minimal) coincides with the Joker attractor $JAttr(G, R)$, and (2) the set of all states having a play reaching a state from R coincide with Joker attractor $JAttr(G, R)$.

Theorem 3. *Let $Reach(G, R) = \{q \in Q \mid q \text{ can reach a state } q' \in R\}$. Then*

$$WinReg(G^\lozenge, R) = JAttr(G, R) = Reach(G, R)$$

3. Joker attractor strategies and minimality.

We show some fundamental results relating Joker attractor strategies to Joker-minimal strategies: Theorem 4 states correctness of Joker attractor strategies: they are indeed cost-minimal. The converse, cost-minimal strategies are Joker attractor strategies, is not true, as shown by Fig. 3 and 4. The game of Fig. 4 also shows that Joker attractor strategies need not take the shortest route to the goal (see also Sect. 6).

Theorem 4. *Any Joker attractor strategy is cost-minimal.*

4. Determinacy.

Unlike arbitrary concurrent games with deterministic strategies, Joker games are *determined*. That is, in each state of $JAttr(G, R)$, either

Player 1 has a winning strategy or Player 2 can keep the game outside R for-ever. Determinacy (Theorem 5) follows from Theorem 3: by $WinReg(G^{\diamond}, R) = JAttr(G, R)$ we have a winning strategy in any state from $JAttr(G, R)$, and by $JAttr(G, R) = Reach(G, R)$ we have that states not in $JAttr(G, R)$ have no play to reach R, so Player 2 wins with any strategy.

Theorem 5. *Joker games are determined.*

5   Joker Games with Randomized Strategies

A distinguishing feature of concurrent games is that, unlike turn-based games, randomized strategies may help to win a game. A classical example is the Penny Matching Game of Fig. 5. We show that randomization is not needed for winning Joker games, but does help to reduce the number of Joker moves. However, randomization in Joker states is never needed. We first set up the required machinery, following [15].

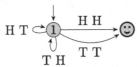

Fig. 5. Penny Matching Game: Each Player chooses a side of a coin. If they both choose heads, or both tails, then Player 1 wins, otherwise they play again. Player 1 wins this game with probability 1, by flipping the coin (each side has probability $\frac{1}{2}$).

Definition 13. *A (probability) distribution over a finite set X is a function $v : X \to [0, 1]$ such that $\sum_{x \in X} v(x) = 1$. The set of all probability distributions over X is denoted $Distr(X)$. Let $q \in Q$. A randomized Player i strategy from q is a function $\sigma_i : Pref(q) \to Distr(Act_i)$, such that $\sigma_i(\pi)(a) > 0$ implies $a \in \Gamma_i(\pi_{end}^q)$. Let $\Sigma_i^r(q)$ denote the randomized strategies for Player $i \in \{1, 2\}$ from q.*

To define the probability of an outcome, we must not only know how player Players 1 and 2 play, but also how the nonderminism is resolved. Given moves a and x by Player 1 and 2, the Player 3 strategy $\sigma_3(\pi, a, x)$ chooses, probabilistically, one of the next states in $Moves(\pi_{end}^q, a, x)$.

Definition 14. *A randomized Player 3 strategy is a function $\sigma_3 : \Pi(q) \times Act_1 \times Act_2 \to Distr(Q)$, such that $\sigma_3(\pi, a, x)(q') > 0$ implies $q' \in Moves(\pi_{end}^q, a, x)$ for all $\pi \in \Pi(q)$. We write $\Sigma_3^r(q)$ for the set of all randomized Player 3 strategies from q. The outcome $Outc(\sigma_1, \sigma_2, \sigma_3)$ of randomized strategies $\sigma_1 \in \Sigma_1^r(q)$, $\sigma_2 \in \Sigma_2^r(q)$, and $\sigma_3 \in \Sigma_3^r(q)$ are the plays $\pi \in \Pi^{\infty}(q)$ such that for all $j \in \mathbb{N}$:*
$$\sigma_1(\pi_{0:j})(\pi_j^a) > 0 \ \wedge \ \sigma_2(\pi_{0:j})(\pi_j^x) > 0 \ \wedge \ \sigma_3(\pi_{0:j}, \sigma_1(\pi_{0:j}), \sigma_2(\pi_{0:j}))(\pi_{j+1}^q) > 0$$

Given randomized strategies for Player 1, Player 2, and Player 3, Definition 15 defines the probability of a play prefix of the game. This probability is computed as the multiplication of the probabilities given by the strategies for the play prefix. A Player 1 strategy is then an *almost sure winning strategy* if it can win from any Player 2 and Player 3 strategy with probability 1.

Definition 15. *Let $\sigma_1 \in \Sigma_1^r(q_0)$, $\sigma_2 \in \Sigma_2^r(q_0)$, and $\sigma_3 \in \Sigma_3^r(q_0)$ be randomized strategies, and let $\pi = q_0\langle a_0, x_0\rangle q_1 \ldots \langle a_{j-1}, x_{j-1}\rangle q_j$ be a finite play prefix. We define its probability as:*

$$P(\pi) = \prod_{i=0}^{j-1} \sigma_1(\pi_{0:i})(a_i) \cdot \sigma_2(\pi_{0:i})(x_i) \cdot \sigma_3\left(\pi_{0:i}, \sigma_1(\pi_{0:i}), \sigma_2(\pi_{0:i})\right)(q_{i+1})$$

The strategies $\bar{\sigma} = (\sigma_1, \sigma_2, \sigma_3)$ define a probability space $(\Omega, \mathcal{F}, \mathcal{P}^{\bar{\sigma}})$ over the set of outcomes. A Player 1 strategy $\sigma_1 \in \Sigma_1^r(q)$ is almost sure winning *for reachability goal R if for all $\sigma_2 \in \Sigma_2^r(q)$, and $\sigma_3 \in \Sigma_3^r(q)$, we have: $\mathcal{P}^{\bar{\sigma}}[\{\pi \in Outc(\sigma_1, \sigma_2, \sigma_3) \mid \pi \text{ is winning}\}] = 1$. Strategy σ_1 is* sure winning *if for all $\sigma_2 \in \Sigma_2^r(q)$, and $\sigma_3 \in \Sigma_3^r(q)$, and for any $\pi \in Outc(\sigma_1, \sigma_2, \sigma_3)$, π is winning.*

Properties of Joker Games with Randomization. In Sect. 4, several fundamental properties were given, which hold for randomized strategies too (Theorem 6). By replacing the standard attractor in the definition of the Joker attractor (Definition 10), by the probabilistic atractor [15], we obtain the definition of the probabilistic Joker attractor. Next, by using this probabilistic Joker attractor instead of the Joker attractor, the definitions for the witnissed probablistic Joker attractor (Definition 11), and probablistic Joker strategies (Definition 12) can be reformulated. From these probablistic definitions, Theorem 6 then follows.

Theorem 6. *Theorem 2, 3, 4 and 5 hold for Joker games with randomized strategies.*

The (Non-)benefits of Randomization in Joker Games. We show that Joker games do not need randomized strategies: if Player 1 can win a Joker game with a randomized strategy, then she can win this game with a deterministic strategy. This result is less surprising than it may seem (Theorem 7(1)), since Joker actions are very powerful: they can determine the next state of the game to be any state reachable in one move. In the Penny Matching Game, Player 1 may in state 1 just take the Joker move $(H, H, \copyright)$ and reach the state $\copyright$ immediately. With randomization, Player 1 can win this game without using Joker moves.

We note however that we only need to use the power of Jokers in Joker states (Theorem 7(2)). We can use a probabilistic attractor [15] to attract to Joker states with probability 1, and then use a Joker move in this Joker state, where even using randomization, the game cannot be won with probability 1. The Jokers used in these Joker states then only needs to be played deterministically, i.e. with probability 1 (Theorem 7(3)). The intuition for this last statement is that a Joker move determines the next state completely, so by choosing the 'best' next state there is no need to include a chance for reaching any other state.

Theorem 7. *If a state $q \in Q$ of Joker game $G^{\diamond}$ has an almost sure winning strategy $\sigma_1^r \in \Sigma_1^{r,\diamond}(q)$, then*

1. *she also has a winning deterministic strategy.*
2. *she also has an almost sure winning strategy that only uses Jokers in Joker states.*
3. *she also has an almost sure winning strategy that only uses Jokers in Joker states, such that these Jokers can all be played with probability 1.*

6   Better Help from Your Friends: Multi-objective and Admissible Strategies

Short Joker Strategies. Although multiple Joker attractor strategies may be constructed via Definition 12, their number of moves may not be minimal. The cause for this is that Joker attractor strategies have to reduce the $ARank(G, R)$ or $JRank(G, R)$ by 1 each step. Figure 4 shows that this is not always beneficial for the total number of moves taken towards the goal: Joker attractor strategies may need more moves in total than other cost-minimal strategies.

To take a shortest path while spending the minimum number of Jokers, we use the structure of the Joker attractor sets to compute a distance function. Definition 17 defines distance for the following four types of states: goal states R, Joker states $JAttr_{\spadesuit}(G, R)$, non-Joker states part of some attractor $JAttr_{\not\spadesuit}(G, R)$, and unreachable states (states not in $JAttr(G, R)$). In a goal state, the distance is 0, and in an unreachable state it is infinite. In a Joker state, we use the Joker action to the state of the next Joker attractor set that has the smallest distance to the goal. In a non-Joker state from some attractor, we choose a Player 1 action that results in reaching a state within the current Joker attractor set, such that this action minimizes the distance to the goal from the reached state. In the latter case we assume that Player 2 and 3 cooperate with decreasing the distance, by using min in the definition. We chose this because we use the definition in Theorem 8, where we consider the situation that Player 2 and 3 cooperate. Less cooperation can be assumed by e.g. replacing min by max. Definition 16 states auxilary definitions used in Definition 17. Most importantly it defines the Joker restricted enabling condition $\Gamma_1^J(q)$ that returns Player 1 actions that surely lead to states within the current Joker attractor set.

Definition 16. *Let $q \in Q$, and $Q' \subseteq Q$. Define the states reachable in one move $Post(q)$, the k-th Joker states $JAttr_{\spadesuit}^k(G, R)$, the non-Joker, attractor states $JAttr_{\not\spadesuit}(G, R)$, the k-th non-Joker states, the restricted enabling condition $\Gamma_1(Q')$, and the Joker restricted enabling condition Γ_1^J as:*

$$Post(q) = \{q' \in Q \mid \exists a \in \Gamma_1(q), \exists x \in \Gamma_2(q) : q' \in Moves(q, a, x)\}$$

$$JAttr_{\spadesuit}^k(G, R) = JAttr_{\spadesuit}^k(G, R) \setminus JAttr^{k-1}(G, R)$$

$$JAttr_{\not\spadesuit}(G, R) = JAttr(G, R) \setminus JAttr_{\spadesuit}(G, R)$$

$$JAttr_{\not\spadesuit}^k(G, R) = JAttr^k(G, R) \setminus JAttr_{\spadesuit}^k(G, R)$$

$$\Gamma_1(Q')(q) = \{a \in \Gamma_1(q) \mid \forall x \in \Gamma_2(q) : Moves(q, a, x) \subseteq Q'\}$$

$$\Gamma_1^J(q) = \begin{cases} \Gamma_1(Attr(G, R))(q) & \text{if } q \in Attr(G, R) \\ \Gamma_1(JAttr^{k+1}(G, R) \setminus JAttr^k(G, R))(q) & \text{if } q \in JAttr_{\not\spadesuit}^{k+1}(G, R) \\ \emptyset & \text{otherwise} \end{cases}$$

Definition 17. *We define the distance function* $d : Q \to \mathbb{N}$ *as follows:*

$$
d(q) = \begin{cases}
0 & q \in R \\
1 + \min_{q' \in Post(q) \cap JAttr^k(G,R)} d(q') & q \in JAttr_\blacklozenge^{k+1}(G,R) \\
1 + \min_{a \in \Gamma_1^J(q)} \min_{x \in \Gamma_2(q)} \min_{q' \in Moves(q,a,x)} d(q') & q \in JAttr_\lozenge(G,R) \\
\infty & q \notin JAttr(G,R)
\end{cases}
$$

A short Joker strategy (Definition 18) minimizes the distance while using the minimum number of Joker actions. The construction of such a strategy from the distance function is straightforward: we use a distance minimizing Player 1 action in a non-Joker state, and a distance minimizing Joker action in a Joker state. This distance minimization follows the structure of Definition 17.

Definition 18. *A strategy* $\sigma \in \Sigma_1(q)$ *in Joker game* $G^\lozenge$ *is a* short Joker strategy *from* q, *if for any play* $\pi \in Outc(\sigma)$ *with* $q' = \pi_{end}$ *the following formulas hold:*

$$
q' \in JAttr_\blacklozenge(G,R) \implies \sigma(\pi) \in \underset{(a,x,q'') \in \Gamma_1^\bullet(q')}{\arg\min} \{d(q'')\}
$$

$$
q' \in JAttr_\lozenge(G,R) \implies \sigma(\pi) \in \underset{a \in \Gamma_1^J(q')}{\arg\min} \{d(q'') \mid x \in \Gamma_2(q'), q'' \in Moves(q',a,x)\}
$$

Unfolding Definition 17 for state 1 of Fig. 4 results in $d(1) = 3$, as expected. With Definition 18 we then obtain a short Joker strategy that is cost-minimal (it uses 1 Joker action), and uses the minimum number of moves (namely 3).

Theorem 8 states that Definition 18 indeed defines cost-minimal strategies using the minimum number of moves for the number of used Joker actions, when helped by Player 2 and 3 (i.e. there is a play). A short Joker strategy prefers the minimum number of Joker actions over the minimum number of moves, so it will not take a shorter route if that costs more than the minimum number of Jokers.

Theorem 8. *A short Joker strategy* σ *is cost-minimal (1), and has a play* $\pi \in Outc(\sigma)$ *using the minimum number of moves to win while using the minimum number of Joker actions (2).*

Admissible Strategies. Various papers [9,10,17] advocate that a player should play *admissible* strategies if there is no winning strategy. Admissible strategies (Definition 20) are the maximal elements in the lattice of all strategies equipped with the dominance order $<_d$. Here, a Player 1 strategy σ_1 dominates strategy σ_1', denoted $\sigma_1' <_d \sigma_1$, iff whenever σ_1' wins from opponent strategy ρ, so does σ_1'. In Definition 20, the set of winning strategies is defined as the pairs of Player 2 and Player 3 strategies, since the nondeterministic choice for the next state affects whether Player 1 wins. Definition 19 defines non-randomized Player 3 strategies, similar to its randomized variant in Definition 14.

Definition 19. *A Player 3 strategy is a function* $\sigma_3 : \Pi(q) \times Act_1 \times Act_2 \to Q$, *such that* $\sigma_3(\pi,a,x) \in Moves(\pi_{end}^q, a, x)$ *for all* $\pi \in \Pi(q)$. *We write* $\Sigma_3(q)$ *for the* *set of all Player 3 strategies from q. The* outcome $Outc(\sigma_1, \sigma_2, \sigma_3)$ *of strategies* $\sigma_1 \in \Sigma_1(q)$, $\sigma_2 \in \Sigma_2(q)$, *and* $\sigma_3 \in \Sigma_3(q)$ *is the play* $\pi \in \Pi^\infty(q)$ *such that:*

$$\forall j \in \mathbb{N}: \ \sigma_1(\pi_{0:j}) = \pi_j^a \wedge \sigma_2(\pi_{0:j}) = \pi_j^x \wedge \sigma_3(\pi_{0:j}, \sigma_1(\pi_{0:j}), \sigma_2(\pi_{0:j})) = \pi_{j+1}^q$$

Definition 20. *Let G be a concurrent game and R a reachability goal. Define the Player 2 and 3 strategy pairs that are winning for a strategy $\sigma_1 \in \Sigma_1(G)$ as:*

$$Win\Sigma_{2,3}(\sigma_1, R) = \{(\sigma_2, \sigma_3) \in \Sigma_2(G) \times \Sigma_3(G) \mid Outc(\sigma_1, \sigma_2, \sigma_3) \in Win\Pi(G, R)\}$$

For any $q \in Q$, a strategy $\sigma_1 \in \Sigma_1(q)$ is dominated by a strategy $\sigma_1' \in \Sigma_1(q)$, denoted $\sigma_1 <_d \sigma_1'$, if $Win\Sigma_{2,3}(\sigma_1, R) \subset Win\Sigma_{2,3}(\sigma_1', R)$. Strategy $\sigma_1 \in \Sigma_1(q)$ is admissible if there is no strategy $\sigma_1' \in \Sigma_1(q)$ with $\sigma_1 <_d \sigma_1'$.

To compare Joker attractor strategies and admissible strategies, we note that Joker attractor strategies are played in Joker games, where Joker actions have full control over the opponent. Admissible strategies, however, are played in regular concurrent games, without Joker actions. To make the comparison, Definition 21 therefore associates to any Player 1 strategy σ in $G^\diamond$, a Joker-inspired strategy σ_{insp} in G: if σ chooses Joker action (a, x, q), then σ_{insp} plays Player 1 action a.

Definition 21. *Let $\sigma \in \Sigma(q)$ be a strategy in $G^\diamond$. Define the Joker-inspired strategy σ_{insp} of σ for any $\pi \in \Pi(G)$ as:*

$$\sigma_{insp}(\pi) = \begin{cases} a & \text{if } \sigma(\pi) = (a, x, q) \\ \sigma(\pi) & \text{otherwise} \end{cases}$$

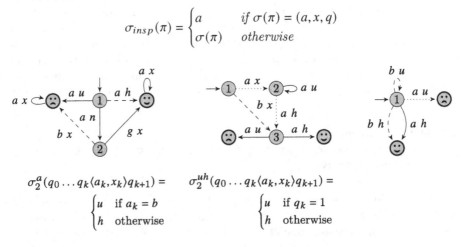

$$\sigma_2^a(q_0 \ldots q_k \langle a_k, x_k \rangle q_{k+1}) = \begin{cases} u & \text{if } a_k = b \\ h & \text{otherwise} \end{cases}$$

$$\sigma_2^{uh}(q_0 \ldots q_k \langle a_k, x_k \rangle q_{k+1}) = \begin{cases} u & \text{if } q_k = 1 \\ h & \text{otherwise} \end{cases}$$

Fig. 6. Left: the dashed cost-minimal strategy uses bad action b in state 2 instead of good action g, because using Joker $(a, h, \odot)$ in state 1 will make Player 1 win the game. Hence, the Joker-inspired strategy of this winning cost-minimal strategy is not admissible, as it is dominated by strategies choosing g in state 2. Middle: the dotted strategy uses 2 Jokers, and is admissible, since it wins from strategy σ_2^a while the dashed cost-minimal strategy (using 1 Joker) does not. Right: the dashed cost-minimal strategy dominates dotted cost-minimal strategy, because dashed strategy wins from σ_2^{uh} while dotted strategy does not.

It turns out that Joker-inspired strategies of cost-minimal strategies need not be admissible, for a rather trivial reason: a cost-minimal strategy that chooses a losing move in a non-visited state is not admissible. See Fig. 6(left). Therefore, Theorem 9 relates admissible and *global* cost-minimal strategies (Definition 22): strategies that are cost-minimal for any initial state of the Joker game. Then still, the classes of admissible and of the Joker-inspired variants of global cost-minimal strategies do not coincide. Figure 6(middle,right) shows two examples, with Player 2 strategies using memory, for both parts of Theorem 9: (1) an admissible strategy need not be cost-minimal, and (2) vice versa. We conjecture that the converse of Theorem 9 holds for memoryless Player 2 and 3 strategies.

Definition 22. *Let $\sigma \in \Sigma_1^{\diamond}(q)$ be a strategy in Joker game $G^{\diamond}$. Then σ is global cost-minimal if σ is cost-minimal from any $q' \in Reach(G, R)$.*

Theorem 9.

1. *A Joker-inspired strategy of a global cost-minimal strategy is not always admissible.*
2. *A admissible strategy is not always a Joker-inspired strategy of a global cost-minimal strategy.*

7   Experiments

We illustrate the application of Joker games in model-based testing.

Testing as a Game. We translate input-output labeled transition systems describing the desired behaviour of the System Under Test (SUT) to concurrent games, as described in [6]. In each game state, Player 1/Tester has 3 options: stop testing, provide one of the inputs to the SUT, or observe the behaviour of the SUT. Player 2/SUT has 2 options: provide an output to the SUT, or do nothing. Hence Player 1 and 2 decide concurrently what their next action is. The next state is then determined as follows: if the Tester provides an input, and the SUT does nothing, the input is processed. If the Tester observes the SUT (virtually also doing no action of its own), the output is processed. If the Tester provides an input, while the SUT provides an output, then several regimes are possible, such as input-eager, output-eager [6]. We opt for the *nondeterministic* regime, where picked action is chosen nondeterministically (this corresponds with having a set of states $Moves(q, a, x)$). In this set up, we investigate the effectiveness of Joker-based testing through a comparison with randomized testing. In Joker-based testing we take the Joker-inspired strategies of Joker attractor strategies, to allow for a fair and realistic (no use of Joker actions) comparison.

Case Studies. We applied our experiments on four case studies from [8]: the opening and closing behaviour of the TCP protocol (26 states, 53 transitions) [18], an elaborate vending machine for drinks (269 states,687 transitions) [12,22] the Echo Algorithm for leader election (105 states, 275 transitions) [19], and a tool for file storage in the cloud (752 states, 1520 transitions) [21,24].

Experimental Setup. For each case study, we randomly selected the different goal states: 5 for the (relatively small) TCP case study and 15 for the other cases. For each of these goals, we extract a Joker attractor strategy, and translate it via its corresponding Joker-inspired strategy, without Joker actions, to a test case, as described in [6]. We run this Joker test case 10.000 times. Also, we run 10.000 random test cases. A random test case chooses an action uniformly at random in any state. Test case execution is done according to the standard model-against-model testing approach [8]. In this setup, an impartial SUT is simulated from the model, by making the simulation choose any action with equal probability. From the 10.000 test case runs for each goal of each case study, we compute: (1) the number of runs that reach the goal state, and (2) the average number of actions to reach the goal state, if a goal state was reached.

Results. Figure 7 shows the experimental results. In the left graph, a point represents one goal state of a case study, and compares the averages of the Joker test case, and random test case. For the right graph, for each goal, the number of actions needed for reaching the goal for Random testing has been divided by the number of actions for the Joker test case. Results for all goals of one case study are shown with one bar. We omitted results for 5 goal states of the Vending Machine case study, as these states were not reached in any of the 10.000 runs of random testing, while there were > 3500 successful Joker runs for each of those goals. Clearly, the graphs show that Joker test cases outperform random testing. The experimental results can be reproduced with the artefact of this paper [1].

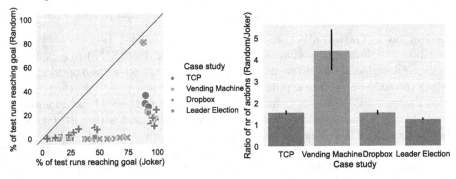

Fig. 7. Experimental results: Joker-based versus randomized testing.

8   Conclusions

We introduced the notion of Joker games, showed that its attractor-based Joker strategies use a minimum number of Jokers, and proved properties on determinacy, randomization, and admissible strategies in the context of Joker games.

In future work, we would like to extend the experimental evaluation of Joker strategies on applications, prove (or disprove) that, against memoryless Player 2 and 3 strategies, admissible strategies are global cost-minimal and vice versa, and investigate other multi-objective Joker strategies, a.o. to quantify the 'badness' of adversarial moves [13], where a bad move is e.g. a move that takes the game to a state where many Jokers need to be spend to reach the goal again.

References

1. The artefact of this paper for reproducing the experimental results of Section 7. https://doi.org/10.5281/zenodo.7712109
2. Bartocci, E., Bloem, R., Maderbacher, B., Manjunath, N., Ničković, D.: Adaptive testing for specification coverage in CPS models. IFAC-PapersOnLine **54**(5), 229–234 (2021). 7th IFAC Conference on Analysis and Design of Hybrid Systems ADHS 2021
3. Bertsekas, D.P.: Dynamic Programming and Optimal Control. Athena Scientific (1998)
4. Berwanger, D.: Admissibility in infinite games. In: Thomas, W., Weil, P. (eds.) STACS 2007. LNCS, vol. 4393, pp. 188–199. Springer, Heidelberg (2007). https://doi.org/10.1007/978-3-540-70918-3_17
5. Bloem, R., Ehlers, R., Könighofer, R.: Cooperative reactive synthesis. In: Finkbeiner, B., Pu, G., Zhang, L. (eds.) ATVA 2015. LNCS, vol. 9364, pp. 394–410. Springer, Cham (2015). https://doi.org/10.1007/978-3-319-24953-7_29
6. van den Bos, P., Stoelinga, M.: Tester versus bug: a generic framework for model-based testing via games, vol. 277, pp. 118–132 (2018)
7. van den Bos, P., Stoelinga, M.: With a little help from your friends: semi-cooperative games via joker moves (2023). Extended version with appendix. arXiv:2304.13417
8. van den Bos, P., Vaandrager, F.: State identification for labeled transition systems with inputs and outputs. Sci. Comput. Program. **209**, 102678 (2021)
9. Brenguier, R., et al.: Non-zero sum games for reactive synthesis. In: Dediu, A.-H., Janoušek, J., Martín-Vide, C., Truthe, B. (eds.) LATA 2016. LNCS, vol. 9618, pp. 3–23. Springer, Cham (2016). https://doi.org/10.1007/978-3-319-30000-9_1
10. Brenguier, R., Pérez, G.A., Raskin, J.-F., Sankur, O.: Admissibility in quantitative graph games. CoRR, abs/1611.08677 (2016)
11. Chatterjee, K., Henzinger, T.A.: Assume-guarantee synthesis. In: Grumberg, O., Huth, M. (eds.) TACAS 2007. LNCS, vol. 4424, pp. 261–275. Springer, Heidelberg (2007). https://doi.org/10.1007/978-3-540-71209-1_21
12. ComMA: Introductory ComMA tutorial. https://www.eclipse.org/comma/tutorial/intro.html
13. Dallal, E., Neider, D., Tabuada, P.: Synthesis of safety controllers robust to unmodeled intermittent disturbances. In: 2016 IEEE 55th Conference on Decision and Control (CDC), pp. 7425–7430. IEEE (2016)
14. David, A., Larsen, K.G., Li, S., Nielsen, B.: A game-theoretic approach to real-time system testing. In: Design, Automation and Test in Europe, DATE 2008, pp. 486–491. IEEE (2008)
15. de Alfaro, L., Henzinger, T.A., Kupferman, O.: Concurrent reachability games. In: FOCS 1998: Proceedings of the 39th Annual Symposium on Foundations of Computer Science, p. 564. IEEE Computer Society (1998)
16. de Alfaro, L., Stoelinga, M.: Interfaces: a game-theoretic framework for reasoning about component-based systems. Electron. Notes Theor. Comput. Sci. **97**, 3–23 (2004)

17. Faella, M.: Admissible strategies in infinite games over graphs. In: Královič, R., Niwiński, D. (eds.) MFCS 2009. LNCS, vol. 5734, pp. 307–318. Springer, Heidelberg (2009). https://doi.org/10.1007/978-3-642-03816-7_27

18. Fiterău-Broştean, P., Janssen, R., Vaandrager, F.: Combining model learning and model checking to analyze TCP implementations. In: Chaudhuri, S., Farzan, A. (eds.) CAV 2016. LNCS, vol. 9780, pp. 454–471. Springer, Cham (2016). https://doi.org/10.1007/978-3-319-41540-6_25

19. Fokkink, W.: Distributed Algorithms - An Intuitive Approach, 2nd edn (2018)

20. Hessel, A., Larsen, K.G., Mikucionis, M., Nielsen, B., Pettersson, P., Skou, A.: Testing real-time systems using UPPAAL. In: Formal Methods and Testing, An Outcome of the FORTEST Network, Revised Selected Papers, pp. 77–117 (2008)

21. Hughes, J., Pierce, B.C., Arts, T., Norell, U.: Mysteries of dropbox: property-based testing of a distributed synchronization service. In: 2016 IEEE International Conference on Software Testing, Verification and Validation (ICST), pp. 135–145. IEEE (2016)

22. Kurtev, I., Schuts, M., Hooman, J., Swagerman, D.-J.: Integrating interface modeling and analysis in an industrial setting. In: Proceedings of the 5th International Conference on Model-Driven Engineering and Software Development - MODELSWARD, pp. 345–352. INSTICC, SciTePress (2017)

23. Neider, D., Weinert, A., Zimmermann, M.: Synthesizing optimally resilient controllers. Acta Informatica **57**(1–2), 195–221 (2020)

24. Tretmans, J., van de Laar, M.: Model-based testing with TorXakis: the mysteries of Dropbox revisited. In: Strahonja, V. (ed.),CECIIS : 30th Central European Conference on Information and Intelligent Systems, 2–4 October 2019, Varazdin, Croatia. Proceedings, pp. 247–258. Faculty of Organization and Informatics, University of Zagreb, Zagreb (2019)

25. Zhu, Q., Alpcan, T., Panaousis, E., Tambe, M., Casey, W. (eds.): GameSec 2016. LNCS, vol. 9996. Springer, Cham (2016). https://doi.org/10.1007/978-3-319-47413-7

26. Zielonka, W.: Infinite games on finitely coloured graphs with applications to automata on infinite trees. Theoret. Comput. Sci. **200**(1), 135–183 (1998)

Efficient Dynamic Model Based Testing
Using Greedy Test Case Selection

P. H. M. van Spaendonck[(✉)] [iD]

Department of Mathematics and Computer Science, Eindhoven University of
Technology, Eindhoven, The Netherlands
P.H.M.v.Spaendonck@tue.nl

Abstract. Model-based testing (MBT) provides an automated approach for finding discrepancies between software models and their implementation. If we want to incorporate MBT into the fast and iterative
software development process that is Continuous Integration Continuous Deployment, then MBT must be able to test the entire model in as
little time as possible.

However, current academic MBT tools either traverse models at random, which we show to be ineffective for this purpose, or use precalculated optimal paths which can not be efficiently calculated for large
industrial models. We provide a new traversal strategy that provides an
improvement in error-detection rate comparable to using precalculated
paths. We show that the new strategy is able to be applied efficiently to
large models. The benchmarks are performed on a mix of real-world and
pseudo-randomly generated models. We observe no significant difference
between these two types of models.

Keywords: model based testing · test case selection · efficient testing

1 Introduction

Testing has become a core tenet of modern-day software engineering. It has been
repeatedly shown that having thoroughly tested software leads to higher quality
software with significantly lower maintenance and development costs [3,5]. This
has led to test-driven engineering, in which tests for a component or feature are
written before its actual implementation commences, and the implementation is
deemed to be correct only once all tests succeed.

Similarly, we see a rise in the usage of model-driven engineering, in which
software components are first described on a higher level of abstraction as a state
machine/model. Model-based techniques can then be used to deliver correct and
verified software. For example, in [4], UMLsec models are used to verify that
the security requirements of a single-sign-in software application are correctly
enforced.

Model-Based Testing (MBT), such as the **ioco**-based approach originally
outlined in [14] by Tretmans, sits at the intersection of these two engineering

This publication is part of the PVSR project (with project number 17933) of the
MasCot research programme which is financed by the Dutch Research Council (NWO).

approaches and allows us to use an abstract model to automatically test its implementation. The ability to automatically generate tests makes MBT very useful for software development by, in theory, removing the need to spend time manually writing tests. In practice, however, the exhaustive approach of MBT can easily lead to testing the same behavior multiple times. This contrasts with manually written test suites which are often designed to have as little overlap in tested behavior as possible. Reducing the overlap in tested behavior when using MBT should thus be considered a critical step for applying it for the testing of large complex systems.

The focus of our research is reducing overlap in tested behavior when applying the **ioco**-based MBT technique. For this technique, we confine ourselves to discrete datatypes and we formalize systems as directed graphs in which edges can be labeled with inputs or outputs that use these datatypes. As such, a test run through the model should have as little overlap with itself as possible. Visiting the same part of the model multiple times means that the behavior corresponding to that part of the model would also be tested multiple times.

In [6], van den Bos and Tretmans provide a possible solution to reducing this overlap by automatically calculating test paths that cover all symbolic transitions of a given model. The MBT tool then uses an SMT solver to calculate concrete values for the queries while traversing the pregenerated path. Their approach shows a significant speedup over the classic random test-case selection approach when used to detect non-conformances in several mutants of the Bounded Retransmission Protocol [8].

However, calculating such a global optimal path is *NP*-hard and thus becomes computationally too expensive when applied to large industrial systems. Another issue, which van den Bos and Tretmans also acknowledge, is that using the same test path every time might cause the test to miss bugs that do not present themselves along the given path [6]. Likely because of these reasons, academic MBT tools, such as TorXakis [15], opt to traverse the model at random instead.

We investigate whether a simple and straightforward greedy test-case selection strategy can be used to attain a similar speedup to the one attained through the usage of pre-generated paths, whilst also being able to be applied to large models. For the initial comparison, we use our greedy strategy to run the same experimental setup used for the global optimal strategy in [6], i.e. mutation detection on the Bounded Retransmission Protocol [8]. Our greedy strategy performs 8.2 times better than the random strategy according to the arithmetic mean.

Second, we test the scalability of the greedy solution by applying it to large real-world models, as well as randomly generated statespaces of varying sizes. These random statespaces are approximations of complex systems running under run-to-completion semantics. The greedy strategy provides a noticeable speedup over the random test-case selection strategy when aiming to cover at least 70% of the states of the given models. We also observe that the generated models provide similar results to those of the real-life use case.

In Sect. 2, we briefly discuss related work on model-based testing techniques and optimizations. In Sect. 3, we give the underlying formalization of the theory of **ioco**-based MBT. In Sect. 4, we discuss the algorithm used for **ioco**-based MBT. In Sect. 5, we discuss our new optimizations. In Sect. 6, we show and discuss our benchmarks. We give our final conclusion and discuss other areas of research that might be important for the usage of MBT within the software development cycle in Sect. 7.

2 Related Work

When formalizing systems as abstract models, we often prefer abstracting away over data and formalizing them as discrete datatypes, as this significantly reduces the complexity of the system. However, when formalizing low-level cyber-physical components, we see that the exact value of data, e.g. the angle of an air-intake vent, can not be abstracted away over, as they are central to the correctness of such components. In such cases, systems can be formalized as continuous or hybrid automata [10]. We highlight some of the state-of-the-art test optimization techniques used for systems with continuous data.

For systems with continuous data, MBT is done through search-based testing in which meta-heuristics, such as genetic algorithms or simulated annealing, are used to automatically generate test data. Reducing overlap in tested behavior can, in these instances, be reformulated as an optimization problem. As an example, in [2], meta-heuristics are used to find optimal inputs that maximize the distance between the expected optimal input, thus increasing the likelihood of a fault occurring, and between previous inputs, decreasing the possible overlap with previously tested behavior. In [12], a combination of dimensionality reduction and surrogate modeling techniques based on supervised learning is used to scale up similar techniques to be able to be applied to the incredibly large search spaces encountered within the cyber-physical domain of the automotive industry.

The systems that we describe in Sect. 3 and use throughout the paper, are models with discrete datatypes, often with no direct interrelation. As such, there is no continuous search space to optimize over and the test case selection comes down to optimizing the traversal of the graph that is the specification model. However, these two techniques are not exclusive, and can very well be combined, such as is shown in [11], in which search-based techniques are used to pick viable candidates for the data parameters of functions.

Last, we discuss work on reducing overlap in tested behavior when using online, i.e. a finite test suite is generated a priori, model-based conformance testing techniques. In [7], Cartaxo et al. provide a solution to reducing overlap in tested behavior by measuring the similarity of different tests in the generated test suite and picking a subset of tests such that the similarity measure between the tests in the subset is as low as possible. By doing so, they are able to reduce the number of run tests with 80% while still maintaining a similar fault detection rate to that of a full run test suite. In [1], Aichernig et al. use model-based mutation testing in which mutant models i.e. models containing faulty behavior, are generated from the correct specification model, which, in turn, are used to generate tests aimed at detecting the faults contained in the mutant models. Aichernig et al. use a bounded equivalence checker to find and remove identical mutants that would lead to tests being generated with an overlapping tested behavior. Offline MBT techniques, such as the one used by us, are generally more suited for testing behavior that only occurs after long specific sequences of inputs and outputs.

3   Theory of Model Based Testing

In this section, we give the theory needed to understand how the behavior of a given system is formalized, and how these formal models are used during dynamic MBT. The MBT theory presented here is the same as the original theory described in [14] with only some notational differences.

The expected behavior of a system is expressed as an input-output labeled transition system (IOLTS), a variation of labeled transition systems in which the action labels are split into disjoint input- and output-action sets. We define an IOLTS as follows:

Definition 1. *An IOLTS L is defined as the 5-tuple $L = \langle Q, q_0, A_I, A_O, \rightarrow \rangle$, where:*

- *Q is the finite set of states,*
- *$q_0 \in Q$ is the initial state,*
- *A_I and A_O are the sets of input- and output-actions, respectively, such that $A_I \cap A_O = \emptyset$ and $\tau, \delta \notin A_I \cup A_O$.*
- *$\rightarrow \subseteq Q \times (A_I \cup A_O \cup \{\tau, \delta\}) \times Q$ is the transition relation, such that $\langle q, \delta, q' \rangle \in \rightarrow$ iff $q = q'$ and the state q has no outgoing transitions labeled with an output action $a_{out} \in A_O$ or τ-action.*

Given states p, q, and some action label a, we use the shorthand notation $p \xrightarrow{a} q$ instead of $\langle p, a, q \rangle \in \rightarrow$.

In the set of actions $A_I \cup A_O$, each element corresponds to a function in the implementation. We make a distinction between input actions A_I, functions that we call as inputs to the system, and output actions A_O, functions of other components that can either trigger as a response to inputs given to the system, or spontaneously, e.g. by some internal timer timing out.

We further extend our set of actions with the special actions τ and δ. The τ-action represents an externally non-observable action, e.g. some internal calculation that occurs as a result of calling a function. The δ-action, referred to as quiescence, represents the system remaining idle. A transition with a δ-action occurs exactly in all states in which it is not possible to take an output transition nor an internal action and must be a self-loop, i.e. the begin- and endpoint must be the same.

For readability, we write A_δ as shorthand for $A_I \cup A_O \cup \{\delta\}$ and we write A as shorthand for $A_I \cup A_O$.

During MBT, a sequence of actions referred to as a *suspension trace*, is used to keep track of the actions performed thus far. We define the set of suspension traces using Definitions 2, and 3.

Definition 2. *Let* $L = \langle Q, q_0, A_I, A_O, \rightarrow \rangle$ *be an IOLTS. We define the observable path relation* $\Rightarrow \subseteq Q \times A_\delta^* \times Q$ *as the smallest relation satisfying:*

- $q \xrightarrow{\epsilon} q$ *given any state* $q \in Q$, *where* ϵ *refers to the empty sequence,*
- *given states* $q, q', q'' \in Q$ *and some word* $w \in A_\delta^*$, *if* $q \xrightarrow{\tau} q'$ *and* $q' \xRightarrow{w} q''$ *then* $q \xRightarrow{w} q''$, *and*
- *given states* $q, q', q'' \in Q$, *an observable action* $a \in A_\delta$, *and a word* $w \in A_\delta^*$, *if* $q \xrightarrow{a} q'$ *and* $q' \xRightarrow{w} q''$ *then* $q \xRightarrow{aw} q''$.

Definition 3. *Let* $L = \langle Q, q_0, A_I, A_O, \rightarrow \rangle$ *be some IOLTS. Given a state* $q \in Q$, *the set of suspension traces* $straces(q) \subseteq A_\delta^*$ *is defined as follows:*

$$straces(q) = \{w \in A_\delta^* \mid \exists_{q' \in Q}[q \xRightarrow{w} q']\}.$$

Model Based Testing tests whether the behavior of the implementation conforms to the behavior of the specification, i.e. the implementation never gives an output that the specification does not allow. This conformance is described using the **input-output-conformance** relation **ioco** on IOLTSs, originally defined in [14], and is given in Definition 5.

Definition 4. *Let* $L = \langle Q, q_0, A_I, A_O, \rightarrow \rangle$ *be an IOLTS. We define the mappings* $out_L : \mathcal{P}(Q) \rightarrow \mathcal{P}(A_O)$ *and* L **after** $: A_\delta^* \rightarrow \mathcal{P}(Q)$ *as follows:*

- *given some set of states* $qs \subseteq Q$, *we have*

$$out_L(qs) = \{a_{out} \in A_O \mid \exists_{q \in qs, q' \in Q}[q \xrightarrow{a_{out}} q']\}, \text{ and}$$

- *given some suspension trace* $\sigma \in straces(q_0)$, *we have*

$$L \text{ after } \sigma = \{q \in Q \mid q_0 \xRightarrow{\sigma} q\}.$$

Definition 5. *Given an IOLTS* L_{impl} *of the implementation and an IOLTS* $L_{spec} = \langle Q, q_0, A_I, A_O, \rightarrow \rangle$ *of the specification, the conformance* L_{impl} **ioco** L_{spec} *holds iff given any trace* $\sigma \in traces(q_0)$, *we have*

$$out_{L_{impl}}(L_{impl} \text{ after } \sigma) \subseteq out_{L_{spec}}(L_{spec} \text{ after } \sigma).$$

4   The MBT Algorithm

We now discuss the MBT algorithm from [14], for which we give a pseudocode description in Algorithm 1. The MBT algorithm uses the set qs, which initially contains the initial state q_0 and all states reachable from there using only τ-actions, to keep track of which states it could be in at the start of each iteration.

Algorithm 1: MBT algorithm

Data: A specification IOLTS $L = \langle Q, q_0, A_I, A_O, \rightarrow \rangle$ and a timeout time t.

1 $qs \leftarrow \{q \in Q | q_0 \overset{\epsilon}{\Rightarrow} q\}$

2 **while** $\text{next}(L, qs) \neq \emptyset$ **do** :

3   **do either** :

4   **if** $\text{next}(L, qs) \cap A_I \neq \emptyset$ **then** :

5   **select** a_{in} **from** $\text{next}(L, qs) \cap A_I$

6   **send**(a_{in})

7              $qs \leftarrow \{q \in Q | \exists q' \in qs : q' \overset{a_{in}}{\Longrightarrow} q\}$

8   **or** :

9   **try** $a_{out} \leftarrow \text{rcv}(t)$

10   **if** $a_{out} \in \text{next}(L, qs)$ **then** :

11                 $q \leftarrow \{q \in Q | \exists q' \in qs : q' \overset{a_{out}}{\Longrightarrow} q\}$

12   **else** :

13   **return** *false*

14   **on** *timeout* :

15   **if** $\delta \in \text{next}(L, qs)$ **then** :

16                 $qs \leftarrow \{q \in qs | q \overset{\delta}{\rightarrow} q\}$

17   **else** :

18   **return** *false*

We define $\text{next}(L, qs)$ to be the set of possible actions that can be taken from at least one state in qs, i.e. $\text{next}(L, qs) = \{a \in A_\delta | \exists_{q \in qs, q' \in Q} [q \overset{a}{\rightarrow} q']\}$.

The function $\text{send}(a)$ on line 6 causes the implementation to execute the function corresponding to the input action a. Whenever the implementation calls a function corresponding to some output action a_{out}, the label a_{out} is sent back to the MBT algorithm and added to a response queue. Messages in the queue are read first-in-first-out using the $\text{rcv}(t)$ function on line 9, removing the read message in the process. If $\text{rcv}(t)$ is called and the queue is empty, it will wait till a new message is received. If no message is received within the timeout time t, the function throws a *timeout*.

The algorithm repeatedly does one of two things:

- Some input action a_{in} that is possible from any state in qs is picked and the implementation is requested to execute the corresponding function using $\text{send}(a_{in})$. The tool then updates the set of possible states qs accordingly and continues.
- The MBT tool listens for a possible output action a_{out} using $\text{rcv}(t)$. If an action is received, we verify whether it is an allowed action. If the action is allowed, the set of states qs is updated accordingly and we continue. If a_{out} is not a possible action from any state in qs, then we can conclude that the implementation is not **ioco** with the specification model, and the test has failed. If no response is received within the timeout time t, we assume the implementation to be idle/quiescent. The algorithm reduces the set qs to only the quiescent states in qs, i.e. states with a δ-loop. If none of the states in qs

are quiescent, then the implementation is also not **ioco** with the specification model, and the test has failed.

Note that the MBT algorithm does not terminate if no behavioral differences are ever detected. The tester must decide when to terminate. The termination criterion that is used throughout the paper is state coverage, i.e. the percentage of states that have been reached/tested throughout the run.

5   The Greedy Test Case Selection Strategy

To reduce the amount of overlap in tested behavior, we want to avoid querying inputs leading to already tested states. However, calculating a global optimal path, i.e. finding the shortest path visiting each state at least once, is too computationally expensive to be done on complex systems which have a large number of states. Instead, our proposed strategy intends to approximate the global optimal path by picking locally optimal solutions. This is done by, calculating all possible paths originating from our current set of states qs, of a given length n, and then picking the input action corresponding to the path with the least states that have already been visited. If more than one such action is available, a random contender is picked.

We make use of two optimizations to reduce the amount of work required to find these local-optimal paths. To highlight the need for these optimizations, let us consider an IOLTS in which each state has, on average, λ outgoing transitions. Simply calculating all possible paths of length n and picking the most optimal one, would still be in the order of $O(|qs| \cdot \lambda^n)$.

For the first optimization, we note that once an optimal path of length n has been found, and a singular action has been performed, it is unnecessary to reconsider all possible paths of length n, since we already have a near-optimal path of length $n - 1$. Instead, we only consider the extensions of our leftover path. In Definition 6 we outline the path-tree data structure that we use to keep track of the previously performed calculations.

Definition 6. *Given an IOLTS* $L = \langle Q, q_0, A_I, A_O, \rightarrow \rangle$, *a path-tree is a 6-tuple* $pt = \langle a, q, next, d, v, v_{max} \rangle$, *where*

- *we have projection functions* a, q, next, d, v *and* vmax *defined on pt such that* $a(pt) = a$, $q(pt) = q$, $next(pt) = next$, $d(pt) = d$, $v(pt) = v$, *and* $vmax(pt) = v_{max}$,
- *a is an action label leading to state q, i.e.* $\exists_{q' \in Q} [q' \xrightarrow{a} q]$,
- *next is a set of path-trees such that* $\forall_{pt' \in next} [q \xrightarrow{a(pt')} q']$,
- *d is the depth of the tree, i.e. 1 plus the highest depth among the path-trees in next,*
- *v, i.e. the value of a path-tree, equals the maximum amount of unvisited states that can be reached through a sequence of d transitions, starting with the transition* $q' \xrightarrow{a} q$, *and*
- v_{max} *is used to store the maximum value among the path-trees in next.*

Algorithm 2: The $\texttt{grow}(L, pt, n)$ algorithm for path-trees

---

Data: The IOLTS $L = \langle Q, q_0, A_I, A_O, \rightarrow \rangle$, a path-tree
$pt = \langle a, q, next, d, v, v_{max} \rangle$, and a target depth of $n \geq d$.

1 **if** $d = n$:
2   **return**;
3 **else if** $next = \emptyset$:
4   **for** $a{:}A, q'{:}Q$ s.t. $q \xrightarrow{a} q'$ **do:**
5   add $\langle a, q', \emptyset, 1, covered(q'), 0 \rangle$ to $next$
6 **for** $pt' \in next$ **do:**
7   **if** $\texttt{v}(pt') + ((n-1) - \texttt{d}(pt')) \geq v_{max}$:
8          $\texttt{grow}(L, pt', n-1)$
9          $v_{max} \leftarrow \texttt{max}(v_{max}, \texttt{v}(pt'))$
10 $v \leftarrow v_{max} + covered(q)$
11 $d \leftarrow n$

We now discuss the $\texttt{grow}$ function outlined in Algorithm 2, which extends a given path-tree $pt = \langle a, q, next, d, v, v_{max} \rangle$ to depth n. The *covered* function, that is used on lines 5 and 10, returns 1 if the state q has not been visited yet, and otherwise returns 0. If the target depth n and path-tree depth d are equal, then no further calculations will be necessary and we immediately terminate (line 1 and 2). Otherwise, we first check whether $next$ is empty, i.e. no calculations belonging to this path-tree have been performed past the state q. If $next$ is empty, a new path tree of depth 1 is inserted for each transition originating from the state q (lines 3 through 5). The $\texttt{grow}$ function is then called recursively on each path-tree in $next$ using a target depth of $n-1$, and the variables d, v and v_{max} are updated accordingly (lines 6 and 8 through 11).

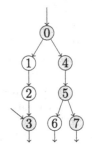

Fig. 1. Preemptive termination example

The **if** statement on line 7 corresponds to our second optimization which consists of pre-emptively terminating the calculation of a given path when we can determine that it will no longer be able to beat or the value of the current optimal path candidate. For example, take Fig. 1 in which a part of a partially explored IOLTS is shown. For readability, the transition labels have been left out and previously visited states have been colored gray. The MBT algorithm is currently in state 0 and wants to find an optimal path of length 3. It first calculates a possible path of length 3 along state 1 and finds a possible path containing 2 unvisited states. It then calculates a path along state 4 but after seeing that the first two states, i.e. 4 and 5, have already been visited, the calculation is terminated since we can determine that the path along state 4 can not contain 2 or more unvisited states.

To use the greedy test-case selection strategy we make use of a variable *paths* to store our current set of path trees originating from qs and replace the statement on line 5 of the MBT algorithm shown in Algorithm 1 with the

---

Algorithm 3: The greedy test case selection strategy.

Data: The IOLTS L, the set of currently maintained path-trees *paths*, the set of current states *qs*, the target depth of n, and a set of possible actions *options*.

```
1  pick_input(L, paths, qs, n, options) :=
2      paths ← {pt ∈ paths | a(pt) ∈ options}
3      if paths = ∅ :
4          for q ∈ qs do:
5              for a ∈ options, q' ∈ Q s.t. q →ᵃ q' do:
6                  insert ⟨a, q', ∅, 1, covered(q'), 0⟩ in paths
7      v_best ← 0
8      pref ← ∅
9      for pt ∈ paths do:
10         grow(L, pt, n)
11         if v(pt) > v_best :
12             v_best ← path.v
13             pref ← {a(pt)}
14         else if v(pt) = v_best :
15             insert a(pt) in pref
16         return pref
```

---

following statement:

$$\text{select } a_{in} \text{ from } \texttt{pick\_input}(L, paths, qs, n, \texttt{next}(L, qs) \cap A_I).$$

The `pick_input` function is given in Algorithm 3 and takes care of growing all current path-trees to the target depth n, and reducing the set of possible input actions *options* to the ones belonging to a local-optimal path of length n. Whenever some action a is performed by the implementation, i.e. an action a is sent to or received from the implementation, the set of paths *paths* is updated to the union of *next* of all path trees whose action equals a. This allows us to reuse the already performed calculations.

6   Benchmarking Results

We split up our benchmarks into two sets. In Sect. 6.1, we test whether our greedy strategy shows improvements over the random test case selection strategy similar to those of the global optimal solution provided in [6]. This is done by benchmarking our strategy to the same set of benchmarks used for the global optimal solution. In Sect. 6.2, we benchmark the scalability of our solution by using both the greedy and the random strategy on a variety of large and complex generated and real-world models.

For both sets of benchmarks, we are interested in the number of transitions each traversal strategy needs to reach a certain goal. For the first set, this goal is detecting non-conformance and for the second set, this goal is a specific percentage of state coverage. We measure the number of transitions instead of the amount of time required, since the throughput, i.e. the number of transitions per second, is largely dependent on the quiescence time, which can vary greatly per system.

The systems that we look at in both sections are deterministic and internal-choice, i.e. in each state, it is possible to query inputs to the implementation or receive outputs from the implementation.

6.1 Fault Detection Speed

The benchmarks used in [15] come from the automata wiki [13], which is an online repository containing various formalized models that can be used for benchmarking. One set of these models pertains to the Bounded Retransmission Protocol [8] by Philips. For this communication protocol, the Wiki provides both a formalization of its intended behavior, as well as 6 mutants. This protocol is a variation of the alternating-bit protocol and provides ordered and partially reliable communication for a sequence split into three messages over a possibly unreliable communication channel. As such, a sequence of messages will always arrive in a clearly marked sequencing, however, the transmission of the entire sequence is terminated if the transmission of a given message has failed a fixed number of times. Each of the six mutants represents incorrect implementations of the communication protocol. We refer the reader to the wiki [13] for exact explanations of the differences between the mutants and the correct implementation.

As was done in [6], we measure the average amount of transitions required to find a non-conformance caused by each mutation using MBT for both the random strategy and our greedy strategy. For each strategy, the average is calculated over a total of 100 runs per mutant. The averages of these runs, as well as the results by van den Bos and Tretmans [6], are shown in Table 1. For reference, the last two columns contain the original benchmarks, where switch coverage is their global optimal solution and TorXakis is the symbolic random test case selection strategy. Since our tool does not allow for infinite data types, the variables representing the three messages have been replaced with constants. As such, we could not properly capture mutant six, since it makes assertions about the three messages that are used, and we omit this mutant from our benchmarks. We calculate the arithmetic mean of the averages of all 5 experiments for each test case selection strategy.

We observe a significant difference in the average detection speed when testing mutant 2 or 6. In mutant 2, the number of permitted failed transmissions after which communication is terminated is reduced from 5 to 4 In mutant 5, an incorrect final response message is sent if only the first 2 messages have been transmitted correctly. Both mutations require a very specific sequence of inputs to become observable and, as the probability of such a specific sequence being picked at random is very low, the random test case selection strategies require significantly longer to observe these mutants.

We observe that the greedy strategy performs ≈ 8.2 times better than the random (non-symbolic) strategy. With the exclusion of Mutant 6, the global optimal solution actually performs ≈ 20.6 times better than the random (symbolic) strategy instead of the ≈ 7.7 times improvement that occurs when Mutant 6 is included. The original authors note that the decreased performance of the global optimal strategy applied to Mutant 6 is caused due the lack of randomness in deciding which values to use for the message variables. Therefore, we believe that the slight randomness of the greedy strategy would lead to similar performance results as those of random test case selection strategies and the performance improvement should stay the same as it is now if Mutant 6 were added to the set of benchmarks.

Table 1. Average number of transitions required to different detect mutations of the Bounded Transmission Protocol though MBT using greedy test case selection, a priori generated path [6], and random test case selection

	Explicit data (2.9k states)		Symbolic data (6 states)	
	greedy w. $N=5$	random	A Priori	TorXakis
Mutant 1	20	22	44	12
Mutant 2	95	412	16	234
Mutant 3	16	21	8	12
Mutant 4	27	29	6	18
Mutant 5	180	2280	18	1620
Mutant 6	–	–	164	76
mean	67.6	552.8	42.7	328.7

6.2 Applicability on Large Models

To investigate the effectiveness of our strategy when used on large systems, we measure the average amount of transitions required by both our greedy strategy and the random strategy, to cover a given percentage of states on such large models. These measurements are performed on both real-world models as well as generated models. We opt to also generate representative models since acquiring a large variety of large complex industrial models is rather difficult. The generated models are based on previous research by Groote et al. [9], in which random LTSs are generated and are shown to be representative of real-world models. This is done by comparing fault-detection results to real-life models and statistical analysis.

The models generated in [9], are generated as follows: An LTS with N states is generated, and each state is given λ outgoing transitions with the target states being uniformly distributed. This process is repeated p times, after which all p random LTSs are parallel composed. The resulting model is then used as a representative LTS.

The models which we generate, are meant to be representative of systems under run-to-completion semantics which dictates that once a system has begun processing some input, it will not start processing another input until the first input has been fully processed, even if both inputs could be processed simultaneously. These semantics are very useful as they significantly reduce the complexity of a model, both in terms of state-space as well as in terms of cognitive complexity.

Since we can see the processing of a given input as a single monolithic action, we end up with similar-looking models to the aforementioned generated LTSs. We thus decide to generate our models as follows: We generate p LTSs as was done before, each transition is labeled with some label representing an arbitrary input action followed by an arbitrary sequence of r output action that forms the processing of the input action. Once all p processes have been parallelly composed, the singular transitions are replaced with a sequence of transitions, labeled with the corresponding input action and the sequence of r output actions.

We require the resulting IOLTS to be deterministic and to be fully connected, i.e. there is always some path from each state to any other state. Using deterministic IOLTSs simplifies the problem situation, reduces variation during testing, and allows us to focus solely on the efficient traversal of the given model. The fully-connected requirement is imposed such that it is always possible to eventually test all states. Intuitively, a system that would not meet this requirement would favor an intelligent strategy that can avoid taking wrong transitions, i.e. a transition that causes yet untested states to become unreachable, in favor of the at-random approach.

We implemented an LTS simulator, that mimics the behavior of the model, and use this as the implementation for all of our benchmarks since we are only interested in the exploration of our LTS. This eliminates a significant portion of the time spent on running the implementation and communication between this and the tool.

For our first set of benchmarks, we apply MBT on the model of an industrial component from Philips. This component is part of the larger set of software used on the Philips Azurion, a large and complex x-ray machine that allows for live imaging during critical heart-surgery operations. Fig. 2 shows the results of these benchmarks. The benchmarks consist of 10 runs per strategy. The average of these runs is indicated by the dashed line $(--)$. The dotted lines $(\cdots)$ show the average plus/minus the standard deviation of these runs. We see that the greedy strategy requires ≈ 6 times fewer steps than the random strategy to cover 90% of the states of the model at Philips. We note that the model contains transitions that, once traversed, cause certain states to no longer be reachable. As such, the random strategy could not consistently test more than $\approx 90\%$ of the states.

For our second set of benchmarks, we use a subsystem of a large Dezyne specification of a sorting robot. This model is part of the set of example models that come with the Dezyne tool, and we believe that, while being an example model, it is representative of machinery that can be encountered in the real world. The model is composed of a large set of modeled subcomponents and, as a result of this, consists of approximately 220 000 states. Since exploring such a large model would take a considerable amount of time, we use statespace

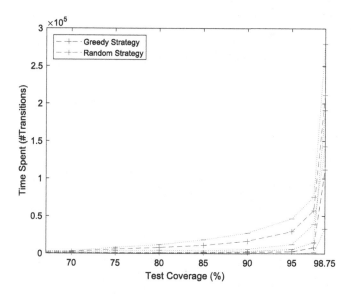

Fig. 2. Number of transitions required to achieve given percentages of state coverage of the model at Philips by both the greedy and random strategies

reduction techniques to reduce its size whilst still maintaining all of the behavior. To do so, we make all quiescence labels explicit and then reduce our LTS modulo branching-bisimulation equivalence. This reduces the model from 220 000 states to only 617 states.

Figure 3 shows the results of the benchmarks performed on the Dezyne sorting machine and shows the greedy strategy requiring $\approx$ 5 times fewer transitions than the random strategy to cover 95% of the sorting machine model. The benchmarks consist of 10 runs per strategy. The average of these runs is indicated by the dashed line $(--)$. The dotted lines $(...)$ show the average plus/minus the standard deviation of these runs.

For our final set of benchmarks, we apply both strategies to several randomly generated statespaces. All random statespaces are generated using the aforementioned technique. We used three different sets of generation parameters. Each set of parameters was used to generate 3 random statespaces. Each randomly generated statespace was then used to perform 10 separate runs per strategy. The set of benchmarks thus consists of 30 runs per strategy per set of generation parameters. The statespaces used for the top-left benchmark are generated using the parameters $N = 10, \lambda = 6$, $r = 1$, and $p = 2$. The statespaces used for the top-right benchmark are generated using the parameters $N = 10, \lambda = 6$, $r = 1$, and $p = 3$. The statespaces used for the bottom benchmark are generated using the parameters $N = 800, \lambda = 6, r = 1$, and $p = 1$.

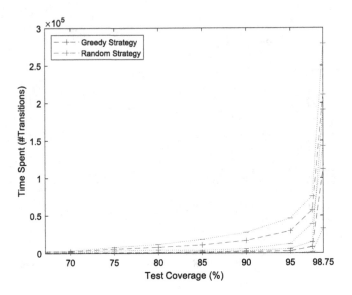

Fig. 3. Number of transitions required to achieve given percentages of state coverage of the sorting machine model by both the greedy and random strategies

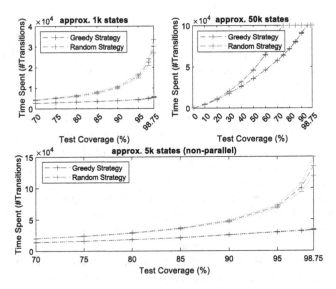

Fig. 4. Number of transitions required to achieve given percentages of state coverage of several generated statespaces

Figure 4 shows the results of the benchmarks performed on the generated statespaces. The greedy strategy, on average, required ≈ 5.5× fewer transitions than the random strategy to reach 98.75% of all states, significantly fewer transitions on the much larger statespaces that were used in the top-right benchmarks, and $\approx 4.2\times$ fewer transitions on the non-parallel statespaces used for the bottom benchmarks. All of the benchmarks showcase similar improvements over the old random strategy.

7   Conclusion and Future Work

We conclude that our greedy solution is a significant improvement over the old at-random exploration strategy when we want to thoroughly test complex systems using dynamic MBT. Our strategy has shown to have a significant speedup over the random strategy when applied to both the industrial model and the sorting machine, as well as the large set of generated statespaces.

However, how often we can query the tested implementation within a given timeframe still remains to be a big bottleneck for MBT. And we believe this to be an important area for future research if we want to be able to efficiently use MBT in software development. More future work lies in studying non-fully connected models, in which a wrong decision could cause a significant portion of states to no longer be visitable. One might propose to solve this, by allowing the test suite to reset the system. Resetting real-world systems is however time-consuming, and thus knowing when to trigger a reset could be crucial in speeding up testing. Another interesting aspect of such systems is finding and comparing strategies that aim to maximize the possible state coverage, by avoiding such wrong decisions.

References

1. Aichernig, B.K., Jöbstl, E., Tiran, S.: Model-based mutation testing via symbolic refinement checking. Sci. Comput. Program. **97**, 383–404 (2015). https://doi.org/10.1016/j.scico.2014.05.004. Special Issue: Selected Papers from the 12th International Conference on Quality Software (QSIC 2012)
2. Araujo, H., Carvalho, G., Mousavi, M.R., Sampaio, A.: Multi-objective search for effective testing of cyber-physical systems. In: Ölveczky, P.C., Salaün, G. (eds.) SEFM 2019. LNCS, vol. 11724, pp. 183–202. Springer, Cham (2019). https://doi.org/10.1007/978-3-030-30446-1_10
3. Beck, K.: Test-Driven Development: By Example. Addison-Wesley Professional, Boston (2003)
4. Best, B., Jurjens, J., Nuseibeh, B.: Model-based security engineering of distributed information systems using UMLsec. In: 29th International Conference on Software Engineering (ICSE 2007), pp. 581–590 (2007). https://doi.org/10.1109/ICSE.2007.55
5. Bhat, T., Nagappan, N.: Evaluating the efficacy of test-driven development: industrial case studies. In: Proceedings of the 2006 ACM/IEEE International Symposium on Empirical Software Engineering, ISESE 2006, pp. 356–363. Association for Computing Machinery, New York (2006). https://doi.org/10.1145/1159733.1159787
6. van den Bos, P., Tretmans, J.: Coverage-based testing with symbolic transition systems. In: Beyer, D., Keller, C. (eds.) TAP 2019. LNCS, vol. 11823, pp. 64–82. Springer, Cham (2019). https://doi.org/10.1007/978-3-030-31157-5_5

7. Cartaxo, E., Machado, P., de Oliveira Neto, F.: On the use of a similarity function for test case selection in the context of model-based testing. Softw. Test. Verif. Reliab. **21**, 75–100 (2011). https://doi.org/10.1002/stvr.413

8. Groote, J.F., van de Pol, J.: A bounded retransmission protocol for large data packets. In: Wirsing, M., Nivat, M. (eds.) AMAST 1996. LNCS, vol. 1101, pp. 536–550. Springer, Heidelberg (1996). https://doi.org/10.1007/BFb0014338

9. Groote, J.F., van der Hofstad, R., Raffelsieper, M.: On the random structure of behavioural transition systems. Sci. Comput. Program. **128**, 51–67 (2016). https://doi.org/10.1016/j.scico.2016.02.006. https://www.sciencedirect.com/science/article/pii/S0167642316000599. Special issue on Automated Verification of Critical Systems (AVoCS'14)

10. Henzinger, T.A.: The Theory of Hybrid Automata. In: Inan, M.K., Kurshan, R.P. (eds.) Verification of Digital and Hybrid Systems, pp. 265–292. Springer, Heidelberg (2000). https://doi.org/10.1007/978-3-642-59615-5_13

11. Lefticaru, R., Ipate, F.: Functional search-based testing from state machines. In: 2008 1st International Conference on Software Testing, Verification, and Validation, pp. 525–528 (2008). https://doi.org/10.1109/ICST.2008.32

12. Matinnejad, R., Nejati, S., Briand, L., Brcukmann, T.: Mil testing of highly configurable continuous controllers: scalable search using surrogate models. In: Proceedings of the 29th ACM/IEEE International Conference on Automated Software Engineering, ASE 2014, pp. 163–174. Association for Computing Machinery, New York (2014). https://doi.org/10.1145/2642937.2642978

13. Neider, D., Smetsers, R., Vaandrager, F., Kuppens, H.: Benchmarks for automata learning and conformance testing (2019). https://doi.org/10.1007/978-3-030-22348-9-23

14. Tretmans, J.: Model based testing with labelled transition systems. In: Hierons, R.M., Bowen, J.P., Harman, M. (eds.) Formal Methods and Testing. LNCS, vol. 4949, pp. 1–38. Springer, Heidelberg (2008). https://doi.org/10.1007/978-3-540-78917-8_1

15. Tretmans, J., van de Laar, P.: Model-based testing with torxakis. In: Central European Conference on Information and Intelligent Systems, pp. 247–258 (2019). https://www.proquest.com/conference-papers-proceedings/model-based-testing-with-torxakis/docview/2366658121/se-2

Minimal Generating Sets for Semiflows

Gerard Memmi[✉]

LTCI, Telecom-Paris, Institut polytechnique de Paris, Palaiseau, France
gerard.memmi@telecom-paris.fr

Abstract. We discuss important characteristics of finite generating sets for $\mathcal{F}^+$, the set of all semiflows with non-negative coordinates of a Petri Net. We endeavor to regroup a number of algebraic results dispersed throughout the Petri Nets literature and also to better position the results while considering semirings such as $\mathbb{N}$ or $\mathbb{Q}^+$ then fields such as $\mathbb{Q}$. As accurately as possible, we provide a range of new algebraic results on minimal semiflows, minimal supports, and finite minimal generating sets for a given family of semiflows. Minimality of semiflows and of support are critical to develop effective analysis of invariants and behavioral properties of Petri Nets. Main results are concisely presented in a table and our contribution is highlighted. We conclude with the analysis of an example drawn from the telecommunication industry underlining the efficiency brought by using minimal semiflows of minimal supports.

Keywords: Formal verification · Petri Nets · invariant · linear algebra · semiflow · generating set

1 Introduction and Motivations

The notion of generating sets for semiflows is well known and efficiently supports the handling of an important class of invariants sometimes unduly called linear invariants in the literature. Several results have been published starting from the initial definition and structure of semiflows [18] to a large array of applications used especially to analyze Petri Nets [9,10,12,27]. Several algorithms were independently developed to compute a generating set of semiflows [26] or later in [1,17]. All of them can be considered as variations of Farkas or Fourier algorithms related to integer linear programming and convex geometry (see [7] for a comparative study or [23] for the underlying mathematical theory).

Semiflows are intimately associated with home spaces and invariants to prove fundamental properties of Petri Nets (even including parameters as in [4]) such as safeness, boundedness, or more complex behavioral properties such as liveness.

Minimality of semiflows and minimality of their supports are critical for accelerating analysis compared to using other semiflows. Invariants deduced from minimal semiflows relate to smaller quantities of resources. Furthermore, the smaller the support of semiflows, the more local their footprint. In the end, these two notions of minimality will foster analysis optimization.

Our main motivation was to go beyond regrouping a number of algebraic results dispersed throughout the Petri Nets literature and to compare and better

© IFIP International Federation for Information Processing 2023
M. Huisman and A. Ravara (Eds.): FORTE 2023, LNCS 13910, pp. 189–205, 2023.
https://doi.org/10.1007/978-3-031-35355-0_12

position these results in considering semirings such as $\mathbb{N}$ or $\mathbb{Q}^+$ then over a field such as $\mathbb{Q}$. In this regard, we were able to complete the current state of the art as accurately as possible with a range of new results on minimal semiflows, minimal supports, and finite minimal generating sets for a given family of semiflows.

1.1   Outline

In Sect. 2, after a brief description of Petri Nets, semiflows, and the set $\mathcal{F}^+$ of all semiflows with non-negative coordinates of a Petri Net, the notions of generating sets, minimal semiflows, and minimal supports are then defined in Sect. 3. Moreover, in this section, it's important to relate semiflow theory to mathematical concepts from linear algebra, convex geometry, or discrete mathematics such as Sperner's theorem to provide with a bound for the number of minimal supports or Gordan's lemma about the existence of finite generating sets. This last connection has never before been attempted.

The three decomposition theorems of Sect. 4 were first published in [19]. Here, two of them are extended to better characterize minimal semiflows and generating sets over $\mathbb{N}$ and better covering $\mathbb{N}$, $\mathbb{Q}^+$, and $\mathbb{Q}$. They are at the core of this paper, since they have made it possible to consolidate results scattered in the literature in a meaningful way and are at the source of the new results presented in the following sections.

Succinct examples and counterexamples are provided to illustrate various results throughout Sects. 4 to 6. Differences between minimal and canonical semiflows are made precise in the Lemma 2 in Sect. 5, which is dedicated to this notion; the section ends with a theorem which states under which condition the number of canonical semiflows is infinite (Sect. 5.2).

The notion of minimal generating sets for semiflows described in Sect. 6 can already be found in [18], then by Colom, Silva, and Teruel in [24] p. 319 and later by the same authors in [8], p. 68 or more recently, in [6]. However, Theorem 5 is new, to the best of our knowledge, and proves the coincidence between a least generating set and a minimal generating set which is not always true in order theory. Uniqueness of particular generating sets is presented in Sect. 6.3.

In Sect. 7, a table is summarizing main results, in particular showing differences[1] when considering $\mathbb{N}$, $\mathbb{Q}^+$, or $\mathbb{Q}$ and highlighting our contribution.

A concrete example is drawn from the telecommunication industry Sect. 8; it illustrates how the choice of minimal semiflows of minimal support is an important factor in simplifying the proof of safeness and liveness for a given Petri Net. Section 9 concludes and provides possible avenues of future research.

2   Petri Nets and Semiflows

A *Petri Net* is a tuple $PN = \langle P, T, Pre, Post \rangle$, where P is a finite set of *places*, T a finite set of *transitions* such that $P \cap T = \emptyset$. A transition t of T is defined by

---

[1] A few inaccuracies found in the literature (e.g. in [6,7]) stem from these differences.

its $Pre(\cdot, t)$ and $Post(\cdot, t)$ conditions[2]: $Pre : P \times T \rightarrow \mathbb{N}$ is a function providing a weight for pairs ordered from places to transitions, $Post : P \times T \rightarrow \mathbb{N}$ is a function providing a weight for pairs ordered from transitions to places. d will denote the number of places: $d = |P|$.

The dynamic behavior of Petri Nets is modeled via markings. A *marking* $M :$ $P \rightarrow \mathbb{N}$ is a function that evolves with the execution (or *firing*) of transitions. When $M(p) = k$, it is often said that the place p contains k *tokens*.

Extensive definitions, properties, and case studies can be found in particular in [5,11].

Semiflows can be defined as solutions of the following homogeneous system of $|T|$ diophantine equations:

$$f^\top Post(\cdot, t) = f^\top Pre(\cdot, t), \quad \forall t \in T, \tag{1}$$

where $x^\top y$ denotes the scalar product of the two vectors x and y since f, Pre and $Post$ can be considered as vectors once the places of P have been ordered.

Considering an initial marking M_0 and the set of reachable markings from M_0, any non-null solution f of the system of Eq. (1) allows to directly deduce the following *invariant* of the Petri Net defined by its Pre and $Post$ functions (used in the system of equations that f satisfies):

$$\forall M \text{ reachable from } M_0 : f^\top M = f^\top M_0. \tag{2}$$

In the rest of the paper, we will only consider the set $\mathcal{F}^+$ of semiflows with non-negative coordinates[3]. $\mathcal{F}^+$ can be defined by:
$\mathcal{F}^+ = \{f \in \mathbb{N}^d \mid \forall t \in T, f^\top Post(\cdot, t) = f^\top Pre(\cdot, t)\}$.

We abusively use the same symbol '0' to denote $(0, ..., 0)^\top$ of $\mathbb{N}^n$, $\forall n \in \mathbb{N}$. The *support* of a semiflow f is denoted by $\|f\|$ and is defined by:
$\|f\| = \{x \in P \mid f(x) \neq 0\}$.

We will use the usual componentwise partial order in which
$(x_1, x_2, \ldots, x_d)^\top \leq (y_1, y_2, \ldots, y_d)^\top$ if and only if $x_i \leq y_i \ \forall i \in \{1, \ldots, d\}$.

3   Generating Sets and Minimality

3.1   Basic Definitions and Results

A subset $\mathcal{G}$ of $\mathcal{F}^+$ is a *generating set over a set* $\mathbb{S}$ if and only if $\forall f \in \mathcal{F}^+$ we have $f = \sum_{g_i \in \mathcal{G}} \alpha_i g_i$ where $\alpha_i \in \mathbb{S}$ and $\mathbb{S} \in \{\mathbb{N}, \mathbb{Q}^+, \mathbb{Q}\}$, where $\mathbb{Q}^+$ denotes the set of non-negative rational numbers.

Since $\mathbb{N} \subset \mathbb{Q}^+ \subset \mathbb{Q}$,[4] a generating set over $\mathbb{N}$ is also a generating set over $\mathbb{Q}^+$, and a generating set over $\mathbb{Q}^+$ is also a generating set over $\mathbb{Q}$. However, the

---

[2] We use here the usual notation: $Pre(\cdot, t)(p) = Pre(p, t)$ and $Post(\cdot, t)(p) = Post(p, t)$.

[3] Semiflows with negative coordinates can also be defined, for instance [7]; however, they are not the object of this paper.

[4] Where $\subset$ denotes the strict inclusion between sets.

reverse is not true and, in our opinion, one source of some of the inaccuracies found in the literature.

The notion of the generating set is strongly related to algebraic concepts especially when it is finite. Let's consider $\mathcal{G}$ a finite generating set of $\mathcal{F}^+$ such that $\mathcal{G} = \{g_1, ...g_k\}$, the following definitions can be recalled.

- If $\mathcal{G}$ is a generating set over $\mathbb{N}$ then
  $\mathcal{S}(\mathcal{G}) = \{f \in \mathbb{N}^d \mid f = \sum_{i=1}^{i=k} \alpha_i g_i \text{ and } \alpha_i \in \mathbb{N}\}$ is a *semigroup* and $\mathcal{F}^+ = \mathcal{S}(\mathcal{G})$.
- If $\mathcal{G}$ is a generating set over $\mathbb{Q}^+$ then
  $\mathcal{C}(\mathcal{G}) = \{f \in (\mathbb{Q}^+)^d \mid f = \sum_{i=1}^{i=k} \alpha_i g_i \text{ and } \alpha_i \in \mathbb{Q}^+\}$ is a *convex polyhedral cone* and $\mathcal{F}^+ = \mathcal{C}(\mathcal{G}) \cap \mathbb{N}^d$. It is interesting to recall a result from [15] stating that $\mathcal{F}^+ \neq \{0\}$ if and only if $\mathcal{C}(\mathcal{G}) \neq \{0\}$.
- If $\mathcal{G}$ is a generating set over $\mathbb{Q}$ then
  $\mathcal{V}(\mathcal{G}) = \{f \in \mathbb{Q}^d \mid f = \sum_{i=1}^{i=k} \alpha_i g_i \text{ and } \alpha_i \in \mathbb{Q}\}$ is a *vector space* and $\mathcal{F}^+ = \mathcal{V}(\mathcal{G}) \cap \mathbb{N}^d$. We can extract from $\mathcal{G}$ a basis of $\mathcal{V}(\mathcal{G})$ (see, for instance, [14] p. 85) which also is a generating set of $\mathcal{F}^+$ over $\mathbb{Q}$ since the elements of this basis are in $\mathcal{F}^+$.

The fact that there exists a finite generating set over $\mathbb{N}$ is non trivial. This result was proven by Gordan circa 1885 then Dickson circa 1913. Here, we directly rewrite Gordan's lemma [2] by adapting it to our notations.

Lemma 1 *(Gordan circa 1885). Let $\mathcal{F}^+$ be the set of non-negative integer solutions of the system of Eq. (1). Then, there exists a finite generating set of vectors in $\mathcal{F}^+$ such that every element of $\mathcal{F}^+$ is a linear combination of these vectors with non-negative integer coefficients.*

In the next sections, we will not come back on the question of the existence of a finite generating set. Being shown for $\mathbb{N}$, it is necessarily true for $\mathbb{Q}^+$ and $\mathbb{Q}$.

3.2   Minimal Supports and Minimal Semiflows

Several definitions of the notion of minimal semiflow were introduced in [24] p. 319, in [8] p. 68, [6,13], or in [19,20]. It can be confusing to look into these in details. In light of this, we propose to consider only two basic notions in order theory: minimality of support with respect to set inclusion and minimality of semiflow with respect to the componentwise partial order on $\mathbb{N}^d$ since the various definitions we found in the literature as well as the results of this paper can be described in terms of these sole two classic notions.

A non-empty support $\|f\|$ of a semiflow f is *minimal* with respect to set inclusion if and only if $\nexists \, g \in \mathcal{F}^+ \setminus \{0\}$ such that $\|g\| \subset \|f\|$.

Since P is finite, the set $\mathcal{MS}$ of minimal supports in P is a *Sperner family* (i.e., a family of subsets such that none of them contains another one) and we can apply Sperner's theorem [25] over $m = |\mathcal{MS}|$ which states that:

$$m \leq \binom{d}{\lfloor d/2 \rfloor}. \tag{3}$$

This result, which was already mentioned in [20,24], provides us with a general upper bound for the number of minimal supports in a given Petri Net. To the best of our knowledge, this bound can be reached only by three families of degenerate Petri Nets containing isolated elements: only one, two, or three places and as many isolated transitions as desired. We conjecture that this bound cannot be reached for Petri Nets with more than three places and should be refined on a case-by-case basis by exploiting connectivity between places and transitions as hinted in the example Sect. 8.

A non-null semiflow f is *minimal* with respect to $\leq$ if and only if $\nexists\, g \in \mathcal{F}^+ \setminus \{0, f\}$ such that $g \leq f$.

In other words, a minimal semiflow cannot be decomposed as the sum of another semiflow and a non-null non-negative vector. This remark yields initial insight into the foundational role of minimality regarding the decomposition of semiflows. We are looking for characterizing generating sets such that they allow analyzing various behavioral properties as efficiently as possible. First, if we consider a generating set over $\mathbb{N}$, then we may have to explore every minimal semiflow. Although finite, the number of minimal semiflows can be quite large. Second, considering a basis over $\mathbb{Q}$ may not capture behavioral constraints quite easily (see the example of Sect. 8).

4   Three Decomposition Theorems

Generating sets can be characterized thanks to a set of three decomposition theorems that can be found in [19] with their proofs. Here, Theorem 1 is extended to better characterize minimal semiflows and generating sets over $\mathbb{N}$, and is provided with a new proof using Gordan's Lemma 1. Theorem 2 was only valid over $\mathbb{N}$ and is now extended to include $\mathbb{Q}^+$ and $\mathbb{Q}$. Theorem 3 is only valid over $\mathbb{Q}^+$ and is unchanged.

4.1   Decomposition over Non-negative Integers

Theorem 1. *If a semiflow is minimal then it belongs to any generating set over* $\mathbb{N}$.

The set of minimal semiflows of $\mathcal{F}^+$ is a finite generating set over $\mathbb{N}$.

Let's consider a semiflow $f \in \mathcal{F}^+ \setminus \{0\}$ such that $\exists f_1, ..., f_k \in \mathcal{F}^+ \setminus \{0, f\}$ and $a_1, ..., a_k \in \mathbb{N}$ such that $f = \sum_{i=1}^{i=k} a_i f_i$. Since $f \neq 0$ and all coefficients a_i are in $\mathbb{N}$, $\exists j \leq k$ such that $a_j > 0$. Therefore, $a_j f_j \leq f$, since $f_j \neq f$, we have $f_j < f$ so f is not minimal. Hence, if a semiflow is minimal then it has to belong to every generating set over $\mathbb{N}$.

Applying Gordan's lemma, there exists $\mathcal{G}$, a finite generating set. Since any minimal semiflow is in $\mathcal{G}$, the subset of all minimal semiflows is included in $\mathcal{G}$ and therefore finite. Let $\mathcal{E} = \{e_1, ...e_n\}$ be this subset.

For any semiflow $f \in \mathcal{F}^+$, we can always define $r \in \mathcal{F}^+$ and a set of n non-negative integers $\{k_1, ...k_n\}$ such that:

i) $r = f - \sum_{j=1}^{j=n} k_j e_j$, where k_i are defined by:

ii) $\forall i \leq n, (f - \sum_{j=1}^{j=i} k_j e_j) \in \mathcal{F}^+$ and $(f - \sum_{j=1}^{j=i} k_j e_j - e_i) \notin \mathcal{F}^+$

By construction of the non-negative integers k_i, we have $r \in \mathcal{F}^+ \setminus \{0\}$ and $\nexists e_i \in \mathcal{E}$ such that $e_i \leq r$. This means that r is minimal or null. $\mathcal{E}$ includes all minimal semiflows, therefore, if r were minimal, then $\exists i \leq n$ such that $e_i = r$. Again, this would contradict the way the coefficients k_i were defined. Therefore, $r = 0$, any semiflow can be decomposed as a linear combinations of minimal semiflows, and $\mathcal{E}$ is a generating set.[5]   □

Let's point out that since $\mathcal{E}$ is not necessarily a basis, the exhibited decomposition may not be unique and depends on the order in which the minimal semiflows are considered as shown in Fig. 1 where the semiflow $h^\top = (9, 9, 6, 0, 3)$ can be decomposed in three different ways: $h = f_2 + g_1 + f_1 = 3f_1 = 2g1 + g3$ just by changing the order in which the 5 minimal semiflows are considered.

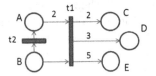

Fig. 1. $f_1^\top = (3, 3, 2, 0, 1)$, $f_2^\top = (4, 4, 1, 0, 2)$, $g_1^\top = (2, 2, 3, 0, 0)$, $g_2^\top = (1, 1, 0, 1, 0)$, $g_3^\top = (5, 5, 0, 0, 3)$ are five canonical and minimal semiflows. $\|f_1\|$ or $\|f_2\|$ are not minimal. f_1 and f_2 are linear combinations of g_1, g_2, g_3 over $\mathbb{Q}^+$: $f_1 = \frac{1}{3}(2g_1 + g_3)$ and $f_2 = \frac{1}{3}(g_1 + 2g_3)$. Therefore, the decomposition of a semiflow on $\{f_1, f_2, g_1, g_2, g_3\}$ is not unique. Moreover, $\mathcal{G}_1 = \{g_1, g_2, g_3\}$ is a generating set over $\mathbb{Q}^+$ or over $\mathbb{Q}$.

However, a minimal semiflow does not necessarily belong to a generating set over $\mathbb{Q}^+$ or $\mathbb{Q}$. In Fig. 1, $\mathcal{G}_1$ does not include f_1, which is minimal or in Fig. 2 where $\mathcal{G}_3$ does not include g_4 which is of minimal support.

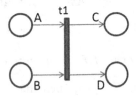

Fig. 2. $f^\top = (1, 1, 1, 1)$, $g_1^\top = (0, 1, 1, 0)$, $g_2^\top = (0, 1, 0, 1)$, $g_3^\top = (1, 0, 1, 0)$, $g_4^\top = (1, 0, 0, 1)$ are five canonical semiflows. f is not minimal and $\|f\|$ is not minimal. $\mathcal{G}_2 = \{g_1, g_2, g_3, g_4\}$ is the unique generating set over $\mathbb{N}$ and $f = g_1 + g_4 = g_2 + g_3$ has exactly two different decompositions in $\mathcal{G}_2$. $\mathcal{G}_3 = \{g_1, g_2, g_3\}$ is a generating set over $\mathbb{Q}$.

---

[5] If $\mathcal{E}$ were infinite, the construction could still be used since the decreasing sequence is bounded by 0 and $\mathbb{N}$ is nowhere dense, and we would have:
$\lim_{n \to \infty} f - \sum_{j=1}^{j=n} k_j e_j = 0$ with the same definition of the coefficients k_j as in ii).

4.2   Decomposition over Semiflows of Minimal Support

Theorem 2. *If I is a minimal support then*

i) there exists a unique minimal semiflow f such that $I = \|f\|$ and $\forall g \in \mathcal{F}^+$ such that $\|g\| = I, \exists k \in \mathbb{N}$ such that $g = kf$,

ii) any non-null semiflow g such that $\|g\| = I$ constitutes a generating set over $\mathbb{Q}^+$ or $\mathbb{Q}$ for $\mathcal{F}_I^+ = \{g \in \mathcal{F}^+ |\ \|g\| = I\}$.

In other words, $\{f\}$ is a unique generating set over $\mathbb{N}$ for $\mathcal{F}_I^+ = \{g \in \mathcal{F}^+ \mid \|g\| = I\}$. However, this uniqueness property is indeed lost in $\mathbb{Q}^+$ or in $\mathbb{Q}$, since any element of $\mathcal{F}_I^+$ is a generating set of $\mathcal{F}_I^+$ over $\mathbb{Q}^+$ or $\mathbb{Q}$.

From Sperner's theorem, any support I of a semiflow contains a finite number m of minimal supports of semiflows. The following theorem states that these m supports cover I, and provide a generating set deduced from these m supports.

Theorem 3. *(decomposition)   Any support I of semiflows is covered by the finite subset $\{I_1, I_2, \ldots, I_m\}$ of minimal supports of semiflows included in I:*
$$I = \bigcup_{i=1}^{i=m} I_i.$$
Moreover, $\forall f \in \mathcal{F}^+$ such that $\|f\| = I$, one has $f = \sum_{i=1}^{i=m} \alpha_i g_i$ where $\alpha_i \in \mathbb{Q}^+$ and the semiflows g_i are such that $\|g_i\| = I_i$.

A sketch of proof of Theorem 3 can be found in [5], a complete proof in [19].

5   Canonical Semiflows

A semiflow is *canonical* ([7,8] p. 68) if and only if the gcd of its non-null coordinates is equal to one. In [6], such a semiflow is said to be *scaled back*.

5.1   Canonical and Minimal Semiflows

Minimal semiflows and canonical semiflows are two different notions. The following lemma and theorem help to compare them.

Lemma 2. *If a semiflow is minimal then it is canonical.*
If a semiflow is canonical and its support is minimal then it is minimal.

The first point is quite evident: if f is not canonical its gcd k is such that $k > 1$ so $\exists g \in \mathcal{F}^+$ such that $f = kg$ and f would not be minimal.

The second point is a direct application of Theorem 2.   □

However, canonical semiflows are not necessarily minimal semiflows; minimal semiflows do not necessarily have a minimal support. For example, Fig. 1, f_1 and f_2 are canonical and minimal, but their support is not minimal. Any semiflow $f = a g_1 + g_2 + b g_3$ where $a, b \in \mathbb{N}$ and $a + b > 0$ is canonical and clearly not minimal. As a and b can be arbitrarily large, this shows that the number of canonical semiflows can be infinite.

5.2   About the Number of Canonical Semiflows

We can observe in the previous example that the infinite sequence of canonical semiflows is constituted of semiflows with non-minimal support. This is hinted on the following theorem.

Theorem 4. *Given a support I, $c_I = |\{f \text{ canonical semiflow} \mid \|f\| = I\}|$,*
  If I is a minimal support, then $c_I = 1$, else c_I is infinite.
  If $c_I = 1$, then I is minimal.

From Theorem 2, there is a unique minimal semiflow having a given minimal support. From Lemma 2, a minimal semiflow is canonical. Hence, if I is minimal, then $c_I = 1$.

If I is not minimal, then $\exists\ e,\ f \in \mathcal{F}^+$ such that $\|e\| \subset \|f\| = I$. We can build an infinite sequence of semiflows f_i, $i \in \mathbb{N}$, such that $f_i = \alpha_i(f + k_i e)$, where $k_i \in \mathbb{N}$ and $1/\alpha_i$ is the gcd of the non-null coordinates of $f + k_i e$. $\forall i \in \mathbb{N}.f_i$ is canonical by construction. Let's consider i, j such that $f_i = f_j$; then $\alpha_i(f + k_i e) = \alpha_j(f + k_j e)$. This leads to: $(\alpha_i - \alpha_j)f = (k_i - k_j)e$. However, since $\|e\| \subset \|f\|$, we must have $\alpha_i = \alpha_j$ and $k_i = k_j$. Hence, we built an infinite sequence of canonical semiflows based upon an infinite sequence of non-negative integers.

If $c_I = 1$ then let f be the unique canonical semiflow of support I. Let's consider $g \in \mathcal{F}^+$ such that $\|g\| \subseteq I$. With the same construction as before, we can build a canonical semiflow $h = \alpha(f + kg)$ where $1/\alpha$ is the gcd of the non-null coordinates of $f + kg$, and $k \in \mathbb{N}$. We have $\|h\| = I$ and $c_I = 1$; therefore, $h = \alpha(f + kg) = f$. Then, $g = ((1 - \alpha)/k\alpha)f$ which means that any semiflow of support included in I is a multiple of f. Hence, I is minimal.   □

The fact that the number of canonical semiflows can be infinite was already pointed out in [6,7,13]. The fact that this number is infinite only when the considered support is non minimal as described in Theorem 4 is new to the best of our knowledge.

6   Minimal Generating Sets, Least Generating Sets, and Fundamental Sets

Minimal generating sets have been defined over $\mathbb{N}$ in [19] and over $\mathbb{Q}^+$ in [19,20], and least generating sets over $\mathbb{Q}$ in [7,11]. Similarly to the notion of generating set defined in Sect. 3.1, we slightly extend their definition to hold over a set $\mathbb{S} \in \{\mathbb{N}, \mathbb{Q}^+, \mathbb{Q}\}$.

From [20] p. 39, a *minimal generating set* over $\mathbb{S}$ is a generating set that does not strictly include any generating set.

From [7] p. 82, or [8] p. 68, a *least generating set of semiflows* "is made up of the least number of elements to generate any semiflow" over $\mathbb{S}$[6] In other words, $\mathcal{G}$ is a least generating set if and only if it does not exist a generating set $\mathcal{H}$ such that $|\mathcal{H}| \leq |\mathcal{G}|$.

---

[6] More precisely, the least generating set is defined over $\mathbb{Q}$ in [7,8] and over $\mathbb{N}$ in [6].

6.1   Coincidence Between Minimal and Least Generating Sets

A minimal generating set is defined with respect to set inclusion while a least generating set is defined with respect to its cardinality. In the case of generating sets of semiflows, Theorem 5 hereunder is a new result stating that these two different notions are in fact equivalent over $\mathbb{S}$.

Lemma 3. *If $\mathcal{G}$ is a generating set over $\mathbb{Q}^+$ or $\mathbb{N}$, I a minimal support, then $\exists g \in \mathcal{G}$ such that $I = \|g\|$.*

We consider e a semiflow of minimal support, $\mathcal{G} = \{g_1, ... g_k\}$, a generating set over $\mathbb{Q}^+$ or $\mathbb{N}$. Then, $e = \sum_{i=1}^{i=k} \alpha_i g_i$. All the coefficients are non-negative and $e \neq 0$, then $\exists j \leq k$ such that $\alpha_j > 0$ and $e \geq \alpha_j g_j$. Since $\|e\|$ is minimal, $\|e\| = \|g_j\|$.   □

This lemma states that any generating set over $\mathbb{Q}^+$ or $\mathbb{N}$ contains at least one semiflow per minimal support. Indeed, this property is not true over $\mathbb{Q}$. In Fig. 2, $\mathcal{G}_2$ is a minimal generating set over $\mathbb{Q}^+$ and $\{g_2, g_3, g_4\} \subset \mathcal{G}_2$ is a generating set over $\mathbb{Q}$ since $g_1 = g_2 + g_3 - g_4$ is of minimal support but generated over $\mathbb{Q}$ (since one coefficient is negative) by the other minimal semiflows of minimal support.

Theorem 5. *If $\mathcal{G}$ is a generating set over $\mathbb{S}$, where $\mathbb{S} \in \{\mathbb{N}, \mathbb{Q}^+, \mathbb{Q}\}$ then the two following properties are equivalent:*
   $\mathcal{G}$ is a minimal generating set,
   $\mathcal{G}$ is a least generating set.

First, the fact that a least generating set is a minimal generating set is straightforward.

Let's consider $\mathcal{G}$, a minimal generating set over $\mathbb{N}$. By applying Theorem 1, we conclude that $\mathcal{G}$ is the set of minimal semiflows and a least generating set.

Next, let's consider $\mathcal{G}$, a minimal generating set over $\mathbb{Q}^+$. Then, Lemma 3 can apply stating that $\mathcal{G}$ includes $\mathcal{G}'$ a family of exactly one semiflow for each minimal support. From Theorem 3, we draw that $\mathcal{G}'$ is a generating set. $\mathcal{G}$ is minimal then $\mathcal{G} = \mathcal{G}'$. This being true for any minimal generating set, $\mathcal{G}$ is also a least generating set.

Finally, let's consider $\mathcal{G}$ a generating set over $\mathbb{Q}$. From $\mathcal{G}$ we can extract a subset $\mathcal{B}$ of linearly independent semiflows (see [14] p. 85 for basic results on vector spaces). Then, $\mathcal{B}$ is a least and minimal generating set over $\mathbb{Q}$.   □

6.2   About Fundamental Sets

Theorem 4 states that there is exactly one canonical semiflow for each minimal support. This particularity characterizes the notion of a fundamental set.

In [24] p. 319, the set of all canonical semiflows of minimal support is called a *fundamental set*.

Corollary 1. *(fundamental set) A fundamental set is a generating set over $\mathbb{Q}^+$ or $\mathbb{Q}$ but not necessarily over $\mathbb{N}$. A fundamental set over $\mathbb{Q}^+$ is a minimal generating set but not necessarily over $\mathbb{Q}$.*

The first point of this corollary is a direct consequence of Theorem 3 and Lemma 2: we conclude that a fundamental set is one possible generating set over $\mathbb{Q}^+$ and therefore over $\mathbb{Q}$.

The second point is directly deduced from the first point and Lemma 3.

The last parts of the two points of the corollary are illustrated by the two following counterexamples.

In Fig. 1, $\mathcal{G}_1 = \{g_1, g_2, g_3\}$ is a fundamental set that is not a generating set over $\mathbb{N}$ since f_1 or f_2 are minimal and cannot be decomposed as a linear combination of elements of $\mathcal{G}_1$ over $\mathbb{N}$ [7].

A fundamental set over $\mathbb{Q}$ is not necessarily a minimal generating set; in Fig. 2, $\mathcal{G}_2$ is the fundamental set and is not a minimal generating set.   □

Belonging to a least generating set, hereunder denoted by *lgs*, does not equip a semiflow f with specific properties[8]:

- if $f \in lgs$ over $\mathbb{N}$, then f is minimal but not necessarily canonical or of minimal support;
- if $f \in lgs$ over $\mathbb{Q}^+$, then f has a minimal support but is not necessarily canonical or minimal;
- if $f \in lgs$ over $\mathbb{Q}$, then f is not necessarily minimal and not necessarily canonical or of minimal support.

6.3   About Uniqueness

Corollary 2. *(uniqueness) The set of minimal semiflows is the unique minimal generating set over $\mathbb{N}$.*

If $\mathcal{G}$ is a least generating set over $\mathbb{Q}^+$ then for any minimal support I of semiflows, $\exists g \in \mathcal{G}$ unique such that $I = \|g\|$.

The fundamental set is the unique minimal generating set of minimal semiflows over $\mathbb{Q}^+$.

The first point can be directly deduced from Theorem 1, the second and third are directly deduced from Theorems 2 and 3 and Lemma 2.   □

The third point of this corollary can be considered as a variation of a statement in [24].

However, a minimal generating set over $\mathbb{Q}^+$ or $\mathbb{Q}$ is not unique even among minimal semiflows of minimal support. In the example of Fig. 2, $\{k_1 g_1, k_2 g_2, k_3 g_3, k_4 g_4\}$ where $k_i \in \mathbb{N}$ constitutes a family of minimal generating sets over $\mathbb{Q}^+$. Moreover, $\mathcal{G}_3 = \{g_1, g_2, g_3\}$ and $\{g_2, g_3, g_4\}$ are two minimal generating sets over $\mathbb{Q}$.

---

[7] In this regard, the statement p. 143–147 of [6] should be rewritten.

[8] The properties 2.2 p. 82 of [7] and 5.2.5 p. 68 of [9] should be rewritten by taking the following statements into account.

7   Results Summary

We have seen through several counterexamples that no result must be taken for granted and that any proposition must be carefully addressed. Figure 3 summarizes the main results presented in this paper.

	$\mathbb{N}$	$\mathbb{Q}^+$	$\mathbb{Q}$
Theorem application domain	Theorems 1, 2, 4, 5	Theorems 2, 3, 4, 5	Theorems 2, 4, 5
Minimality and uniqueness	{minimal semiflows} = unique mgs	mgs={one semiflow per minimal support} fs = unique mgs of minimal semiflows	An mgs is a basis No uniqueness
Theorem 2 I minimal support |{minimal semiflow of support I}|=1	{f minimal semiflow} = unique mgs = fs	Any semiflow of support I is a mgs for {semiflow f | I = ||f||}	Any semiflow of support I is an mgs for {semiflow f| I = ||f||}
Corollary 1 fs= {canonical semiflows of minimal support}	fs not always a gs	fs is a mgs among others	fs is not necessarily an mgs
Theorem 5	mgs = lgs	mgs = lgs	mgs = lgs

Fig. 3. gs, fs, mgs, lgs denote the generating set, the fundamental set, the minimal generating set, and the least generating set respectively.

Our contribution in terms of new results consists of the following:

- the first three theorems in Sect. 4, which have been slightly extended with a new proof for Theorem 1 and could be used for infinite Petri Nets [22];
- Lemma 2 and Theorem 4 of Sect. 5 about comparing minimal and canonical semiflows;
- Lemma 3 and Theorem 5 about the equivalence between minimal and least generating sets;
- Corollaries 1 and 2 about fundamental sets and uniqueness.

8   Reasoning with Invariants, an Example

The example described in Fig. 4 is a reduced[9] version of a Petri Net published in [16] representing two subscribers, "a caller" and a "callee", having a conversation

---

[9] See [5,11] for Petri Nets reduction rules.

(places CLA and CA respectively). Initially, they are in an idle state with places LA and A marked with one token. Signals PU, R are sent from the caller to the callee and signals S, F from the callee to the caller. The overall desired behavior is that caller and callee cannot go back to their idle state as long they have not received all the signals sent to them despite the fact that they both can hang up at any time making the order in which signals F and R are sent and received undetermined.

From their idle state (place LA), the caller can pick up their phone (transitions t_1) sending the signal PU to the callee. From their idle state (place A), the callee, upon receiving the signal PU, can pick up their phone (transition t_7), send the signal S and go to conversation (place CA) from where they can hang up (transition t_8) at any time sending the signal F to the caller. Receiving the signal S, the caller can go (transition t_2) to the conversation (place CLA). They can also hang up at any time (transitions t_3, t_4, t_5) sending the signal R to the callee. After hanging up via t_4 or t_5, the caller will have to wait (place W) until they receive the signal F from the callee before going back (transition t_6) to their initial idle state LA. The callee can go back to their idle state A only upon receiving the signal R (transition t_9).

The initial marking M_0 is such that $M_0(LA) = M_0(A) = 1$, $M_0(p) = 0$ for any other place: the modeled system is in its idle state.

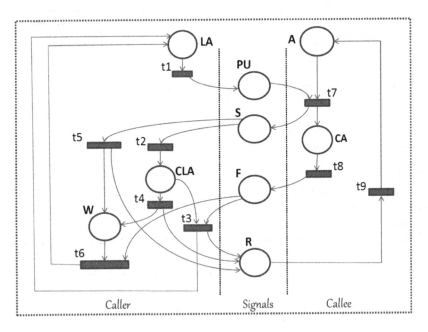

Fig. 4. This Petri Net has exactly three minimal semiflows of minimal support constituting a minimal generating set over $\mathbb{Q}^+$: $\mathcal{GB}_1 = \{f_1, f_2, f_3\}$ such that: $f_1(LA) = f_1(CLA) = f_1(W) = f_1(PU) = f_1(S) = 1$, $f_1(p) = 0$ for any other place, $f_2(LA) = f_2(PU) = f_2(F) = f_2(CA) = 1$, $f_2(p) = 0$ for any other place, $f_3(CLA) = f_3(S) = f_3(R) = f_3(A) = 1$, $f_3(p) = 0$ for any other place.

8.1   Optimizing Sperner's Bound

First, let us notice that inequality (3) gives us the following bound for m, the number of minimal supports: $m \leq \binom{9}{\lfloor 9/2 \rfloor} = 126$. However, it is easy to notice that transitions t_1, t_2, t_8, and t_9 have only one input and one output, which means that any support including such an input also includes the corresponding output to satisfy the equations associated to t_1, t_2, t_8, and t_9. The bound can be optimized to: $m \leq \binom{5}{\lfloor 5/2 \rfloor} = 10$. It can further be improved by reasoning on transitions t_5 and t_6 and reach $m \leq 3$.

8.2   A Proof Scheme Using Minimal Semiflows of Minimal Support

We want to verify the following property (known as safeness [11] p. 489):
   $\mathcal{P} = \forall M$ reachable from $M_0, \forall p \in P, M(p) \leq 1$.
   We also want to prove that the initial marking M_0 is a home state (i.e., a marking such that whatever the evolution of the Petri Net, it is always possible to reach it back) from which it is easy to deduce that the Petri Net is live.
   These two important properties are proven hereunder, starting from $\mathcal{GB}_1 = \{f_1, f_2, f_3\}$ the set of minimal semiflows of minimal support defined Fig. 4 without considering every reachable marking.
   Similarly as in Eq. (2), three invariants can directly be drawn from $\mathcal{GB}_1$: for any reachable marking M from M_0, $f_1^\top M = f_1^\top M_0 = 1$, $f_2^\top M = f_2^\top M_0 = 1$, $f_3^\top M = f_3^\top M_0 = 1$.[10]
   In other words, there is exactly one token in the support of any semiflow of $\mathcal{GB}_1$. Hence, $\mathcal{P}$ is true since $P = \bigcup_{i=1}^{i=3} \|f_i\|$.
   To prove that M_0 is a home state, we start to prove that $\mathcal{HS} = \{M \mid M(LA) = 1\}$ is a home space (i.e., a set of markings such that whatever is the evolution of the Petri Net, it is always possible to reach one element of the set). If we consider the invariant deduced from f_2, we know that any reachable marking M is necessarily in one of the 4 following cases.

   i) $M(LA) = 1$, then $M \in \mathcal{HS}$,
   ii) $M(F) = 1$, since $f_2^\top M = 1$, we have $M(LA) = M(PU) = M(CA) = 0$. $f_1^\top M = f_1(CLA)M(CLA) + f_1(W)M(W) + f_1(S)M(S) = 1$ and it then remains only 3 sub-cases to explore:
   ii-1) $M(CLA) = 1$, t_3 can occur from M and we can reach $M' \in \mathcal{HS}$
   ii-2) $M(W) = 1$, t_6 can occur from M and we can reach $M' \in \mathcal{HS}$
   ii-3) $M(S) = 1$, t_2 can occur from M then we are in the sub-case ii-1).
   iii) $M(CA) = 1$, t_8 can occur from M then we are in the case ii).
   iv) $M(PU) = 1$, then considering the invariants deduced from f_1 and f_2, we have: $M(LA) = M(CLA) = M(W) = M(F) = M(S) = M(CA) = 0$

   From $f_3^\top M = 1$, we have two sub-cases:

   iv-1) $M(A) = 1$, t_7 can occur from M then we are in the case iii).
   iv-2) $M(R) = 1$, t_9 can occur then we are in the case iv-1) again.

---

[10] In the following, we will omit the phrase "for any reachable marking M from M_0".

From these simple 4 cases and 5 sub-cases, we directly deduce that $\mathcal{HS}$ is a home space from where it is easy to conclude that M_0 is a home state and the Petri Net is live.

8.3   Further Remarks

We let interested readers develop the same proof scheme from $\mathcal{GB}_2 = \{f_1, \ g = f_2 + f_3, \ h = f_1 + f_3\}$ or from $\mathcal{GB}_3 = \{g, \ h, \ l = f_1 + f_2\}$ which are minimal generating sets over $\mathbb{Q}$ and find out that the analysis becomes more complex even with small additional changes. We conclude that the smaller the support, the more effective the analysis will be since the number of cases and sub cases of the proof scheme depends on the number of elements of each considered support.

The same proof scheme can be used with a colored Petri Net or the same Petri Net enriched with two parameters to model x callers and y callees. In the latter, the initial marking M_0 becomes: $M_0(LA) = x$, $M_0(A) = y$, $M_0(p) = 0$ for any other place p. $\mathcal{GB}_1$ is unchanged, but its three associated invariants become: $f_1^\top M = f_1^\top M_0 = x$, $f_2^\top M = f_2^\top M_0 = x$, $f_3^\top M = f_3^\top M_0 = y$. To prove that $\mathcal{HS} = \{M|\ M(LA) = x\}$ is a home space, we can start from a marking M that satisfies $f_2^\top M = x$ and build a sequence of transitions σ_1 that will reach a marking M' such that $M'(PU) < M(PU)$. σ_1 can then be iterated until a marking of $\mathcal{HS}$ is finally reached. From there, it becomes easy to prove that the Petri Net is live. At last, with the same scheme, it can be proven that $\mathcal{HS}_c = \{M|\ M(CLA) = M(CA) = z \text{ and } z \leq min(x,y)\}$ is a home space meaning that it is always possible to have z subscribers in a conversation.

9   Conclusion

By considering $\mathbb{N}$, then $\mathbb{Q}^+$, then $\mathbb{Q}$, the size of a minimal generating set decreases as expected since an increasing amount of possibilities to combine semiflows are provided. More interestingly, if m is the number of minimal supports in a Petri Net then:

a minimal generating set over $\mathbb{N}$ is finite and has at least m elements,

a minimal generating set over $\mathbb{Q}^+$ has exactly m elements,

a minimal generating set over $\mathbb{Q}$ has, at most, m elements.

Moreover, we were able to regroup and clarify some key algebraic results scattered in the literature by considering only the two notions of minimality in terms of semiflow and support respectively.

The example of Sect. 8 showed how loose the Sperner's bound is, as well as a first pathway to improve upon it by considering the connections imposed by the homogeneous system of Eq. (1). The same example provides reasons to consider non-negative semiflows of minimal support. With that said, a comprehensive complexity analysis of the complete process of computing a generating set along with analyzing a Petri Net properties is required in order to quantitatively evaluate the trade-off between manipulating a generating set over $\mathbb{Q}^+$ or over $\mathbb{Q}$. Let us also point out that in the literature, there exist additional reasons to consider minimal supports described, for instance in [9].

We claimed that results in [6] or in [8] p. 68 need to be rephrased in considering the formulation by the same authors in one of their previous publications [24].

We believe that these results may be enriched along two different alleys. From a mathematical point of view, the relation with integer linear programming or convex geometry has been investigated many times, particularly in [7], however, we believe it could be fruitful to look at the notion of toric varieties and saturated semigroups [21]. From a Petri Net and, even more broadly, from a transition system theory point of view, applying these new results to a variety of models (for example, colored Petri Nets or any transition system that can be associated with a system of equations such as (1)) remains to be done. On another note, supports of semiflows can be considered as a specific structure of places such as siphons or traps [3,5,11]. It would be worth investigating their relationship since a support of a semiflow is, at the same time, a trap and a siphon.

Finally, we would like to stress the possibility to automate the proof scheme exhibited throughout the example of Sect. 8. Even though some proof steps can be shortened, we chose to develop our proofs in a systematic way to provide a clear road map on how an algorithm could proceed for solving such properties.

Acknowledgements. the author is grateful to Claude Girault who helped with the many comments and the organization of this paper. Many thanks to Pierre Jouvelot, Bethany Cagnol as well as the anonymous reviewers of this conference the help of whom was greatly appreciated and led to its improvement.

References

1. Alaiwan, H., Memmi, G.: Algorithmes de recherche des solutions entières positives d'un système linéaire d'équations homogènes. Revue Technique Thomson-CSF **14**(1), 125–135 (1982)
2. Alon, N., Berman, K.A.: Regular hypergraphs, Gordon's lemma, Steinitz' lemma and invariant theory. J. Comb. Theory A **43**, 91–97 (1986)
3. Barkaoui, K., Pradat-Peyre, J.-F.: On liveness and controlled siphons in petri nets. In: Billington, J., Reisig, W. (eds.) ICATPN 1996. LNCS, vol. 1091, pp. 57–72. Springer, Heidelberg (1996). https://doi.org/10.1007/3-540-61363-3_4
4. Bozga, M., Esparza, J., Iosif, R., Sifakis, J., Welzel, C.: Structural invariants for the verification of systems with parameterized architectures. In: TACAS 2020. LNCS, vol. 12078, pp. 228–246. Springer, Cham (2020). https://doi.org/10.1007/978-3-030-45190-5_13
5. Brams, G.W.: Réseaux de Petri: Théorie et Pratique. Masson, Paris, France (1982)
6. Ciardo, G., Mecham, G., Paviot-Adet, E., Wan, M.: P-semiflow computation with decision diagrams. In: Franceschinis, G., Wolf, K. (eds.) PETRI NETS 2009. LNCS, vol. 5606, pp. 143–162. Springer, Heidelberg (2009). https://doi.org/10.1007/978-3-642-02424-5_10

7. Colom, J.M., Silva, M.: Convex geometry and semiflows in P/T nets. A comparative study of algorithms for computation of minimal p-semiflows. In: Rozenberg, G. (ed.) ICATPN 1989. LNCS, vol. 483, pp. 79–112. Springer, Heidelberg (1991). https://doi.org/10.1007/3-540-53863-1_22
8. Colom, J.M., Silva, M., Teruel, E.: Properties. In: Girault, C., Valk, R. (eds.) Petri Nets for Systems Engineering, pp. 53–72. Springer, Heidelberg (2003). https://doi.org/10.1007/978-3-662-05324-9_6
9. Colom, J.M., Teruel, E., Silva, M., Haddad, S.: Structural methods. In: Girault, C., Valk, R. (eds.) Petri Nets for Systems Engineering, pp. 277–316. Springer, Heidelberg (2003). https://doi.org/10.1007/978-3-662-05324-9_16
10. Dworzanski, L.W., Lomazova, I.A.: Structural place invariants for analyzing the behavioral properties of nested petri nets. In: Kordon, F., Moldt, D. (eds.) PETRI NETS 2016. LNCS, vol. 9698, pp. 325–344. Springer, Cham (2016). https://doi.org/10.1007/978-3-319-39086-4_19
11. Girault, C., Valk, R.: Petri Nets for Systems Engineering, A guide to Modeling, Verification, and Applications. Springer, Heidelberg (2003). https://doi.org/10.1007/978-3-662-05324-9
12. Johnston, M.D., Anderson, D.F., Craciun, G., Brijder, R.: Conditions for extinction events in chemical reaction networks with discrete state spaces. J. Math. Biol. **76**(6), 1535–1558 (2018)
13. Krückeberg, F., Jaxy, M.: Mathematical methods for calculating invariants in petri nets. In: Rozenberg, G. (ed.) APN 1986. LNCS, vol. 266, pp. 104–131. Springer, Heidelberg (1987). https://doi.org/10.1007/3-540-18086-9_22
14. Lang, S.: Algebra. GTM, 3rd edn. Springer, New York (2002). https://doi.org/10.1007/978-1-4613-0041-0
15. Lasserre, J.B., Mahey, P.: Using linear programming in petri net analysis. RAIRO RO **23**(1), 43–50 (1989)
16. Martin, R., Memmi, G.: Specification and validation of sequential processes communicating by FIFO channels. In: 4th International Conference on Software Engineering for Telecommunication Switching Systems, Warwick U. Conventry, U.K., pp. 54–57. SIEE (1981)
17. Martinez, J., Silva, M.: A simple and fast algorithm to obtain all invariants of a generalised petri net. In: Girault, C., Reisig, W. (eds.) Application and Theory of Petri Nets, pp. 301–310. Springer, Heidelberg (1982). https://doi.org/10.1007/978-3-642-68353-4_47
18. Memmi, G.: Semiflows and invariants. Application in petri nets theory. In: Journées d'Etudes sur les Réseaux de Petri AFCET-Institut de Programmation), pp. 145–150 (1977)
19. Memmi, G.: Fuites et Semi-flots dans les Réseaux de Petri. Thèse de Docteur-Ingénieur, U. P. et M. Curie, Paris, France (1978)
20. Memmi, G.: Methodes d'analyse de Réseaux de Petri, Réseaux a Files, Applications au temps reel. Thèse d'Etat, U. P. et M. Curie, Paris, France (1983)
21. Oda, T.: Convex Bodies and Algebraic Geometry (An Introduction to the Theory of Toric Varieties). Springer, Heidelberg (2012)
22. Petri, C.A.: Nets, time, and space. TCS **153**(1), 3–48 (1996)
23. Schrijver, A.: Theory of Linear and Integer Programming. Wiley, Hoboken (1987)
24. Silva, M., Terue, E., Colom, J.M.: Linear algebraic and linear programming techniques for the analysis of place/transition net systems. In: Reisig, W., Rozenberg, G. (eds.) ACPN 1996. LNCS, vol. 1491, pp. 309–373. Springer, Heidelberg (1998). https://doi.org/10.1007/3-540-65306-6_19

25. Sperner, E.: Ein satz *über* untermengen einer endlichen menge. Mathematische Zietschrift **27**, 544–548 (1928)
26. Toudic, J.M.: Algorithmes d'Analyse structurelle des Réseaux de Petri. Thèse de 3eme cycle, U. P. et M. Curie, Paris, France (1981)
27. Wolf, K.: How petri net theory serves petri net model checking: a survey. In: Koutny, M., Pomello, L., Kristensen, L.M. (eds.) Transactions on Petri Nets and Other Models of Concurrency XIV. LNCS, vol. 11790, pp. 36–63. Springer, Heidelberg (2019). https://doi.org/10.1007/978-3-662-60651-3_2

Relating Reversible Petri Nets and Reversible Event Structures, Categorically

Hernán Melgratti[1]([⊠]), Claudio Antares Mezzina[2]([⊠]), and G. Michele Pinna[3]([⊠])

[1] ICC - Universidad de Buenos Aires, Buenos Aires, Argentina
hmelgra@dc.uba.ar
[2] Dipartimento di Scienze Pure e Applicate, Università di Urbino, Urbino, Italy
claudio.mezzina@uniurb.it
[3] Dipartimento di Matematica e Informatica, Università di Cagliari, Cagliari, Italy
gmpinna@unica.it

Abstract. Causal nets (CNs) are Petri nets where causal dependencies are modelled via inhibitor arcs. They play the role of occurrence nets when representing the behaviour of a concurrent and distributed system, even when reversibility is considered. In this paper we extend CNs to account also for asymmetric conflicts and study (i) how this kind of nets, and their reversible versions, can be turned into a category; and (ii) their relation with the categories of reversible asymmetric event structures.

1 Introduction

Reversible models of concurrent computation [1] have gained momentum in recent years, as witnessed by the variety of models available today: RCCS [6], CCSK [22], rhoπ [10], Rπ [5], reversible Petri nets [15], reversible event structures [20], to name a few. As expected, the attention has turned to the question of how these models relate to each other (see e.g. [9,12,13]). This work addresses such goal by revisiting, in the context of reversibility, the connection between *Event Structures* (ESes) [24] and *Petri Nets* (PNs) established by Winskel [17].

Reversible Asymmetric Event Structures (rAESes) [20] are a reversible counterpart of *Asymmetric Event Structures* (AESes) [3], which in turn are a generalisation of *Prime Event Structures* (PESes) [17]. A PES describes a computational process as a set of events whose occurrence is constrained by two relations:

This work has been supported by the Italian MUR PRIN 2020 project *NiRvAna*, the French ANR project ANR-18-CE25-0007 *DCore*, the INdAM-GNCS project CUP_E55F22000270001 *Proprietà Qualitative e Quantitative di Sistemi Reversibili*, and the European Union - NextGenerationEU program Research and Innovation Program PE00000014 *SEcurity and RIghts in the CyberSpace* (SERICS), projects *Secure and TRaceable Identities in Distributed Environments* (STRIDE) and *Securing softWare frOm first PrincipleS* (SWOPS), the EU H2020 RISE programme under the Marie Skłodowska-Curie grant agreement 778233, UBACyT projects 20020170100544BA and 20020170100086BA.

© IFIP International Federation for Information Processing 2023
M. Huisman and A. Ravara (Eds.): FORTE 2023, LNCS 13910, pp. 206–223, 2023.
https://doi.org/10.1007/978-3-031-35355-0_13

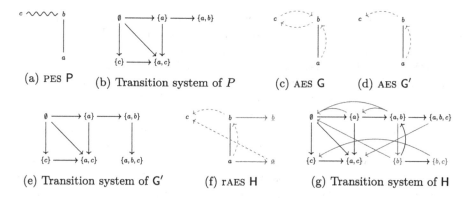

(a) PES P   (b) Transition system of P   (c) AES G   (d) AES G′

(e) Transition system of G′   (f) rAES H   (g) Transition system of H

Fig. 1. PES, AES, rAES and their transition systems.

causality and (symmetric) *conflicts*. A simple PES is depicted in Fig. 1a, where causality ($<$) is drawn with straight lines (to be read from bottom to top) and conflicts ($\#$) with curly lines. In this PES, b causally depends on a (i.e., $a < b$): b cannot occur if a does not occur first; additionally, b and c are in conflict (i.e., $b\#c$): b and c are mutually exclusive and cannot occur in the same execution of the process. The behaviour of a PES can be understood in terms of a transition system defined over *configurations* (i.e., sets of events), as illustrated in Fig. 1b. For instance, the transition $\emptyset \to \{a, c\}$ indicates that the initial state $\emptyset$ (i.e., no event has been executed yet) may evolve to $\{a, c\}$ by concurrently executing a and c. Neither $\{b\}$ nor $\{a, b, c\}$ are configurations because b cannot occur without a; and b and c cannot happen in the same run.

In order to accommodate asymmetries that may arise, e.g., in shared-memory concurrency, AESes relax the notion of conflicts by considering *weak causality*. Intuitively, an event e weakly causes the event e' (written $e \nearrow e'$) if e' can happen after e but e cannot happen after e'. This can be considered as an asymmetric conflict because e' forbids e to take place, but not the other way round. Symmetric conflicts can be recovered by making a pair of conflicting events to weakly cause each other. The PES P in Fig. 1a can be rendered as the AES G in Fig. 1c, where weak causality is depicted with red, dashed arrows. Now the conflict between b and c is represented as $b \nearrow c$ and $c \nearrow b$. Unsurprisingly, the transition system associated with G coincides with that of P in Fig. 1b. Differently, the AES G′ relaxes the conflict between b and c by making it asymmetric: we keep $b \nearrow c$ but drop $c \nearrow b$. Now c can be added to the configuration $\{a, b\}$ but b cannot be added to $\{a, c\}$, as rendered by the transition system in Fig. 1e.

A reversible model embodies two different flows of computation: the *forward* one and the *backward* one, which undoes the effects of the forward one. In rAESes, the backward flow is described in terms of a set of reversing events, each of them representing the undoing of some event of the forward flow. Two relations, dubbed *reverse causation* ($\prec$) and *prevention* ($\lhd$), describe the backward flow and regulate the way in which reversing events occur: $\prec$ prescribes the events required for the undoing while $\lhd$ stipulates those that preclude it. The rAES H in

Fig. 1f extends G' with a backward flow represented by blue arrows: solid arrows correspond to reverse causation and dashed ones to prevention. Then, $a \prec \underline{a}$ says that $\underline{a}$ can be executed (meaning a can be undone) only when a has occurred. Prevention $\underline{a} \lhd c$ states that a can be reversed only if c has not occurred. The transition system of H is in Fig. 1g. Interestingly, a can be reversed in $\{a, b\}$ leading to $\{b\}$, which is not reachable by the forward flow (black arrows). This is known as out-of-causal order reversibility [21].

Event structures have played a central role in developing denotational semantics for PNs [24]. It is well-known that different classes of ESes correspond to different classes of PNs [3,4,24] and that different relations in ESes translate into different operational mechanisms of PNs. Causality and conflicts are typically modelled in nets via places *shared* among transitions. However, shared places fall short when translating other kinds of dependencies, such as weak causality, which require contextual arcs [3]. Reversible ESes have introduced further questions about the required features of their operational counterpart, suggesting that shared places are not always a suitable choice ([13,18,19]). It has been shown that the operational model of (reversible) PESes can be recovered as a subclass of contextual Petri nets, called *(reversible) Causal Nets* (rCNs), in which causality is modelled via inhibitor arc instead of using a shared place in which one transition produces a token that another one consumes [13]. Inhibitor arcs neither produce nor consume tokens but check for the *absence* of them. This idea is rendered by the nets in Fig. 2. We recall that a PN gives an operational description of a computation in terms of *transitions* (boxes) that consume and produce *tokens* (bullets) in different *places* (circles). According to the black arrows in Fig. 2a, the transition a consumes a token from s_1 producing a token in s_4; similarly b consumes from s_4, s_2 and s_3 producing in s_5. Note that b and c are in mutual exclusion (i.e., conflict) because they both compete for the shared resource (i.e., token) in s_3. The arc connecting s_4 to b indicates that b cannot be fired if s_4 does not contains any token; consequently, b can happen only after a has produced the token in s_4. The causal relation between a and b arises because of s_4. The ES P in Fig. 1a corresponds to N_P in Fig. 2a. Causality and conflicts in N_P could be represented instead via inhibitor arcs, as shown in Fig. 2b. The inhibitor arc (depicted as a red line ending with a circle) between s_1 and b models $a < b$, whereas the inhibitor arcs (s_5, c) and (s_6, b) represent the symmetric conflict between b and c. A reversible version of the net in Fig. 2b is obtained by adding a reversing transition for each reversible event, as shown in Fig. 2c (in gray). The added transitions $\underline{a}$ and $\underline{b}$ respectively reverse the effects of a and b: each of them consumes (produces) the tokens produced (resp., consumed) by the associated forward transition. Inhibitor arcs model also reverse causation and prevention as, e.g., the inhibitor arc connecting $\underline{a}$ with s_6 stands for $\underline{a} \lhd c$.

In this paper we generalise the results in [13] to deal with rAESes. We use inhibitor arcs for representing, not only causal dependencies, but also (symmetric) conflicts. Hence, all the dependencies are modelled *uniformly* via inhibitor arcs. We identify a subclass of rCNes, dubbed *reversible Asymmetric Causal Nets* (rACNes), which are the operational counterpart of rAESes. We show that the correspondence is tight and it is expressed in categorical terms (following

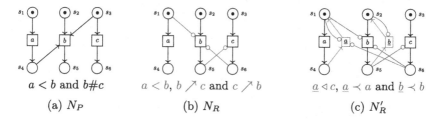

$a < b$ and $b\#c$ $a < b,\, b \nearrow c$ and $c \nearrow b$ $\underline{a} \lhd c,\, \underline{a} \prec a$ and $\underline{b} \prec b$

(a) N_P (b) N_R (c) N'_R

Fig. 2. Occurrence net N_P and (Reversible) causal nets N_R and N'_R

the literature [17,24,25]). We first turn rAESes and rACNes into categories by providing suitable notions of morphisms. Then, we relate both categories via two functors. We show that the functor that associates rAESes with rACNes is the left adjoint of the one that gives rACNes out of rAESes.

2 Reversible Asymmetric Event Structures

In this section we recall the basics of *Asymmetric Event Structures* (AESes) [3] and their reversible version [8,20].

An AES consists of a set of events and two relations: *causality* ($<$) and *weak causality* or *precedence* ($\nearrow$). If e weakly causes e', written $e \nearrow e'$, then e cannot occur after e'; i.e., if both events occur in a computation, then e precedes e'. In this case we say that e' is in an *asymmetric* conflict with e. Events e and e' are in *(symmetric) conflict*, written $e\#e'$, iff $e \nearrow e'$ and $e' \nearrow e$; intuitively, they cannot take place in the same computation.

Definition 1. *An* Asymmetric ES *(AES) is a triple* $\mathsf{G} = (E, <, \nearrow)$ *where*

1. *E is a countable set of* events;
2. *$< \subseteq E \times E$ is an irreflexive partial order, called* causality, *defined such that* $\forall e \in E.\ \lfloor e \rfloor = \{e' \in E \mid e' \leq e\}$ *is finite; and*
3. *$\nearrow \subseteq E \times E$, called* weak causality, *is defined such that for all $e, e' \in E$:*
   (a) $e < e' \Rightarrow e \nearrow e'$;
   (b) $\nearrow \cap (\lfloor e \rfloor \times \lfloor e \rfloor)$ is acyclic; and
   (c) if $e\#e'$ and $e' < e''$ then $e\#e''$.

Each event has a finite set of causes (2). Moreover, weak causality is consistent with causality: if e is a cause of e', then e is also a weak cause of e' (3a); and there cannot be circular dependencies on the causes of an event (3b). Finally, (symmetric) conflicts (#) are required to be inherited along causality (3c).

Example 1. Each event of the AES in Fig. 3a has a finite set of causes, i.e., $\lfloor c \rfloor = \{a, b, c\}$, $\lfloor a \rfloor = \{a\}$ and $\lfloor b \rfloor = \{b\}$. Also $a < c$ implies $a \nearrow c$ and $b < c$ implies $b \nearrow c$. Moreover, $\nearrow$ is acyclic on $\lfloor a \rfloor, \lfloor b \rfloor$ and $\lfloor c \rfloor$; and G does not have any symmetric conflict. On the contrary, the weak causality relation of the AES G' in Fig. 3b induces symmetric conflicts, i.e. $b\#'a$ and $b\#'c$. Such conflicts are inherited along causality, i.e. $b\#'a$ and $a < c$ imply $b\#'c$.

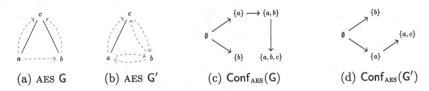

Fig. 3. Two AESes and their configurations

Definition 2. *A* configuration *of an* AES G *is a set* X *of events such that*

1. *$\nearrow$ is well-founded on X (events are not in conflict),*
2. *$\forall e \in X. \lfloor e \rfloor \subseteq X$ (it contains all the causes for each event); and*
3. *$\forall e \in X. \{e' \in X \mid e' \nearrow e\}$ is finite (events have finite sets of weak causes).*

We write $\mathsf{Conf}_{\mathrm{AES}}(\mathsf{G})$ for the configurations of G. The configurations of the AESes G and G' in Example 1 are shown in Figs. 3c and 3d, respectively.

Definition 3. *An* AES-morphism $f : \mathsf{G}_0 \to \mathsf{G}_1$ *is a partial function* $f : E_0 \to E_1$ *such that for all* $e, e' \in E_0$

1. *if $f(e) \neq \bot$ then $\lfloor f(e) \rfloor \subseteq f(\lfloor e \rfloor)$; and*
2. *if $f(e) \neq \bot \neq f(e')$ then*
   (a) *$f(e) \nearrow_1 f(e') \Rightarrow e \nearrow_0 e'$; and*
   (b) *$f(e) = f(e') \wedge e \neq e' \Rightarrow e\#_0 e'$.*

AES-morphisms preserve causes (condition 1) and reflect weak causes (condition 2a). If two different events e and e' are mapped to the same event then they are in conflict (condition 2b).

We remark that AES-morphisms preserve computations (i.e., configurations), i.e. if $X \in \mathsf{Conf}_{\mathrm{AES}}(\mathsf{G}_0)$, then $f(X) \in \mathsf{Conf}_{\mathrm{AES}}(\mathsf{G}_1)$ [3]. Since AES-morphisms compose [3], we write **AES** for the category of AESes and AES-morphisms.

We now summarise the *reversible* AESes introduced in [8, 20]. Let U be a set of events and $u \in U$ an event, we write $\underline{u}$ for the *undoing* of u, and $\underline{U} = \{\underline{u} \mid u \in U\}$ for *undoings* of U.

Definition 4. *A* Reversible AES *is a sextuple* $\mathsf{H} = (E, U, <, \nearrow, \prec, \lhd)$ *where E is the set of events, $U \subseteq E$ is the set of* reversible *events, and*

1. *$\nearrow \subseteq E \times E$, called* weak causality;
2. *$\lhd \subseteq \underline{U} \times E$, called* prevention;
3. *$< \subseteq E \times E$, called* causation, *is an irreflexive relation defined such that for all $e \in E, \lfloor e \rfloor_< = \{e' \in E \mid e' \leq e\}$ is finite and $(\nearrow \cup <)$ is acyclic on $\lfloor e \rfloor_<$;*
4. *$\prec \subseteq E \times \underline{U}$, called* reverse causation, *is defined such that*
   (a) *$\forall u \in U. u \prec \underline{u}$;*
   (b) *for all $u \in U, \lfloor \underline{u} \rfloor_\prec = \{e \in E \mid e \prec \underline{u}\}$ is finite and $(\nearrow \cup <)$ is acyclic on $\lfloor e \rfloor_\prec$;*
5. *for all $e \in E, \underline{u} \in \underline{U}. e \prec \underline{u} \Rightarrow \neg(\underline{u} \lhd e)$; and*
6. *$(E, \overline{\nnearrow}, \nearrow)$ with $\overline{\nnearrow} = < \cap \{(e, e') \mid e \notin U \text{ or } \underline{e} \lhd e'\}$ is an* AES.

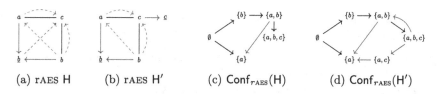

(a) rAES H   (b) rAES H'   (c) Conf$_{rAES}$(H)   (d) Conf$_{rAES}$(H')

Fig. 4. Two rAESes and their configurations

An rAES is defined in terms of a set of events E; the ones in U are reversible. Causation ($<$) and weak causality ($\nearrow$) specify the forward flow, while reverse causation ($\prec$, drawn as solid blue arrows) and prevention ($\lhd$, as dashed blue arrows) describe the backward flow. Weak causality plays the same role as in AESes: $e \nearrow e'$ states that e cannot occur after e'. Prevention constrains the undoing of events: $\underline{e} \lhd e'$ indicates that e cannot be undone if e' has occurred. Causation (like causality in AESes) indicates causal dependencies. As in AESes, every event has a finite set of causes $\lfloor e \rfloor_<$, which does not contain cyclic dependencies according to $< \cup \nearrow$ (Condition 3). Acyclicity of $\lfloor e \rfloor_<$ implies that for all $e, e' \in E$. $e < e' \Rightarrow \neg(e' \nearrow e)$. Reverse causation specifies the causes for the undoing of each event: $e \prec \underline{e'}$ states that e' can be undone only if e has occurred. Hence, condition 4a simply states that an event u can be undone only if it has occurred. Condition 4b establishes that each undoing has a finite set of causes. Condition 5 requires causation and weak causality to be consistent, i.e. an event cannot have precedence over some of its causes. Note that the definition does not require $(E, <, \nearrow)$ to be an AES, because conflicts may not be inherited along causation. Condition 6 relies instead on the *sustained causation* relation $\twoheadleftarrow$, which is obtained from $<$ by removing those pairs $e < e'$ where e can be undone even when e' has occurred (i.e., when $\underline{e} \lhd e'$ does not hold). This is essential for accommodating out-of-causal order reversibility (see the example below). When $U = \emptyset$, $\twoheadleftarrow$ coincides with $<$ and $(E, \emptyset, <, \nearrow, \emptyset, \emptyset)$ is indeed an AES.[1]

Example 2. Consider the rAES H in Fig. 4a. The (forward) events are $\{a, b, c\}$, with b reversible (i.e. $U = \{b\}$). Causation is such that $a < c$ and $b < c$, and weak causality states $a \nearrow c$, $b \nearrow c$, and $b \nearrow a$. Hence, c is caused by a and b, and b is a weak cause of a. Reverse causation is such that $a \prec \underline{b}$ and $b \prec \underline{b}$, while prevention states that $\underline{b} \lhd c$. Hence, b can be reversed when a is present and c has not been executed. Sustained causation coincides with causation, because b cannot be reversed when c, which causally depends on b, is present.

The rAES H' in Fig. 4b has the same events of H as well as the same causation and weak causality. In this case, both b and c are reversible, and reverse causation establishes also that $c \prec' \underline{c}$ (in addition to $a \prec' \underline{b}$ and $b \prec' \underline{b}$). Prevention is empty. Hence, b can be reversed even when c, which causally depends on b, has occurred. The sustained causation in H' consists only of $a \twoheadleftarrow' c$, i.e. the pair

---

[1] Definition 4 differs in style from the one in [20] where $<$ and $\prec$ are glued in one relation as also are $\nearrow$ and $\lhd$. We explicitly require $(E, \twoheadleftarrow, \nearrow)$ to be an AES instead of restating conditions. The correspondence is straightforward.

$b < c$ is removed because b can be reversed despite c has occurred, which is an out-of-causal order reversibility.

The definition for configurations of rAESes has an operational flavour, which relies on the notion of enabling. Let $\mathsf{H} = (E, U, <, \nearrow, \prec, \lhd)$ be an rAES and $X \subseteq E$ a set of events such that $\nearrow$ is acyclic on X. For $A \subseteq E$ and $B \subseteq U$, we say $A \cup \underline{B}$ is *enabled* at X if $A \cap X = \emptyset$, $B \subseteq X$, $\nearrow$ is acyclic on $A \cup X$ and

1. for every $e \in A$, if $e' < e$ then $e' \in X \setminus B$ and if $e \nearrow e'$ then $e' \notin X \cup A$; and
2. for every $u \in B$, if $e' \prec \underline{u}$ then $e' \in X \setminus (B \setminus \{u\})$ and if $\underline{u} \lhd e'$ then $e' \notin X \cup A$.

Thus X must contain all the causes of the events in A (to be added) and none of their preventing events. Furthermore X must contain all the reverse causes of the events in B (to be undone) and none of their preventing ones. If $A \cup \underline{B}$ is *enabled* at X then $X' = (X \setminus B) \cup A$ can be reached from X, written $X \xrightarrow{A \cup \underline{B}} X'$.

Let H be an rAES and X a set of events that is well-founded with respect to $(\nearrow \cup <)$. We say X is a *(reachable) configuration* if there exist a sequences of pairs of sets A_i and B_i, for $i = 1, \ldots, n$, such that

- $A_i \subseteq E$ and $B_i \subseteq U$ for all i, and
- $X_i \xrightarrow{A_i \cup \underline{B_i}} X_{i+1}$ $X_1 = \emptyset$ and $X_{n+1} = X$.

The set of configurations of H is denoted by $\mathsf{Conf}_{r\text{AES}}(\mathsf{H})$.

Example 3. The configurations of the rAESes in the Example 2 (and how they are reached) are depicted in Figs. 4c and 4d. Note that $\{a, c\}$ is a configuration of H' but not of H. It can be reached from $\{a, b, c\}$ by the undoing of b.

Definition 5. *Let H_1 and H_2 be rAESes. An rAES-morphism $f : \mathsf{H}_0 \to \mathsf{H}_1$ is an AES-morphism $f : (E_0, <_0, \nearrow_0) \to (E_1, <_1, \nearrow_1)$ such that*

- $f(U_0) \subseteq U_1$;
- *for all $u \in U_0$, if $f(u) \neq \bot$ then $\lfloor f(u) \rfloor_{\prec_1} \subseteq f(\lfloor \underline{u} \rfloor_{\prec_0})$; and*
- *for all $e \in E_0$ and $u \in U_0$, if $f(e) \neq \bot \neq f(u)$ then $\underline{f(u)} \lhd_1 f(e) \Rightarrow \underline{u} \lhd_0 e$.*

Recall that rAES-morphisms preserve causes (and reverse causes) of events (resp., reversing events), and reflect prevention. Hence, they preserve behaviour, i.e. if $X \in \mathsf{Conf}_{r\text{AES}}(\mathsf{H}_0)$ then $f(X) \in \mathsf{Conf}_{r\text{AES}}(\mathsf{H}_1)$.

As shown in [8], rAES-morphisms compose; hence rAESes and rAES-morphisms form a category, denoted by **RAES**. Moreover, **AES** is a full and faithful subcategory of **RAES**.

3   Nets with Inhibitor Arcs

We summarise the basics of Petri net with inhibitor arcs along the lines of [2,16]. A *multiset* over a set A is a function $m : A \to \mathbb{N}$, with $\mathbb{N}$ the natural numbers. We assume the usual operations of union (+) and difference (−) on multisets, and write $m \subseteq m'$ if $m(a) \le m'(a)$ for all $a \in A$. We write $[\![m]\!]$ for the underlying set of m, 0 for the multiset with empty underlying set, and μA for the set of all multisets over A.

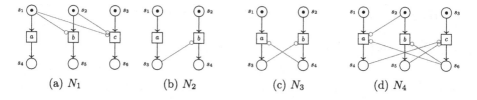

(a) N_1 (b) N_2 (c) N_3 (d) N_4

Fig. 5. Some simple IPTs

Definition 6. *A Petri net with inhibitor arcs* (IPT *for short*) *is a tuple* $N = \langle S, T, F, I, \mathsf{m} \rangle$, *where* S *is a set of* places, T *is a set of* transitions *such that* $S \cap T = \emptyset$, $F \subseteq (S \times T) \cup (T \times S)$ *is the* flow *relation,* $I \subseteq S \times T$ *is the* inhibiting *relation, and* $\mathsf{m} \in \mu S$ *is the* initial marking.

Given an IPT $N = \langle S, T, F, I, \mathsf{m} \rangle$ and $x \in S \cup T$, the *pre-* and *postset* of x are respectively the (multi)sets $^\bullet x = \{y \mid (y, x) \in F\}$ and $x^\bullet = \{y \mid (x, y) \in F\}$. If $x \in S$ then $^\bullet x \in \mu T$ and $x^\bullet \in \mu T$; analogously, if $x \in T$ then $^\bullet x \in \mu S$ and $x^\bullet \in \mu S$. The *inhibitor set* of a transition t is the (multi)set $^\circ t = \{s \mid (s, t) \in I\}$. The definition of $^\bullet \cdot, \cdot^\bullet, {}^\circ\cdot$ generalise straightforwardly to multisets of transitions.

Example 4. The IPT N_1 in Fig. 5a has six places (named s_i) and three transitions a, b, and c; the initial marking is $\mathsf{m} = \{s_1, s_2, s_3\}$. For instance, the transition b consumes a token from s_2 and produces a token in s_5 and it is inhibited by s_1, i.e., $^\bullet b = \{s_2\}$, $b^\bullet = \{s_5\}$ and $^\circ b = \{s_1\}$. In N_2 a and b are in asymmetric conflict which is a symmetric one in N_3.

A (multi)set of transitions $A \in \mu T$ is *enabled* at a marking $m \in \mu S$, written $m\,[A\rangle$, if (i) $^\bullet A \subseteq m$, (ii) $^\circ A \cap \llbracket m \rrbracket = \emptyset$, and (iii) $\forall t \in \llbracket A \rrbracket$. $^\circ t \cap (A - \{t\})^\bullet = \emptyset$. Intuitively, A is enabled at m if m contains the tokens to be consumed by A and none of the transitions in A is inhibited in m. $\forall t \in \llbracket A \rrbracket$. $^\circ t \cap (A - \{t\})^\bullet = \emptyset$ avoids cases in which the firing of $t \in A$ produces tokens in inhibitor places of other transitions in A. 0 is enabled at every marking. A set A enabled at m can *fire* and its firing produces the marking $m' = m - {}^\bullet A + A^\bullet$, written $m\,[A\rangle\,m'$. We assume that transitions cannot fire *spontaneously*, i.e. $^\bullet t \neq \emptyset$ for all t.

A marking m is *reachable* if there exists a sequence of firings $m_i\,[A_i\rangle\,m_{i+1}$ originated in the initial marking and leading to m. We write $\mathcal{M}_N$ for the set of reachable markings of N. An IPT N is *safe* if every reachable marking is a set, i.e., $\forall m \in \mathcal{M}_N.m = \llbracket m \rrbracket$. From now on, we will only consider safe IPTs.

Example 5. Consider N_4 in Fig. 5d. Both b and c are enabled at $m = \{s_1, s_2, s_3\}$. On the contrary, a is not enabled because it is inhibited by the token in s_2. The firing of b on m produces the marking $m' = \{s_1, s_3, s_5\}$, i.e. $m\,[b\rangle\,m'$. The transition a is enabled at m' while c is disabled and cannot be fired because of the token in s_5. The firing of a on m' produces $m'' = \{s_3, s_4, s_5\}$. The reachable markings of N_4 are $\{s_1, s_2, s_3\}$, $\{s_1, s_3, s_5\}$ $\{s_1, s_2, s_6\}$ and $\{s_3, s_4, s_5\}$.

4 Reversible Asymmetric Causal Nets

4.1 Asymmetric Causal Nets

We now introduce *Asymmetric Causal Nets*, a class of IPTs that generalises the *Causal Nets* of [13] to account for asymmetric conflicts. We focus on IPTs where all the dependencies between transitions arise because of *inhibitor* arcs. As in causal nets, $t^\bullet \cap {}^\bullet t' = \emptyset$ holds for all t, t': if a place appears in the preset of a transition, it does not appear in the postset of any transition, and vice versa. Hence, the flow relation induces an empty causal relation. However, causality can be recovered from inhibitor arcs. Intuitively, a transition t connected via an inhibitor arc to some place in the preset of another transition t' cannot be fired before t' (if we assume that the preset of t' is marked). This is the case, e.g., of the transitions a and b in Fig. 5d, where a can be fired only after b. The induced (immediate) causality relation $\lessdot$ is defined by $t \lessdot t'$ iff ${}^\bullet t \cap {}^\circ t' \neq \emptyset$, i.e. the firing of t consumes (at least) one of the tokens that inhibit the firing of t'.

Asymmetric causal nets additionally impose places not to be shared between the presets and postsets of transitions, i.e., $t^\bullet \cap t'^\bullet \neq \emptyset \lor {}^\bullet t \cap {}^\bullet t' \neq \emptyset$ implies $t = t'$ for all t, t'. As a consequence, the flow relation does not introduce forward or backward conflicts, which need to be recovered from inhibitor arcs. Note that a transition t inhibited by some place in the postset of another transition t' cannot be fired if t' has been fired, i.e., t' prevents t. The induced prevention relation $\curvearrowleft$ is defined by $t \curvearrowleft t'$ iff $t^\bullet \cap {}^\circ t' \neq \emptyset$. We write $\rightsquigarrow$ for the inverse of $\curvearrowleft$. Observe that $\rightsquigarrow$ is analogous to the weak causality of an AES: if $t' \rightsquigarrow t$ then $t^\bullet \cap {}^\circ t' \neq \emptyset$; hence t' cannot be fired if t has been fired, however t can be fired after t'. As in AES, *symmetric* conflicts are recovered from prevention, i.e., t and t' are in *symmetric* conflict, written $t \natural t'$, whenever $t \curvearrowleft t'$ and $t \rightsquigarrow t'$.

Definition 7. *Let $C = \langle S, T, F, I, \mathsf{m} \rangle$ be an IPT. C is a* pre asymmetric causal net *(pACN) if the following conditions hold:*

1. $\forall t, t' \in T.\ t^\bullet \cap {}^\bullet t' = \emptyset$;
2. $\forall s \in S.\ |{}^\bullet s| \leq 1 \land |s^\bullet| \leq 1$ *and* $\mathsf{m} = {}^\bullet T$;
3. $\forall t \in T.\ |{}^\bullet t| = |t^\bullet| = 1$;
4. $\lessdot^+$ *is a partial order;*
5. $\forall t \in T.\ \lfloor t \rfloor_\lessdot = \{t' \in T \mid t' \lessdot^* t\}$ *is finite and* $(\rightsquigarrow \cup \lessdot)$ *is acyclic on* $\lfloor t \rfloor_\lessdot$;
6. *for all* $t, t' \in T.\ t \lessdot^+ t'$ *implies* $t \lessdot t'$.

Condition 1 states that causal dependencies do not arise because of the flow relation. The second one implies that a place may appear in the preset/postset of at most one transition and that the places in the presets of all transitions are initially marked. Condition 3 forbids that transitions may fire spontaneously or tokens may disappear. Since $\lessdot$ is meant to model causal dependencies, we require its transitive closure $\lessdot^+$ to be a partial order (condition 4). Condition 5 requires each transition to have a finite set of causes; hence, $\lessdot^+$ is a well-founded partial order. By requiring $(\rightsquigarrow \cup \lessdot)$ to be acyclic on the causes of every transition

t we ensure that the causes can be ordered so as to satisfy causality and prevention. More precisely, we exclude situations in which (i) prevention contradicts causality (e.g., $t \lessdot t'$ and $t' \leadsto t$), (ii) there are circular chains of prevention (i.e., $t_0 \leadsto t_1 \leadsto \ldots \leadsto t_n \leadsto t_0$), where symmetric conflicts are a particular case, and (iii) self-blocked transitions (i.e., $\lessdot$ needs to be irreflexive and hence ${}^\bullet t \cap {}^\circ t = \emptyset$ for all t). Condition 6 imposes that all dependencies among transitions have to be explicitly represented in the structure of the net, namely causality is saturated.

Definition 8. *Let* $C = \langle S, T, F, I, \mathsf{m} \rangle$ *be a* pACN. *Then* C *is an* asymmetric causal net *(*ACN*) whenever for all* $t, t', t'' \in T$. $t \natural t' \wedge t' \lessdot t''$ *imply* $t \natural t''$.

The added condition implies that there are inhibitor arcs for all inherited symmetric conflicts.

Example 6. The IPTs in Fig. 5 are ACNs. The first two conditions of Definition 7 hold for the four nets since transitions do not share places in their pre and postsets. Moreover, the places in the presets of all transitions are the only ones that are initially marked. For N_1 (Fig. 5a), we have that $a \lessdot b$ and $b \lessdot c$; consequently, $\lessdot^+$ is a total order, and causality is saturated as we also have $a \lessdot c$. Moreover, $\leadsto$ is empty (because none of the transitions has an inhibitor arc connected to the postset of another transition). For N_2 in Fig. 5b, causality is empty while prevention contains the unique pair $a \leadsto b$. For N_3 in Fig. 5c, a and b are in symmetric conflict ($a \natural b$): their executions prevent each other. Figure 5d shows a net where $b \lessdot a$, $b \natural c$ and $a \natural c$, and conflicts are inherited along causality $\lessdot$.

For the definition of (p)ACNs morphisms we take into account that inhibitor arcs correspond to two different dependencies: causality and prevention. In particular, the inhibitor arcs representing prevention demand a peculiar treatment of markings if compared against the classical notions of morphisms for nets [24, 25]. We introduce some technical machinery. A partial mapping $f : A \to B$ extends to a mapping $f : \mu A \to \mu B$ by stipulating that $f(\sum_{a \in A} n_a \cdot a) = \sum_{b \in B}(\sum_{a \in f^{-1}(b)} n_a) \cdot b$. A multirelation f is a multiset on $A \times B$; it is *finitary* if $\{b \in B \mid f(a, b) > 0\}$ is finite for all a. A multirelation f is a relation if $f = [\![f]\!]$, i.e., if it is a set. The composition of two multirelations f on $A \times B$ and g on $B \times C$, written $f; g$, is the multirelation on $A \times C$ defined such that $[f; g](a, c) = \sum_{b \in B} f(a, b) \cdot g(b, c)$ for all $a \in A, c \in C$. A finitary multirelation f on $A \times B$ induces a partial mapping from $\mu f : \mu A \to \mu B$ defined such that $\mu f(\sum_{a \in A} n_a \cdot a) = \sum_{b \in B} \sum_{a \in A}(n_a \cdot f(a, b)) \cdot b$. Conversely, a partial mapping $\mu f : \mu A \to \mu B$ induces a mapping $[\![f]\!] : \mu A \to B$ defined such as $[\![f]\!](m) = [\![\mu f(m)]\!]$.

Definition 9. *An* ACN-*morphism from* C_0 *to* C_1 *is a pair* (f_S, f_T) *consisting of a relation* $f_S \subseteq S_0 \times S_1$ *and a partial function* $f_T : T_0 \to T_1$ *defined such that*

1. *for all* $t \in T_0$ *if* $f_T(t) \neq \bot$ *then*
    (a) ${}^\bullet f_T(t) = \mu f_S({}^\bullet t)$ *and* $f_T(t)^\bullet = \mu f_S(t^\bullet)$;
    (b) $\forall (s, f_T(t)) \in I_1. \forall s' \in f_S^{-1}(s). (s', t) \in I_0$; *and*
2. $\forall t, t' \in T_0$ *if* $f_T(t) \neq \bot \neq f_T(t')$ *then* $f_T(t) = f_T(t') \Rightarrow t \natural_0 t'$;

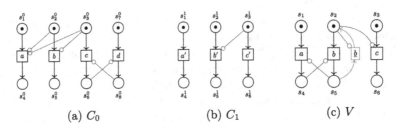

Fig. 6. Two simple ACNs and a rACN

3. $\forall s_1 \in S_1. \; \forall s_0, s_0' \in f_S^{-1}(s_1). \; s_0 \neq s_0'$ implies $s_0^\bullet \uparrow_0 s_0'^\bullet$ or $^\bullet s_0 \uparrow_0 {}^\bullet s_0'$;
4. $[\![f_S]\!](m_0) = m_1$.

Conditions 1 and 2 are standard: presets and postsets are preserved and inhibitor arcs are reflected; only conflicting transitions can be identified. Differently from usual requirements, Condition 3 allows f_S to *identify* different places in the preset of different transitions. This may be seen as problematic because a place in the target of the morphism may represent different tokens in the source, which in principle may evolve independently. However, according to Condition 3, f_S may only identify places connected to transitions that are in (symmetric) conflict.

Example 7. Consider the ACNs C_0 and C_1 in Fig. 6. A morphism $(f_S, f_T) : C_0 \rightarrow C_1$ can be defined as follows. The mapping for transitions is $f_T(a) = a'$, $f_T(b) = b'$ and $f_T(c) = c' = f_T(d)$. Note that the conflicting transitions c and d are identified. The relation on places is as expected, i.e., $f_S(s_i^0, s_i^1)$ for $1 \leq i \leq 6$, $f_S(s_7^0, s_3^1)$, and $f_S(s_8^0, s_6^1)$. The inhibitor arc (s_3^1, b') of C_1 is reflected in the one (s_3^0, b) of C_0. The remaining arcs of C_0 are not preserved by the mapping.

As expected, it can be shown that ACN-morphisms preserve the tokens game, i.e., if $m\,[A\rangle\,m'$ then $[\![f_S]\!](m)\,[\mu f_T(A)\rangle\,[\![f_S]\!](m')$. Also, ACN-morphisms preserve behaviours and are closed under composition, as stated below.

Lemma 1. *Let* $(f_S, f_T) : C_0 \rightarrow C_1$ *and* $(g_S, g_T) : C_1 \rightarrow C_2$ *be two* ACN-*morphisms. Then* $(f_S; g_S, f_T; g_T) : C_0 \rightarrow C_2$ *is an* ACN-*morphism as well.*

pACNs and ACN-morphisms form a category, denoted by **pACN**. We write **ACN**, for the full and faithful subcategory that has ACNs as objects.

4.2   Reversible Asymmetric Causal Nets

Reversible Asymmetric Causal Nets are defined by following the approach in [13]: pACNs are enriched with *backward* transitions that undo the effects of previously executed *forward* transitions (i.e., the ordinary ones). We assume that the set T of transitions is partitioned into a set $\overline{T}$ of forward transition and $\underline{T}$ of backward transition. Every backward transition $\underline{t} \in \underline{T}$ undoes the effect of one and only one forward transition $t \in \overline{T}$. However, there could be forward transitions that are irreversible. With slightly abuse of notation, we write t for the forward transition and $\underline{t}$ for the associated reversing transition (when it exists).

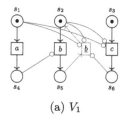
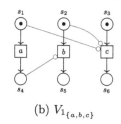
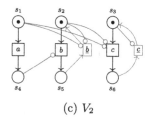

(a) V_1 (b) $V_{1\{a,b,c\}}$ (c) V_2

Fig. 7. Simple rACNes

Definition 10. *An* IPT $V = \langle S, T, F, I, \mathsf{m} \rangle$ *is a reversible Asymmetric Causal Net (rACN) if there exists a partition $\{\overline{T}, \underline{T}\}$ of T, with $\overline{T}$ the forward transitions and $\underline{T}$ the backward ones, such that:*

1. $V_{\overline{T}} = \langle S, \overline{T}, F_{|\overline{T} \times \overline{T}}, I_{|\overline{T} \times \overline{T}}, \mathsf{m} \rangle$ *is a pACN net;*
2. $\forall \underline{t} \in \underline{T}.\ \exists!\ t \in \overline{T}$ *such that* $t^{\bullet} = {}^{\bullet}\underline{t},\ {}^{\bullet}t = \underline{t}^{\bullet},$ *and* ${}^{\bullet}t \subseteq {}^{\circ}\underline{t}$;
3. $\forall \underline{t} \in \underline{T}.\ K_{\underline{t}} = \{t' \in \overline{T} \mid {}^{\circ}\underline{t} \cap {}^{\bullet}t' \neq \emptyset\}$ *is finite and* $\rightsquigarrow$ *acyclic on $K_{\underline{t}}$;*
4. $\forall \underline{t} \in \underline{T}.\ \forall t \in \overline{T}$ *if* ${}^{\bullet}t \cap {}^{\circ}\underline{t} \neq \emptyset$ *then* $t^{\bullet} \cap {}^{\circ}\underline{t} = \emptyset$;
5. $\forall t, t', t'' \in \overline{T}.\ t \natural t' \wedge t' \lll t'' \Rightarrow t \natural t''$ *with* $\lll$ *being the transitive closure of* $< \cap\ \{(t, t') \mid \underline{t} \notin \underline{T}$ *or* ${}^{\circ}\underline{t} \cap t'^{\bullet} \neq \emptyset\}$.

The underlying net $V_{\overline{T}}$ containing just the forward transitions of V must be a pACN. Condition 2 establishes that each backward transition $\underline{t}$ reverses exactly one forward transition t. Note that $\underline{t}$ consumes the tokens produced by t (i.e., $t^{\bullet} = {}^{\bullet}\underline{t}$) and produces the tokens consumed by t (i.e., $\underline{t}^{\bullet} = {}^{\bullet}t$). The condition ${}^{\bullet}t \subseteq {}^{\circ}\underline{t}$ amounts to saying that $\underline{t}$ (i.e., the reverse of t) cannot be fired if t has not been executed: a transition can be reversed only if it has been fired. Condition 3 can be read as requiring a finite set of causes for the undoing of each transition; in fact, ${}^{\bullet}K_{\underline{t}}$ contains all the forward transitions t' that enable the execution of $\underline{t}$. By Condition 4, if a backward transition $\underline{t}'$ causally depends on the forward transition t (i.e., ${}^{\bullet}t \cap {}^{\circ}\underline{t}' \neq \emptyset$) then $\underline{t}'$ cannot be prevented by the same transition t, i.e. $t^{\bullet} \cap {}^{\circ}\underline{t}' = \emptyset$ since otherwise will be blocked. The relation $\lll$ in the last condition, which is analogous to the *sustained causation* of rAES, coincides with causality except for the cases in which a cause can be reversed even when a causally-dependent transition has been fired. The conflicts should be inherited along $\lll$, not along the $<$. We shall write $V^{\underline{T}}$ for a rACN V whose set of backward transitions is $\underline{T}$.

Inhibitor arcs induce the previously discussed relations $<$ and $\rightsquigarrow$ over the forward flow (i.e. on $\overline{T} \times \overline{T}$). They also induce two relations regulating the backward flow (i.e. on $\overline{T} \times \underline{T}$): (i) the *reverse causation* $\prec$ defined by $t \prec \underline{t}'$ iff ${}^{\bullet}t \cap {}^{\circ}\underline{t}' \neq \emptyset$; and (ii) the *prevention* $\lhd$ defined by $\underline{t}' \lhd t$ iff $t^{\bullet} \cap {}^{\circ}\underline{t}' \neq \emptyset$.

Example 8. Figure 7a shows the rACN V_1, exhibiting an asymmetric conflict between a and b, and b can be reversed (i.e., $\underline{b}$ can happen) only if a and b have been fired and c has not. Removing $\underline{b}$ we get the pACN $V_{1\{a,b,c\}}$ in Fig. 7b.

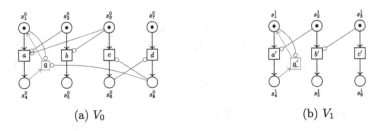

(a) V_0 (b) V_1

Fig. 8. Two rACNs related by a rACN-morphism

Example 9. In the rACN V_2 in Fig. 7c both b and c are reversible and $V_{2_{\{a,b,c\}}} = V_{1_{\{a,b,c\}}}$. In this rACN the transition c depends on b, however $\underline{b}$ can be executed (b can be reversed) even if the transitions depending on b have not been reversed. In this way the configuration $\{a, c\}$ can be reached by mixing forward and backward computations, but not by only forward computations. This is an example of out-of-causal order reversibility in rACN.

Morphisms for rACNs are defined below.

Definition 11. *Let $V^{\underline{T_0}}$ and $V^{\underline{T_1}}$ be two rACNs. An rACN-morphism is a pair (f_S, f_T) consisting of a relation $f_S \subseteq S_0 \times S_1$ and a partial function $f_T : T_0 \to T_1$ satisfying the following conditions*

1. $f_T(\overline{T_0}) \subseteq \overline{T_1}$ *and* $f_T(\underline{T_0}) \subseteq \underline{T_1}$;
2. $(f_S, f_T|_{\overline{T_0}}) : V_{\overline{T_0}} \to V_{\overline{T_1}}$ *is a* ACN-*morphism,*
3. $\forall \underline{t} \in T_0.$ *if* $f_T(t) \neq \bot$ *then*
   (a) $f_T(\underline{t}) \neq \bot$ *and* $f_T(\underline{t}) = \underline{f_T(t)}$; *and*
   (b) $\forall (s, f_T(t)) \in I_1. \forall s' \in f_S^{-1}(s). (s', t) \in I_0.$

By Condition 1, forward (resp. backward) transitions are mapped to forward (resp. backward) transitions. Condition 2 implies that when we restrict f_T to $\overline{T_0}$, i.e., only consider forward transitions, we obtain an ACN-morphism on the underlying nets consisting of forward transitions, i.e., $V_{\overline{T_0}}$ and $V_{\overline{T_1}}$. Condition 3a ensures that the transition $\underline{t}$ that reverses t is mapped to the transition $\underline{f_T(t)}$ that reverses $f_T(t)$. Condition 3b prevents the collapse of inhibitor arcs, i.e., it avoids the identification of different causes that may prevent the reversing of a transition.

Example 10. An rACN-morphism $(f_S, f_T) : V_0 \to V_1$ for the rACNs V_0 and V_1 in Fig. 8 is as follows: f_S is as in Example 7 and f_T is the mapping in Example 7 extended for the reversing transition $\underline{a}$ as $f_T(\underline{a}) = \underline{a}'$. Clearly $\underline{f_T(a)} = f_T(\underline{a})$.

It can be shown that rACN-morphisms preserve behaviours [14], i.e. if $m\,[A\rangle\,m'$ in $V^{\underline{T_0}}$, then $[\![f_S]\!](m)\,[\mu f_T(A)\rangle\,[\![f_S]\!](m')$ in $V^{\underline{T_1}}$. Moreover, they are closed under composition as stated below.

Lemma 2. *Let $(f_S, f_T) : V_0 \to V_1$ and $(g_S, g_T) : V_1 \to V_2$ be two rACN-morphisms. Then $(f_S; g_S, f_T; g_T) : V_0 \to V_2$ is a rACN-morphism as well.*

rACNs and rACN-morphisms form a category, which is denoted by **RACN**.

5 Relating Models

We now study the relationship between the categories of (reversible) asymmetric causal nets and (reversible) asymmetric event structures. We start by showing how to recover an rAES out of the flow and inhibitor arcs of an rACN. The relations induced by the inhibitor arcs of a rACN, namely $<$ (causality), $\rightsquigarrow$ (weak causality), $\prec$ (reverse causality), $\lhd$ (prevention), and $\lll$ (sustained causation) contribute to the definition of the relations of the associated rAES.

Definition 12. *Let $V^{\underline{T}} = \langle S, T, F, I, \mathsf{m} \rangle$ be an rACN. Then, $\mathcal{E}_r(V^{\underline{T}})$ is the tuple $(\overline{T}, U, <, \lll \cup \rightsquigarrow, \prec, \lhd)$ where $U = \{t \in \overline{T} \mid \underline{t} \in \underline{T}\}$ are the reversible events and $<, \rightsquigarrow, \prec, \lhd$ and $\lll$ are the causation, weak causality, reverse causality, prevention and sustained causation induced by F and I.*

Theorem 1. *Let $V^{\underline{T}}$ be an rACN. Then $\mathcal{E}_r(V)$ is an rAES.*

Example 11. Consider the rACN V_1 in Fig. 7, the corresponding rAES $\mathcal{E}_r(V_1)$ is H_1 in Example 2.

An rACN without reversing transitions (i.e., $V^\emptyset$) is an ACN, hence the construction in Definition 12 works also for ACNes: if C is an ACN then $\mathcal{E}_r(C)$ is an AES.

$\mathcal{E}_r$ extends to a functor by observing that an rACN-morphism $(f_S, f_T) : V_0 \to V_1$ induces an rAES-morphism $\mathcal{E}_r(f_S, f_T) = f_T$.

Proposition 1. *$\mathcal{E}_r : \mathbf{RACN} \to \mathbf{RAES}$ is a well-defined functor.*

The construction that associates a net to an event structure follows the usual intuition: places are suitable subsets of events, and transitions are connected to places according to the relations in the event structure.

Definition 13. *Let $H = (E, U, <, \nearrow, \prec, \lhd)$ be a rAES. Then, $\mathcal{N}_r(H)$ is the net $\langle S, E \cup \{(\underline{u}, \mathbf{r}) \mid u \in U\}, F, I, \mathsf{m} \rangle$ where*

$S = \{(A, B) \mid A, B \subseteq E \wedge |A| \leq |B| \leq 1 \wedge A \subseteq B\}$

$F = \{((\emptyset, \{e\}), e) \mid e \in E\} \cup \{(e, (\{e\}, \{e\})) \mid e \in E\} \cup$
$\qquad \{((\{u\}, \{u\}), (\underline{u}, \mathbf{r})) \mid u \in U\} \cup \{((\underline{u}, \mathbf{r}), (\emptyset, \{u\})) \mid u \in U\}$

$I = \{((\emptyset, \{e'\}), e) \mid e' < e\} \cup \{((\{e'\}, \{e'\}), e) \mid e \nearrow e' \wedge \neg(e' < e)\} \cup$
$\qquad \{((\emptyset, \{e\}), (u, \mathbf{r})) \mid e \prec \underline{u}\} \cup \{((\{e\}, \{e\}), (u, \mathbf{r})) \mid \underline{u} \lhd e\}$

$\mathsf{m} = \{(\emptyset, A) \mid (\emptyset, A) \in S\}$

Events E are the forward transitions, and each event e has two associated places: $(\emptyset, \{e\})$ indicates that e has not occurred whereas $(\{e\}, \{e\})$ indicates that it has occurred. A transition $(\underline{u}, \mathbf{r})$ reverses the forward transition u, i.e. it consumes from $(\{u\}, \{u\})$ and produces in $(\emptyset, \{u\})$. The inhibitor arcs in I model causality (forward or backward) and precedence (forward or backward). the initially marked are those appearing in the preset of some forward transition.

Theorem 2. *Let $H = (E, U, <, \nearrow, \prec, \lhd)$ be an rAES. Then $\mathcal{N}_r(H)$ is an rACN.*

Again, if $G = (E, <, \nearrow)$ is an AES then $\mathcal{N}_r((E, \emptyset, <, \nearrow, \emptyset, \emptyset))$ is an ACN.

Example 12. Consider the rAES H′ in Example 2. The associated net $\mathcal{N}_r(\mathsf{H}')$ has $(\emptyset, \emptyset)$, $(\emptyset, \{a\})$, $(\emptyset, \{b\})$, $(\emptyset, \{c\})$, $(\{a\}, \{a\})$, $(\{b\}, \{b\})$ and $(\{c\}, \{c\})$ as places, a, b, c as forward transitions, and $(\underline{b}, \mathsf{r}), (\underline{c}, \mathsf{r})$ as reversing transitions. The flow arcs are as in Definition 13, while inhibitor arcs are those induced by the different relations in H′. The resulting net is analogous to the one in Fig. 7c, where places bear different names and the isolated place $(\emptyset, \emptyset)$ has been omitted.

$\mathcal{N}_r$ extends to a functor. For an rAES-morphism $f : \mathsf{H}_0 \to \mathsf{H}_1$ and $\mathcal{N}_r(\mathsf{H}_i) = \langle S_i, E_i, F_i, I_i, \mathsf{m}_i \rangle$ for $i = 0, 1$, we take $\mathcal{N}_r(f) = (f_S, f_T)$ where $f_S \subseteq S_0 \times S_1$ is defined such that $(s_0, s_1) \in f_S$ iff one of the following holds:

- $s_0 = (\emptyset, A)$; $s_1 = (\emptyset, B)$; $A \subseteq f^{-1}(B)$; and $A = \emptyset \Rightarrow f^{-1}(B) = \emptyset$; or
- $s_0 = (A, A)$; and $s_1 = (f(A), f(A))$;

and $f_T : E_0 \cup \{(\underline{u}, \mathsf{r}) \mid u \in U_0\} \to E_1 \cup \{(\underline{u}, \mathsf{r}) \mid u \in U_1\}$ defined such that

- $f_T(t) = f(e)$ if $e \in E_0$;
- $f_T(\underline{u}, \mathsf{r}) = (\underline{f(u)}, \mathsf{r})$ if $f(u) \neq \perp$.

Proposition 2. *Let* $f : \mathsf{H}_0 \to \mathsf{H}_1$ *be an rAES-morphism. Then* $\mathcal{N}_r(f) : \mathcal{N}_r(\mathsf{H}_0) \to \mathcal{N}_r(\mathsf{H}_1)$ *is a well defined rACN-morphism.*

Proposition 3. $\mathcal{N}_r : \mathbf{RAES} \to \mathbf{RACN}$ *is a well-defined functor.*

Our main result below states the precise relation between **RACN** and **RAES**, namely, the functor $\mathcal{N}_r$ is the left adjoint of $\mathcal{E}_r$.

Theorem 3. *The functor* $\mathcal{N}_r : \mathbf{RAES} \to \mathbf{RACN}$ *is the left adjoint of the functor* $\mathcal{E}_r : \mathbf{RACN} \to \mathbf{RAES}$.

Let $\mathcal{E}$ and $\mathcal{N}$ be the respective restrictions of the functors $\mathcal{E}_r$ and $\mathcal{N}_r$ respectively on ACNes or AESes, i.e. we restrict our attention to the full and faithful subcategories of **ACN** and **AES**. Then, we have the following connection.

Theorem 4. *The functor* $\mathcal{N} : \mathbf{AES} \to \mathbf{ACN}$ *is the left adjoint of the functor* $\mathcal{E} : \mathbf{ACN} \to \mathbf{AES}$.

6   Discussion

In this paper we complete previous efforts [13,18,19] aimed at relating classes of reversible event structures with classes of Petri nets. To the best of our knowledge, the only previous attempt to relate reversible event structures and nets is in [13]. In contrast to the (pre) causal nets proposed in [13], the notion of (pre) asymmetric causal net considers forward symmetric conflicts represented by asymmetric ones, rather than via shared places. As a result, rACNs are obtained from pre ACNs by incorporating reversibility. Regarding the philosophy behind our nets, it may be asked whether we adhere to the *individual token philosophy* or the *collective token philosophy*, as defined in [23]. In the individual token philosophy, each place can be uniquely marked, whereas in the collective token philosophy, there can be multiple ways to place a token in a given place. If we only consider the forward flow of our nets, they adhere to the individual token philosophy. However, asymmetric conflicts suggest that the *past* of the transition putting a token in a given place may not be unique. Moreover, when considering the reversing flow, things become more complex, particularly with out-of-causal order reversibility, as a forward transition may only be executed because some reversing transition has been executed. To settle this question, it may be necessary to seek a different definition for the individual token philosophy, perhaps by focusing on the forward dependencies of the pre-asymmetric causal net in the rACN, rather than considering the entire rACN.

Establishing a correspondence between these two different models has not only theoretical relevance, but it can also be exploited in concrete scenarios. For instance, one successful application of reversibility is causal-consistent *reversible debugging* [7,11]. Reversible debuggers extend classical ones by allowing the user to go back in the execution, thereby making it easier to find the source of a bug. Causal-consistent reversible debuggers further improve on reversible ones by leveraging causal information while undoing computations. While this technique has been applied to message-passing concurrent systems (e.g., actor-like languages), it has not been applied to shared-memory-based concurrency so far.

Consider the next snippet of code

```
1  pthread_mutex_t m = //initialization     9  int main()
2  int *x=malloc(sizeof(int));             10  {   pthread_t t;
3  void thread(void *arg)                  11      pthread_create(&t, NULL, thread,
4  {   pthread_mutex_lock(&m);                     NULL);
5      if(x != NULL)                       12      pthread_mutex_lock(&m);
6          doSomething(x);                 13          free(x);
7      pthread_mutex_unlock(&m);           14      pthread_mutex_unlock(&m);
8  }                                       15      return 0;}
```

The behaviour of the program can be thought in terms of events. Be a the event corresponding to the initialisation of x at line 2, b for the instruction at line 6 and c for the one at line 13. Both b and c causally depend on a ($a < b$ and $a < c$); while c can happen after b, b cannot happen after c, that is $b \nearrow c$. Moreover, the reversal of a complete execution of the program should ensure that c is reversed (i.e., the memory is allocated) before b is reversed, hence $\underline{b} \lhd c$. Consider instead a version of the program in which c is executed outside a critical section. In this case, the execution may raise a *segmentation fault* error. When debugging such a faulty execution, the programmer would observe that the execution violates $b \nearrow c$ because b happened after c. On the one hand, an execution can be visualised in terms of events, i.e., the programmer can be provided with a high-level description of the current state of the system (a configuration of the event structure) along with the relevant dependencies. On the other hand, the instrumented execution of the program and of its reversal can be handled by the underlying operational model (i.e., a reversible causal net). Also, one could think of the undoing of an event as a backward breakpoint. That is, one could trigger the undoing of an event from the net and then the debugger will execute all the necessary backward steps in the code, to undo such event. The seamless integration of rAES and rACN with causal-consistent reversible debuggers can be a nice exploitation of our results, which we will consider in future work.

References

1. Aman, B., et al.: Foundations of reversible computation. In: Ulidowski, I., Lanese, I., Schultz, U.P., Ferreira, C. (eds.) RC 2020. LNCS, vol. 12070, pp. 1–40. Springer, Cham (2020). https://doi.org/10.1007/978-3-030-47361-7_1

2. Baldan, P., Busi, N., Corradini, A., Pinna, G.M.: Domain and event structure semantics for petri nets with read and inhibitor arcs. Theor. Comput. Sci. **323**(1–3), 129–189 (2004)

3. Baldan, P., Corradini, A., Montanari, U.: Contextual Petri nets, asymmetric event structures, and processes. Inf. Comput. **171**(1), 1–49 (2001)

4. Boudol, G.: Flow event structures and flow nets. In: Guessarian, I. (ed.) LITP 1990. LNCS, vol. 469, pp. 62–95. Springer, Heidelberg (1990). https://doi.org/10.1007/3-540-53479-2_4

5. Cristescu, I., Krivine, J., Varacca, D.: A compositional semantics for the reversible π-calculus. In: 28th Annual ACM/IEEE Symposium on Logic in Computer Science, LICS, pp. 388–397 (2013)

6. Danos, V., Krivine, J.: Reversible communicating systems. In: Gardner, P., Yoshida, N. (eds.) CONCUR 2004. LNCS, vol. 3170, pp. 292–307. Springer, Heidelberg (2004). https://doi.org/10.1007/978-3-540-28644-8_19

7. Giachino, E., Lanese, I., Mezzina, C.A.: Causal-consistent reversible debugging. In: Gnesi, S., Rensink, A. (eds.) FASE 2014. LNCS, vol. 8411, pp. 370–384. Springer, Heidelberg (2014). https://doi.org/10.1007/978-3-642-54804-8_26

8. Graversen, E., Phillips, I., Yoshida, N.: Towards a categorical representation of reversible event structures. J. Log. Algebraic Methods Program. **104**, 16–59 (2019)

9. Lanese, I., Medic, D., Mezzina, C.A.: Static versus dynamic reversibility in CCS. Acta Informatica **58**(1–2), 1–34 (2021)

10. Lanese, I., Mezzina, C.A., Stefani, J.: Reversibility in the higher-order π-calculus. Theor. Comput. Sci. **625**, 25–84 (2016)

11. Lanese, I., Nishida, N., Palacios, A., Vidal, G.: CauDEr: a causal-consistent reversible debugger for erlang. In: Gallagher, J.P., Sulzmann, M. (eds.) FLOPS 2018. LNCS, vol. 10818, pp. 247–263. Springer, Cham (2018). https://doi.org/10.1007/978-3-319-90686-7_16

12. Medic, D., Mezzina, C.A., Phillips, I., Yoshida, N.: A parametric framework for reversible π-calculi. Inf. Comput. **275**, 104644 (2020)

13. Melgratti, H.C., Mezzina, C.A., Pinna, G.M.: A distributed operational view of reversible prime event structures. In: 36th Annual ACM/IEEE Symposium on Logic in Computer Science, LICS, pp. 1–13. IEEE (2021)

14. Melgratti, H.C., Mezzina, C.A., Pinna, G.M.: Relating reversible Petri nets and reversible event structures, categorically. Technical report (2023). https://arxiv.org/pdf/2302.14195.pdf

15. Melgratti, H.C., Mezzina, C.A., Ulidowski, I.: Reversing place transition nets. Log. Methods Comput. Sci. **16**(4) (2020)

16. Montanari, U., Rossi, F.: Contextual nets. Acta Informatica **32**(6), 545–596 (1995)

17. Nielsen, M., Plotkin, G., Winskel, G.: Petri nets, event structures and domains. In: Kahn, G. (ed.) Semantics of Concurrent Computation. LNCS, vol. 70, pp. 266–284. Springer, Heidelberg (1979). https://doi.org/10.1007/BFb0022474

18. Philippou, A., Psara, K.: A collective interpretation semantics for reversing Petri nets. Theor. Comput. Sci. **924**, 148–170 (2022)

19. Philippou, A., Psara, K.: Reversible computation in nets with bonds. J. Log. Algebraic Methods Program. **124**, 100718 (2022)

20. Phillips, I., Ulidowski, I.: Reversibility and asymmetric conflict in event structures. J. Log. Algebraic Methods Program. **84**(6), 781–805 (2015)

21. Phillips, I., Ulidowski, I., Yuen, S.: Modelling of bonding with processes and events. In: Dueck, G.W., Miller, D.M. (eds.) RC 2013. LNCS, vol. 7948, pp. 141–154. Springer, Heidelberg (2013). https://doi.org/10.1007/978-3-642-38986-3_12

22. Phillips, I.C.C., Ulidowski, I.: Reversing algebraic process calculi. J. Log. Algebraic Methods Program. **73**(1–2), 70–96 (2007)

23. Glabbeek, R.J.: The individual and collective token interpretations of petri nets. In: Abadi, M., de Alfaro, L. (eds.) CONCUR 2005. LNCS, vol. 3653, pp. 323–337. Springer, Heidelberg (2005). https://doi.org/10.1007/11539452_26

24. Winskel, G.: Event structures. In: Brauer, W., Reisig, W., Rozenberg, G. (eds.) ACPN 1986. LNCS, vol. 255, pp. 325–392. Springer, Heidelberg (1987). https://doi.org/10.1007/3-540-17906-2_31

25. Winskel, G.: Petri nets, algebras, morphisms, and compositionality. Inf. Comput. **72**(3), 197–238 (1987)

Author Index

© IFIP International Federation for Information Processing 2023
M. Huisman and A. Ravara (Eds.): FORTE 2023, LNCS 13910, p. 225, 2023.
https://doi.org/10.1007/978-3-031-35355-0

Printed in the United States
by Baker & Taylor Publisher Services